The Informed Student Guide to
HUMAN RESOURCE MANAGEMENT

Dedication

To Vera and Tommy
Brian and Margaret

The Informed Student Guide to
HUMAN RESOURCE MANAGEMENT

Edited by Tom Redman and Adrian Wilkinson

Australia • Canada • Mexico • Singapore • Spain • United Kingdom • United States

The Informed Student Guide to Human Resource Management

Copyright © Thomson Learning 2002

The Thomson Learning logo is a registered trademark used herein under licence.

For more information, contact Thomson Learning, Berkshire House, 168–173 High Holborn, London, WC1V 7AA or visit us on the World Wide Web at:
http://www.thomsonlearning.co.uk

British Library Cataloguing-in-Publication data
A catalogue record for this book is available from the British Library

ISBN 1-86152-541-9

Typeset by J&L Composition Ltd, Filey, North Yorkshire

Printed in Great Britain by TJ International, Padstow, Cornwall

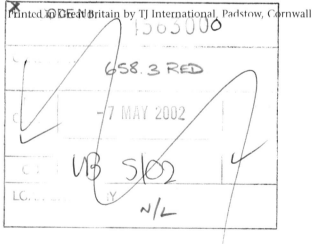

Introduction

This book arises out of a flourishing interest in the practice of human resource management (HRM) in recent years. In part this interest has been triggered by the growing number of studies that support what human resource (HR) managers have always claimed: that good HR practice delivers improved organizational performance. This organizational interest in HRM has been matched by a steep growth in the number of students enrolling on HRM courses and individual HRM modules. To meet the needs of these students there has been a large increase in the production of HRM texts (see the lists at the end of the book). The International Encyclopedia of Business Management series has itself produced *A Handbook of Human Resource Management* (edited by Poole and Warner) but this is a large and thus expensive library resource book with a collection of extended scholarly essays. In contrast this book is intended for students to purchase directly as a companion to, rather than as a straight replacement for a standard text on HRM.

The target audience of this book are those students who are maybe encountering HRM for the first time and are faced with an often bewildering array of new terms, technical HRM 'jargon' and especially acronyms. The language of HRM (particularly that of HRM lecturers and tutors) is perhaps far too abbreviated and this text will help the student familiarize themselves in an easily accessible way with what the like of ACAS, TUC, JIT, TQM IIP, PRP, etc. actually mean. Equally we believe the clear and concise nature of the entries will help students who are looking for a compact examination revision aid. One recent trend in HRM examinations has been to incorporate sections (such as the Chartered Institute of Personnel and Development examinations) where the student has to produce short condensed answers on a wide range of HRM topics.

Our aim has been to produce an authoritative and comprehensive reference book of briefings on key HRM topics. Each entry has a list of references and further reading to enable students to gain a deeper awareness and understanding of the topic. The further reading provided aims to present the reader with a range of appropriate types of material from classic texts, prescriptive managerial approaches, surveys and case studies of practice, heavyweight theoretical and empirical journal articles as well as web sites, seminal and up-to-date papers for the interested student to follow up. Each entry provides a short introductory overview of the topic area, theory, technique or practice. Each term is briefly defined (based on research) and there is then a move evaluative commentary. The 279 entries are arranged in an alphabetical sequence to enable the reader to quickly locate the entry they are interested in. All the entries' authors and their organizational affiliations are listed in the List of Contributors.

Obviously the completing of such a work is somewhat idiosyncratic in that there are no clearly defined limits to the subject of HRM, and the boundaries between, for example, HRM and 'organizational behaviour' and 'management' are far from distinct. Thus entries can be found on such 'core' HR areas as performance appraisal, discipline and industrial conflict, key organizational behaviour terms such as organizational culture and organizational commitment, and on broader management terms such, total quality management and business process re-engineering. The rationale here is that such terms are likely to be used in an HRM course that seeks to link HR issues with broader business practice rather than teaching it as an isolated and self-contained area of management practice. Each entry reflects the views of an expert and authoritative author. We have tried to make it forward looking by examining current trends and to clearly show the origins of the technique, theory or practice etc. Entries are cross-referenced to other relevant entries where appropriate.

We would like to thank the authors and the in-house publishing team, especially Kay Larkin, So-Shan Au and Melody Woollard, for their invaluable contribution to this project. We are also grateful to Rebecca White for co-ordinating the exercise.

Tom Redman and Adrian Wilkinson

List of contributors

PA – Peter Ackers
JA – John Arnold
AA – Alan Arthurs
NB – Nicolas Bacon
GJB – Greg J. Bamber
JB – Jean Barclay
YB – Yehuda Baruch
DB – David Beale
IB – Ian Beardwell
JBe – John Berridge
AB – Alison Bone
JBr – Jim Bradley
CB – Chris Brewster
SC – Susan Cartwright
MAC – Margaret A. Chapman
TC – Tim Claydon
DSC – David S. Collins
AC – Annette Cox
NC-A – Nick Creaby-Attwood
Scr – S Crowther
PD – Penny Dick
TD – Tony Dundon
JE – Jill Earnshaw
DF – David Farnham
JG – Jim Grieves
IG – Irena Grugulis
JH – Jerry Hallier
PH – Peter Hanafin
HH – Hilary Harris
RH – Rosemary Harrison
FH – Frances Hill
LH – Len Holden

JHy – Jeff Hyman
PJ – Philip James
SJ – Stephen James
DK – Don Keithley
DL – Deborah Lee
JL – John Leopold
JL-C – John Loan-Clarke
HM – Hedley Malloch
MM – Mick Marchington
PM – Pat McColl
MMo – Marie Morley
KM – Kevin Morrell
SP – Stephen Proctor
TR – Tom Redman
DR – Douglas Renwick
SR – Sadie Reynolds
DRo – Derek Rollinson
CR – Chris Rowley
YS – Yoko Sano
SS – Sue Shaw
ASm – Alison Smith
ES – Ed Snape
LS – Lynda Stansfield
JS – Jim Stewart
AS – Anne Story
JSk – John Stredwick
ST – Stephen Taylor
DT – Derek Torrington
BvdH – Beatrice van der Heijden
AW – Adrian Wilkinson
JW – John Wilson
DW – Diana Winstanley

Peter Ackers is Reader in Employment Relations and Co-ordination or REAM (Research in Employment and Management) at Loughborough University Business School, UK. His PhD was a study of coal mining labour history. Co-author of *New Developments in Employee Involvement* (Employment Department, 1992) and co-editor of *The New Workplace and Trade Unionism* (Routledge, 1996), he has been published widely in academic journals and edited collections on industrial relations, the sociology of work and labour history. He is joint editor of *Labour History Review*, the journal of the British Society for the Study of Labour History, and is currently co-editing (with Adrian Wilkinson) a book for Oxford University Press on industrial relations as an academic discipline and its relationship to other social science perspectives.

John Arnold is Subject Area Co-ordinator for the OB/HRM group at the Loughborough University Business School, and is also a member of the school's management group. He has directed several research projects on career development, especially in his early career, and also conducts consultancy work in this area. Current research includes a major project funded by the Department of Health's Human Resource Research Initiative concerning recruitment and retention of nurses and professionals allied to medicine, and an ESRC-funded project on professionals' perceptions of managers and management. He has published numerous articles on career development in leading academic and practitioner journals, and together with Professors Ivan Robertson and Cary Cooper has written the successful textbook *Work Psychology*, published by FT/Prentice-Hall in 1995. John is also author of the 1997 book *Managing Careers into the 21st Century*, published by Sage. He is a chartered psychologist registered with the British Psychological Society.

Alan Arthurs is lecturer in industrial relations and personnel management at the University of Bath. Formerly a plant manager and personnel manager with ICI, National Co-ordinator of the ESRC's Open Door Scheme and Acas-appointed Independent Expert on Equal Pay, he was also the Institute of Personnel and Development's Associate Examiner for 'Reward Management'. Current research interests are equal pay, particularly the operation of the concept of equal value, single status and harmonization of employment policies.

Nicolas Bacon is Reader in Human Resource Management at Nottingham University Business School. He has published widely on industrial relations and human resource management issues. His current work includes studies of the introduction of teamworking, integrative bargaining and the impact of financial and accounting control systems on the personnel function.

Greg J. Bamber is Director of the Graduate School of Management, Griffith University, Queensland, Australia. His publications include many articles and books, for example: *Militant Managers?* (Gower, 1985); *Managing Managers* (Blackwell, 1993); *Organisational Change Strategies* (Longman, 1995); *Employment Relations in the Asia-Pacific* (Allen & Unwin/Thomson Learning, 2000); *New Technology* (Routledge/Allen & Unwin, 1989) and *International and Comparative Employment Relations* (Sage/Allen & Unwin, 1998). His publications have been translated into several languages including French, German, Spanish, Indonesian, Italian, Russian, Chinese, Korean and Japanese. He is President of the International Federation of Scholarly Associations of Management. Formerly, he was at Durham University Business School (UK) and an arbitrator for the Advisory, Conciliation and Arbitration Service.

Jean Barclay is Lecturer in Human Resource Management at Glasgow Caledonian University. Her research interests include the use of behavioural interviewing in selection, ethics in selection, learning logs, and assessment methods used in selection and in education. She has been published in various journals including *Personnel Review, Education & Training* and *Management Education and Development*. She is a member of the Chartered Institute of Personnel and Development and a member of the Institute of Learning and Teaching.

Yehuda Baruch is a reader in organizational behaviour and human resource management at UEA Norwich and formerly a visiting research fellow at London Business School. He holds a BSc in electronic engineering (Ben Gurion, Israel), MSc and DSc in management and behavioural sciences (The Technion, Israel). After being a project manager in high technology industry he entered a career in academia. His research interests are HRM, mainly career management systems and international HRM, tele-working, and organizational culture. He published in these fields in a number of journals, including *Human Relations, Organizational Dynamics, Human Resource Management* and *Organization Studies*.

David Beale is a senior lecturer in human resource management at Staffordshire University. He was awarded a PhD from UMIST (entitled 'New Management Initiatives and Trade Union Response in the Public Sector'), and previously worked in the further education college sector, including ten years as a trade union education tutor. He has had considerable experience as a union branch officer and workplace representative, was for many years a local trades union council delegate, and is also the author of *Driven by Nissan? A Critical Guide to New Management Techniques* (Lawrence and Wishart Ltd, 1994).

Ian Beardwell, BSc, MSc, PhD, is Professor of Industrial Relations at Leicester Business School. He is a Vice President of the CIPD and chairs the Education and Membership committee. Experienced in industrial relations and human resource management policy with the public and private sectors, he has researched and published in the areas of low pay, union recognition, public sector labour relations and the management of industrial relations, and has recently been engaged in a study of personnel career development sponsored by the CIPD. He was a member of the Workplace Employee Relations Survey (WER 98) development team in 1998. He is the joint editor of the text *Human Resource Management: a Contemporary Approach* (FT Prentice Hall, 2000), published in its 3rd edition and one of the best selling HRM books in the UK and international markets.

John R. Berridge is Visiting Senior Lecturer in Personnel Policy in the Manchester School of Management, UMIST, where he has worked for the past 21 years, having been Director of the postgraduate programme in Personnel Management and Industrial Relations and latterly, Director of International Studies. He has taught and researched widely in Europe and the U.S., and written seven books including *Employee Assistance Programmes and Employee Counselling* (John Wiley and Sons 1997) co-authored with Cary L. Cooper and Carolyn Highley-Marchington, based on the largest British research project on this topic.

Alison Bone is head of the law group at Brighton Business School at the University of Brighton and the Examiner in Employment Law for the Chartered Institute of Personnel and Development. She writes on both employment law and management development issues and acts as a representative for applicants at employment tribunals. She is involved in the training of HR professionals and lectures on a wide range of undergraduate, post-graduate and post-experience programmes.

Jim Bradley is Principal Lecturer in Business Process Improvement in the Business School at the University of Teeside. After a ten year career in human resource management at undergraduate and postgraduate levels in three UK Universities, he now teaches business strategy and small business consulting. He has also carried out research and consultancy projects in both large and small organizations, and publishes in strategic benchmarking with particular reference to the process industries and SMEs in the UK service sector.

Chris Brewster is Professor of International Human Resource Management at Cranfield School of Management in the UK. He is Director of the school's Centre for European HRM. He has substantial experience in trade unions, government, specialist journals, personnel management and consultancy prior to joining Cranfield. In addition to his teaching role, Professor Brewster has acted as a consultant to UK and international organizations mainly in the areas of personnel policies (the subject of his PhD) and management training. He is a frequent conference speaker around the world and has recently presented papers at the Association of International Business, the Academy of Management and the European Association of Personnel Management. He is the author of some dozen books, including *The Management of Expatriates* (Kogan Page, 1991), *European Community Social Policy* (IPD, 1989), *The European Human Resource Management Guide* (Academic Press, 1992), *European Developments in Human Resource Management* (Kogan Page, 1993), *Policy and Practice in European Human Resource Management* (Thomson Learning, 1993) and numerous articles. He is currently directing a major research programme on international strategic human resource management, which is assessing developments across Europe.

Susan Cartwright is a chartered psychologist and senior lecturer in organizational psychology at Manchester School of Management, UMIST. She has written or co-edited eleven books, twenty one book chapters and over forty published articles. She is joint editor of the *Leadership & Organisation Development Journal*. Her research and consultancy interests are in the area of occupational stress and organizational change. Susan is a fellow of the Royal Society of Arts and a council member of the British Academy of Management.

Margaret A. Chapman, BSc (Hons), MSc, AdvDipEdn, MANLP, FCIPD is a work/ organizational psychologist based at Loughborough University. Here she is undertaking doctoral work into emotional intelligence and exploring its implications for individual and organizational learning. Prior to receiving two ESRC awards for her Masters' and doctoral work she was head of human resources for two software companies for which she achieved Fellowship of the Chartered Institute of Development (CIPD). She has published in the area of mentoring, small firms, personal development and emotional intelligence. Margaret combines her work as an academic with consultancy specializing in coaching. She is also a visiting facilitator on a range of postgraduate HRM and professional programmes at Cambridge and Leeds universities.

Tim Claydon is a principal lecturer in the Department of Human Resource Management at De Montfort University Leicester, UK. He has written on various topics such as industrial relations history, trade union derecognition, ethics and HRM, HRM and the labour market, and HRM in the USA. His current research interests are changes in public service trade unionism and the nature of contemporary patterns of organizational change.

David S. Collins is Senior Lecturer in Management at the university of Essex. He is the author of *Organizational Change: Sociological Perspectives* (1998) and *Management Fads and Buzzwords: Critical-Practical Perspectives* (2000), both published by Routledge.

Annette Cox is a lecturer in employment studies at Manchester School of Management, UMIST. Her research interests and publications centre on the management of variable pay systems and HRM in small companies. She teaches reward and generalist HRM topics on both undergraduate and postgraduate courses.

Nick Creaby-Attwood is a lecturer at the University of Teesside and a member of the Chartered Institute of Personnel and Development. He holds an MA from the University of Newcastle upon Tyne, and is currently undertaking doctoral research in the interaction of trade union structure and the development of collective identity. He is the course leader for the MSc in International Management, and the MSc in Enterprise Management and has previously worked in local government and as a researcher for a major British trade union.

Penny Dick, BA, MSc, PhD, C.Psychol., is a lecturer in organizational behaviour and human resource management at the Sheffield University Management School. She is a chartered occupational psychologist in the public and private sector. Her research interests include stress among emergency service workers and diversity management. She has published in both these areas.

Tony Dundon, BA (Hons), MA, PhD, MICPD, is a lecturer in employment relations at the Department of Management, National University of Ireland, Galway. He was previously programme director for the PricewaterhouseCoopers programme at Manchester School of Management, UMIST. His main areas of published research include non-union industrial relations, union renewal, workplace union organization and HRM in small to medium-sized enterprises.

Jill Earnshaw is a senior lecturer in employment law at the Manchester School of Management, UMIST and Dean of Management Studies. Since 1990 she has also acted as a part-time chairman of employment tribunals. Her current research interests are in the resolution of employment disputes and the role of workplace procedures.

David Farnham is Professor of Employment Relations at the University of Portsmouth Business School. He is active nationally in the Chartered Institute of Personnel and Development, where he is Chief Examiner Core Personnel and Development. Internationally, he is co-chair of the Personnel Policy Study Group of the European Group of Public Administration. His major research interests are people management and employment relations in the public sector, managerialism in public organizations and public management in Europe. His recent books include: *Managing Academic Staff in Changing University Systems* (Open University Press, 1999); *Public Management in Britain* (Macmillan, 1999); *Human Resources Management in the Public Services* (Macmillan, 2000) and *Employee Relations in Context* (CIPD, 2000).

Jim Grieves is Senior Lecturer at the Teesside Business School, University of Teesside U.K. He teaches and researches organizational development. He is editor of *The Learning Organization*.

Irena Grugulis is a lecturer in employment studies at Manchester School of Management, UMIST, and an associate fellow of SKOPE, University of Warwick/University of Oxford. Her main area of interest is vocational education and training and she has researched into and published on NVQs, management training, the nature of managerial work and managing culture, having been funded by both the ESRC and the ERDF. She was a founding organizer of the International Critical Management Studies Conference and is currently working on a project funded under the ESRC's Future of Work series.

Jerry Hallier is a senior lecturer in human resource management at the University of Stirling. He joined the University of Stirling in 1991 having previously worked for thirteen years in the electronics and computing industry. His published work has mainly focused on work transitions, HRM in Greenfield sites, and ageism in work and employment. A major strand has been how enforced job changes affect workers' psychological contracts and employment security. These related interests have evolved further into the study of managers' own psychological contracts under new and harsher regimes and how these colour their treatment of workers. Research into HRM on Greenfield sites includes the development of a two-dimensional framework of analysis for categorizing Greenfield HRM practices over time and the employer rhetorics used to legitimate departures from the espoused culture (with John Leopold).

Peter Hanafin is a senior lecturer in human resource management at Teesside Business School, University of Teesside. He is a Fellow of the Chartered Institute of Personnel and Development and has worked in personnel and training for 30 years. His previous experience includes consultancy work in both the private and public sector. For the last eleven years he has been an academic specializing in employee relations.

Hilary Harris is Director of the Centre for Research into the Management of Expatriation (CReME). This is a new centre focusing on the strategic management of expatriates, which has been established by Cranfield School of Management and Organisation Resources Counsellors, Inc. The Centre aims to provide rigorous and practical information and research on the effective management of expatriates to both practitioners and academics.

Dr Harris has had extensive experience as an HR practitioner with organizations in the security, engineering and computing sectors. In addition, she has undertaken consultancy with a broad range of leading edge organizations in the public and private sectors in the areas of equal opportunities and HR information systems.

Her specialist areas of interest are international HRM, expatriate management, cross-cultural management and women in management. She runs women's management development courses in Britain and in the USA. She is co-author, with Chris Brewster, of *International HRM: Contemporary Issues in Europe* (Routledge, 1999). She teaches, consults and writes extensively in these areas.

Hilary is currently a member of the Institute of Personnel and Development's International Forum and was part of the working group that produced the IPD's *Guide on International Management Development*. She is a visiting lecturer at the Swedish Institute of Management and the Centre for International Briefing and regularly works with groups of managers from Scandinavia on cross-cultural management programmes. She has lived and worked in Australia and New Zealand.

Frances Hill is a senior lecturer in the School of Management and Economics at Queen's University Belfast. She holds BA, MBA and PhD degrees. Her teaching specialisms are in the areas of organizational behaviour and theory, while her research interests are in the field of organizational change, particularly in the context of business improvement/business excellence. Her numerous research papers have dealt with quality circles, total quality management, service quality, business process reengineering and organizational learning. She is Chairperson of the Women's Research Network based in the School of Management and Economics at Queen's.

Jeff Hyman is Professor of Human Resource Management at Glasgow Caledonian University. He has written several articles and books on industrial democracy at work and has recently spent a sabbatical at the International Labour Organization Headquarters in Geneva. His current research is focused on the future of work and on work–life balance.

Philip James is Professor of Employment Relations at Middlesex University Business School. Philip has researched and written extensively in the fields of both human resource management and occupational health and safety. He has served on the editorial board of the *Human Resource Management Journal*, edited the *Health and Safety Information Bulletin* and currently sits on the executive committee of the Institute of Employment Rights.

Stephen James is Senior Lecturer in Economics at Teeside Business School at the University of Teeside and he also works as a consultant. His current research interests include labour market economics and the economic and monetary union.

Don Keithley is a principal lecturer in human resource management at Sunderland Business School. He has a doctorate from Durham University in industrial relations, and is a fellow of the Chartered Institute of Personnel and Development. His research interests include work-based learning and life long learning. With Tom Redman, he has co-authored a number of articles and conference papers.

Deborah Lee is Lecturer in Sociology at the University of Derby. She previously completed a PhD at the Centre for the Study of Women and Gender, University of Warwick. Deborah has published articles exploring women's and men's experiences of sexual harassment and bullying in the workplace and in higher education (which have appeared in *Gender and Education*, *Women's Studies International Forum*, the *Journal of Gender Studies* and *Personnel Review*). Currently, her main research interest is contrapower bullying.

John Leopold is Associate Dean and Head of Department of Human Resource Management at Nottingham Business School. He was co-guest editor of a special issue of *Personnel Review* on Managing the Employment Relationship on Greenfield Sites (Vol. 30, no. 3, 2001) and has published on the topic in *Employee Relations, Human Resource Management Journal, International Journal of Human Resource Management* and *Industrial Relations Journal*. He is co-editor of *Strategic Human Resourcing* (FT Pitman, 1999) and editor of *Human Resources in Organisations* (Pearson 2001).

John Loan-Clarke is Lecturer in Organizational Development at the Business School, Loughborough University. He has previously worked in human resource roles in local government and the National Health Service. He has published in numerous journals, primarily in relation to the topics of management development and organizational issues relating to healthcare.

Hedley Malloch PhD, MSc, BSc (Econs) is an associate professor at the IESEG School of Management at the Catholic University of Lille, France, where he teaches and researches in human resource management and strategic management.

Mick Marchington is Professor of Human Resource Management at Manchester School of Management, UMIST. His principal research interests are in the fields of employee participation, workplace employment relations and the links between business strategy and HRM. He has written 12 books and monographs and about 100 articles in academic and practitioner journals. His most recent books are *Core Personnel and Development*, published by CIPD in 2000, *Managing with Total Quality Management*, published by Macmillan in 1997 and *HRM: The New Agenda*, published by Pitman in 1998. He is currently running a major project at UMIST on Changing Organizational Forms and the Reshaping of Work which is part of the ESRC Future of Work Programme. He has been Dean of Management Studies at UMIST and one of the CIPD's Chief Examiners. He has been external examiner at several universities and is currently external examiner at Leeds and Cranfield. Professor Marchington is a Companion of the CIPD.

Pat McColl is a senior lecturer at the University of Teesside where she teaches in the areas of employee resourcing and employee development and is currently Programme Leader for the BA (Hons) in HRM. Her previous experience includes over 12 years of professional practice in the public and private sectors.

Marie Morley is a research associate at the Employment Studies Research Unit, Bristol Business School, the University of the West of England and a doctoral student at the School of Management, the University of Bath.

Kevin Morrell BA, MA Cantab, MSc, is a doctoral candidate at Loughborough University Business School, researching the turnover of nursing staff in the NHS. He is testing a model of decision making, which challenges conventional thinking about how and why people choose to leave their employers, and has published on labour turnover in the *International Journal of Management Reviews*.

Stephen Proctor is Alcan Chair of Management in the School of Management, University of Newcastle. His main research interests are in the contemporary restructuring of work and organizations, and among his many publications in this area is *Teamworking* (Macmillan, 2000, co-edited with Frank Mueller). He is founder and co-organizer of the International Workshop on Teamworking.

Douglas Renwick is Lecturer in HRM at Sheffield University Management School, where he teaches HRM, HR strategy and employee relations. His research interests include HR-line work relations, line manager involvement in HRM, e-HR and HRM in Russia and Central and Eastern Europe.

Sadie Reynolds is an independent training and development consultant specializing in management competencies covering a wide spectrum of skills. She has carried out work for numerous organizations in both the private and public sectors. Her previous full-time work experience includes: Course Director for the Chartered Institute of Personnel and Development courses, working in recruitment at British Airways and as Employee Development Manager where she was responsible for all learning and development events for the organization. Sadie is nearing the end of her research into internal marketing of HRM and hopes to complete her PhD at UMIST later in the year. She already holds a BA and MBA and is a fellow of the CIPD.

Derek Rollinson is an independent researcher writer, who is also a principal lecturer at the University of Huddersfield Business School, where he teaches organizational behaviour and analysis, and employee relations. He holds degrees in social psychology and business administration. His doctoral research was in industrial relations and he is a chartered psychologist and member of the Chartered Institute of Personnel and Development. Previous publications include: *Understanding Employee Relations: A Behavioural Approach* (Addison Wesley, 1993); *Organisational Behaviour and Analysis: An Integrated Approach* (Addison Wesley, 1998), and numerous journal articles on the handling of discipline and grievance. His current research interests are: the internal dynamics of discipline and grievance handling; employee relations in non-union organizations and power and control in organizations.

Chris Rowley is a senior lecturer at City University Business School, London. His previous experience includes a variety of work in the public and private sectors. His qualifications include a BA and MA from Warwick University and a DPhil from

Nuffield College, Oxford University. He researches and teaches in a range of areas, including international and comparative employee relations, human resource management, technological change, flexibility and Asia Pacific business. He has been published widely in journals (over 40 articles) and books (over 40 chapters and other contributions) and has edited 8 books. He is an editor of the academic journal, *Asia Pacific Business Review* and is also an editorial board member, a reviewer and was a recent guest editor, of the journal *Personnel Review.*

Yoko Sano is Professor of Human Resources and President of Kaetsu University in Tokyo. She has been a visiting professor in a number of universities: Canberra, Glasgow, Cranfield, Cerge-Pontoise and Manila. She has published numerous papers in academic journals, and her books in English include *Human Resource Management in Japan* (Keio University Press, Inc., 1995) and *Frontiers of Human Resource Practices in Japan* (The Japan Institute of Labour, 1997). One of her recent contributions is 'Global competitive pressures, labour market and employment issues in the Japanese service sector' in *Work and Employment in a Globalized Era* (Frank Cass, 2001).

Sue Shaw is Head of Department of Management at Manchester Metropolitan University. She is a past chair of the CIPD and a member of its Quality Assurance Panel. She researches and publishes in the areas of human resource practitioner careers and equal opportunities.

Alison Smith is Director of Professional Programmes at Loughborough University Business School and is also Deputy Director of the Management Development Centre at Loughborough University Business School. Previously a lecturer in further education, involved in vocational training, she is currently employed on the design, direction and delivery of management development programmes. Her main research interests are training needs analysis, the effectiveness of management development, learning methods in management development and communications. She has published widely in management journals and presented at national and international conferences. She has co-edited and authored a book on flexible approaches to management learning called *Flexible Learning in Higher Education* (Kogan Page, 1996).

Ed Snape is a professor in the Department of Management, The Hong Kong Polytechnic University. His previous posts were Professor of Human Resource Management at the University of Bradford Management Centre and Reader in the Department of Human Resource Management at the University of Strathclyde. His teaching and research interests are in human resource management and employee/industrial relations.

Lynda Stansfield lectures in human resource management at the University of Bradford School of Management, chairs the evening MBA programme and is leader of courses in core HRM and strategic HRM at post-graduate level. Prior to Bradford, Lynda lectured in HRM at Cranfield School of Management. Before pursuing an academic career, she gained extensive professional experience, principally as UK head of personnel and training for a multi-national company and as a management consultant with an international firm. Lynda's research interests include strategic human resource development, management development and workplace assessment. She has published several articles in learned journals and has presented numerous papers at academic and professional conferences.

Jim Stewart is Professor of Human Resource Development at Nottingham Business School where he is also Joint Course Leader of the Doctorate in Business Administration programme. He is the author and joint author of seven books on the subject of HRD, the latest of which will be published in the autumn of 2001. In addition, he is the author of numerous articles and conference papers, and he is Chair of the UK-based and European wide research network: the University Forum for HRD. Along with Professor Jean Woodall and Dr Monica Lee, Jim is currently organizing an ESRC funded Research Seminar Series on HRD.

Anne Story is a principal lecturer in human resource management at Teesside Business School, University of Teesside. She holds a BSc from Edinburgh University and an MSc in human resource development from Nottingham Trent University. Her teaching and research interests are in the area of human resource development. She is a member of the CIPD and one of the team of national examiners for CIPD Employee Development examinations.

John Stredwick FCIPD, B.Com., has published four books including *Flexible Working Practices* (CIPD, 1998) and *An Introduction to Human Resource Management* (Butterworth-Heinneman, 2000). His career has spanned senior HR positions in publishing, shipbuilding, home improvement and local authority services. He is currently Senior Lecturer at Luton Business School and a consultant in reward issues and flexible working practices.

Stephen Taylor is a senior lecturer in HRM at Manchester Metropolitan University Business School and a national examiner for the Chartered Institute of Personnel and Development. He formerly taught at UMIST and held a number of personnel management posts in the NHS and in the hotel industry. He teaches and researches in the fields of employee resourcing, reward management and employment law.

Derek Torrington is Emeritus Professor of Human Resource Management at UMIST and Chair of the Manchester Federal School of Business and Management. He has written 36 books and is a companion of both the Institute of Personnel and Development and the Institute of Management.

Beatrice van der Heijden PhD, is working as an associate professor in the HRM department at the University of Twente in the Netherlands. Her background is in work and organizational psychology and she has been an academic researcher for more than ten years. She has published both in text books as well as in (inter)national journals on professional expertise, career development, ageing and work and employability.

John Wilson is Director of Teesside Business School, University of Teesside. He is a qualified member of the Chartered Institute of Public Finance and Accountancy and the Chartered Institute of Marketing and has an academic background in politics and economics. His main research interests concern the management and economics of public service provision.

Diana Winstanley, BSc, PhD, Dip. Couns., FCIPD, is a senior lecturer in human resource management at Imperial College Management School. She is author of four books and over 30 articles on management, including co-editor of *Ethics and Contemporary Human Resource Management* (Macmillan, 2000), and co-author of *Management Development: Strategy and Practice* (Blackwell, 1998). She is also a qualified counsellor and a fellow of the Chartered Institute for Personnel and Development. She is currently researching ethics and values of consultants in the charity and voluntary sectors.

A

Absence management

Around 3 per cent of working time in Britain is lost each year through staff absence, although this average figure conceals marked variations between occupational groups and industry sectors. Such absence stems from a variety of causes that have been usefully classified by Rhodes and Steers into two main categories. First, factors, such as individual work ethics, job satisfaction and reward systems, which affect worker motivation to attend. Second, factors, including transport difficulties, child-care responsibilities and ill health, which affect their ability to attend. As a result, the management of absence can be seen to be multifaceted and extend to encompass a wide range of areas of action, for example:

- the redesign of jobs and the work environment to increase employee satisfaction and motivation,
- the establishment and operation of disciplinary rules and procedures,
- the adoption of strategies to prevent worker illness and injury,
- the provision of childcare support
- the provision of rehabilitation and other forms of assistance aimed at facilitating the return to work of those who are ill and injured.

Existing evidence indicates that employers see the control of absence as an important issue and have in recent years often sort to revise their disciplinary rules and procedures. However, it also appears that relatively few employers have placed as much emphasis on the other types of action identified above and therefore adopted broad-ranging strategies towards the reduction of workforce absence. **PJ**

References and further reading
Barmby, T., Ercolani, M. and Treble, J. (1999) 'Sickness absence: new quarterly and annual series from the GHS and LFS', *Labour Market Trends*, August: 405–13.
Edwards, P. and Whitson, C. (1993) *Attending to Work: The Management of Attendance and Shopfloor Order*, Oxford: Blackwell.
Huczynski, A. and Fitzpatrick, M. (1989) *Managing Employee Absence for a Competitive Edge*, London: Pitman.
Institute of Personnel and Development (IPD) (2000) *Employee Absence: A Survey of Management Policy and Practice*, London: Institute of Personnel and Development.
Rhodes, S. and Steers, R. (1990) *Managing Employee Absenteeism*, Reading, MA: Addison-Wesley.

Accreditation of prior learning (APL)

> The accreditation of prior learning (APL) permits the award of credit towards a qualification on the basis of evidence drawn from an individual's past achievements. (City and Guilds)
>
> APL is a process which enables the identification, assessment and certification of a person's vocationally relevant past achievements. (Business and Technology Council – BTEC)

The above quotations from the literature of awarding bodies identify the link between APL and qualifications, particularly National Vocational Qualification (NVQ) awards which are based upon the demonstration of competence. However, APL may be used also to demonstrate prior learning which will give access to a course of study. This prior learning need not necessarily be accredited, just evidenced to a required level. APL is also accepted in some academic courses (i.e. not only for the award of competence-based qualifications) for the purpose of granting exemptions.

APL originated in the USA where it is known as Prior Learning Assessment (PLA). In the UK it is also known as APA (Accreditation of Prior Achievement), APEL (Accreditation of Prior Experiential Learning) and the MCI term, Crediting Competence. The UK variants have, as the acronyms suggest, sophisticated differences in meaning, but APL tends to be the generic term.

APL is an assessment process whereby skills, knowledge, experience and achievements can be credited and formally recognized. The attainment of competence can be acquired in previous, current, unpaid and voluntary work. In theory, an individual's lifetime is available for assessment although awarding bodies may well restrict usable time to, for example, three years.

The benefits of APL are that it widens access to education and training opportunities to populations which previously, through lack of formal qualifications, had been disadvantaged. It also encourages candidates to take greater responsibility for learning since they must demonstrate appropriate evidence. It is not seen as a 'soft option' and, indeed, cannot be if APL candidates are to join traditionally qualified candidates on courses. It is also perceived as an opportunity to reduce time and expense spent undertaking courses to qualify in existing competence (although, clearly there is time expended in demonstrating that competence).

Concerns around APL centre upon the difficulties of measuring and applying standards to important qualities such as creativity, flexibility and sensitivity. The need to apply a standard can lead to an overly rigid approach which, it is argued, at higher levels of management, for example, is not appropriate. There is another danger that APL is retrospective, in giving credit for past experience, and therefore is not developmental. If it is used for certification and exemption only, this may well be the case. For these reasons APL is viewed somewhat sceptically, particularly by academics and not all higher education institutions have an APL policy.
AS

References and further reading

Challis, M. (1993) *Introducing APEL*, London: Routledge.

Nyatanga, L., Foreman, D. and Fox J. (1998) *Good Practice in the Accreditation of Prior Learning*, London: Cassell.

Simosko, S. (1991) *APL: A Practical Guide for Professionals*, London: Kogan Page.

Simosko, S. (1992) *Get Qualifications for What You Know and Can Do: A Personal Guide to APL*, London: Kogan Page.

Smith, A. J. and Preston, D. (1993) 'APL: the relationship between rhetoric and reality' *Management Education and Development* 24(4): 395–405.

Action learning

A particularly interesting learning method pioneered by Professor Reg Revans is that of action learning. Many books have been written about this topic, but in essence, it is a learner-centred method of solving problems using learning in small groups of people. Participants meet to discuss and work on real-life issues and potential solutions, leading to action being taken to resolve the problem and learning from the experience. Revans's premise was that 'there can be no learning without action and no (sober and deliberate) action without learning'.

The basic underlying theory is that organizations and their people cannot succeed unless their rate of learning exceeds or is at least the same as, the rate of change they are experiencing. This has been expressed as a simple formula: $L \geq C$, where L stands for rate of learning, and C stands for rate of change. Revans suggests that learning itself is made up of two essential parts: *programmed knowledge* (P) and *questioning insight* (Q). He defines programmed knowledge as traditional instruction (for example, the kind of things one would learn on a formal course) and questioning insight as the seeking out of unresolved problems and engaging in critical reflection. Using these definitions, Revans derived another formula, this time for learning, which is $L = P + Q$.

In essence, there need to be four elements to action learning. These are the individual who seeks out an issue or problem, a group of individuals usually called a 'learning set' who meet to discuss members' problems, a 'problem' or issue to be resolved and action taken on the problem. It is essential that learning results from the action, therefore critical reflection is encouraged. The method relies very heavily on the concept of *experiential learning* (see separate entry). The 'learning sets' are often initially facilitated by outside people, in order to bring an element of form and structure to the proceedings until the set can operate for itself. Action learning is mostly utilized in organizations as a form of management development. It has been employed successfully in organizations across different sectors. Several academic institutions in the UK have also embraced action learning recently. More formal academic management programmes (for example, some MBA courses) are beginning to utilize action learning techniques, especially for projects. Arguably, there are business advantages to be gained by both individual students and their sponsoring organizations from this form of development. **LS**

References and further reading

Pedler, M. (1996) *Action Learning for Managers,* London: Lemos and Crane.
Revans, R. (1998) *ABC of Action Learning,* London: Lemos and Crane.

Added value bonus schemes

Added value schemes are a form of gainsharing that measures the workforce's increased performance in order to calculate the bonus to be paid. Using sales as the base rate figure, deductions are made for materials and services brought into the company. This produces a net company growth figure which takes account of the various inputs of the workforce in areas such as increased production, income generated from new ideas or research and development, improved efficiency savings, continuous improvement schemes and customer service. It therefore recognizes the contribution made by all levels of the organization in generating capital for the company.

This type of pay scheme seeks to foster co-operation, corporate citizenship, loyalty, employee alignment with the corporate goals and the development of a positive psychological contract. Possible disadvantages are that a scheme of this nature relies on communication of the strategic focus of the company, so that the employees understand the business plan and can question it if necessary. It therefore requires a degree

of openness on the part of management and a necessary degree of worker empowerment in the decision-making processes to extract the maximum amount of value
from the scheme.

There is also the possibility of the free-rider problem, whereby, one (or more) sections of the organization does not perform to the optimum. This reduces the overall
effectiveness of the organization, which impacts on the bottom line and ultimately
affects bonus. Therefore, instead of generating a culture of solidarity, it can polarize
the employees into those who are working for the company and those who appear
to be working for themselves. **MMo**

References and further reading

Armstrong, M. and Murlis, H. (1998) *Reward Management*, 4th edn, London: Kogan Page.
Incomes Data Services (IDS) (1999) *'Bonus schemes'*, IDS Study 665, March.

Advisory, Conciliation and Arbitration Service (ACAS)

The 1975 Employment Protection Act provided for an independent statutory body
to provide for the 'machinery for promoting the improvement of industrial relations'. Part 1 of the Act stated 'There shall be a body to be known as the Advisory,
Conciliation and Arbitration Service'. There was nothing new about the concept of
a publicly funded industrial advisory and peace-making service conducted by a third
party with the voluntary co-operation of those involved in the dispute. The first voluntary conciliation and arbitration service was set up in 1896. ACAS is staffed by
almost 750 people and has a head office in London, together with offices in Scotland
and Wales and eight English regions. The service is directed by a council comprising
a full-time chairperson and 12 other members all appointed by the Secretary of State
for Education and Employment. The ACAS mission statement is to 'improve the
performance and effectiveness of organisations by providing an independent and
impartial service to prevent and resolve disputes and to build harmonious relationships at work'. ACAS staff advise on a wide range of issues, for example:

- industrial relations policies
- payment systems
- job evaluation
- personnel records
- labour turnover
- absence
- recruitment and selection
- staff induction
- workplace communications
- disciplinary practice and procedures
- equal opportunities, etc.

Staff are specialist trained in the field of industrial relations and personnel management. They are recruited from both industry and the trade union movement.

Most of the work of ACAS begins with an inquiry from an employee, employer or
employee representative. Many inquiries for information are dealt with over the telephone. However, more complicated problems may involve a visit or a series of visits
to the organisation concerned. Advisers also become involved in training on industrial relations matters as well as contributing to conferences and seminars. In collective conciliation ACAS staff act as impartial and independent third parties to assist
employers and trade unions to reach mutually acceptable settlements of their disputes. The essential characteristic of such conciliation is that it involves the voluntary participation of both sides to the dispute who also hold the joint responsibility
for any agreement that is reached. The settlement belongs to them and is not the
'property' of the ACAS official.

To ensure the continuation of ACAS staff impartiality, with arbitration and mediation, ACAS appoint mediators or arbitrators from persons who are not employed by ACAS. The Industrial Relations Information Service, based in the ACAS head office, collects and provides information on a wide range of subjects in industrial relations and personnel management. The information service is responsible for monitoring developments in current industrial relations/personnel management practices. Much of this information is becoming available on ACAS's web site (see References). The special characteristics of ACAS are its impartial third party role and the general acceptability of its advisory services to both sides of industry. It is agreed almost universally that the history of ACAS is one of overwhelming success. ACAS continually gets good press from both the employers and trade unions. Its publications are well received. Its advice considered authoritative and helpful. Its work in conciliation, mediation and arbitration is respected and trusted by both sides of the employment world. Recently ACAS began to prepare for how they will set up and administer the voluntary arbitration scheme for resolving unfair dismissal claims, as provided for by the Employment Rights (Dispute Resolution) Bill.

Traditionally all political parties and governments of either persuasion have supported ACAS. The last Conservative government in its latter years changed the objectives of ACAS by removing the responsibility to promote collective bargaining. They also made proposals to charge for ACAS services. Following vociferous opposition mounted from industry and the trade unions this idea was dropped and in its place the then government cut ACAS's budget cut by 25 per cent. The moves by the last Conservative government to reduce its effectiveness seem to stem from ideological misgivings. There is no evidence from industrial relations practitioners, whether trade unionists or industrial relations managers, that the need for ACAS has diminished or is somehow bypassed by recent events in the UK industrial relations systems. **PH**

References and further reading

ACAS web site at www.acas.org.uk

Industrial Relations Service (IRS) (2001) 'ACAS to the rescue', *Employment Trends* (719) January: 6–10.

Mumford, K. (1996) 'Arbitration and ACAS in Britain: a historical perspective', *British Journal of Industrial Relations* 34(2): 287–305.

Sanderson, M. and Taggert, J. (1999) 'ACAS advice - a lost cause', *Employee Relations* 21(1–2): 128–30.

Age discrimination

Older workers have often encountered age discrimination from employers, for example through explicit age bars on job advertisements and less favourable treatment in recruitment, promotion and training. A possible reason for this discrimination is that older workers may be perceived as having certain undesirable characteristics, including:

- poor health
- an inflexible attitude
- resistance to change
- low trainability.

There is now a significant amount of research on such stereotypical beliefs in Western societies. Such beliefs about older workers, held by work colleagues, employers and customers, may influence employment decisions and thus give rise to age discrimination. However, it must not be forgotten that younger workers can also experience age discrimination, particularly when they are perceived as lacking the experience and maturity necessary for a particular post or promotion.

There is evidence of persistent and widespread discrimination against older workers in both the private and public sectors in the UK. Although the UK has well-established legislation on sex and race discrimination, and has recently passed legislation on disability, it lags behind countries such as the USA, Canada, Spain, France, New Zealand and Australia in having no laws prohibiting discrimination on grounds of age. Those in favour of such legislation have argued that it is needed to highlight the problem of age discrimination and to provide for redress for those effected. Opponents, particularly employers' organizations such as the Confederation of British Industry and the Chartered Institute of Personnel and Development, prefer voluntary self-regulation and claim that legislation would be difficult to enforce, would do little to change attitudes about older workers and would pose an additional administrative burden on employers. Some UK employers have argued that legislation is unnecessary, since demographic and labour market changes have obliged them to reconsider any negative attitudes to older workers, whilst a growing number of the over-50s are in any case taking early retirement. However, the extent to which such early retirements are 'voluntary' is open to question, with suggestions that employers are targeting older employees for redundancy, which may itself point to a need for protective legislation.

Thus far, UK governments have preferred to adopt a voluntary approach, for example by promoting 'good practice' via the *Code of Practice on Age Diversity in Employment*, distributed to over 34 000 workplaces during 1999 (DfEE, 1999). The code shows employers how to enhance equality of opportunity by eliminating the use of age as an employment criterion in decisions on recruitment, selection, promotion, training, redundancy and retirement. The government will review the effectiveness of the code during 2001 but early indications are that it has made little impact on discriminatory practice, with many employers unaware of the code's existence and others reporting that it has made no difference to their employment practices. However, the European Commission's Anti-Discrimination Directive will give rise to discrimination on the basis of age being made unlawful from 2006 in the UK. **TR**

References and further reading

Arrowsmith, J. and McGoldrick, A. (1996) *Breaking the Barriers: A Survey of Managers' Attitudes to Age and Employment*, London: Institute of Management.

Chiu, W., Snape, E., Chan, A. and Redman, T. (2001) 'Age stereotypes and discriminatory attitudes towards older workers: an East-West comparison', *Human Relations* (forthcoming).

Department for Education and Employment (DfEE) (1999) *Code of Practice on Age Diversity in Employment*, London: DfEE.

McKay, S. (1998) 'Older workers in the labour market', *Labour Market Trends*, July: 365–9.

Taylor, P. and Walker, A. (1994) 'The ageing workforce: employers' attitudes towards older people', *Work, Employment and Society* 8(4): 569–91.

Taylor, P. and Walker, A. (1997) 'Age discrimination and public policy', *Personnel Review*, 26(4), 307–18.

Alternative work arrangements

The conventional, traditional mode of work consists of a full-time job, conducted in one workplace, for a single employee, with a stable and cyclic schedule (e.g. 0900–1700). However, there is a wide range of modes of employment, labelled 'alternative work arrangements', 'flexible work', 'atypical work'; all are non-conventional. Gottlieb, Kelloway and Barham (1998) listed an array of flexible work arrangements and practices. At the core of these practices is the need for organizations to recognize and be proactive in dealing with the individual and the home/family – work interface. This variety of flexible ways of managing people have been developed to enable better utilization of the human assets. Competitive advantage is based on the internal resources of the firm, and in particular the human capital. While optimizing the human asset is cited as the most important aspect for increasing competitiveness, managing it becomes a crucial element in gaining competitive advantage.

One of the most effective and successful methods of alternative work arrangements is teleworking (also labelled home-working or telecommuting; – see also **Teleworking**). Novel flexible modes of work do not start or end with teleworking. Lobel, Googins and Bankert (1999), offer a wide framework which takes into account contemporary trends: globalization, increasing organizational flexibility, changing family structures and technological changes to examine both operational and strategic implications for managers, as well as research implications.

Part-time work has been growing quickly over the last quarter of the twentieth century and gains high attention in the theoretical academic development (cf. Feldman, 1990, and Barling and Gallagher, 1996, on the nature and consequences of part-time work). This evolution has been mainly linked to four factors:

1. The high rate of unemployment in several European countries.
2. The increased participation of women in the labour force; women's rate of part-time work is higher than that of men.
3. The need to cut down costs, to enhance operational flexibility, or to increase access to scarce human capital and to enlarge the pool of talent upon which the organization can build.
4. State incentives aiming to increase employment rate have supported and increased the use of part-time jobs.

At another level of work flexibility and employment relationship we can find the phenomenon of multiple part-time (MPT) work patterns. MPT is a new alternative work arrangement, forming part of the emerging 'new psychological contracts' in employment. MPT involves a shift away from paternalistic and benevolent secure employment, to an emphasis on continuous responsibility for self-development and employability on the part of the employee.

A different flexible work arrangement that enables people to keep to work and career effectively is flexitime. By this term we mean the ability to shift time of work in an unorthodox schedule. This can be an option to start and end work earlier or later than the 'standard', or to arrange work according to pressure that can be subject to different demands. Such demands can be on a weekly, monthly or annual basis. For example, in accounting there is more work pressure at the end of the month, and on a yearly base, in April and December.

Job sharing is another alternative work arrangement that enables more than one person to share a certain role. It came mostly as a response for working females and mothers, but might mean lost opportunities for advancement when such arrangements are necessary.

Another form of labour market flexibility is the use of contingent work. It has become questionable whether employers are still looking for a highly committed workforce. They may wish to have this commitment from their 'core' people. However, new evidence suggests that temporary workers may have a similar psychological contract and even higher job satisfaction and commitment to the organization. Krausz, Sagie and Bidermann (2000) found no difference between part-time and full-time workers in their work attitudes. In fact, they identify advantages for the control of work scheduling, which can be more in the hands of contingent workers. Contingent work can be an invaluable source of knowledge and learning for the organization (Matusik and Hill, 1998). Nevertheless, finding an appropriate career system to fit the needs of a contingent workforce is a challenging task for organizations. **YB**

References and further reading

Barling, J. and Gallagher, D. (1996) 'Part-time employment', in C. L. Cooper and I. T. Robertson (eds) *International Review of Industrial and Organizational Psychology*, vol. 2, Chichester: Wiley, 243–77.

Feldman, D. C. (1990) 'Reconceptualizing the nature and consequences of part-time work', *Academy of Management Review* 15: 103–12.

Gottlieb, B. H., Kelloway, E. K. and Barham, E. (1998) *Flexible Work Arrangements*, Chichester: Wiley.

Krausz, M., Sagie, A. and Bidermann, Y. (2000) 'Actual and preferred work schedules and scheduling control as determinants of job-related attitudes', *Journal of Vocational Behavior* 56(1): 1–11.

Lobel, S. A., Googins, B. K. and Bankert, E. (1999) 'The future of work and family: critical trends for policy, practice, and research' *Human Resource Management* 38(3): 243–54.

Matusik, S. F. and Hill, C. W. (1998) 'The utilization of contingent work, knowledge creation, and competitive advantage', *Academy of Management Review* 23(4): 680–97.

Annual hours

Annual hours is a system whereby employees contract to work a number of hours over a year, instead of per week. It has been introduced to allow flexibility in working, especially where the organization's context is one of seasonality or a degree of uncertainty. In a frozen food factory, the employees may work 48 hours a week at harvest time and 34 hours a week the rest of the year. Although mostly operating in manufacturing, it has spread into contracting, installation and has been formalized in a number of professional occupations, particularly teaching. There are also innovative schemes in the media and the health service, public and private. Around 3 per cent of full-time employees (485 000) currently work under some form of annualized hours scheme. (IDS, 1999)

Annual hours' schemes are often integrated with changes in working practices, including job design and pay systems. For example, the agreed annual hours may represent a reduction in the working week but will aim to eliminate all overtime payments, with employees covering for any absence or holidays by training to enhance their skills. Employees will have a work schedule for an extended period, say three months or six months, but this may not take up all of their contracted hours, the remainder being 'reserve' hours when they can be called upon in response to difficulties caused by machine breakdowns or absence. Management strategy here is to try to change the work culture from one of indifference to work problems (which help to creating overtime) to one of concern for continuous, problem-free output (where their reserve hours are not required). Employees generally receive the same monthly payment throughout the year.

For employers, the schemes can lead to substantial savings and better continuity of work. It should also produce greater commitment from employees and reduced absenteeism. The benefits for employees can include the evenness of payment each month and generally some reduction in hours. However, where the context is very uncertain, such as in the media, employees may be required to work long hours at short notice. Other difficulties associated with the scheme are the complexity of operation and the forecasting of required hours. If the forecasts are wrong and employees run out of hours before the end of the year, then a reversion to overtime becomes necessary which undermines the whole basis of the scheme. **JS**

References and further reading

Hutchinson, S. (1993) *Annual Hours Working in the UK*, London: Institute of Personnel and Development.

Income Data Services (IDS) (1999) 'Annual hours', Study 674, August.

Stredwick, J. and Ellis, S. (1998) *Flexible working practices*, London: Institute of Personnel and Development.

Application form

Application forms are used for shortlisting, the first step in selection of new staff. They are widely used by organizations, particularly in the public sector, for all but the most senior posts, the alternative being to allow candidates to construct their own CV, or to use telephone screening. The advantages of using application forms are that the employer can ensure all the required information is included on the form, they provide a more systematic way to compare candidates, and they can provide information which can be used as a structure for interviews. Some organizations even link the form to their competency framework asking questions such as 'provide an example of when you have demonstrated your leadership skills'.

On the downside, some candidates, especially for professional and senior posts, may feel that application forms are too restrictive to allow them to present themselves effectively, and at the other end of the range, form filling may be off-putting for candidates with poor language skills, a concern if the post is a manual one anyway. To minimize these concerns employers may use several forms for different levels of post, allowing a more tailored approach, and different formats should be available, such as braille, for those with disabilities.

Current concerns about application forms centre around the sorts of questions which may be included. Good practice in avoiding unfair discrimination suggests that questions relating to title (e.g. Mr or Miss), names (first names and surnames), gender, schools attended, marital status, dependant children and union membership should all be avoided, and with concerns about age discrimination, reference to date of birth is also becoming contentious. Another approach is to have all such information on a separate form for monitoring race, sex and disability so that those making shortlisting decisions are not affected by possible unfair bias. There is also some debate on the usefulness of questions about hobbies and interests, since such information is of limited relevance to potential job performance and many candidates may not answer these honestly anyway. **JB**

References and further reading

Industrial Relations Service (IRS) (1990) 'Application forms', *Industrial Relations Review and Report, Recruitment and Development Report*, 472, September: 16.

Industrial Relations Service (IRS) (1994) 'Ensuring effective recruitment: developments in the use of application forms', *Industrial Relations Review and Report, Employee Development Bulletin*, 556, March: 2–8.

Leighton, P. (2000) 'Don't ask, don't tell', *People Management* 6(10), 11 May: 42–4.

Examples of application forms used by various organizations can be found on the Chartered Institute of Personnel and Development's web site: www.cipd.co.uk/

Apprenticeships

The principle of modern apprenticeships is that for the first time in Britain the state supports part-time education and training for young people who are employed. The subsidy provided by the government varies between localities and occupations Nevertheless it is an important step towards establishing the principle of providing financial support for employers who may be unable, or unwilling, to pay the full costs of training young people. The employer still pays the wages of the modern apprentice and from its inception the Modern Apprenticeship (MA) scheme was designed to give control to employers. Therefore, traditional certifying bodies and trade unions have taken on a scaled down role to emphasize that it is the employer's responsibility for training and developing young people within a modern apprenticeship scheme.

To date, approximately 70 sectors covering the majority of British industry and commerce have developed model apprenticeship programmes. Many have been built on the more traditional models, particularly in engineering and electrical installation and to a much greater extent revived the construction industry's previous apprenticeship programmes. According to Gospel, the only large new sectors that have embarked on MA programmes are business administration, retailing, health, social and childcare. It would appear from published figures that sectors such as information technology, chemical, textiles and telecommunications have been slow in organizing MAs for young people. However, it is important to note that the MA schemes are new to these sectors and need to be fully established with increased numbers.

The aim of the MAs is fundamentally to attract young women and ethnic groups because of the former embedded philosophy that apprenticeships were only applicable and, indeed, suitable for, young males especially in engineering and construction. The new design of MAs is to encourage employers to take a young person onto the payroll as an employee as a means of attracting other young people. The apprenticeship in entered into by agreement between employer and employee, specifying rights and obligations. The agreement incorporates the training to be provided qualifications to be attained and a commitment to completion. This agreement is underwritten or countersigned by the local Training and Enterprise Council, (TEC – soon to become Training Skills Councils) If the employer ceases trading, it is the responsibility of the local TEC to find an alternative employer for the young person.

The government's intention is to create an apprenticeship culture in Britain but make it quite clear that, because of devolution of the British government, i.e. the Welsh Assembly, and Scotland with its own Parliament, the apprenticeship will apply to England only. The culture will emphasize:

1. Meeting the needs of the individual in a learning environment, which is broader and more coherent than before.
2. Offers even greater opportunities for progression including higher education by 2010.
3. Secures highest possible standards and is part of a coherent vocational learning system for all young people from the age of 14 years.

The modern apprenticeship framework is based on competencies with the basic idea that a nationwide and rationalized system of transparent and transferable qualifications will be achieved. The qualifications will be based on the National Vocational Qualification (NVQ) system and range from level 1 at the bottom up to degree level (level 5). The statistics that are currently available show:

- Britain's apprenticeships represent less that 1 per cent of the workforce
- Germany 5 per cent
- Australia 2 per cent.

From these figures it is apparent that there is still a long way to go to develop a workforce with the skills that are appropriate to the intense competitive market in which the UK operates. However, it is worth noting that in retailing and health care the numbers are increasing and this is congruent with the system operating for many years in Germany. Many National Health Service (NHS) hospitals in the UK have completely revamped their training and development programmes. Modern apprenticeships are offered in a wide range of occupations, for example, radiography, midwifery, pharmacy, physiotherapy and even hotel services within the NHS. **SR**

References and further reading

Creating more apprenticeships (1997) *European Industrial Relations review* no. 276: 21–3. (Comparisons with other European countries especially Germany.)

Gospel, H. F. (1998) 'Reinventing apprenticeship' *CentrePiece* 3(3): 19–23.

Gospel, H. F. (1997) *The Revival of Apprenticeship Training in Britain?* London: London School of Economics, Centre for Economic Performance.

Government consultative document (2000), 'Modern apprenticeships', July, DfEE.

Industrial Relations Service (IRS) (1998) 'Trainees' IRS Employment Review, *Industrial Relations Law Bulletin* no. 655, May: 12–16. (This article is an overview of the special employment law considerations applying to trainee workers who do not necessarily have employee status.)

NHS recruitment leaflet, Heatherwood and Wexham Park Hospitals NHS. (With special thanks for their help.)

Arbitration

In industrial relations terms, arbitration can be seen as a method of settling a dispute by referring it to an independent body or arbitrator, both parties having agreed beforehand to abide by the arbitration decision.

Arbitration within industry in Britain has a long history. In 1800 there existed a system of compulsory binding arbitration in disputes between the employer and individual employees. However, the model for a system of arbitration emerged following the 1891 Royal Commission on Labour. The resulting 1896 Conciliation Act repealed earlier provisions for compulsory and binding arbitration and allowed the Labour Department of the Board of Trade to appoint an arbitrator to settle disputes. The emphasis of the approach from 1896 has been to settle disputes first through conciliation, and then *voluntary* arbitration. Only during wartime has this approach altered with the introduction of compulsory *binding* arbitration. This is unlike most other countries who operate a system of compulsory arbitration in labour disputes.

The voluntary arbitration service started by the government in 1896 was operated from 1960 by the Industrial Relations Service, the Manpower and Productivity Service from 1969, and the Conciliation and Advisory Service from 1972. Finally, the Advisory, Conciliation and Arbitration Service (ACAS) was established in 1975 to facilitate (amongst other functions) an arbitration service independent of the state.

The Industrial Court, established in 1919 as a permanent and independent tribunal of employers and employee representatives, plus independents, was a body to which the Minister of Labour dould refer any actual or anticipated dispute to the court for voluntary arbitration, but only if both parties consented. The Industrial Court was renamed the Industrial Arbitration Board on 1971, and was replaced by the Central Arbitration Committee (CAC) in 1976. The CAC can:

- Provide voluntary arbitration.
- Determine claims by the trade unions for disclosure of information for collective bargaining purposes.
- Arbitrate claims for statutory recognition and de-recognition of trade unions under the Employment Relations Act, 1999. This arbitration is compulsory, and thus unique in the UK.

Although arbitration is part of the remit of ACAS, it is not ACAS officials but independent experts drawn from an approved panel who arbitrate in a dispute. At the request of one party to a dispute, but normally with the consent of both, ACAS can appoint an arbitrator, or refer a matter to the CAC. The parties can, however, choose not to go through ACAS, instead appointing their own arbitrator.

The process of arbitration usually involves the arbitrator hearing the arguments put forward by both sides and deciding on a compromise. The approach has been criticized as resulting in arbitration awards which 'split' the difference between the parties. This has encouraged some organizations to use pendulum arbitration where the arbitrator chooses between the employer's final offer or employee's final claim. In theory this should encourage both sides to take less extreme positions, increasing the potential for a voluntary settlement. However, a disadvantage is that pendulum arbitration assumes one side is right , and the other side is wrong.

Arbitration has not been seen as relevant for all types of disputes. Usually it is used for 'disputes of rights', i.e. issues arising over disputes about the parties rights in existing collective agreements. Arbitration is not seen as appropriate in 'disputes of interest', i.e. disputes arising from negotiating new collective agreements.

During the 1980s and 1990s the types of issues dealt with through arbitration have covered job grading, discipline and dismissals, and pay (but not annual pay increases) and conditions. However, the use of arbitration has now declined significantly. This appears to be mainly because of employer reluctance; they perceive arbitration as a process whereby they lose control of events, unlike with processes such as conciliation and mediation. Thus, whilst arbitration will continue to have a role on industrial relations in Britain, it is unlikely to be more extensively used. **DK**

References and further reading
Elkouri, F. and Elkouri, E. (1997) *How Arbitration Works*, New York: BNA Books.
Goodman, A. (1993) *Basic Skills for the New Arbitrator*, New York: Solomon.
Kheel, T. W. and Lurie, W. L. (1999) *The Keys to Conflict Resolution*, New York: Four Walls.

Assessment and development centres

Assessment centres are most commonly used as a method of selection to management and professional posts. They consist of sets of exercises such as presentations, group discussions, management simulations, psychometric tests and interviews. These are designed to reveal the extent to which candidates possess the attributes required for the post for which they are being considered. Candidates are observed by trained assessors who score their performance on predetermined criteria on the basis of candidates' behaviour. The criteria are competencies and other personal attributes required to perform well in the post, and perhaps also of strategic importance to the organization's future direction. Assessors usually meet at the end of the centre to discuss the candidates and arrive at overall judgements and decisions. Assessment centres typically last about two days, but one-day and three-day versions are not uncommon. They are often experienced as quite intensive by all involved. It is important that exercises are carefully designed to test the required attributes, that assessors are trained well and that the centre is run efficiently. Where this is the case, assessment centres tend to be one of the more valid selection techniques, in the sense that candidates' performance at the centre predicts fairly well their success in the job.

Development centres use the same technology as assessment centres, but are normally not used to select for particular posts. Instead, they are used to identify individuals' current strengths and limitations, and ways in which they can best be developed in future. In order to achieve this, it is essential that feedback is given to candidates. The feedback needs to be comprehensive and expressed in ways which make it as easy as possible to form plans for future development. There needs to be commitment within the organization to the implementation of individuals' development plans. Development centres often have an element of selection about them – for example, entry to a 'fast track' development stream may depend on performance at the centre. This mixing of selection and development can often create difficulties. For example, candidates may try to hide their weaknesses because there is something at stake. **JA**

References and further reading
Ballantyne, I. and Povah, N, (1995) *Assessment and Development Centres*, Aldershot: Gower.
Carrick, P. and Williams, R. (1999) 'Development centres – a review of assumptions', *Human Resource Management Journal* 9(2): 77–92.
Gaugler, B., Rosenthal, D., Thorton, G. and Bentson, C. (1987) 'A survey of assessment center practices in organizations', *Journal of Applied Psychology* 72: 493–511.
Jackson, C. and Yeates, J. (1993). *Development Centres: Assessing or Developing People?* Brighton: Institute for Manpower Studies.
Jones, R. G., and Whitmore, M. D. (1995) 'Evaluating developmental assessment centers as interventions', *Personnel Psychology* 48: 377–88.
Robertson, I. T., Iles, P. A., Gratton, L. and Sharpley, D. (1991) 'The impact of personnel selection and assessment methods on candidates', *Human Relations* 44(9): 963–81.

B

Ballots

Ballots ensure that each voter can make a choice in secret. Ballots are used by trade unions to make decisions about industrial action, to elect union members to some senior positions within the union (particularly to union national executive committees) and to decide upon the continuation or establishment union political funds. Legal obligations for unions to use ballots in these circumstances were defined in the 1984 Trade Union Act, and the 1988 Employment Act required that these ballots be postal. These provisions were later incorporated in the 1992 Trade Union and Labour Relations (Consolidation) Act. If, in the event of industrial action, unions fail to adhere to the legally defined ballot procedures, they are denied immunity from civil action by employers and employers may seek an injunction initially to obstruct such industrial action. Under the 1999 Employment Relations Act secret ballots can also be used to establish trade union recognition (Gennard and Judge, 1999: 170–3). If there are particular doubts about the union's case for recognition, under this Act the Central Arbitration Committee can invoke a ballot of the relevant workforce.

In the late 1970s and early 1980s, there were widespread employer and media accusations that union voting systems were undemocratic, and that union militancy was unrepresentative of union membership. Most unions argued that this was an excuse for government interference in their internal affairs. Traditionally, unions had operated a variety of voting methods, including secret ballots in some circumstances and *show of hands* votes in others. However, following the 1984 and 1988 Acts, unions quickly adjusted to the new situation, and the outcome of this legislation was often not quite what the Conservative government had intended. Large majorities of union members decided to retain union political funds, secret ballots did not necessarily obstruct the election of union militants, and sometimes ballot results in favour of industrial action have proved to be enough in themselves to secure significant concessions from employers. (See also **Strikes** and **Political funds**.) **DB**

References and further reading
Elias, P. (1990) 'Law and union democracy: the changing shape', in P. Fosh and E. Heery (eds) *Trade Unions and their Members: Studies in Union Democracy and Organization*, London: Macmillan.

Gall, G. and McKay, S. (1996) 'Injunctions as a legal weapon in industrial disputes', *British Journal of Industrial Relations* 34 (4): 567–82.

Gennard, J. and Judge, J. (1999) *Employee Relations*, 2nd edn, London: Institute of Personnel and Development, pp. 170–3.

Labour Research Department (LRD) (1998) 'Ballot laws cause legal attacks', *Labour Research*, 87 (10): 15–16.

Labour Research Department (LRD) (1998) *The Law at Work*, London: LRD Publications.

McIlroy, J. (1995) *Trade Unions in Britain Today*, 2nd edn, Manchester: Manchester University Press.

Behavioural event interviewing

Behavioural event interviewing (also known as patterned behaviour description interviewing, or criterion-based, competency-based or skills-based interviewing) poses in-depth questions about candidates' actual past behaviour to gather evidence about skills or competencies. For example, where a job requires persuasiveness, behavioural questions ask candidates to describe how they persuaded someone to change their view or gain support for something. The interviewer seeks evidence of successful persuasive skills from past events, the inference being that the candidate would display similar behaviour in the future. This approach is used mainly in selection interviewing, but can also be used in other interviewing scenarios such as appraisal, discipline, and selection of consultants. Research suggests that these questions give a more accurate prediction of performance than more general questions. It also has the benefit of being flexible, and respondents can discuss skills they have used in situations outside work.

Interviewers tend to be positive about the technique in practice because it gives them more relevant, detailed information on which to judge candidates, particularly in relation to critical incidents, and from the candidates' perspective it gives them a good opportunity to explain their skills, although they may need to prepare in advance to give detailed examples from their past.

There is evidence that the use of this questioning technique is becoming more commonplace. To use this approach interviewers need to have clearly defined competencies for each post, and it does require more time to prepare and conduct the interview. It is also important to use a structured scoring system to evaluate responses. Because it focuses exclusively on the past, a concern is that this type of questioning may disadvantage young candidates who have not had the opportunity to demostrate their potential. In these cases, it may be preferable to use some situational interview questions or assessment centre exercises. **JB**

References and further reading

Anderson, N. and Shackleton, V. (1993) *Successful Selection Interviewing*, Oxford: Blackwell.

Barclay, J. (2001) 'Improving selection interviews with structure: organizations' use of "Behavioural" Interviews', *Personnel Review*, (forthcoming).

Campion, M. A., Palmer, D. K. and Campion, J. E., (1997) 'A review of structure in the selection interview', *Personnel Psychology* 50 (3): 655–702.

Taylor, P. J. and O'Driscoll, P. (1995) *Structured Employment Interviewing*, Aldershot: Gower.

Belbin teams

Teamworking has become increasingly important in the workplace, but effective teamwork is not easy to achieve. It depends, among other things, on the members of a team being able to adopt different and complementary roles. If this is done successfully, the result of the team's efforts can be greater than the sum of the individuals' efforts. One particularly influential perspective on team roles has been developed by Meredith Belbin. He identified nine roles that team members need to fulfil if the team is to be successful:

1. Co-ordinator: keeps team focused on goals without offending other members.
2. Shaper: energetic, lots of drive to achieve team goals.
3. Plant: supplies new and innovative ideas.
4. Monitor evaluator: analytical and detached evaluator of plans and ideas.
5. Implementer: identifies and carries out the routine methodical tasks conscientiously.
6. Team worker: builds harmony and team spirit by supporting other members.
7. Resource investigator: finds information and resources from outside the team.
8. Completer finisher: makes detailed plans and ties up loose ends.
9. Technical specialist: provides specialist knowledge and/or skills.

Of course, not all teams are composed of exactly nine people, each of whom takes one role. Usually it is necessary for each person to fill more than one role. Most individuals are capable of doing this, though each of us has roles we would find it very difficult to fill effectively. An important part of team-building using Belbin's roles involves assessing the preferred roles of each team member and encouraging all members to appreciate the characteristics and strengths of the others. Belbin has developed a self-assessment questionnaire for identifying individuals' preferred team roles. It is a useful tool for raising awareness of team roles, and research has uncovered some connections between it and theory in personality and leadership. However, it also seems to have a number of psychometric weaknesses which cast doubt on its ability to measure stable aspects of personality. Nevertheless, it helps team members understand the alternative roles and why their team performs as it does. For example, a team oversupplied with Shapers and Implementers, but lacking Plants and Team Workers would probably formulate plans quite quickly, but these might well be insufficiently creative and discussed in a combative fashion which could leave some team members upset or alienated.

JA

References and further reading

Belbin, R. M. (1993) *Team Roles at Work*: *A Strategy for Human Resource Management*, Oxford: Butterworth–Heinemann.

Belbin, R. M. (1996) *Management Teams*: *Why They Succeed or Fail*, Oxford: Butterworth–Heinemann.

Belbin, R. M. (1996). *How to Build Successful Teams. . . the Belbin Way*, CD-ROM published by Butterworth–Heinemann, Oxford.

Dulewicz, V. (1995) 'A validation of Belbin's team roles from 16PF and OPQ using bosses' ratings of competence', *Journal of Occupational and Organizational Psychology* 68: 81–99.

Fisher, S. G. , Hunter, T. A., and Macrosson, W. (1998). 'The structure of Belbin's team roles', *Journal of Occupational and Organizational Psychology* 71: 283–8.

Furnham, A., Steele, H. and Pendleton, D. (1993) 'A psychometric assessment of the Belbin Team-Role Self-Perception Inventory', *Journal of Occupational and Organizational Psychology* 66: 245–57.

Benchmarking

Benchmarking is the process of measuring and comparing organizational performance and practices against relevant criteria (benchmarks), and using the results as a basis for improving organizational performance. Benchmarking first became popular in the 1950s when used by the Japanese, who imported Western consumer goods and stripped them down to understand how they were made and to improve their own manufacturing practices and performance as a result. More recently this process of learning was reversed as Western managers travelled to Japan to learn their techniques of world-class manufacturing and we came full circle.

In the West, benchmarking became popular as a result of the pioneering work of Robert Camp at Rank Xerox in the USA. Benchmarking methods consist of a set of tools and techniques for measuring specific business results, such as productivity or absenteeism, and comparing them with competitors or industry averages or even world-class standards in order to gain some insight into company competitiveness in key areas of performance. The outcome is normally a performance improvement programme designed to increase output or reduce costs or in some way to improve an organization's competitive position in its markets. Competitor benchmarking consists of directly comparing organizational performance with industry leaders in order to understand and try to surpass their level of achievement. The problem with this idea, of course, is that such information is hard to obtain when companies consider that this is what gives them competitive advantage.

Benchmarking methods can be either tailored to a specific organization and its needs or they can be standardized through the use of generic questionnaires, which have grown in popularity in recent years. Generic methods are cheaper and quicker to use and provide a ready-made database of benchmarks. Some standardized methods of benchmarking can be found on the World Wide Web (WWW) and can be completed and analysed on-line (see References). The Confederation of British Industry (CBI) has a family of four generic benchmarking methods available to its members. Based on the use of self-assessment questionnaires, these tools can be used to benchmark manufacturing performance, customer service standards and environment health and safety standards in organizations. Human Resource Management (HRM) professionals may wish to note that in 2000 the CBI added a method of benchmarking the human resource function itself. It is called 'Headstart' and would provide HRM professionals with valuable insight into the advantages and disadvantages of this kind of approach. Some industries, such as motor manufacturing, have devised their own industry-based benchmarking tools. More recently, benchmarking theorists and practitioners have progressed towards 'process benchmarking', which seeks to identify and map the processes which underlie superior performance in organizations. Process mapping has become a new skill in some organizations as they seek to identify 'best practice' in organizations. This is sometimes called best practice benchmarking. Software packages are now available to support process mapping. Benchmarking is no longer the preserve of private industry. It is being used extensively by UK police forces and the health sector. Local government has also taken up benchmarking as a way of demonstrating that it can challenge and compare its existing practices with external best practice. **JBr**

References and further reading

Brewster, C., Farndale, E. and Van Ommren, J. (2000) *HR Healthcheck: Benchmarking HRM Practice across the UK and Europe*, London: Financial Times Prentice Hall.

Bullivant, J. (2000) *Practical Benchmarking to Make a Difference*, London: Office for Public Management.

Camp, R. C. (1998) *Global Cases in Benchmarking*, New York: McGraw-Hill.

Reider, R. (2000) *Benchmarking Strategies*, Chichester: Wiley.

Spendolini, M. J. (2000) *The Benchmarking Book*, New York: AMACOM.

World Wide Web (WWW) (1999) *Industry Weeks Manufacturing Best Practices Survey*, httrx 11205.179141.1 70/Surveysliw 1/survey. hUn

Zairi, M. (1998) *Benchmarking for Best Practice*, Oxford: Butterworth-Heinemann.

'Best practice' human resource management (HRM)

'Best practice' HRM is the notion that human resource (HR) practices work most effectively when introduced in related and mutually reinforcing 'bundles'. In contrast to 'contingency' theorists (who argue that the efficacy of employment policy and practice may be dependent on a business's product market, the competitive context and, perhaps most significantly, its strategy (see **Contingency approach**), most advocates of 'best practice' maintain that it provides a suitable model for *all* businesses to follow.

Although the precise practices vary between individual studies (cf. Pfeffer, 1994; 1998; Wood, 1995; Huselid, 1995; Ichniowski *et al.*, 1996) there are some common elements. Pfeffer (1998), one of the best known American writers on 'best practice' includes seven practices (a reduction from the 16 described in 1994):

- employment security
- selective hiring
- self-managed teams or teamworking
- high compensation contingent on organizational performance
- extensive training
- the reduction of status differences
- sharing information with employees.

Crucially, it is argued that the impact of such benefits is quantifiable. In a survey of more than 1 000 US-owned firms, Huselid (1995) argued that a one standard deviation increase in these practices is associated with a 7.05 per cent decrease in labour turnover and $27 044 more in sales per employee.

There are difficulties with this literature and with some of the studies used to illustrate the notion. While at a commonsensical level it is reasonable to assume that consistent and complementary HR practices will be more effective than isolated interventions, it is not clear that any particular 'bundle' (or, if it is, *which* of the numerous 'bundles' advocated in the literature) is universally beneficial. Moreover, detailed study of the literature reveals that individual practices may not be as 'best' as originally presented or as consistently applied (see Marchington and Grugulis, 2000, for a more detailed discussion of this). **IG and MM**

References and further reading

Huselid, M (1995) 'The impact of human resource management practices on turnover, productivity and corporate financial performance', *Academy of Management Journal* 38(3): 635–72.

Ichniowski, C., Kochan, T., Levin, D., Olson, C. and Strauss, G. (1996), 'What works at work: overview and assessment', *Industrial Relations* 35(3): 299–333.

Marchington, M. and Grugulis, I. (2000) ''Best Practice' human resource management: perfect opportunity or dangerous illusion?', *International Journal of Human Resource Management* 11(5), December: 1104–24.

Pfeffer, J. (1994) *Competitive Advantage through People,* Boston, MA: Harvard Business School Press.

Pfeffer, J. (1998) *The Human Equation; Building Profits by Putting People First*, Boston, MA: Harvard Business School Press.

Wood, S. (1995) 'The four pillars of HRM; are they connected?' *Human Resource Management Journal* 5(5): 49–59.

Biodata

Using biodata (short for biographical data) in selection is an attempt to relate the characteristics of job applicants to the characteristics of successful job holders to predict job performance. It might be argued that this is what all selection involves, but the use of biodata requires a very systematic approach. The process involves first categorizing existing employees in a specific post as good, average or poor performers, and then identifying the key work and personal characteristics of good and poor performers. New applicants answer a detailed questionnaire about their work and personal history. These answers are scored according to how closely these match those of existing good performers.

It is a technique which is not commonly used (fewer than 5 per cent of large organizations use it) because it is costly and controversial. Practical concerns include the need for large numbers of existing job holders (several hundred) to take part in the development stage of identifying key data, which is also time-consuming. The key data cannot be transferred between jobs: the criteria for each job must be identified separately and updated regularly.

More fundamental are the concerns about the fairness of the technique. It tends to be considered unfair by candidates since decisions may be based on seemingly irrelevant and sometimes intrusive information, such as whether they are the first born in their family, or if their parents divorced. It is also criticized because it is potentially discriminatory, using criteria such as sex, marital status, number of children and nationality to shortlist or reject applicants. While some of these attributes may be shared by the best existing employees, these may in fact have no direct influence on performance: these may be simply be a matter of coincidence or more likely, the result of hiring similar employees in the past.

Biodata can therefore only be used cost-effectively where there are a large number of applications for a standard, unchanging position and where there are also large numbers of existing staff in that position from which to identify the selection criteria. Even in these limited situations employers should be wary of the potential for unfairness inherent in the approach. **JB**

References and further reading

Gunther, B., Furnham, A. F. and Drakely, R. J. (1993) *Biodata: Biographical Indicators of Business Performance*, London: Routledge.

Industrial Relations Service (IRS) (1990) 'Biodata – past tense, future perfect?', *Industrial Relations Review and Report, Recruitment and Development Report*, no. 456, July: 9–16.

Industrial Relations Service (IRS) (1997) 'The state of Selection 2: developments in basic methods', *Industrial Relations Review and Report, Recruitment and Development Bulletin*, no. 89, May: 6–11.

Strebler, M. (1991) *Biodata in Selection*, Brighton: Institute of Manpower Studies.

Taylor, S. (1998) *Employee Resourcing*, London: Institute of Personnel and Development, pp. 142–5.

Wilkinson, L. (1993) 'An alternative view of biodata: the model', *Recruitment, Selection and Retention* 2(3): 23–9.

Boardroom pay

Concerns expressed during most of the 1990s in the media and elsewhere about the level and transparency of directors' pay led to the setting up of three committees, chaired by Cadbury (1993), Greenbury (1995) and Hampel (1998). The committees were set up by the interested financial parties, including the London Stock Exchange, the accountancy profession and the Financial Reporting Council. All three committees were attempts at self-regulation to try to prevent legislation being forced upon them. Any company wishing to be listed on the Stock Exchange now has to agree to certain recommendations, which each committee has gradually tightened. A summary of the main points are as follows:

- A separation of the roles of chairman and chief executive is to be preferred and companies should justify a decision to combine the roles.
- Independent non-executive directors should make up at least one-third of the board members.
- A Remuneration Committee should be in place made up only of non-executive directors which should determine remuneration policy and the reward packages of individual executive directors. The committee's report should be part of the company's annual report.
- Full disclosure should be given in the accounts of named individual director's remuneration (basic pay, various bonuses and the criteria for awarding them, pension provision, contracts of service, share option and termination arrangements).

- Service contract periods should not exceed two years and should, preferably, be no longer than a year.
- Remuneration packages should become more geared to measurable performance factors and take account of wider issues, including the pay and employment conditions elsewhere in the company. **JS**

References and further reading
Armstrong, M. and Murlis, H. (1998) *Reward Management*, 4th edn, London: Kogan Page.

Laing, D. and Weir, C. (1999) 'Governance structures, size and corporate performance in UK firms', *Management Decision* 37(8): 457–65.

Main, G. (1993) 'Pay in the board room: practice and procedures', *Personnel Review* 22(7): 2–13.

Potter, S. (1995) 'Disclosing more on top rewards', *People Management* 1(11): 41–2.

Broad-banded pay

As opposed to classical graded pay structures, broad-banded pay structures, as the name suggests, have a wide range of possible pay rates within them. There is often a considerable degree of overlap with other bands in the organization so that employees who are at different levels in the company hierarchy may be in receipt of the same remuneration.

There are usually only four or five bands present in a broad-banded pay structure. This reflects the trend towards flatter organizations as it conveys the message that a career can progress horizontally and not just vertically. This type of structure also supports role flexibility and team working strategies.

The bands consist of two parts, a Pay Zone for a particular role, followed by a further zone, which allows scope for further progression. This ensures that progressive reward is not only linked to promotion and this type of arrangement allows pay to be linked to some form of performance or skill measurement and not just position in the organization.

Some of the advantages claimed for broad-banding are that:

- It provides scope for greater task flexibility in moving staff between jobs within the same band.
- The consolidation of older narrow grades into a broad band usually raises the ceiling of the grade maximum, providing greater scope for upward employee progress.
- The bureaucracy and maintenance associated with a number of grading structures is removed.

Disadvantages which have been identified are:

- Salary progression and pay determination becomes more opaque; in the absence of fixed increments employees are uncertain about where they will move to.
- Pay can drift upwards in an uncontrolled way in the absence of fixed increments.
- Employee expectations can be thwarted if it is difficult to achieve the higher rate. **MM**

References and further reading
Armstrong, M. (2000) '*Feel the Width*', People Management, 3 Feb., p.34

Incomes Data Services (2000) '*Job Evaluation*', IDS StudyPlus , Autumn.

Institute of Personnel and Development (2000) *Study of broad-banded and job family pay structures*, January.

Leymann, H. (1996) 'The content and development of mobbing at work' *European Journal of Work and organizational Psychology*, 5(2): 165–84.

MSF (1995) *Bullying at Work*: *How to Tackle It. A Guide for MSF Representatives and Members*. London: MSF.

NASUWT (1996) *No Place to Hide. Confronting Workplace Bullies*. Birmingham: NASUWT.

Bullying

The concept of workplace bullying originated in Scandinavia. In the 1980s, workplace bullying was identified as part of the workplace health and safety agenda (Hoel, 1997).

Workplace bullying migrated to the UK in the 1990s. The problem has been defined as: 'persistent, offensive, abusive, intimidating, malicious or insulting behaviour, abuse of power or unfair penal sanctions which makes the recipient feel upset, threatened, humiliated or vulnerable, which undermines their self-confidence and which may cause them to suffer stress, (MSF, 1995: 12). This may include:

- having your opinions and views ignored
- someone withholding information which affects your performance
- being exposed to an unmanageable workload
- being given tasks with unreasonable or impossible targets or deadlines
- being ordered to do work below competence
- being ignored or facing hostility when you approach
- being humiliated or ridiculed in connection with your work
- excessive monitoring of your work
- spreading gossip
- having insulting or offensive remarks made about your person (i.e. habits and background), your attitudes or your private life
- having key areas of responsibility removed or replaced with more trivial or unpleasant tasks (Hoel and Cooper, 2000: 11).

Yet while many experiences count as workplace bullying, most researchers have insisted that these problems must be persistent in order to be understood as workplace bullying (Leymann, 1996, says it has to happen at least once a week for six months). However, Lee (2000) argues that even one incident of workplace bullying is one too many – workers should always be treated with dignity and respect.

Workplace bullying is usually presented in terms of abuse of organizational position. The current character of workplace bullying is often said to be related to the changing nature of work. The National Association of Schoolmasters and Union of Women Teachers (NASUWT) report (1996) points out that there are 'pathological bullies who will persecute and torment any victim they can find for the sheer pleasure of the exercise', yet most researchers focus upon 'situational bullies' (who threaten and bully subordinates when they are under pressure), 'role playing bullies' (who think they are expected to act in a bullying fashion because of the culture of the organization in which they work) and 'punishing bullies' (who believe that you get more out of staff by punishment and reward).

Research has focused upon the way in which workplace bullying is damaging to individuals and – perhaps most importantly – organizations. Field's workplace bullying web site lists a range of costs of workplace bullying:

- Six million working days are lost annually because of stress caused by bullying, job insecurity, shift work and long hours.
- On average, stress-related sickness absence costs employers between £530 and £545 per employee.
- The cost of replacing one employee is at least £5 000 for advertising and basic recruitment costs.
- Employment tribunals will cost in excess of £10 000 per stage.
- Workplace bullying victims frequently remain unemployed, dependent upon state benefits.

Workers are, therefore, significantly in need of protection. There have been attempts to introduce a law against workplace bullying – the Dignity at Work Bill. This failed in 1997. **DL**

References and further reading

Hoel, H. (1997) 'Bullying at work – a Scandinavian perspective', *Proceedings of the First Annual Conference of the National Harassment Network Higher and Further Education Branch*, University of Central Lancashire, 13–14 March.

Hoel, H. and Cooper, C. (2000) *Destructive Conflict and Bullying at Work*, Manchester: UMIST.

Lee, D. (2000) 'An analysis of workplace bullying in the UK', *Personnel Review* 29(5): 593–608.

Leymann, H. (1996) 'The content and development of mobbing at work', *European Journal of Work and Organisational Psychology* 5(2): 165–84.

Manufacturing, Science and Finance union (MSF) (1995) *Bullying at Work: How to Tackle It. A Guide for MSF Representatives and Members*, London: MSF.

National Association of Schoolmasters and Union of Women Teachers (NASUWT) (1996) *No Place to Hide. Confronting Workplace Bullies*, Birmingham: NASUWT.

Tim Field's workplace bullying web site: http://www.successunlimited.co.uk/

Business process re-engineering (BPR)

BPR emerged as a strategy for organizational change at the start of the 1990s and became a dominant theme for bringing about the radical transformation of businesses for the next decade.

BPR can be seen as a reaction to the theories of Continuous Improvement and Total Quality Management (see also entries on *Continuous Improvement* and *Total Quality Management*) which had become so well established in the 1980s. BPR theorists, such as Michael Hammer , took the view that incremental improvements in business performance were not sufficient to close the international competitiveness gap which was emerging between the USA and the so-called ' tiger economies ' of the Pacific rim, especially Japan and Korea. In the late 80s , this was the background to the development of theories of the need for radical organizational change.

Michael Hammer, a Professor of Computer Science at MIT , became the 'guru' of BPR and published a seminal article on the subject in Harvard Business Review in 1990. This was followed up by ' Reengineering the Corporation', co-authored with James Champy in 1993 , which became a bestseller and which is generally taken to be the foundation text of the BPR movement.

Hammer defines BPR as 'the radical transformation of business processes, structures, management systems and values to achieve quantum leaps in performance.' Proponents of BPR laid great emphasis on identifying core business processes and using customer focussed process reengineering (redesign) principles , usually driven by the transformational power of new information and communications technologies , to effect radical change in business methods leading to fundamental improvements in performance. Many companies undertook BPR programmes in the United States , including GEC , Hewlett-Packard and IBM. The ideas spread to Europe where they were taken up particularly by companies in telecommunications such as BT and in the petroleum , chemicals and financial services sectors.

But the theory did not always work out in practice and researchers into the effects of BPR programmes generally conclude that most of the programmes failed to achieve their objectives. BPR programmes were often used as the theoretical basis for 'downsizing' activities by companies in the 1990s. BPR came to be seen as a euphemism for job losses and its value as a management strategy began to be questioned.

Hammer himself came to revise his original views of BPR at the end of the 1990s and acknowledged that his ideas had undervalued the importance of Human Resources in organizations as compared to processes and technology.

With the erosion of the competitive threat from the far-east economies , at least for the moment , the peak of BPR activity is probably over but it has left a legacy of business process thinking and redesign skills which is still being felt across the UK economy and has lafterly made headway in the Public Sector, underpinning radical change programmes in ,for example, Local Government and the Health Service. **JB**

References and further reading
Armistead,C and Rowland,P (1996) *'Managing Business Processes:BPR and Beyond '*, Wiley
Burke,G and Peppard J (1995) *'Examining Business Process Reengineering, Current Perspectives and Research Directions'* Kogan Page, London
Hammer, M (1990) 'Re-engineering Work: Don't Automate, Obliterate' *Harvard Business Review,* 67(4), July–August
Hammer, M and Champy J (1993) ' *Reengineering the Corporation A Manifesto For Business Revolution* , Nicolas Brearley Publishing, London
Hammer, M (1996) *'Beyond Reengineering '*,Harper Collins

Business strategy and contingency approaches to human resource management

A well-established idea within the literature on human resource management (HRM) is that policies relating to the core functions of human resource (relations, reward, resourcing, training and development) should be integrated with business strategy. To this end, a number of theorists have developed existing ideas within mainstream business strategy or marketing to examine the different implications for HRM. Four of these are discussed below: the BCG Matrix, Porter's framework of competitive advantage, lifecycle models and, finally, Miles and Snow's typology. The reason such outlines of businesses are called 'contingency' approaches (sometimes 'matching' approaches) is because the focus and character of human resource (HR) initiatives is dependent on (contingent on) the underlying competitive position of the organization.

BCG Matrix

Developed by the Boston Consulting Group (hence BCG), this matrix describes the competitive position of a business in terms of two dimensions: market share, and overall market growth. The business can have either a high or low market share, and market growth can either be fast-growing or stagnant/declining. Thus there are four possible positions for a business, each of which has implications for HR:

1. Low share of fast-growing market – labelled *'wildcat/question mark'*; this business would be seeking growth via innovation and flexibility with de-emphasis on rules and bureaucracy. It is likely there would be little formal HR presence but employees might be expected to work 'beyond contract' to help the business grow.
2. Low share of a stagnant/declining market – labelled *'dog'*; this business would be one struggling to survive in a dwindling market with poor prospects for employees and managers alike. Emphasis for HR is likely to be on cutting labour costs and managing redundancy.
3. High share of fast-growing market – labelled *'star'*; this business is one with a profitable present and potentially even more profitable future. As a major player (high market share), it is unlikely there would be as much emphasis on risk as in a 'wildcat/question mark' firm and care would be taken to maintain and build on its competitive position. Emphasis for HR is likely to be on recruitment and selection, internal promotion and training and development.
4. High share of a stagnant/declining market – labelled *'cash cow'*; this business would be characterized by order and desire to maintain the (profitable) status quo. There may be elements of complacency and inflexibility or even arrogance given the well-established nature of the firm and given high profit margins. The HR function is likely to be similarly well established with specialist expertise in areas such as administration of pay systems, training and development and recruitment.

Porter's competitive advantage framework

This is developed from Porter's idea that organizations have three generic strategies to achieve competitive advantage. The three strategies are cost reduction, quality enhancement and innovation. Each has HR implications.

1. *Cost reduction*: labour costs are minimized; HR function is likely to be minimal and many policies ad hoc; pay would also be low; the firm is likely to be non-unionized.
2. *Quality enhancement*: in many ways likely to be the opposite of the above; the HR function will use ideals of 'best practice'.
3. *Innovation*: a premium on flexibility, informality (e.g. in communication networks) and problem-solving. Human resource may assist teamworking or specific development needs.
4. *Lifecycle approach*: This is based on the idea that organizations go through various stages of a lifecycle from start-up to growth, maturity and decline, and is similar in some ways to the BCG model (start-up – wildcat/question mark; growth – rising star; maturity – cash cow; decline – dog). During *start-up* there is a premium on flexibility and entrepreneurship and HR functions (such as recruitment) may be outsourced. During *growth*, formalization may emerge and although there will still be a premium on flexibility, it will be important to retain committed employees. In *maturity* it is likely the most formalized HR systems will have developed, but the prospect of future decline may encourage emphasis on maintaining productivity and controlling cost. In *decline* emphasis will be on reducing labour costs and managing redundancies or reducing pay levels, both of which are likely to cause conflict even where there is no union presence.

Miles and Snow's types of effective strategy

These are defender, prospector and analyser, and are outlined briefly as follows:

1. *Defender*: organization has a narrow, stable product line in predictable markets and seeks growth through market penetration. Characterized by consistency, the HR focus is on internal promotion, training and development, and equity in reward systems to encourage high commitment.
2. *Prospector*: organization has a broad, changing product line in changing markets and seeks growth through product and market development. Characterized by change, the HR focus is on buying in relevant skills (recruitment) and rewarding results in the short term. Training and development may focus on ad hoc requirements.
3. *Analyser*: organization has both stable and changing product lines, operates in predictable and changing markets, and seeks growth mainly through market development. This is a combination of the other two strategies and so the HR implications are more diverse, or even mixed. The administration of pay systems, training and development initiatives and recruitment and selection will all need to be sensitive to this diversity.

It is perhaps best to use these conceptual tools as a means of guidance or shorthand way of collecting together related ideas of business strategy and HR *as a starting point for further thought*. They have limitations. They give no real sense of process or development, but offer a static or lock-step account of the strategy–HR interface. They also portray a very 'rational' view of strategy. Other theorists would emphasize that corporate strategy is often not planned, but emerges or evolves on an ad hoc basis, and is as much influenced by politics, personality and power struggles as it is by product line or market share. These models may represent what ought to be, rather than what is. Many organizations do not even have a coherent business strategy and it is hard to find clear evidence to show the strategy–HR interface working in the real world. An argument could also be made that if an organization's assets truly reside in its employees, then it should be that business strategy is determined by the HR function, or at least co-determined, rather than the picture here, which is of 'strategy first, people later'. A more mundane assessment would suggest that a final limitation of these contingency approaches is that they misrepresent the degree to which considerations of an overall strategy affect day-to-day operations in an HR department, which in practice may have little scope or power to influence even the core HR functions. **KM**

References and further reading
Legge, K. (1995) *Human Resource Management*: *Rhetorics and Realities*, London: Macmillan.
Marchington, M. and Wilkinson, A. (2000) *Core Personnel and Development*, London: IPD.
Purcell, J. and Ahlstrand, B. (1994) *Human Resource Management in the Multi-Divisional Company*, Oxford: Oxford University Press.
Schuler, R. (1992) 'Strategic human resource management: linking the people with the strategic needs of the business', *Organizational Dynamics*, 21(1): 18–32.
Schuler, R. and Jackson, S. F. (1987), 'Organizational strategy and organization level as determinants of human resource management practices', *Human Resource Planning*, 10(3): 125–41.
Storey, J. (ed.) (1995) *Human Resource Management*: *A Critical Text*, London: Thomson Learning.

Career anchors

Career anchor is a term introduced by Ed Schein. It began with some research he conducted in the 1960s on the careers of 44 high-flying American graduates. Schein concluded that these people developed during early career a core set of values and attitudes which guided their career decisions and strategies, though they were often unaware of this. He used the metaphor of an anchor to symbolize being attached to a fixed point, and being dragged back to it if one drifted too far away. Schein subsequently developed this work, and suggests that there are nine different anchors an individual may hold.

1. Technical/functional competence: specialization in the skills and knowledge of a specific function.
2. General managerial competence: interpersonal and analytical competence, managing things, seeking income and responsibility.
3. Autonomy/independence: doing things in one's own way, unfettered by rules, procedures or close supervision.
4. Security (geographic): staying in one's home area, staying local.
5. Security (tenure): having job security, staying loyal.
6. Entrepreneurial creativity: creating new organizations, products or services of one's own.
7. Service/dedication: having work which reflects important aspects of one's identity, and often (but not always) concern for others.
8. Pure challenge: wanting to overcome obstacles and win against the odds.
9. Lifestyle: integrating the different aspects of one's life.

Schein has produced a user-friendly workbook to enable people to identify their anchor. He suggests that during early career one anchor, and one only, becomes dominant. It reflects the things we will not sacrifice when confronted by difficult choices. People with different anchors may need to be managed and motivated in different ways. For example, those with a technical/functional career anchor will not appreciate being promoted into management roles. Clearly, some anchors are better suited to twenty-first century work than others. The security anchors may be quite hard to satisfy, whereas there may be ample opportunity for expression of the pure challenge and entrepreneurial creativity. **JA**

References and further reading

Nordvik, H. (1991) 'Work activity and career goals in Holland's and Schein's theories of vocational personalities and career anchors', *Journal of Vocational Behavior* 38: 165–78.
Schein, E. H. (1993) *Career Anchors: Discovering your Real Values*, London: Pfeiffer.

Career breaks

A career break is an extended period of unpaid leave from work. The intention is that, at some future date, the employee will return to work with the same employer at either the same level or to the same job, retaining all or some of the service-related rights and benefits. They are sometimes called 'employment breaks' as the break may not be related to a conventional career path.

These breaks were introduced as a formal scheme in the late 1980s by the high street banks and were first aimed at women who wanted to stay at home in their childrens' early years and would therefore leave their employment. The scheme allowed the banks to retain the skills and experience of these staff and the staff themselves would be assured of a soft re-entry to work. Originally they were only available to 'high-flyers' but most schemes today do not distinguish by rank, sex or age. In recent years, schemes have applied in many other situations, including caring for terminally ill relatives, departure overseas to accompany a spouse and even writing film scripts.

Schemes usually require a minimum period of work each year (two to four weeks is common) to update skills and retain contact. This often helps with staffing peak periods. The time limit for the break is usually five years, although some schemes extend to seven. Contact is also maintained through the staff receiving company magazines and being invited to social events.

Introducing such a scheme clearly demonstrates the employer's belief in a long-term commitment to its staff and contributes towards an effective and active equal opportunities programme. There are few reported difficulties, although clarification is required over the contractual situation (most schemes make it clear that service is broken but this has not been tested legally) and the details of re-entry. **JSk**

References and Further Reading

Institute of Employment Studies (IES) (1992) 'Beyond the Career Break', IMS Report, no. 223.
Stredwick, J. and Ellis, S. (1998) *Flexible Working Practices*, London: IPD.

Career management

Careers can be thought of as the sequence of employment-related positions, roles, activities and experiences encountered by a person. Career management is any attempt to influence one or more aspects of a person's career. This could include what job moves people make, the training to which they are exposed, the type of work they search for, and even the way they interpret their past. Individuals bear considerable responsibility for managing their own careers. It is not necessarily easy to find the time and space to do this, given the work and family demands experienced by many people, and the rapid changes in some labour markets brought about by economic and technological change.

In managing their own careers, individuals need to be aware of both their own changing skills, interests and values, and also the changing requirements and opportunities of the world of work. They also need to be able to match up information about self with information about world of work. Career management also includes identifying appropriate training and learning opportunities, developing and maintaining a network of contacts and presenting oneself effectively during selection processes, as well as performing well in one's work.

Employing organizations can also play a part in career management of people within them. If done well, this should help to ensure that individuals experience roles to which they are well suited, and that the organization benefits from their commitment and from their skills which are well matched to changing organizational needs. organizational career management techniques include mentoring (where relatively inexperienced individuals are guided by more experienced ones), personal development plans, development centres, succession planning and career counselling. The success of these interventions depends upon many factors, especially the commitment of, and training for all those involved. There also need to be clear benefits from participation for both individual and organization. **JA**

References and further reading

Arnold, J. (1997) *Managing Careers into the 21st Century*, London: Paul Chapman Publishing.

Arnold, J. (2001). 'Careers and career management', in N. Anderson, D. Ones, H. Kepir Senangil and C. Viswesvaran (eds) *International Handbook of Work and Organizational Psychology*, London: Sage.

Gutteridge, T. G., Leibowitz, Z. B. and Shore, J. E. (1993) *Organizational Career Development*, San Francisco: Jossey-Bass.

Herriot, P. and Pemberton, C. (1995) *New Deals*, Chichester: Wiley.

Hirsh, W. and Jackson, C. (1996). *Strategies for Career Development: Promise, Practice and Pretence*, Brighton: Institute for Employment Studies.

Tharenou, P. (1997) 'Managerial career advancement', In I. T. Robertson and C. L. Cooper (eds) *International Review of Industrial and Organizational Psychology*, vol. 12, Chichester: Wiley.

Careers

Careers are often thought of as involving entry to a relatively high status occupation and/or organization, with subsequent progression up a hierarchy offering increasing responsibility and reward. Kanter (1989) has termed this the bureaucratic career, and pointed out that nowadays it is not the only or even the most common form that careers can take. It is probably more helpful to adopt a much more flexible definition of career, as Arnold (1997: 16) has done: 'the sequence of employment-related positions, roles, activities and experiences encountered by a person'. This avoids the connotations of high status and upward movement inherent in more traditional conceptions of careers, which tend to contrast them with jobs. It also includes both subjective and objective elements of career. So, for example, one person might view his or her work history as enjoyable and successful while another person with an identical work history might experience it as monotonous and disappointing.

Careers are less predictable and, for some, less pleasant than they once were. Widespread downsizing and delayering combined with rapid technological and economic change starting in the last part of the twentieth century have meant that many people find themselves making unexpected, and sometimes unwelcome, transitions into different kinds of work or unemployment. These transitions often involve a loss of security and income. They may require unwanted relocation and retraining. Sideways and even downward hierarchical moves in organizations have become more common. Michael Arthur and colleagues have coined the term 'boundaryless career' (Arthur and Rousseau, 1996; Arthur, Inkson and Pringle, 1999) to express how careers take people across different organizations, settings, locations and types of work. Innovative individuals who are flexible with a range of up-to-date skills, the ability to market themselves and with a clear sense of their own values are more than ever likely to be those who experience satisfying and successful careers. **JA**

References and further reading
Arnold, J. (1997) *Managing Careers into the 21ˢᵗ Century*, London: Paul Chapman Publishing.
Arnold, J. (2001) 'Careers and career management', in N. Anderson, D. Ones, H. Kepir Senangil and C. Viswesvaran (eds) *International Handbook of Work and Organizational Psychology*, London: Sage
Arthur, M. and Rousseau, D. (1996) *The Boundaryless Career*, Oxford: Oxford University Press.
Arthur, M., Inkson, K. and Pringle, J. (1999) *The New Careers*, London: Sage.
Howard, A. (ed.) (1995) *The Changing Nature of Work*, San Francisco: Jossey-Bass.
Kanter, R. M. (1989) *When Giants Learn to Dance*, New York: Simon and Schuster.

Cellular manufacturing

Cellular manufacturing is a system of production in which machines and workers in a factory are organized into groups or 'cells', each of which is responsible for as much as possible of the manufacture of a 'family' of related products. Where a factory produces a range of products, it thus serves as an alternative to a 'process' layout, in which machines and workers are grouped together according to the function they perform. From the point of view of production or operations management, its chief advantage is that it reduces the amount of time semi-finished products spend in unproductive 'travelling' around the factory.

Although the historical origins of cellular manufacturing are obscure, the academic and consultant, John Burbidge, is credited with popularizing the idea in the UK during the 1960s and 1970s. It was not until the 1980s, however, that it became widespread, in part because of its association with other 'new wave' manufacturing strategies such as just-in-time (JIT) production.

From a human resource perspective the importance of cellular manufacturing lies in its association with two things: flexibility and teamworking. Workers' flexibility between tasks is likely to increase with the introduction of cells, as a relatively small group is now expected to be run as 'a factory within a factory'. This flexibility might be something effectively forced onto workers, however, rather than something accompanied by more opportunities for training and increases in pay and status. Teamworking in this context is likely to involve workers in a cell becoming jointly responsible for such things as the scheduling of work.

Although often thought of in terms of enhancing the autonomy of the work group, the introduction of teamworking is perhaps better understood as increasing the degree of interdependence between workers. While both cellular manufacturing and teamworking are associated with the development of 'high performance' work organization, the relationship between the restructuring of work and the overall performance of organizations has been a difficult one to establish. **SP**

References and further reading
Alford, H. (1994) 'Cellular manufacturing: the development of the idea and its application', *New Technology, Work and Employment* 9(1): 3–18.
Badham, R., McLoughlin, I. and Buchanan, D. (1998) 'Human resource management and cellular manufacturing', in N. Suresh and J. Kay (eds) *Group Technology and Cellular Manufacturing*, London: Kluwer.
Benders, J. and Badham, R. (2000) 'A history of cell-based manufacturing', in M. Beyerlein (ed.) *Work Teams: Past, Present, Future*, London: Kluwer.
Buchanan, D. (1994) 'Cellular manufacture and the role of teams', in J. Storey (ed.) *New Wave Manufacturing Strategies: Organizational and Human Resource Dimensions*, London: Paul Chapman Publishing
Drucker, P. (1990) 'The emerging theory of manufacturing', *Harvard Business Review* 68(3): 91–102.
Procter, S., Rowlinson, M. and Hassard, J. (1995) 'Introducing cellular manufacturing: operations, human resources and high-trust dynamics', *Human Resource Management Journal* 5(2): 46–64.

Central Arbitration Committee (CAC)

The Central Arbitration Committee is a permanent independent arbitration body. Its history can be traced back to the Industrial Courts Act of 1919. In its modern guise it was established under section 10 of the Employment Protection Act (EPA) of 1975 and is now embodied in the 1992 Trade Union and Labour Relations (Consolidation) Act. As well as having powers to adjudicate on certain claims made unilaterally under various enactment's (e.g. the EPA itself, the Equal Pay Act, disclosure of information for collective bargaining claims and most recently over disputes involving recognition issues), it arbitrates in trade disputes ranging from matters affecting a single company or a group of employees to national disputes. Such issues can be referred to the CAC by the Advisory, Conciliation and Arbitration Service (ACAS) or at the request of both parties to the dispute.

The independent chairperson and deputy chairperson of the CAC and its two panels of members who have experience as representatives respectively of employers and employees, are all appointed by the Secretary of State after consultation with ACAS. Cases are normally heard by a committee of three, consisting of the chairperson or deputy chairperson and two members, one from each panel. Central Arbitration Committee awards can only be published with the consent of all parties to the dispute. Such awards become part of the contract of employment of those affected by the award. According to Lewis and Sargeant (2000) no decision of the CAC can be overturned unless it has made an error in law, breached natural justice or acted outside their jurisdiction. New responsibilities under the trade union recognition regulations provided for by the 1999 Employee Relations Act have provided CAC with rejuvenation and rescued it from relative obscurity. **PH**

References and further reading

Gall, G. and Hammond, D. (2000) 'Spectre of CAC prompts first wave of voluntary recognitions', *People Management* 6(24):14–15.
Lewis, D. and Sargeant, M. (2000) *Essentials of Employment Law*, 6th edn, London: CIPD.
Warren, M. (2000) 'Guiding rights', *People Management* 6(24):18–19.

Certification Officer

Established through the 1975 Employment Protection Act, the provisions of the Certification Officer are now contained in the 1992 Trade Union and Labour Relations (Consolidation) Act. The 1999 Employee Relations Act also has made changes in the duties undertaken by the Certification Officer. Under these provisions the Certification Officer is required to submit an annual report to the Secretary of State for Trade and Industry and the chairperson of the Advisory, Conciliation and Arbitration Service (ACAS). Members of the public are entitled to a copy of the Certification Officer's report and one will be sent, free of charge, on receipt of a request. The main role of the Certification Officer, who is appointed by the Secretary of State, is to maintain two lists. One is a list of trade unions that the Certification Officer has verified as having truly independent status from an employer, employers or an employers association. The other is a list of employers' associations.

Although the benefits to employers' associations of being listed are minimal, for trade unions there are number of benefits. Certification that a trade union is independent gives it rights in two areas. First there are tax advantages allowable for trade union income and expenditure and, second, an independent trade union can claim certain rights in the area of collective bargaining. According to Rose (2001) these include such benefits as:

- time off for employees to take part in union activities
- the right of access to information needed by union representatives for collective bargaining purposes

- information and consultation when there is a transfer of the employee business
- information about pensions
- time off for representatives to have industrial relations training
- notification and consultation about redundancies.

The 1999 Employee Relations Act gave additional responsibilities to the Certification Officer stemming from the abolition of the Commissioner for the Rights of Trade Union Members (CROTUM). Other duties of the Certification Officer include the scrutiny of employers' associations and trade unions accounts to ensure that they have been maintained and audited in line with statutory requirements. The Certification Officer now has the duty to investigate complaints from trade union members that regulations incumbent on trade unions have not been complied with, e.g. failing to maintain an accurate listing of members or failing to hold secret ballots for the election of executive committees, general secretaries and presidents. The Certification Officer is charged with the scrutiny of the operation of political funds both of trade unions and employers' associations and to investigate any complaints that there has been malpractice. The area of mergers and transfers of undertakings of both trade unions and employers' associations also falls into the remit. The Certification Officer's report is very useful source of information on industrial relations. However, it is clear that the work is skewed towards trade unions at the expense of information on employers' associations. **PH**

References and further reading
Bland, P. (1999) 'Trade union membership and recognition 1997–98: an analysis of data from the Certification Officer and the Labour Force Survey', *Labour Market Trends* 107(7): 343–52.
Cully, M. and Woodland, S. (1998) 'Trade union membership and recognition 1996–97: an analysis of data from the Certification Officer and the LFS', *Labour Market Trends* 106(7): 353–65.
Rose, E. (2001) *Employment Relations*, London: Financial Times Prentice Hall.

Chartered Institute of Personnel and Development (CIPD)

The Chartered Institute of Personnel and Development is the principal professional body for personnel and development specialists in the UK. It was formed in 1994 as a result of a merger between the Institute of Personnel Management (IPM representing personnel specialists) and the Institute of Training and Development (ITD representing training and development specialists). It gained chartered status on 1 July 2000. At the beginning of 2001 its membership stood at approximately 105 000 of whom some 25 000 were in membership as Studying Affiliates undertaking formal programmes of professionally recognized study.

The antecedents of the CIPD go back across the greater part of the last century. The IPM traces its roots to the foundation of the Welfare Workers Association in 1913, which became the Central Association of Welfare Workers in 1918. Later in 1919 it became the Welfare Workers Institute. In 1931 this body became the Institute of Labour Management and in 1946 the Institute became the Institute of Personnel Management. The ITD owes its origins to the foundation of the British Institute of Training Officers in 1964. In 1967 this latter body changed its name to the Institute of Training Officers which became the Institute of Training and Development in 1979.

The principal objectives of the CIPD are to provide professional education and development of its members and to research and provide appropriate information to support practitioners in their professional roles. These two objectives are supported by the work of the Membership and Education Committee and the Professional Policy Committee (PPC). In the case of the former, a nationally representative committee is responsible for the establishment and maintenance of professional educational standards across a wide range of provision, whether within universities, by means of national examinations set by CIPD or by assessment of prior experience and qualifications. In the case of the PPC, relevant research, work which materially assists in the analysis and dissemination of personnel and development issues, is commissioned from leading academic and policy analysts both within the UK and internationally. In addition to these two main functions the CIPD runs a number of conferences each year, the two largest of which are concerned with human resource development and human resource management in London and Harrogate respectively. **IB**

Check-off

Check-off is a system of deduction of trade union subscriptions from pay at source, and therefore it requires the co-operation of the employer to operate it. Traditionally, in most manual unions shop stewards carried out regular workplace collections of union subscriptions through personal contact with their own members. In the 1960s and 1970s these methods were increasingly replaced by check-off, and by the 1980s check-off had become the main method of collection employed by manual and white-collar unions in both private and public sectors. However, as a result of the 1993 Trade Union Reform and Employment Rights Act, union members had to provide their employer with individual written notification every three years that they wished their check-off arrangements to continue. This was a cause of concern for unions. However, in 1998 the notification requirements of the 1993 Act were repealed by the in-coming Labour government.

Initially there were fears that the replacement of unions' traditional methods of collection with check-off would destroy close links between shop stewards and their members, but such fears appear to have been ill-founded, and check-off has provided considerable financial advantages to unions in terms of cash flow. Whilst the price paid by unions has been a greater dependence upon the co-operation of employers, many employers are evidently sympathetic to conventional systems of check-off, as demonstrated by their opposition to the legal changes incorporated in the 1993 Act (Atkinson and Hillage, 1994; Cully *et al.*, 1999: 89). However, with wages paid directly into employees bank accounts, some unions – particularly white-collar – decided to promote direct debit as an alternative to check-off (Millward *et al.*, 1992: 124–7). In spite of this, check-off still remains the predominant method of collection, with 66 per cent of unionized workplaces continuing to operate such methods in 1998 (Cully *et al.*, 1999: 89). **DB**

References and further reading

Atkinson, J. and Hillage, J. (1994) 'Employers policies and attitudes towards check-off', IMS Report no. 271.

Cully, M., Woodland, S., O'Reilly, A. and Dix, G. (1999) *Britain at Work*: *As depicted by the 1998 Workplace Employee Relations Survey*, London: Routledge, pp. 89–90.

Labour Research Department (1996) 'Signing up for a good deal', *Labour Research* 85(7): 19–21.

Labour Research Department (1998) 'Complex check-off rules abolished', *Labour Research* 87(8): 6.

Millward, N., Stevens, M., Smart, D. and Hawes, W. R. (1992) *Workplace Industrial Relations in Transition*: *The ED/ESRC/PSI/ACAS Surveys*, Aldershot: Dartmouth, pp 124–7.

Morris, T. and Willman, P. (1994) 'The check-off challenge', *Centre for Organizational Research Working Paper*, London Business School.

Closed shops

The term 'closed shop' does not indicate only one configuration of union organization. Although McCarthy (1964: 211) defined the closed shop as: 'a situation in which employees come to realize that a particular job is only to be obtained or retained if they become and remain union members", in practice the organization of the closed shop and the precise rules that governed it varied considerably. Some closed shops were termed 'pre-entry closed shops' where prospective employees had to be a member of the relevant trade union prior to appointment to a post in the organization. In such circumstances, if a manager appointed a non-union member, considerable industrial relations problems could ensue with the rest of the workforce refusing to work with the new recruit. Some closed shops were termed 'post-entry closed shops' and the requirement here was that new recruits must join the union on the commencement of their appointment. In particular circumstances, where an individual had a deeply held moral or religious conviction opposed to the principle of trade unionism, then they may have been allowed to remain in non-membership and employment if they paid an equivalent sum to membership dues to a charity of their choice.

There has been great controversy over the operation of closed shops. This stems from ideological differences that people hold. For some the notion of closed shops implies a fundament infringement of individual liberty to seek employment wherever and in whichever organization they choose. For others it is a perfectly rational approach to workplace organization. Any small loss of individual freedom is in keeping with the same loss associated with collective bargaining and, in any case, is worth it because of the solidarity of the workforce that ensues and the delivery of better terms and conditions because of that solidarity. An associated argument here is that the contract of employment is in effect an agreement to subservience. Such subservience is a loss of freedom and the closed shop goes some way to redressing the imbalance of power that results from this subservience.

From a management perspective a similar range of belief can be identified. Some managers may believe fundamentally that any instrument that adds to the potency of a trade union in advancing employees' interests in the workplace is dangerous and likely to lead to inefficiency and unrest. From a different perspective, those managers who identify collective bargaining as a legitimate and effective instrument for the resolution of workplace problems and the advancement of management objectives as well as employee objectives, may welcome the closed shop as a powerful discipline on the workforce in bringing to fruition managerial aspirations for change.

Certainly the last Conservative government was of the opinion that closed shops were an infringement of individuals' freedoms and, with a strong element of the 'libertarian right' in their ranks, an anathema to their beliefs. Also the economic philosophies based on the neo-monetarist principles of Hayek would view any instrument that added to trade union power as highly dangerous. The result of this ensured the viability and legality of the closed shop was reduced by inclusion in a number of disabling statutes in the 1980s and early 1990s. The final 'nail in the coffin' was the 1992 Trade Union and Labour Relations (Consolidation) Act which provides that it is illegal to refuse employment to people because they are or are not members of a trade union. **PH**

References and further reading

Black-Branch, J. L. (1998) 'Closing the door on closed-shop agreements: labor law, trade unionism, and the right to freedom of assembly and freedom of association under the European Convention on Human Rights', *Journal of Collective Negotiations in the Public Sector* 27(4): 307–30.

Dunn, S. and Wright, M. (1994) 'Maintaining the "status quo"? An analysis of the contents of British collective agreements: 1979–1990', *British Journal of Industrial Relations* 32(1): 23–46.

McCarthy, W. (1964) *The Closed Shop in Britain*, Oxford: Blackwell

Naylor, R. and Cripps, M. (1993) 'An economic theory of the open shop trade union', *European Economic Review* 37(8): 1599–621.

Coaching

Coaching is a current trend in management development. It essentially consists of (usually) a one-to-one relationship between a manager (or a competent other) and an individual with the purpose of developing within that person a new skill or enhancing performance in some way. The analogy of the 'coach' is taken from the sporting world. The sportsperson needs to know how to develop valuable skills and positive attitudes, to train and practise towards achieving their goals. Sports coaches help them to develop those skills and attitudes. Rather like a sports coach, in a coaching relationship at work, the manager or competent person will work with the individual or with groups of individuals to improve aspects of their performance, acting as role model, teacher and provider of encouragement to help people achieve their best in their jobs, or aspects of them.

Coaching is not the same as teaching or training. It is a more learner-centred approach. Coaching is about helping people to take responsibility for their own development. It aims to draw out the full potential in the individual. For this to happen, the quality of the relationship between the two parties is crucial. Therefore the coach needs to have a highly developed set of skills. Woodall and Winstanley (1998) provide a list of the skills required in coaching. First there is observation, the ability to take a step back from a situation and view it in an objective manner. Next there is active listening, not just hearing but truly understanding what the individual is saying, making a distinction between truth and imagination. The skills of active listening include using the right kind of 'body language' and encouraging people to 'open up' through communication skills. The skill of facilitating discussion is important. The focus in coaching is on encouraging people to answer their own issues through effective challenging and questioning techniques. The coach must encourage the individual to take his or her own action through delegation and effective review and feedback. Finally, the coach must be able to set aside the necessary uninterrupted time and to judge accurately when coaching interventions will have their optimum effect.

A related one-to-one development relationship is that of the mentor (see **Mentoring**). This has become a popular concept in recent years. Mentoring is very similar to coaching, but tends to be less specific in its focus. It is not unusual, for example, for a new employee to be assigned to a 'mentor' when they join an organization, so that he or she can show them 'the ropes', help them find their way around the organization and then, sometimes, maintain an interest in that person's progress as they move through their career. Mentoring relationships, however, do not have to involve just new entrants. They can have value for more established members of staff.

Coaching as a concept has become so popular in recent times that some organizations even engage external 'executive' coaches, usually for the benefit of senior managers. There are several providers of 'coaching schools' to help people develop the skills they need to become effective coaches to others. **LS**

References and further reading
Bee, R. and Bee, F. (1999) *Constructive Feedback*, London: IPD.
Parsloe, E. (1999) *The Manager as Coach and Mentor*, London: IPD.
Woodall, J. and Winstanley, D. (1998) *Management Development: Strategy and Practice*, Oxford: Blackwell.

Codes of practice

Codes of practice are a set of guidelines that seek to promote good industrial relations and human resource management. They can be issued by both regulatory agencies and professional bodies, which means there can be some significant difference between voluntary guidance and legal compliance (Whincup, 1991).

Voluntary codes of practice issued by professional bodies outline a minimum level of behaviour expected of their members. For example, organizations such as the Institute of Personnel and Development (IPD) and the British Psychological Society (BPS) advocate the fair treatment of employees in areas such as recruitment, selection and employee confidentiality.

In contrast, approved codes of practice (ACOP) often carry a legal weight. These are issued by state agencies such as the Equal Opportunities Commission (EOC), the Commission for Racial Equality (CRE), the Health and Safety Executive (HSE) and the Advisory, Conciliation and Arbitration Service (ACAS). Many codes are not legally binding, although they can be cited in employment tribunals as best practice in areas such as equal treatment, discipline, grievance and redundancy. For example, the approved ACAS *Code of Practice* on dismissal outlines the procedures that an employer should follow when contemplating dismissal, such as the need for a thorough investigation of alleged misconduct, the employee's right to information, representation and an appeal. The most recent ACAS *Code of Practice* is concerned with the rights and obligations of employers and trade unions concerning union recognition as a result of the Employment Relations Act (1999). For employers, the code explains what is required in terms of allowing trade unions access to communicate with workers during a recognition ballot. If an employer fails to comply, then the Central Arbitration Committee (CAC) of ACAS can declare union recognition without the need for a ballot.

Codes of practice are one important way to promote equitable standards of human resource management (HRM) that can institutionalize industrial relations practices (Clegg, 1979). However there are limitations. Winstanley and Woodall (2000) comment that the some of the practical effects of many codes of practice do little more than ensure legal compliance. Employers see them as a 'magical shield' that provide a minimum set of standards rather than thinking through the practices and building upon these to develop more sophisticated HRM practices. **TD**

References and further reading

Advisory, Conciliation and Arbitration Service (ACAS) (1985) *Code of Practice on Disciplinary Practices and Procedures in Employment*, London: HMSO.

Advisory, Conciliation and Arbitration Service (ACAS) (2000) *Draft Code of Practice on Union Recognition*, London: HMSO.

Clegg, H. (1979) *The Changing System of Industrial Relations in Great Britain*, Oxford: Blackwell.

Whincup, M. (1991), *Modern Employment Law*, 7th edn, London: Butterworth.

Winstanley, D. and Woodall, J. (2000) *Ethical Issues in Contemporary Human Resource Management*, London: Macmillan.

Collective bargaining

Collective bargaining refers to the process of negotiation and the establishment of agreements between representatives of trade unions and employers in respect of substantive issues (e.g. pay, hours, holidays, work practices) and procedural arrangements (e.g. the handling of disciplinary cases and grievances). Agreements may be negotiated at local or national level, though in the 1980s and 1990s there has been a considerable decentralization of collective bargaining in Britain. In the engineering and manufacturing sectors industry wide bargaining has essentially disappeared. In some cases this has been replaced by company-level bargaining, but often by bargaining at divisional or plant level. However, unlike the experience of the 1960s, such plant-level bargaining is not a means for unions to improve upon national agreements, but instead it has increasingly replaced national bargaining. Government attempts to promote decentralization of bargaining in the public sector have proved more problematic, particularly in relation to pay (Bach and Winchester, 1994: 263–82).

The changes to the pattern of collective bargaining in Britain in the 1980s and 1990s need to be understood within the context of the major shift in power in favour of employers. The decentralization of collective bargaining can also be linked to the decentralizing developments in business organization and management in this period. However, by 1998 41 per cent of public sector workplaces were still covered by multi-employer bargaining compared with 14 per cent of all workplaces (i.e. those with 25 employees or more), and some of the decline in public sector multi-employer pay bargaining which has occurred can be explained by the substitution of pay review bodies for such bargaining arrangements (Cully *et al.*, 1999: 228–9, 241–2). Overall, the union recognition provisions of the 1999 Employment Relations Act may encourage some increase in the extent of collective bargaining arrangements in the near future. In the longer term, it is possible that a gradual decline in unemployment will help to bring about a renewed emphasis upon trade unionism and collective bargaining in both private and public sectors. (See also **Trade Unions**.) **DB**

References and further reading

Arrowsmith, J. and Sisson, K. (1999) 'Pay and working time: towards organization-based systems?', *British Journal of Industrial Relations* 37(1): 51–75,

Bach, S. and Winchester, D. (1994) 'Opting out of pay devolution? Prospects of local bargaining in UK public services', *British Journal of Industrial Relations* 32(2): 263–82.

Blyton, P. and Turnbull, P. (1998) *The Dynamics of Employee Relations*, 2nd edn, London: Macmillan, ch. 7.

Brown, W., Marginson, P. and Walsh, J. (1995) 'Management, pay determination and collective bargaining', in P. Edwards (ed.) *Industrial Relations: Theory and Practice in Britain*, Oxford: Blackwell.

Cully, M., Woodlands, S., O'Reilly, A. and Dix, G. (1999) *Britain at Work: As Depicted by the 1998 Workplace Employee Relations Survey*, London: Routledge, 241–2, 228–9 and ch. 5.

Incomes Data Services (1999) *Pay and Conditions in the United Kingdom 1999*, IDS Research Report.

Collectivism

At least three different uses of 'collectivism' can be found in the human resource management (HRM) field. First, collectivism is often used synonymously to refer to the pattern of industrial relations in post–war Britain. organizations managing through 'collectivism' therefore rely heavily upon traditional union–management arrangements based on principles such as 'mutuality' (joint agreement to any proposed changes). For example, such organizations consult and/or bargain with trade union representatives to set the terms and conditions of employment and rely upon standardized procedural agreements for handling organizational change and the resolution of conflicts. Collective industrial relations are thought to decline if industrial relations procedures fall into disuse along with decreases in union recognition and union membership.

Second, collectivism is sometimes used to suggest a standardized approach (whether union influenced or not) in areas other than industrial relations (see Storey and Bacon, 1993). For example, 'collective' employment practices are detected in teamworking and team-briefing (Storey and Sisson, 1993), certain types of performance-related pay schemes (Kessler and Purcell, 1995) and even in the standardized forms which many 'individual contracts' adopt in practice (Evans and Hudson, 1993). Third, both Purcell (1987) and Marchington and Parker (1990) identify 'high' collectivism with a partnership approach between management and unions (see Bacon and Storey, 2000). However, individualism and collectivism are not simply either/or alternatives as there is always an 'individual' component to the employment relationship and indeed much of what unions do is regulate individual contracts (cf. Flanders, 1970). See also **Individualism. NB**

References and further reading

Bacon, N. and Storey, J. (2000) 'New employee relations strategies in Britain: Towards individualism or partnership?', *British Journal of Industrial Relations*, 38(3): 407–27.

Evans, S. and Hudson, M. (1993) 'From collective bargaining to personal contracts: the case studies in port transport and electricity supplies', *Industrial Relations Journal* 25: 305–14.

Flanders, A. (1970) *Management and Unions: The Theory and Reform of Industrial Relations*, London: Faber.

Kessler, I. and Purcell, J. (1995) 'Individualism and collectivism in theory and practice: management style and the design of pay systems', in P. Edwards, (ed.) *Industrial Relations: Theory and Practice in Britain*, Oxford: Blackwell, 337–67.

Marchington, M. and Parker, P. (1990) *Changing Patterns of Employee Relations,* Hemel Hempstead: Harvester Wheatsheaf.

Purcell, J. (1987) 'Mapping management styles in employee relations', *Journal of Management Studies* 24:533–48.

Storey, J. and Bacon, N. (1993) 'Individualism and collectivism: into the 1990s', *International Journal of Human Resource Management* 4:665–84.

Storey, J. and Sisson, K. (1993) *Managing Human Resources and Industrial Relations*, Milton Keynes: Open University Press.

Commission for Racial Equality (CRE)

The Commission for Racial Equality was established under the Race Relations Act (RRA) 1976 to tackle racial discrimination and promote racial equality. It is funded by government but nominally independent of it. The commissioners are public appointees chosen by the government or nominated by the Confederation of British Industry (CBI) and the Trades Union Congress (TUC).

The CRE has three statutory duties:

- to work towards the elimination of discrimination
- to promote equality of opportunity and good relations between people of different racial groups in general
- to keep the working of the legislation under review through proposing reform.

The legislation invests the commission with a number of powers to enable it to perform its duties. It has the power:

- to advise or assist people with individual complaints about discrimination, harassment or abuse
- to conduct formal investigations of organizations where there is evidence of possible discrimination
- to take enforcement action against discriminatory advertising and where there is pressure and instruction to discriminate.

Individual help ranges from general guidance and dispute resolution to legal advice and representation. Where action is taken against an employer suspected of discrimination, the route is through formal investigation and enforcement as in most situations the commission does not have the power to institute proceedings directly. If a formal investigation reveals discrimination, the commission can order the organization to revise its policies and procedures through the issue of a Non-Discrimination Notice. In this way, discrimination is tackled at a structural level. In practice the CRE's preferred approach is a voluntary one, working with organizations and using its powers of investigation and enforcement only as a last resort. A key part of the practical guidance for employers on the RRA is the CRE's *Code of Practice* for the elimination of racial discrimination and the promotion of equality of opportunity in employment which can be used in evidence during an industrial tribunal. The commission's advisory role is also reinforced through its various research reports and other publications, which provide guidance on every aspect of employment from equal opportunities policies to ethnic monitoring.

Racial inequality in employment still exists in Britain and in this context a number of shortcomings has been identified in the commission's structure and powers. In addition to giving the commission wider legal investigative powers, it has also been suggested that the CRE should be merged with the Equal Opportunities Commission and Disability Rights Commission to form one overarching Human Rights Commission. **SS**

References and further reading

Commission for Racial Equality (1984) *Code of Practice*: *For the Elimination of Racial Discrimination and the Promotion of Equality of Opportunity in Employment*, London: HMSO.

Honeyford, R. (1999) *The Commission for Racial Equality – British Bureaucracy and the Multi-Ethnic*, London: Transaction.

Townshend-Smith, R. J. (1998) *Discrimination Law*: *Text, Cases and Materials*, London: Cavendish.

Also visit the CRE's web site at http://www.cre.gov.uk

Company unionism

The terms *company unionism*, *enterprise unionism* and *business unionism* have similar meanings. Narrowly interpreted, company unionism refers to unions which have members within one particular company only, the implication of which is that such unions are likely to be relatively isolated from wider trade union interests and concerns. Company unions collaborate closely with management over many issues, and therefore lack independence. Examples of this narrower concept of company unionism are relatively unusual in Britain, and where examples do occur they are more likely to be in the form of staff associations. Company unions are common in the car industry in Japan, however, and in companies like Toyota and Nissan, the career routes of union representatives and managers may be closely integrated. The terms *business unionism* and *enterprise unionism* are sometimes used to refer to broader interpretations of the concept, based on a common union–management approach over a wide range of issues, achieved at the expense of union independence.

Various forms of company and business unionism have had considerable influence in the USA. In Britain, the growth of single union no-strike agreements in the 1980s can be interpreted as a particular expression of the broader notion of business unionism. These agreements were pioneered at greenfield sites by Japanese motor vehicle and consumer electronics companies, which invited unions to compete for the opportunity to sign them. Most unions condemned this situation as a 'beauty contest' and refused to participate. A minority, particularly the electricians and engineering unions (now merged as the Amalgamated Engineering and Electrical Union), embraced such deals, and were accused of promoting business unionism. Whilst in the mid-1980s such unions were largely ostracized within the Trades Union Congress (TUC), with the subsequent embrace of 'new realism' and concepts of social partnership, the TUC has managed to mend the rift arguably at the price of making significant concessions to business unionism philosophy. (See also **No-strike deals**.) **DB**

References and further reading

Babson, S. (ed.) (1995) *Lean Work*: *Empowerment and Exploitation in the Global Auto Industry*, Detroit, MI: Wayne State University Press, chs 3, 5 and 6.

Bassett, P. (1987) *Strike Free*: *New Industrial Relations in Britain*, London: Macmillan.

Benson, J. (1996) 'A typology of Japanese enterprise unions', *British Journal of Industrial Relations* 34(3): 371–86.

Gall, G. (1993) 'What happened to single union deals?', *Industrial Relations Journal* 24(1): 71–5.

Monks, J. (1998) 'Trade unions, enterprise and the future', in P. Sparrow and M. Marchington (eds) *Human Resource Management*: *the New Agenda*, London: Financial Times and Pitman.

Whittaker, D. H. (1998) 'Labour unions and industrial relations in Japan: crumbling pillar or forging a *third way*?', *Industrial Relations Journal* 29(4): 280–94.

Comparative human resource management

While not new, comparative approaches can be usefully applied to the analysis of human resource management (HRM). Several important benefits flow from this. These include a questioning of what might otherwise be taken as 'natural' states of affairs in HRM, putting them into perspective and reducing ethnocentric views and parochial analysis. Also, HRM differences in similar countries or similarities in different countries can be more rigorously analysed. Levels of analysis for comparative HRM can include the macro, state/economy level, exploring the influence of national factors in a particular country. Such approaches are written to varying levels and degrees of detail and sophistication. However, making manageable and meaningful comparisons of multiple whole country HRM systems can be difficult. Regions or blocs, i.e. 'Europe' or 'Asia', have also been utilized. Yet, even these are diverse internally. A second level concerns comparing HRM practices and policies, not least as organizations in all states address similar issues, such as how to resolve the dilemma of worker control and commitment. There is a wealth of work in this mould. There can also be attempts to mix these two by explicitly examining a number of the same elements and practices across countries.

As in much comparative research, we should be aware of its potential restrictions. The issue of actually comparing 'like with like' and representativeness of any analysis remains cogent. A reliance on stereotypes, often for simplicity and quickness may result in only partial pictures. The lack of common languages, terminology and meanings can create problems and confusion. Furthermore, the same institutions in different locations and contexts operate differently in practice. In short, we simply may not be able to isolate and compare so easily. Nevertheless, comparative HRM remains important, not least for the insights into your own country's practice and features it produces. **CR**

References and further reading

Bamber, G. and Lansbury, R. (eds) (1998) *International and Comparative Employment Relations*, London: Routledge.

Hollinshead, G. and Leat, M. (1995) *HRM: An International and Comparative Perspective*, London: Pitman.

Locke, R., Kochan, T. and Piore, M. (1995) *Employee Relations a Changing World Economy*, Cambridge, MA: MIT Press.

Rowley, C. (ed.) (1998) *Human Resource Management in the Asia Pacific Region: Convergence Questioned*, London: Cass.

Competence/competency

The use of the words competence, competency and competencies, when applied to management, has become exceptionally popular. However the words are used in a way which lacks clarity of meaning. Boyatzis (1982), in the USA, is generally considered to have introduced these words into common usage in the management field. A job competency was defined as 'an underlying characteristic of a person which results in effective and superior performance in a job' (ibid.: 21). This underlying characteristic 'may be a motive, trait, skill, aspect of ones self image or social role, or a body of knowledge which he/she uses' (ibid.).

In contrast, within the UK, the Management Charter Initiative guidelines (MCI, undated: xvii) define competence as 'the ability to perform the activities within an occupational area to the level of performance expected in employment'.

Perhaps the most useful attempt to clarify these terms has been proposed by Woodruffe (1991). He suggests the terminology:

1. Can be used to refer to areas of work at which the person is competent. This is the job related sense of the word, and the terms competent or competence should be used.
2. Can also be used to refer to the dimensions of behaviour that lie behind competent performance; here the words competency or competencies should be used.

As Woodruffe also points out, different methodologies are used to derive areas of competence rather than personal competencies. Areas of competence are derived from an analysis of job functions known as functional analysis. Analysis of an individual's competencies uses techniques such as repertory grid analysis or behavioural event interviewing.

In the UK many major blue chip organizations, e.g. Barclays, National Westminster Bank, Cadbury Schweppes have invested considerably in the development of competency models based around Boyatzis' approach.

Albanese (1989) provides a useful discussion of the assumptions underpinning the competency model. Loan-Clarke (1996) offers a useful critique of the MCI model of competence. **JL-C**

References and further reading

Albanese R. (1989) 'Competency-based management education', *Journal of Management Development* 8(2): 66–76.

Boam, R. and Sparrow, P. (1992) *Designing and Achieving Competency*, Maidenhead: McGraw-Hill.

Boyatzis, R.E. (1982) *The Competent Manager*, New York:Wiley.

Loan-Clarke, J. (1996) 'The Management Charter Initiative: a critique of management standards/NVQs', *Journal of Management Development* 15(6): 4–17.

Management Charter Initiative (MCI) (undated) Standards implementation pack, London: MCI.

Woodruffe, C. (1991) 'Competent by any other name', *Personnel Management*, September: 30–3.

Conciliation

From unitary perspectives conciliation may be viewed as irrelevant, in contrast to pluralist type approaches. In the human resource management (HRM) area conciliation may be seen as an assisted continuation of negotiation and related to conflict. An intervention process, conciliation involves an independent, neutral third party acting as interpreter and messenger in identifying the causes of differences and relative significance of issues and positions to develop mutually acceptable solutions. However, agreement to these remains the parties' joint decision as conciliators do not impose or recommend solutions. There is a long history of support in the UK, including the 1896 Conciliation Act. Conciliation may be provided by private or public facilities. In the UK the most well known is the Advisory, Conciliation and Arbitration Service (ACAS). Conciliation by its full time staff, almost all civil servants, is voluntary and arises via the parties' request, procedural agreements or its volunteering of its services. In 1999–2000 ACAS received 1 500 requests for collective conciliation (52 per cent over pay and terms and conditions), plus 164 525 cases of individual conciliation (52 791 on unfair dismissal, 36 837 on protection of wages and 29 053 over breach of contract).

There are several issues around conciliation. Calling for conciliation can be seen as a sign of weakness and undermining authority. Varied amounts of 'compulsion', removing some of the parties' freedom, could be used as it avoids giving third parties power to resolve issues on uncongenial terms. Conciliation provides 'public relations' aspects, being used to shift some 'blame' and responsibility for settlements. Yet, reliance on conciliation can become 'addictive', it can 'chill' processes such as negotiation, making earlier settlement less likely. Nevertheless, conciliation forces the sides to re-examine cases, making some movement possible, while conciliators approach issues with fresh minds. The area of conciliation will remain an important one for HRM. **CR**

References and further reading

Advisory, Conciliation and Arbitration Service (ACAS), Annual Reports.

International Labour Organization (ILO) (1980) *Conciliation and Arbitration Procedures in Labour Disputes*, Geneva: ILO.

Lowry, P. (1990) *Employment Disputes and the Third Party*, London: Macmillan.

Salaman, M. (2000) *Industrial Relations: Theory and Practice*, London: Pearson.

Confederation of British Industry (CBI)

The CBI is a voluntary organization made up of a direct corporate membership employing over 4 million and an employers' and trade association membership who employ a further 6 million.

It was formed in 1965 by the amalgamation of three existing bodies, the Federation of British Industry (FBI), the National Association of British Manufacturers (NABM) and the British Employers Confederation (BEC), all at the time having slightly different objectives. Although the process of merger was not easily achieved there was an imperative for this to happen. This was brought about by the government of the day's wish to operate a tripartite approach to economic management and thus the need for single body to represent the opinion of industry. In the Trades Union Congress (TUC), the government had the single body to represent the opinions of the trade unions and with the formation of the CBI, the mechanisms in place for a corporatist labour market.

The functions of the CBI are much wider than just those of assisting with the employee relations of its members. Primarily the CBI exists today to act as a pressure group to influence the government (both Westminster and Whitehall), the European Commission, the trade union movement and the general public. The CBI champions the cause of British industry. It seeks to disseminate both the needs of UK business and the contribution that business makes to British society. As well as attempting to shape policy domestically, in Europe and internationally, the CBI provides its members with professional information garnered through analysis of surveys and disseminated through forecasts of economic and business trends. It also provides a variety of conferences and forums where its members can meet to find a better understanding of the issues that face them.

The CBI's organization can be divided into three basic parts. First is the ruling Council, chaired by the President, who is elected annually and normally serves for two periods of office. The Council, which is made up of 400 representatives from the various categories of membership, meets monthly to set policy. Various Standing Committees who are in turn supported by CBI permanent staff undertake the formulation of these policy proposals. Although it may seem that the ruling Council is the locus of power, in reality power is in the hands of the CBI's President and full-time Director General. It is they who not only appoint the members of the various Standing Committees but also the centrally important President's Committee which has a wide remit including advice on strategy and major policy. The annual National Conference does not make policy but provides advice on it to the Council and acts as a public showcase for industries' interests.

The second aspect of organization is the thirteen Regional Councils which exist to provide an important communications link between national structures and local opinion.

The third aspect is the CBI's permanent staff. In its headquarters at Centre Point in the heart of London's West End the CBI employs 200 staff to support the work of the Standing Committees and to service the membership. The CBI also has 13 offices around the UK and one in Brussels.

The CBI does not represent all of British industry with many small firms feeling that their interests are not being met and many large, especially service, companies feeling that they do not need the CBI's affiliation. This affects its role as a pressure group as it cannot claim to be truly representative. Its success as a pressure group has often been criticized when compared to that of the TUC. The major success it can point to is its successful campaigning, in the mid-1970s, against the recommendations of the Bullock Report on industrial democracy. In hand with the TUC its influence declined from 1979 when the Thatcher government abandoned corporatist decision making in favour of a laissez-faire, free market approach to economic operation.

The CBI is identified as having a number of ongoing problems. The lack of comprehensive membership issue has already been discussed. It also suffers from disparity in the type of organizations in membership in that policy always needs to accommodate the diverse interests its membership generates. This diversity of interests also makes it difficult for the CBI to achieve solidarity of action over any given issue. It is argued that it is underresourced for the breadth of its interests and that it lacks cohesion. This results in a tension between the membership 'doves' who wish to seek co-operation with and concession from the government and the 'hawks' that favour a more outspoken criticism of government policy and action.

For all the criticisms that are levelled at the CBI there is no doubt that it is has been active in the pursuance of its objectives. It is now being consulted again following the change of government. It remains active on such bodies as the Advisory, Conciliation and Arbitration Service, the Commission for Racial Equality and the Equal Opportunities Commission. It has influence in Europe through its membership of UNICE, the European Employers' Federation. There also appears to be no great rush of membership disaffiliations. It could be that members are satisfied with the service provision of the CBI. It could also be argued that such members facing similar and complex problems value the affiliation that the CBI provides and that if there were not a CBI then someone would invent one. **PH**

References and further reading
Farnham, D. and Pimlott, J. (1995) *Understanding Industrial Relations*, London: Cassell.
Visit the CBI web site on http://www.cbi.org.uk

Contingency approach

The contingency approach to management developed as a reaction to the classical approach. Where the classical approach had sought to define general principles of management and to argue the case for an organizational structure that would be universal since it was based on principles of rationally coherent design the contingency approach, by contrast, argued that there was no single optimum state for organizational efficiency and effectiveness. Whereas the classical approach viewed organizational design as a mechanism, the contingency approach was informed by the biological analogy of organizmic sociology, also referred to as the system's approach. This suggested that the structure of the organization should be designed in relation to the context in which operates. In other words, the most appropriate structure for an organization depends on (is contingent upon) its environment or market situation, the nature of its technology and its goals. These contingencies should determine organizational change. Thus, the effectiveness of an organization is determined by a structure that is designed to be responsive to all of these factors.

The contingency approach has been linked to research carried out by members of the Industrial Administration Research Unit at Aston University and led by Derek Pugh between 1961 and 1970. This unit included several generations of researchers whose backgrounds range from psychology, sociology, economics and politics. Essentially the contingency approach fused three main perspectives – psychology, sociology and economics. Their research methods were informed by an epistemology that rejected the attempt to study and teach the principles of administration as though they were scientific laws, when in reality, they represented little more than administrative expediency. Their approach can be described as a multicausal explanation of organizations.

In this way, researchers from this tradition sought to identify the various external forces acting upon the organization as well as the way in which the organization deals with these in meeting its objectives. The implication of this is that once each of these have been carefully diagnosed and assessed the organization's structure can be designed to deal with them. Their research approach focused on three main areas. These were:

1. The nature of change and organizational complexity. This required an examination of the forces that acted upon the organization as well as the way in which the organization deal with them.
2. Internal arrangements such as control systems, the degree of hierarchy and authority relationships, communication and leadership.
3. The degree of fit between the external forces and the internal arrangements.

However, in order to understand these relationships researchers used a methodology that provided data from multiple perspectives. For example, by using multiple observers a more rounded picture of an organization could be achieved. As a consequence, various researchers became prominent in different aspects of this approach. Examples include the work of Burns and Stalker who researched the degree of fit between an organization and its environment, Perot and Woodward who researched aspects of technology, and Lawrence and Walsh who considered the influences of internal factors.

The contingency model is not without its critics, who have argued that:

1. Its assumption that organization performance is simply related to organizational structure is simplistic.
2. Consequently, it ignores the skills, attitudes, and performance of managers.
3. It ignores a range of other factors such as the skill of employees, their level of expertise, the morale and motivation of the workforce, the ability of leadership and the exercise of power, each of which are independent of structure but also critically important in delivering organizational efficiency and effectiveness.
4. Its tendency to assume that technology was a neutral variable leads to its failure to recognize how managers make decisions and what processes inform their judgement. **JG**

References and further reading

Child, J. (1972) 'Organizational structures, environment and performance: the role of strategic choice', *Sociology* 6: 2–22.

Hickson, D. J., Hinings, C. R., Lee, C. A., Schneck, R. E. and Pennings, J. M. (1971) 'A strategic contingencies theory of intraorganizational power,' *Administrative Science Quarterly* 16(2): 216–29.

Hickson, D. J. and McMillan, C. J. (eds) (1981) *Organization and Nation: The Aston Programme IV*, Aldershot: Gower.

Hinings, C. R. and Greenwood, R. G. (1988) *The Dynamics of Strategic Change*, Oxford: Blackwell.

Pugh, D. S. (1990) 'The measurement of organization structures: does context determine form?', in D. S. Pugh (ed.) *Organizational Theory*, Harmondsworth: Penguin.

Pugh, D. S. and Hickson, D. J. (1976) *Organizational Structure in its Context: The Aston Programme I*, Aldershot: Gower.

Pugh, D. S. and Hinings, C. R. (eds) (1976) *Organizational Structure – Extensions and Replications: The Aston Programme II*, Aldershot: Gower.

Pugh, D. S. and Payne, R. L. (eds) (1977) *Organizational Behaviour in its Context: The Aston Programme III*, Aldershot: Gower

Continuing professional development

In recent years, there has been a shift in emphasis from the notion that the initiative for training and development should be organization led, to the idea that individuals should take responsibility for their own development throughout their career lifetimes. There are two related concepts to consider here: *continuous development* and *continuing professional development*.

Continuous development reflects the modern notion that a person's development does not end after school, college or university and that learning is a lifelong process.

Today's skills and competencies soon become outdated, so the skills involved in continuous learning itself are now being emphasized as important life skills. For members of professional bodies, this process of continuous development post-qualification has been termed *continuing professional development* (CPD). Promoting and encouraging CPD have become important activities recently for many professional bodies. Examples of professional bodies who have CPD policies include the Royal College of Nursing, the Law Society, the British Psychological Society and the **Chartered Institute of Personnel and Development** (CIPD) (see separate entry).

In order to satisfy the requirements for CPD, the professional body usually stipulates minimum amounts of effort members should expend on their own post-qualification professional development. This is often expressed in terms of time (for example, number of hours). The content of CPD is almost limitless in its scope. It can range from updating oneself with the profession's body of knowledge (for example, attending a session on the Human Rights Act for lawyers and human resource professionals) to engaging in more personalized learning activities such as working on a project in an area outside one's own. Professional bodies differ in the extent of prescription they use in their CPD schemes. Some professional bodies dictate to members exactly what form the development should take at various stages of their professional lives. Other professional bodies adopt a less directive policy, preferring to let their members decide for themselves the nature of their own development. There appears however to be degree of consensus amongst professional bodies that CPD should not just include professional updating. Other desirable elements include the development of management skills, commercial awareness and aspects of personal development such as confidence building. There is also a recognition that there is a wide range of means by which CPD can take place. Again the possibilities are almost limitless, ranging from short courses to reading, engaging in coaching and mentoring activities, voluntary work and secondments.

One of the most difficult issues in CPD is compliance. Here, professional bodies seem to be adopting one of two models: the sanctions model and the benefit model. Several professional bodies attempt to operate a sanctions policy against members who fail to provide evidence of their CPD activities. Some bodies are prepared to strike members off their registers for non-compliance. Others refuse to upgrade members to higher grades of membership without evidence of CPD activity. The Chartered Institute of Personnel and Development prefers to emphasize the benefits to members of engaging in CPD rather than employing a more heavy-handed approach. The question of whether or not the concepts of compliance and sanctions are even appropriate when discussing personal and professional development is in itself a moot point. **LS**

References and further reading

Regular updates on CPD for human resource professionals in the Chartered Institute of Personnel and Development's bi-monthly magazine for practitioners, *People Management.*

The Chartered Institute of Personnel and Development's web site contains valuable information about the institute's CPD scheme. It can be found at www.cipd.co.uk

Jones, N. and Fear, N. (1993) 'Continuing professional development: perspectives from human resource professionals', *Personnel Review* 22(1): 49–60.

Sadler-Smith, E. and Badger, B. (1998) 'The HR practitioner's perspective on continuing professional development', *Human Resource Management Journal* 8(4): 66–75.

Continuous improvement

As a concept, continuous improvement seems innocuous enough and very straightforward. All organizations should seek to improve continuously. What could be more natural? And yet, it was not always so. The scale and pace of change in modem industrial life has made continuous improvement more important than it was. In times of economic stability, where change is slow and incremental, then continuous improvement can take place at an almost imperceptible pace. Over the last two decades, however, increased competition in global markets and the evolution of new technologies like the Internet have made it necessary for world-class organizations to seek proactively to improve operations rather than passively evolve with the general developments in their industries. Continuous Improvement has become an attitude of mind in companies, which seek to gain competitive edge through technological innovation or process improvement. Manufacturing has led the way, as it became clear that change would be a way of life for organizations rather than maintaining the status quo. Markets have become deregulated and competition has increased. Product life cycles have diminished and product development has become critical to long-term success.

Continuous Improvement is associated with other change strategies in organizational life. In one sense, it can be regarded as a mind-set but it can also be seen as the final stage in change processes driven by World-Class Manufacturing standards, quality programmes, **BPR** and **Just-In-Time** manufacturing methods (see entries). Indeed, readers should view the concept in the context of such programmes of organizational change in order to understand it more fully. The change theorists concerned argue that change is no longer a ' one-off 'experience, nor is it a series of discontinuous steps, where management get ' time off' in between the steps. They see change as a continuous process that will never end and advise managers to prepare themselves to manage change it self rather than any particular status quo. According to Michael Hammer, BPR programmes may aim to secure quantum leaps in performance to recover the ground lost through years of strategic drift, but they will need to be followed by programmes of Continuous Improvement to prevent organizations from drifting back to their former standards and to avoid complacency in an ever changing business environment. The same notion applies to programmes of TQM and culture change in organizations.

In the public sector in the UK, notions of Continuous Improvement tend to lag the private sector but are rapidly catching up in the Health sector and in Local Government particularly under the political and economic pressures of the 'Best Value' initiative.

For students of HRM, Continuous Improvement means the steady reinterpretation of training and development needs in organizations. What core competencies will be needed for organizational success in the future? What kind of managers will be needed and how can they be trained? How can organizations cope with the stresses of continuous change and initiative fatigue? What impact will this have on working methods and conditions of employment? How can staff be encouraged to welcome change rather than fear it? The pressures of Continuous Improvement will constitute a major challenge for organizational change agents at all levels. **JB**

References and further reading

Chang R Y and Niedzwicki M E (1994) *Continuous Improvement Tools A Practical Guide to achieve Quality results.* New York: Pfeiffer.
Clark T (1999) *Success through Quality: support guide for the journey to Continuous Improvement.* London: McGraw Hill.
Gallaher M *et al* (1997) *Continuous Improvement in Action* London: Kogan Page.
Goldratt E M (1992) *Goal: Process of Ongoing Improvement* New York: North River Press .

Contract of employment

The employment relationship is based on the law of contract. If the contract under which a person is employed is considered to be a contract of employment, then he or she is an employee and potentially entitled to a range of statutory employment protection rights such as the right not to be unfairly dismissed, maternity rights and the right to a redundancy payment. On the other hand, a person who is employed under a *contract for services* is regarded as self-employed.

Whilst the distinction between the two forms of contractual relationship is important, no legislation has sought to define them and it has therefore been left to case law to attempt to identify the features which characterize them. Features suggesting a contract of employment are, for example:

- provision of tools and equipment by the employer
- control over the work and/or the manner in which it is done
- payment of tax and National Insurance by the employer
- fixed hours
- payment of 'wages' or 'salary'
- provision of sick pay or a pension
- the power to discipline.

In contrast, a contract for services is generally characterized by:

- chance of profit and risk of loss (the 'entrepreneurial' element)
- ability to delegate the work to another
- payment of tax and National Insurance by the individual
- working for a number of employers
- negotiation of a 'fee' or other lump sum payment
- lack of 'mutuality of obligation' (the employer is under no obligation to provide work and the individual is free to refuse it).

Although a court or tribunal will take into account the label the parties have put on the relationship, they are not bound by it.

There is no legal obligation for a contract of employment to be in writing, although for evidential purposes it may be prudent. However, Section 1 of the Employment Rights Act 1996 provides that after eight weeks, an employee is entitled to a written statement of the main terms and conditions of employment. Express terms of the contract may be determined individually or collectively, but it is important to remember that a contract of employment will also contain a number of implied terms – such as the employer's duty of care, the employee's duty of good faith and the duty on both parties not to destroy the relationship of mutual trust and confidence. **JE**

References and further reading
Employment Rights Act 1996, Section 1, London: HMSO.
Express and Echo Publications Ltd v. *Tanton* [1999] IRLR 367.
Hall v. *Lorimer* [1994] IRLR 171.
Kenner, J. (1999) 'Statement or contract? Some reflections on the EC Employee Information (Contract or Employment Relationship) Directive after *Kampelman*', *Industrial Law Journal* 28(3): 205–31.
O'Kelly v. *Trusthouse Forte plc* [1983] IRLR 369.

Convergence theory

Convergence theory is the argument that industrialized societies are gradually becoming more alike, with their different patterns of institutional employment relations behaviour converging on a single model. Kerr *et al.* (1973) were the first to give the theory wide currency. Their core proposition is that there is a global tendency for technological and market forces associated with industrialization to push national industrial relations systems towards uniformity. They argue that a 'logic of industrialism' requires such universal features as the development of a concentrated, disciplined workforce with new and changing skills, a larger role for governments in the provision of infrastructure and the growth or imposition of a pluralistic consensus which provides an integrated body of ideas and beliefs.

Subsequent modifications to the theory have described convergence as a 'tendency' that is not likely to precipitate systems that are absolutely identical. Dore (1973) concluded that employment arrangements are becoming more alike, but that Japan, rather than any Western country, is the model towards which other countries are converging. In recent years some writers have argued that trade liberalization will encourage convergence, either by creating a 'race to the bottom' in labour costs or by facilitating the development of institutions and minimum standards that operate across national borders.

Critics of convergence theory point to the continuing heterogeneity that exists *between* and *within* national industrial relations systems, and argue that the decentralization of employment relations is being accompanied by an increasing incidence of custom-made rules for particular workplaces or enterprises. If convergence is actually occurring, it may only be around moves in a range of industrialized countries towards less regulation of employment relations and a decrease in collective bargaining. **GJB**

Acknowledgement
Thanks to Ken Lovell for his great help.

References and further reading
Bamber, G. J. and Lansbury, R. D. (eds) (1998) *International and Comparative Employment Relations: A Study of Industrialised Market Economies*, London: Sage/Sydney: Allen and Unwin.

Dore, R. (1973) *British Factory, Japanese Factory: The Origins of National Diversity in Industrial Relations*, London: Allen and Unwin.

Eaton, J. (2000) *Comparative Employment Relations: An Introduction*, Cambridge: Polity Press.

Gunderson, M. (1998), 'Harmonization of labour policies under trade liberalization', *Relations Industrielles/Industrial Relations* 53(1) Winter: 24–55.

Kerr, C. (1983) *The Future of Industrial Societies: Convergence or Continuing Diversity?* Cambridge, MA: Harvard University Press.

Kerr, C., Dunlop, J. T., Harbison, F. H and Myers, C. A. (1973) *Industrialism and Industrial Man: The Problems of Labour and Management in Economic Growth*, 2nd edn, London: Penguin (first published in 1960).

Kochan, T. A., Lansbury, R. D. and MacDuffie, J. P. (eds) (1997) *After Lean Production: Evolving Employment Practices in the World Auto Industry*, Ithaca, NY: Cornell University Press.

Poole, M. (1986) *Industrial Relations: Origins and Patterns of National Diversity*, London: Routledge.

Corporate universities

Corporate universities are considered a relatively recent innovation in approaches adopted by companies to employee, or human resource development. However, they can be said to be the result of a long line of evolution which began when firms such as the National Cash Register Company (NCR) in the USA established corporate 'Training Schools' at the end of the nineteenth century. While the NCR focused on sales training and aspects of business administration, the idea was widely adopted in other contexts and, in the UK, the term is commonly associated with craft apprenticeship training. The term 'training school' in some industries and for some levels of staff was replaced with 'staff college' or 'management college'. In the UK, the Civil Service Staff College is probably one of the best known of these. There are though others in the public services such as the Fire Service College and the Police Staff College, and many commercial organizations such as IBM UK, BT and most of the high street banks have well-established management colleges. It was again in the USA, in the form of the Walt Disney Company, where the term 'university' was first used and where, therefore, the idea of a corporate university first emerged.

It is very difficult to define what is and what is not a corporate university (see Walton, 1999 and Lester, 1999). Part of this difficulty is the fact that use of the term itself is considered by many researchers and writers to be insufficient. Thus, more recent terminology such as 'institute of learning' or 'learning academy' are commonly included as examples of a corporate university. The difficulty is compounded when examples of 'virtual universities' such as that established by British Aerospace in 1997 remove the notion of 'place' as a defining characteristic. A review of both academic and practitioner accounts of corporate universities suggests that they are primarily concerned with providing a strategic mechanism for supporting business strategies through the development of employees, suppliers and customers. As part of this, there is a strong focus on facilitating and supporting the creation, dissemination and sharing of knowledge. There are therefore clear connections between the use of corporate universities as a human resource development (HRD) strategy and approaches to knowledge management. It is also clear from the literature that corporate universities can and do vary in both purpose and form. Walton's (1999) notion of 'first, second and third generation' corporate universities is therefore helpful in understanding and analysing the various purposes and forms adopted.

A final and significant difficulty with use of the term 'university' is the relationship between corporate universities and what might be termed 'proper' universities. One element of this difficulty is that it is only the latter that have the power to award qualifications at degree level and above. An additional element is the implications for proper universities, especially their business schools, of the rising number of corporate universities. These two elements suggest both opportunities and threats for both proper universities and organizations either considering or actually adopting the 'corporate university' approach to human resource development. **JS**

References and further reading

Arkin, A. (2000) 'Combined honours', *People Management* 6(20): 42–6.

Lester, T. (1999) 'Degree couture', *Human Resources*, March: 74–8.

Meister, J. C. (1998) *Corporate Universities: Lessons in Building a World-Class Workforce*, New York: McGraw-Hill.

Prince, C. and Stewart, J. (2000) 'The dynamics of the corporate education market and the role of business schools' *Journal of Management Development* 19(3): 207–19.

Stewart, J. and Miller, R. (1999) 'Opened university: Unipart as a learning organisation' *People Management* 5(12): 42–6.

Walton, J. (1999) *Strategic Human Resource Development*, London: Financial Times Prentice Hall.

Counselling

Counselling is defined in various sources (Reddy, 1987; Egan, 1990; Summerfield and van Oudtshoorn, 1995; Berridge, Cooper and Highley-Marchington, 1997) as a process which is intended to help people help themselves, come to terms with feelings which may block decision-making, consider what options for action are open in a problematic situation and make choices leading to valued outcomes.

The counselling process consists of a set of techniques, skills and attitudes to help people manage their own problems using their own resources. This is mirrored in the British Association of Counselling (BAC) definition cited by Berridge, Cooper and Highley-Marchington, (1997):6 'The task of counselling is to give the client the opportunity to explore, discover and clarify ways of living more resourcefully and towards greater well-being.' Counselling therefore has the nature of being empowering and problem-solving.

Models of counselling typically consist of three stages:

- identifying, defining and understanding the present problem
- generating and evaluating possible solutions
- marshalling emotional and practical resources to achieve the outcome.

The skills of active listening, reflecting, challenging and questioning are complemented by attitudes of respect, empathy and genuineness (Reddy, 1987).

'Using counselling skills' is therefore contrasted with 'being a counsellor'. The roles of manager and counsellor are far apart but it can be argued (Megranahan, 1989) that there is common ground in the use of facilitative skills to help others achieve results – the purpose of managerial work.

Counselling skills may be deployed in situations of organizational change (mergers, redundancy) and individual crises – conflict in the workplace (harassment, bullying), career decisions, stress management, family and relationship problems, and substance abuse. It is also a process which can be seen to have relevance to the development of a learning organization.

The development of counselling skills can therefore be seen as of central importance in the context of managing people at work in today's organizational context. However, it is also argued (Ashton, 1994; Nixon and Carroll, 1994) that the demands made on a manager using counselling skills in the workplace are far from straightforward. The issues raised relate to role conflict and the confusion of boundaries, the difficulty of achieving anonymity and maintaining confidentiality, and incompatibility of the values inherent in the counselling process with dominant organizational values and managerial priorities. **PM**

References and further reading

Ashton, F. (1994) 'The politics of staff counselling', *Journal of Workplace Learning* 6(1): 16–20.

British Association of Counselling (BAC) (1989) *Code of Ethics and Practice for Counselling Skills*, Rugby: BAC.

Berridge, J., Cooper, C. L. and Highley-Marchington, C. (1997) *Employee Assistance Programmes and Workplace Counselling*, Chichester: Wiley.

Egan, G. (1990) *The Skilled Helper: A Systematic Approach to Effective Helping*, 4th edn, Pacific Grove, CA: Brookes Cole.

Megranahan, M. (1989) *Counselling: A Practical Guide for Employers*, London: IPM.

Nixon, J. and Carroll, M. (1994) 'Can a line manager also be a counsellor?', *Journal of Workplace Learning* 6(1): 10–15.

Reddy, M. (1987) *Counselling at Work*, Leicester: British Psychological Society.

Summerfield, J. and van Oudtshoorn, L. (1995) *Counselling in the Workplace*, London: IPD.

Custom and practice

Custom and practice is a set of informal rules that evolve from the day-to-day activities that exist between employees, their representatives and management. In a classic study of custom and practice, Brown (1972) notes that such rules arise not from any explicit and formal negotiation, but from a process whereby managerial error or omission establishes a practice that workers then see as legitimate to defend. It is important to note that managerial error or omission can be a conscious act. Terry (1977) provides an example where employees are required to report lateness to a supervisor, who would then be over-tolerant of the workers' excuses for lateness in order to gain co-operation from the employees. The rationale for maintaining customary rules thus becomes a legitimate function of management in meeting production schedules, service delivery targets and co-operative workplace relations (Beynon, 1973; Armstrong, Goodman and Hyman, 1981).

Brown (1972) distinguished between custom and practice rules which are 'transactional' (based on some informal understanding between the parties) from those that are 'unilateral' (rules which occur outside the boundaries set by management). The implication is that the formulation and maintenance of informal rules then become part of a shifting 'frontier of control' (Goodrich, 1975). In other words, both management and workers regard it as legitimate to defend and maintain certain customary practices that have evolved over time.

Custom and practice also has legal connotations with regard to *implied* contractual terms. For customary rules to form part of the contract (regardless of whether or not these rules are actually written in the contract), three factors must be satisfied: the practice must be 'certain', 'well-known' to both parties and 'reasonable'. If workers take 15 minutes to wash-up before the end of a shift (as is often the practice in manufacturing industry), and management know and tolerate this practice, then this is implicit in the contractual terms and conditions of employment. In the classic legal case of *Sagar* v. *Ridehalgh* [1930, Rep 288], the employer's practice of deducting wages for bad workmanship was held to be in accordance with a trade custom which was deemed to be part of the condition of employment.

It is fair to say that custom and practice still forms an extremely important part of the management of people (see Delbridge, 1998), although there is considerable ambiguity regarding the legal position given the subjective nature of the criteria (see Lockton, 1999). **TD**

References and further reading

Armstrong, P., Goodman, J. and Hyman, J. (1981) *Ideology and Shopfloor Industrial Relations*, London: Croom.

Beynon, H. (1973) *Working for Ford*, Harmondsworth: Penguin.

Brown, W. (1972) 'A consideration of custom and practice', *British Journal of Industrial Relations* 10(1): 42–61.

Delbridge, R. (1998) *Life on the Line in Contemporary Manufacturing*, Oxford: Oxford University Press.

Goodrich, C. (1975) *The Frontier of Control*, London: Pluto Press

Lockton, D. (1999) *Employment Law*, 3rd edn, London: Macmillan.

Terry, M. (1977) 'The inevitable growth of informality', *British Journal of Industrial Relations*, 15(1): 76–90.

Customer appraisal

Total quality management (TQM) and customer care programmes are now very widespread in both private and public sectors in the UK. One impact of such initiatives is that organizations are now increasingly setting employee performance standards based upon customer care indicators and appraising staff against these. For example, fast-food restaurants use a mix of 'hard' quantifiable standards such as 'delivery of a customers first drink within two minutes' and 'soft' qualitative standards such as 'a warm and friendly greeting' in its performance appraisal system. Employee performance standards when linked into customer care policies need to be realistic, achievable and measurable. The use of service guarantees, which involve the payment of compensation to customers if the organizations do not reach the standards promised has also led to a greater use of customer data in performance appraisal ratings. Customer service data for use in appraising employees is gathered in a variety of methods. First, there is the use of a range of customer surveys, such as via the completion of customer care cards, telephone surveys, interview with customers and postal surveys. Organizations are now using such surveys more frequently and are increasingly sophisticated in how they gather customer views. Second, there are a range of surveillance techniques used by managers to sample the service encounter (see also mystery shopping entry). Here the electronic work monitoring of factory workers is being extended into the services sector. For example, customer service managers at call centres will review staff performance by taping staff–customer conversations and giving immediate feedback as well as using this and other data for the regular formal review process.

In an increasing number of organizations internal service–level agreements are also being established. The introduction of compulsory competitive tendering and, more recently, 'best value' has given considerable impetus to such agreements in the public sector. Often in these agreements there is an internal customer-service 'guarantee' stating the level and nature of services the supplier will provide. It thus has been a natural progression of such a development for organizations to incorporate performance data from service-level agreements into the appraisal process. A key advantage claimed for using internal customers in this way is that joint goal-setting helps provide both internal customer and service provider with greater understanding of the roles that individuals and departments provide. It thus helps in breaking down internal barriers between departments. **TR**

References and further reading

Arkin, A. (1992) 'Fitting up customer care', *Personnel Management* 24(3): 49–51.
Fuller, L. and Smith, V. (1991) 'Consumers' reports: management by customers in a changing economy', *Work Employment and Society* 4(1): 1–16.

CV

Short for curriculum vitae, the CV is a summary (or résumé) of someone's educational and professional career history, prepared for job applications.

Candidates can present their accomplishments and qualifications to a potential employer without the restrictive format of employers' application forms, and lots of advice is available to job hunters in books and web sites on how to write an effective CV. Different formats may be adopted. A 'reverse chronological' format is the most common, with the most recent job first. This has the benefit to employers of being easy to follow and it can highlight any career 'gaps'.

A 'functional' format is non-sequential and emphasizes key skills and achievements, summarizing all experience together. It allows the applicant to highlight their relevant talents whereas the chronological approach emphasizes the most recent work experience. The functional format can, however, be off-putting to potential employers if they think the applicant is trying to hide something in their career history.

These two approaches can be combined to gain the advantages of both: a chronological format with key skills highlighted at the beginning. Applicants should ensure that their CV highlights skills relevant for the post in question, and it is suggested, therefore, that a new CV should be written for each post applied for.

Whatever format is adopted, the CV should be short and concise, on no more than two sides of plain white A4 paper. The wording is important, as it is an example of the applicant's communication skills and ability to 'sell' themselves to an employer, and key words on skills and qualifications can also be picked out with the increasing use of electronic scanning of CV applications. The overall appearance of the CV can also impress selectors and one poorly presented can be off-putting, irrespective of the actual content, as selectors may be influenced by presentation and first impressions. **JB**

References and further reading

Cornfield, R. (1999) *Preparing your own CV*, London: Kogan Page.
Courtis, J. (1999) *Getting a better job*, London: Chartered Institute of Personnel and Development.
Fowler, A. (1995) 'How to make the best use of CVs', *People Management*, 1(7), 6 April: 44–5.
Johnstone, J. (1996) *'Applying for a Job: How to Sell your Skills and Experience to a Prospective Employer'*, Oxford: How To Books.
McBride, P. (1995) *CVs and Written Applications: How to Present Yourself on Paper*, Cambridge: Hobsons.
Theaker, M. (1995) 'Entering the era of electronic CV's', *People Management* 1(16), 10 August: 34–7.
Web site at www.aiuto.net/uk.htm (a gateway for access to British web resources on careers information and guidance).

D

Department for Education and Employment (DfEE)

This UK government department has as its aim 'to give everyone the chance, through education, training and work, to realise their full potential, and thus build an inclusive and fair society and a competitive economy' (DfEE web site).
It has three prime objectives:

1. 'Ensuring that all young people reach 16 with the skills attitudes and personal qualities that will give them a secure foundation for lifelong learning, work and citizenship in a rapidly changing world.
2. Developing in everyone a commitment to lifelong learning, so as to enhance their lives, improve their employability in a changing labour market and create the skills that our economy and our employers need.
3. Helping those without a job into work' (DfEE web site).

The ministerial team comprises the Ministers for Employment, Welfare to Work and Equal Opportunities, Education and Employment in the Lords and School Standards. These Ministers are supported by Under Secretaries of State as well as a civil service team. A full listing of responsibilities, organization chart, publications, annual report, current and future plans is accessed via the web site on government information and government departments.

This large department is rarely out of the headlines, its remit touching aspects of most people's lives. It is responsible for educational standards and the related issues and initiatives such as the National Curriculum, Standard Assessment Tasks (SATS), Office for Standards in Education (OFSTED) inspections, teachers' pay and the introduction of performance-related pay (PRP). The emphasis on lifelong learning is related to employability and here the DfEE is involved in Training and Enterprise Council (TEC) initiatives such as Individual Learning Accounts, Investors in People (IIP) and National Vocational Qualifications (NVQs). In the higher education area, the DfEE is involved in access issues, student grants, loans and fees. The University of Industry (UFI) is a government initiative. These are only a few areas highlighted from a very broad list of responsibilities. Linking the two areas of employment and education has brought together employers and skills training with teachers and academe to focus upon national economic competitiveness. **ASm**

References and further reading
Web site at http://www.gfee.gov.uk/insidedfee/ministers.htm
Web site at http://www.dfee.gov.uk/insidedfee/aaandob.htm

De-skilling

The de-skilling of jobs and work can result from technological change as well as management actions. This area has increasingly been associated with the labour process school and especially Harry Braverman, who built on Marx's writings. This camp argues, basically, that during the twentieth century there was an underlying tendency within capitalism to substitute less skilled or unskilled work for skilled work. Technology deskilled and degraded manual and mental work. Labour came to increasingly execute only routine and conceptually depleted tasks in the service of capital, while management control was enhanced.

This de-skilling thesis has been criticized on several grounds:

1. For its universalism and US bias. Societies varied with socio-cultural and institutional contexts which impinged on the employment relationship.
2. There are supportive examples where de-skilling has occurred, but there are also cases where upskilling of workers has resulted.
3. Its focus on 'objective' features of skill ignored important 'tacit' skills, those connected to gender or personality and skill transfer.
4. It failed to explore 'social action' and alternative management strategies, treating labour as passive and compliant. In reality workers can resist de-skilling via individual and collective action. It also underestimated the degree of consent and accommodation as employees can consent to their own subordination.
5. It overplays the dominance of labour in managerial thought and management's coherence and strategic abilities. This underemphasizes broader business objectives and the diversity and competing nature of management, with labour and control less central to thoughts and issues dealt with in an ad hoc and expedient manner.

However, it has been argued that perhaps a more subtle reading of the thesis, for example, if it is seen as less of a universal law operating in all cases, and rather as more of a 'tendency', weakens some of these criticisms. **CR**

References and further reading
Armstrong, P. (1988) 'Labor and monopoly capital', in R. Hyman and W. Streeck (eds) *New Technology and Industrial Relations*, Oxford: Blackwell.
Braverman, H. (1974) *Labor and Monopoly Capital: Degradation of Work in the Twentieth Century*, New York: Monthly Review Press.
Kelly, J. (1982) *Scientific Management, Job Design and Work Performance*, London: Academic Press.
Knights, D and Willmott, H. (eds) (1990) *Labour Process Theory*, London: Macmillan.
Littler, C. (1982) *The Development of the Labour Process In Capitalist Countries*, London: Hutchinson.
Wood, S. (ed.) (1982) *The Degradation of Work? Skill, Deskilling and the Labour Process*, London: Hutchinson.
Wood, S. (ed.) (1989) *The Transformation of Work? Skill, Flexibility and the Labour Process*, London: Unwin Hyman.
Zimbalist, A. (ed.) (1979) *Case Studies in the Labour Process*, New York: Monthly Review Press.

Devolution

The term 'devolution' in human resource management (HRM) is normally associated with two developments in modern organizations. First, it denotes a shift in decision-making from the highest organizational bodies to the lowest, i.e. from corporate head quarters to business unit level. Second, it denotes a shift in how human resource (HR) work itself is done, notably indicating a shift away from HR 'specialists' involvement to an increased role for 'generalist' line managers.

The first aspect of devolution is designed to enable managers to effectively complete work without the need to constantly refer it back up an organizational hierarchy before decisions are made. This is thought to keep business costs low, release senior executives to focus on 'strategic' business issues and 'empower' managers in a strictly defined context, as these managers are seen to be closer to customer and business needs as they are at the front line of the organization's work.

The second aspect of devolution is to enable middle-level line managers to take more responsibility for people management – often seen as a key component of an explicitly HR approach. The logic of this latter development is that as generalist line managers and not HR specialists already do day-to-day people management, they should do more of it 'as they know their people best'. Again, this helps to reduce costs of needing an expensive HR function, and also releases HR managers to focus on strategic issues. This aspect of devolution is not straightforward to introduce, as HR and line groups often encourage such changes to their roles – for HR being a release from the 'drudgery' of HR work, and for the line to reject 'interference' from bureaucratic HR managers in their affairs.

Moreover, other issues raised concern the need to get the balance right in how much HR work to devolve from HR to the line – if any. Devolving too much may produce poor people management as HR issues are not handled professionally or properly (due to lack of expertise in HRM), but devolving too little may marginalize HR issues as they are not 'voiced' or 'owned' by line managers, and HR managers omit the business case for them (Marchington, 1999). Further developments in the use of intranet/Internet-based technologies remove the need for HR expertise (as HR services are outsourced), and HR managers are 'absent' in guiding and advising line managers on best HR practice (as HR function's shrink as HR services are delivered on-line). Whether these developments affect the practice of professional people management in organizations remains to be seen, as line manager commitment to, and reward for, undertaking HR tasks is presently unknown, as is HR managers' commitment to a 'strategic' HR role. **DR**

References and further reading

Budhwar, P. S. (2000) 'Evaluating levels of strategic integration and devolvement of human resource management in the UK', *Personnel Review* 29(2): 141–61.

Marchington, M. (1999) 'Professional qualification scheme: core personnel and development exam papers & examiner's reports May 1999', Institute of Personnel and Development, paper given to the IPD Professional Standards Conference, University of Warwick, July, pp. 1–12.

Marginson, P., Edwards, P. K., Martin, R., Purcell, J. with Hubbard, N. (1993) *The Control of Industrial Relations in Large Companies*: *An Initial Analysis of the Second Company Level Industrial Relations Survey*, Warwick Papers in Industrial Relations, no. 45, IRRU, University of Warwick.

Proctor, S. and Currie, G. (1999) 'The role of the personnel function: roles, processes and perceptions in an NHS Trust', *International Journal of Human Resource Management* 10(6): December 1077–91.

Purcell, J. and Ahlstrand, B. (1994) *Human Resource Management in the Multi-Divisional Company*, Oxford: Oxford University Press.

Sisson, K. and Storey, J. (2000) (eds) *The Realities of Human Resource Management*: *Managing the Employment Relationship*, Buckingham: Open University Press.

Disability discrimination

Labour market statistics indicate that those with disabilities occupy a markedly inferior position to those who do not. This inferior position arises from a range of social and labour market factors, including the human resource management strategies and policies of employers. To combat this latter source of disadvantage the Disability

Discrimination Act 1995 imposes requirements on employers in respect of disabled workers, that is, those who have a mental or physical impairment that has lasted or is likely to last at least 12 months and which has a substantial adverse effect on their ability to 'carry out normal day-to-day activities'. The requirements concerned, which apply to employers with 15 or more employees, seek to advance the position of such workers in two main ways:

1. By prohibiting employers from treating them less favourably.
2. By requiring employers to make reasonable adjustments to their premises and the way in which they operate where this is necessary to avoid a disabled person being put at a 'substantial disadvantage'.

Breaches of the Act's requirements can be enforced through individual complaints to an employment tribunal. In addition, a Disability Rights Commission is empowered to conduct formal investigations and to issue non-discrimination notices where such investigations reveal unlawful discrimination. The available evidence shows that many employers, in response to the introduction of the Act, have either adopted or amended their existing policies relating to the treatment of disabled persons. However, it also suggests that the implementation of such policies is often difficult as a result of line management failure to implement them adequately, staff resistance to the provision of 'special treatment' to those with disabilities and the absence within devolved management structures of any centralized budget to fund the costs of any necessary adjustments. **PJ**

References and further reading

Cox, S. (2000) 'Disability Discrimination Act 1995', *Industrial Relations Law Bulletin* 649, September: 2–12.

Cunningham, I. and James, P. (1998) 'The Disability Discrimination Act – an early response of employers', *Industrial Relations Journal* 29(4): 304–15.

Doyle, B. (1996) *Disability Discrimination – the New Law*, Bristol: Jordan.

Industrial Relations Services (IRS) (2000) 'New ways to manage disability', *IRS Employment Trends* 708, July: 9–16.

Meager, N. and Hibbett, A. (1999), 'Disability and the labour market: findings from the DfEE Baseline Disability Survey', *Labour Market Trends*, September: 467–76.

Discipline

In the context of the workplace the term 'discipline' refers to the methods used by managers to secure compliance on the part of staff with specific rules and, more generally, with organizational expectations. At one level there are formal disciplinary procedures which are invariably written and have a constitutional character. Because of the existence of dismissal as a possible sanction, disciplinary procedures are typically designed so as to comply with the guidance given in the Advisory, Conciliation and Arbitration Service (ACAS) *Code of Practice 1: Discipline at Work*. This acts as the standard applied by employment tribunals in determining the reasonableness or otherwise of an employers actions in cases of unfair dismissal. Behaviour which is judged by an organization to comprise 'gross misconduct' and can lead to summary dismissal is thus set out, along with the procedure that is to be used when such incidents arise. Here there is a requirement for management to investigate the matter properly, to convene a disciplinary hearing, to allow the perpetrator to state his or her case, to be accompanied by a representative and, should it be necessary, to appeal against a subsequent dismissal. For lesser offences the procedure is similar, but here there is a commitment not to dismiss without first giving either one or two formal warnings to the individual concerned. Disciplinary sanctions thus frequently fall short of dismissal. Examples range from a formal rebuke, through the allocation of less desirable work, to suspension and demotion.

A broader conception of discipline at work focuses less on formal rules and procedures, and more on the methods used to engender self and peer-based discipline. The emphasis here is on ways in which organizational structures and cultures act more subtly to exercise control over employee activities. Examples are the outcomes associated with the operation of reward systems, approaches to performance management and methods used to determine promotions. Some argue that an important feature of the evolution of human resource management (HRM) as a specific approach to the management of people is the presence of informal, less obvious control mechanisms such as these. **ST**

References and further reading

Advisory, Conciliation and Arbitration Service, (ACAS) (2000): *Code of Practice 1*: *Discipline at Work*, London: ACAS.

Earnshaw, J., Goodman, J., Harrison, R. and Marchington, M. (1998) *Industrial Tribunals, Workplace Disciplinary Procedures and Employment Practice*, London: Department of Trade and Industry.

Edwards, P. (2000) 'Discipline: towards trust and self-discipline', in S. Bach and K. Sisson (eds) *Personnel Management*: *A Comprehensive Guide to Theory and Practice*, Oxford: Blackwell.

James, P. and Lewis, D. (1992) *Discipline*, London: IPD.

Torrington, D. (1998) 'Discipline and dismissal', in M. Poole and M. Warner (eds) *The Handbook of Human Resource Management*, London: Thomson Learning.

Torrington, D. and Hall, L. (1998) *Human Resource Management*, 4th edn, London: Prentice Hall, ch. 29.

Dismissal

Dismissal is the process by which an employee is required to leave an organization involuntarily. Practice in the UK is now heavily influenced by the requirements of unfair dismissal legislation that have evolved since 1971. Employers wishing to avoid the risk and expense of having to justify their actions in court are thus obliged to avoid giving grounds for ex-employees to bring such an action. The right not to be unfairly dismissed is given to any employee (i.e. someone working under a contract of service) who has more completed than a year's continuous employment in the organization concerned and who is under the normal age of retirement. Where it is established that an ex-employee qualifies and has been dismissed, employment tribunals turn to the employer to prove that the reason for the dismissal was one of those permitted in unfair dismissal law. The dismissal is found to be unfair if the tribunal is not satisfied at this stage.

The main categories are misconduct, incapability (either on grounds of performance or ill health) and redundancy, although there are others including the much criticized 'some other substantial reason'. If the tribunal is satisfied that the dismissal was for one of these reasons it goes on to examine the reasonableness of the employer's action in carrying through the dismissal. Here the focus is on the use of a fair procedure, consistency and the appropriateness of dismissal as a sanction in the circumstances. Where the tribunal considers the employer not to have acted reasonably it will declare the dismissal unfair. Compensation is the usual outcome (to a maximum of £50 000), but there are situations in which some form of reinstatement can be ordered.

Dismissals are unquestionably the hardest and most unpleasant activity that human resource (HR) professionals have to undertake. They are particularly difficult where the reason is ill health and where the individual concerned is likely to find difficulty in securing further employment. It is therefore advisable for organizations to provide training for managers with responsibilities in this field. It is also essential that managers prepare well before the meeting at which the dismissal is to take place so that they are able to answer any points with clarity and authority. **ST**

References and further reading
Ferris, G. R., Howard, J. L. and Bergin, T. G. (1995) 'Rationality and politics in organizational exit decisions', in G. Ferris and R. Buckley (eds) *Human Resources Management: Perspectives, Context, Functions and Outcomes*, London: Prentice Hall.
Ford, M. and Gibbons, S. (1996) 'Remedying unfair dismissal law', in A. McColgan (ed.) *The Future of Labour Law*, London: Pinter.
Lewis, D. and Sargeant, M. (2000) *Essentials of Employment Law,* 6th edn, London: IPD, chs 13 and 14.
Willey, B. (2000) *Employment Law in Context*, London: Financial Times Prentice Hall, ch. 8.

Distance learning

Distance learning is a method of employee development which is generally acknowledged to be a subset of open learning. The latter is an approach which attempts to provide greater control and autonomy to individual learners. This autonomy is argued to extend to decisions on the what, where, how, when and pace of learning. Open learning, therefore, is concerned with overcoming both administrative and educational barriers to learning opportunities. An example of the former would be a centrally delivered training programme which occurs at a particular time and place, and only if sufficient numbers of learners wish to or can attend. An example of the latter would be specifications of existing qualifications as entry criteria to the programme or, in an organizational context, specifying programmes as being available only to certain grades or categories of staff. Given its 'openness' to everyone, the Open University (OU) in the UK is often cited as an example of an open learning institution. However, the OU only overcomes some educational barriers. Many administrative barriers, such as timing, pace and cost, remain. Therefore, it is perhaps more accurate to view the OU as a distance learning institution. Its programmes meet the defining characteristics of distance learning in that the individual learner:

- is not continuously and immediately supervised by another person, e.g. trainer or tutor
- benefits from the services of a training/tutorial organization
- utilizes learning materials in a variety of media and forms provided by a training/tutorial organization.

Two points emerge from this discussion. First, distance learning can be incorporated into open learning programmes, but the two concepts are distinct. Second, neither concept represents an absolute and it is more helpful to think of particular programmes as more or less 'open' or 'distance' learning relative to alternative programmes.

Distance learning programmes and materials utilize a variety of technologies. They can be text based, use audio or videotapes, laser discs, DVD or computers. One common feature and claimed advantage of distance learning is the use of a variety of media in one programme. Where new technologies are utilized, the related term technology-based training (TBT) is often applied. More recently, the term 'e-learning' is becoming popular to denote and describe programmes which utilize the potential of intranets, the Internet and the World Wide Web to deliver learning. New computer programmes and associated facilities such as those provided by Lotus Notes are being applied. Such developments may replace the services currently provided by learning resource centres which were created by many companies in the 1990s. They also raise questions about the future role of professional employee development practitioners. However, it is as well to remember that the newer technologies simply provide new media with which to deliver distance learning. They are unlikely to have the ability to fully replace either established technologies in distance learning, or all of the existing alternatives to distance learning. As Professor Ian Angell of the London School of Economics said at the 2000 conference of the Chartered Institute of Personnel and Development, 'technology enthusiasts and e-learning gurus are either knaves or naive'. **JS**

References and further reading

Darling, J. (1999) *The Changing Role of the Trainer*, London: Institute of Personnel and Development.

MacQueen, J. (1996) IRS Employment Review, *Employee Development Bulletin,* 614.

Masie, E. (1999) 'Joined-up thinking', *People Management* 5(23): 32–6.

Rana, E. (1999) 'E-learning "will fail" unless it is focused on the users', *People Management* 5(24): 11.

Salmon, G. (2000) *E-Moderating*: *The Key to Teaching and Learning Online*, London: Kogan Page.

Stewart, J. and Winter, R. (1995) 'Open and distance learning', in S. Truelove, (ed.) *The Handbook of Training and Development,* 2nd edn, Oxford: Blackwell.

See also Kogan Page's Open and Distance Learning Series, F. Lockwood, series editor.

Donovan Commission

As a result of deteriorating industrial relations in the 1960s, the then Labour government established a Royal Commission on Trade Unions and Employer's Associations which sat from 1965 to 1968 under the chairmanship of Lord Donovan. The report (commonly known as the Donovan Report) and 11 research papers, written by various industrial relations experts, provide a comprehensive outline of what were perceived to be the problems at that time with the industrial relations system in Great Britain. The resulting prescriptions for reform influenced industrial relations thinking over the following decade.

The main conclusion of the Donovan Report was that Britain has not one but two systems of industrial relations. The 'formal' system was based on the national system of collective bargaining which produced industry wide collective agreements and institutions for conflict resolution. The 'informal' system had emerged, especially in the 1960s, as a result of a growing level of unstructured workplace bargaining which altered the nationally established terms and conditions of employment, especially pay. Local bargaining was described by Alan Flanders to the Donovan Commission as 'largely informal, largely fragmented, and largely autonomous'.

The move in power towards the workplace resulted in strain on industry-level disputes procedures which struggled to cope with the problems emerging from the growing number of disagreements arising from rough local bargaining, thereby raising the level of industrial conflict. Explanations for the development of local bargaining centred on economic conditions (especially full employment) and the use of piecework payment systems. Local management frequently supported the development of local bargaining as a way of dealing with local problems, despite the evidence that it contributed to inefficiency and a rising number of unofficial disputes.

The Donovan Commission argued the following changes were needed to the industrial relations systems in Britain:

1. Reform of workplace industrial relations should be a major public policy priority. A key element to this should be the development of more formal collective bargaining structures and agreements at workplace level to replace the haphazard structures that had developed under the 'informal' system.
2. The resulting plant level (or company agreements in multiplant companies) should be registered with the Department of Employment and Productivity. These could be scrutinized by an Industrial Relations Commission, and improvements suggested.
3. To improve the conduct of industrial relations, collective bargaining should be encouraged, with no employee being prevented from joining a trade union. The Industrial Relations Commission would have a role here in facilitating union recognition.

4. The issue of control of strike activity was considered. Whilst imposing legal sanctions on individuals and unions pursuing unconstitutional strikes was rejected, Donovan did recommend compulsory strike ballots and a compulsory 'cooling-off period' between a strike ballot and industrial action.
5. In the area of individual rights the commission proposed:
   (a) employees should be protected against unfair dismissal
   (b) the closed shop should not be banned, but employees dismissed because of the operation of a closed shop should be able to complain to an industrial tribunal.
6. The commission proposed trade union reform to include:
   (a) a reduction on multiunionism
   (b) the reform of branch structures.

In the end, the Donovan Commission's report was not directly acted upon, although many of the themes were taken up by later governments. Instead, the Labour government introduced a White Paper in 1969 entitled 'In Place of strife' with proposals such as cooling-off periods before strike action and power to revise trade union election rules. Trade unions did not agree with many of the proposals and a change of government in 1970 meant the measures never reached the statute book. **DK**

Downsizing

Organizational downsizing can be defined as a 'planned elimination of positions or jobs'. Dealing with organizational downsizing (see also **redundancy** and **redeployment**) is a growing demand on the human resource departments' time and expertise. Downsizing has been widespread in the UK. Surveys of redundancy report two-thirds of organizations having reduced their staff over recent years with the number of jobs lost ranging from four to over 10 000 (IRS, 1998a; 1998b). Individual UK-based companies have undergone massive layoffs, for example, BT shed 88 000 out of 237 000 (37 per cent) between 1990 and 1994, BP 118 050 to 66 500 (44 per cent) and Rolls-Royce 65 900 to 43 500 (34 per cent). In the 1980s the brunt of job reductions were borne by the manufacturing sector, with services suffering particularly in the 1990s. For example, financial services alone lost 150 000 jobs between 1990 and 1995. The public sector has also downsized with privatization and outsourcing leading to large-scale redundancies in the former privatized industries and in the public sector more generally. There appears to have been little abatement in the levels of downsizing in recent years. Particularly worrying here are the numbers of organizations downsizing who are actually making healthy profits. organizational size, it seems, is no longer a measure of corporate success

Effectively managing workforce reduction is thus of increasing importance in human resource management practice not least because of its greater scale and frequency but also because of the potentially serious negative effects of its mismanagement. The mismanagement of workforce reduction can clearly cause major damage to both the organization's employment and general business reputations. Damage to the former can seriously effect an organization's selection attractiveness with potential future employees by producing an uncaring, hire and fire image. Similarly, bad publicity over retrenchment can cause customers to worry that the firm may go out of business or give rise to problems in the continuity or quality of supplies and services.

There have been increasing recent concerns about the organizational effectiveness of the post-downsized 'anorexic organization'. The benefits, which organizations claim to be seeking from downsizing centre on savings in labour costs, speedier decision-making, better communication, reduced product development time, enhanced involvement of employees and greater responsiveness. However, reports suggest that the results of downsizing are often illusory. Downsizing, it seems, can have a damaging effect on corporate performance. Paradoxically, restructuring has also been seen as a sign of corporate virility and stock market prices have boomed in a period of downsizing. However, there is some suggestion from the literature that while shares of downsizing companies have outperformed the stock market for six months or so after downsizing, three years later they lag behind. Other studies have found downsizing has an adverse effect on innovation and on the bottom line. Empirical research has found that companies using lay-offs as a strategy for financial improvements failed to achieve this and profit margins, return on assets and return on equity continued to deteriorate, but at an even faster rate than before downsizing.

The potential negative impact of downsizing is not restricted to those who leave but it has also a major effect on the remaining employees. Such employees are by their very nature now much more important to the employer but are often overlooked in downsizing situations. The impact of downsizing on the remaining employees is such that commentators now talk of 'the survivor syndrome'. This is the term given to the collection of behaviours such as decreased motivation, morale and loyalty to the organization, and increased stress levels and scepticism that are exhibited by those who are still in employment following restructuring. **TR**

References and further reading
Cameron, K. (1994) 'Strategies for successful organisation downsizing', *Human Resources Management* 33(2): 189–211.

De Meuse, K. P., Bergmann, T. J. and Vanderheiden, P. A. (1997) 'Corporate downsizing. Separating myth from fact', *Journal of Management Inquiry* 6(2): 168–76.

Industrial Relations Service (IRS) (1998a) 'The 1998 IRS Redundancy Survey Part 1', *Employment Trends*, no. 658, June: 5–11.

Industrial Relations Service (IRS) (1998b) 'The 1998 IRS Redundancy Survey Part 2', *Employment Trends*, no. 659, July: 9–16.

Redman, T. and Keithley, D. (1998) 'Downsizing goes East? Employment restructuring in post-socialist Poland', *International Journal of Human Resource Management* 9(2): 274–93.

Turnbull, P. and Wass, V. (1997) 'Job insecurity and labour market lemons: the (mis)management of redundancy in steel making, coal mining, and port transport', *Journal of Management Studies* 34(1): 27–51.

Drug testing

The Health and Safety Executive estimate that up to 14 million working days are lost each year due to alcohol-related problems, and that drug use costs industry some £800 million each year. Employees who are under the influence of drugs or alcohol are likely to take time off work, and are liable to cause accidents and injury to themselves, other employees and to the public, and it is for these reasons that some employers have introduced drug or alcohol testing of employees. Following a recent rail crash, train drivers are now routinely tested at recruitment as well as during their period of employment. Whilst few would argue with this example, many people, concerned about civil liberty, question the use of random checks. As well as being an invasion of privacy, tests can be inaccurate. It is argued that using soft drugs recreationally does not affect workplace performance and that the employer should not be an arbiter of moral standards, particularly with the ongoing debate about decriminalizing some 'soft' drugs.

However, proponents of random screening argue that drugs can have residual effects which may impact on work performance, and that rather than waiting until after an accident, random checks may save lives. Random testing also avoids the need for managers to identify problems, since they may be untrained to recognize signs of abuse.

Testing should be part of a wider policy on substance abuse and it is advantageous to have clear rules. Addiction should be regarded as an illness and employees should be encouraged to obtain treatment. Other measures, such as provision of confidential advice and counselling to staff, perhaps via an employee assistance programme can be useful. However, where employees refuse to get help, sell drugs or take drugs whilst on duty (especially in high-risk occupations or industries), employers can be justified in applying discipline or dismissal for misconduct. **JB**

References and further reading
Employment Digest (1992) 'Dealing with drug abuse', 339, 17 August.

IDS Brief (1998) 'Drink and drugs – the employment law issues', 625, November.

Jackson, T. (1999) D*rugs and Alcohol policies*, London: CIPD.

Javaid, M. (1998) 'A policy of substance', *People Management* 4(10), December: 20–1.

MacDonald, S., Wells, S. and Fry, R. (1993) 'The limitations of drug screening in the workplace', *International Labour Review* 132(1): 95–113.

Pawsey, V. (2000) 'High time for action', *People Management* 6(10): 24–32

Rockmore, B. W., Zimmerer, T. W. and Jones, F. F. (1997) 'Building a socially responsive drug testing programme', *Journal of Workplace Learning: Employee Counselling Today* 9(7): 220–4.

Dual careers

Greenhaus and Callanan have defined a dual-career couple as two people who share a lifestyle that includes an ongoing love relationship, cohabitation and a work role for each partner. Much of the research on dual careers focuses on married couples with children. It clearly shows the potential benefits of dual careers, such as the opportunity for both people to experience a sense of autonomy and fulfilment, and an equality or near equality of contribution to the household, including in terms of income. The parents may also have more equal relationships with children than would be the case if one was employed and the other a homemaker.

Nevertheless, it remains the case that in most countries women earn less money than men for the same kind of work, and women are more often expected than men to abandon work when a child or elderly relative needs help. In heterosexual dual-career households it still tends to be the woman who does most of the housework. Tensions can therefore arise concerning the relative burdens on each member of the dual-career household. Difficult issues can also arise over whose career takes priority when, for example, one partner has the chance of a job in a different location. Communication between the partners needs to be open and honest, and there needs to be a sense of 'we' in decision-making rather than 'I'.

Some employers take steps to meet the needs of dual-career couples. These include maternity and paternity leave beyond statutory requirements, and the provision of workplace childcare facilities. Flexible arrangements about hours of work (for example an annual number of hours rather than a weekly or daily number) are also sometimes offered, though it is not always easy to reconcile this with business needs. Some organizations offer career breaks where a person (almost always a woman) leaves the workforce for several years, except for a few weeks each year when she works to keep up to date. When men start taking career breaks in numbers, the world really will be changing! **JA**

References and further reading
Cooper, C. L. and Lewis, S. (1993) *The Workplace Revolution: Managing Today's Dual Career Families*, London: Kogan Page.

Davidson, M. (1996) 'Women and employment', In P. Warr (ed.) *Psychology at Work*, 4th edn, London: Penguin.

Greenhaus, J. and Callanan, G. (1994) *Career Management*, 2nd edn, London: Dryden Press.

Lewis, S., Izraeli, D. and Hootsmans, H. (1992) *Dual-Earner Families: International Perspectives*, London: Sage.

Potucheck, J. (1997) *Who Supports the Family? Gender and Breadwinning in Dual-Earner Marriages*, Stanford, CA: Stanford University Press.

E-learning

E-learning is electronically based learning. World Wide Web technologies are now a vital business tool, and their growth means that e-learning is fast becoming the largest delivery vehicle for corporate training and development in an increasing number of organizations. It offers many advantages, including:

- *Speed*: in today's fast-moving competitive environments, e-learning can enable people to rapidly acquire new skills. It can also give fast access to new information, speeding up the generation of new knowledge that, in turn, can enable new developments to be produced at a pace to outstrip the competition.
- *Cost-effectiveness*: it can deliver what the learner needs, when, where and how they need it, and can reach large and far-flung groups of personnel flexibly and cost-efficiently.
- *Skills profiling*: using data from on-line training networks, trainers can produce skills profiles of individuals and jobs. They can then analyse the interaction between profiles, e-learning material and personal learning plans, and use the outcomes for accreditation and other purposes.
- *Fast feedback*: e-learners can receive immediate and effective feedback through the relevant use of computer-based assessment.
- *Collective learning*: e-learning can bring people together in a unique learning process – for example, using organizational intranets, computer conferencing and interactive videos.

The University for Industry provides access through *learndirect*, its delivery arm, to a wide range of electronically based (e-based) courses. Also, many universities in this country are working with partners abroad to develop worldwide e-based networks. These enable the sharing of research and teaching facilities, and give access to high-quality long-distance learning and teaching. A warning note, however: new technology is expensive in terms of capital investment and specialist expertise, so risk factors must be evaluated before deciding what kind of e-learning investment to make:

- On-line packages must be of a high quality, tailored to specific organizational and individual needs and to the workplace environment.
- Packages must be supported by an effective technological and human infrastructure. Where information technology (IT) departments exercise a damaging

stranglehold over trainers' on-line learning plans, external learning providers may have to be used instead, to provide delivery systems better adapted to learners' needs.

- E-learning must fully mimic the human learning process, and should therefore allow for the negative as well as the positive to occur. 'It must induce failure and allow explanation' (Schank, 1999: 57).
- E-learning processes will founder unless learners are motivated and have some human contact. A careful integration of e-based and traditional learning approaches characterizes many innovative and successful e-learning strategies. **RH**

References and further reading

Sloman, M. (2001) *The E-learning Revolution*: *From Proposition to Action*, London: Chartered Institute of Personnel and Development.
Schank, R. (1999) 'Courses of action', *People Management* 5(20): 54–7.
Tucker, B. (ed.) (1997) *Handbook of Technology-Based Training*, Aldershot: Gower.
Web site for *learndirect* is at www.ufiltd.co.uk or free helpline 0800 100 900.
Web site for Technologies for Training is at www.tft.co.uk

Emotional intelligence

The concept of emotional intelligence entered the human resource management lexicon at the end of the twentieth century. Originally devised by two US psychologists, Peter Salovey and John Mayer, emotional intelligence refers to a learned ability to *perceive emotions, to access and generate emotions so as to assist thought, to understand emotions and emotional knowledge, and to reflectively regulate the emotions so as to promote emotional and intellectual growth*. Put simply it is the ability to perceive, understand and express our feelings accurately and to control our emotions so that they work for us, not against us. Emotional intelligence is seen as essential for effective communication, social adeptness, adaptability, self-actualization and personal happiness.

Although coined by Salovey and Mayer, it was Daniel Goleman, another US psychologist and journalist, who popularized the concept and brought it to the attention of human resource professionals and business leaders. By drawing on research that investigated what distinguished top leaders, Goleman argued that as much as 85 per cent of success could be attributed to emotional intelligence (EQ), whilst only 15 per cent to IQ. He identified 20 behavioural competencies of emotional intelligence, such as emotional self-awareness, trustworthiness, change catalyst and empathy, and grouped them under four headings: self-awareness, self-management, social awareness and social skills.

Variously referred to as Ei or EQ, emotional intelligence has seen a meteoric rise in popularity, but it has yet to prove its value to human resource management (HRM) practice. The concept itself is criticized for being poorly specified and speculative thinking. Whilst Goleman's model is the one that has achieved a dominant position in HRM discourse, Stephen Fineman has suggested that it has done so through *aspiring guru rhetoric* but has yet to achieve widespread application. Through its intuitive and timely appeal, emotional intelligence has acted as a catalyst for a whole new industry offering new psychometric tools and the promise of new solutions to age-old organizational performance problems. Whether 'Ei' is a passing fad destined for the conceptual waste-bin or is to emerge as one of *the* great ideas of the twenty-first century, in HRM at least, remains to be seen. **MAC**

References and further reading

Abraham, R. (1999) 'Emotional intelligence in organizations: a conceptualisation', Genetic, Social and General Psychology Monographs.
Fineman, S. (2000) 'Commodifying the emotionally intelligent', in S. Fineman (ed.) *Emotion in Organizations*, 2nd edn, London: Sage.

Fisher, C. D. and Ashkanasy, N. M. (2000) 'The emerging role of emotions in work life: an intro-
duction', *Journal of Organizational Behaviour*, 21: 123–9.
George, J. M. (2000) 'Emotions and leadership: the role of emotional intelligence', *Human
Relations* 53(8): 1027–55.
Goleman, D. (1998) *Working with Emotional Intelligence*, London: Bloomsbury.
Mayer, J. and Salovey, P. (1997) 'What is emotional intelligence: implications for educators',
in P. Salovey and D. Sluyter (eds) *Emotional Development, Emotional Literacy and Emotional
Intelligence*, New York: Basic Books.

Employability

In an ever-changing, global, technologically demanding business environment,
sourcing and retaining talent becomes the competitive battleground. One way to
adapt the activities of firms to the exigencies of the fast-changing technological
change in their environment, is to increase the employability of the personnel.

The time that careers consisted of upward moves within a framework of long-term
employment relations has passed. A new strategy of career development should be
envisaged. Nowadays we talk about the 'protean career' (from the Greek god Proteus,
who could change shape at will) which consists of all the person's varied experiences
in education, training, work in several organizations, changes in organizational field
and so forth. Through permanent learning and by changing jobs and tasks regularly,
employees are expected to change their skills and knowledge in order to increase
their chances at the labour market.

Accordingly, an employability orientation, i.e. the attitudes and behavior of
employees towards their own employability, becomes of crucial importance. Because
of the importance of continuously updating knowledge and skills, both the organization and the individual are responsible for optimizing this development inter-
actively. To enable employees to enlarge their employability, organizations should
also change their practices and provide information, learning opportunities and
experiences to support their careers.

Most employees develop expertise, but mostly in too narrow a field to stay
employable in the long run. At the point that their function or job becomes obsolete
and they require re-employment in another job field, they are left out of account. As
the lifecycle of occupations and functions offered by organizations has shortened
tremendously during the 1980s and 1990s, the mastery of these learning and coping
strategies and the transferability of these strategies are important topics for psychological research in organizations.

Employees are neither willing nor enabled to take advantage of the opportunity to
continue their development and to develop a new expertise. In addition, possibilities
for a development of broader expertise are scarcely explored at all. Furthermore, they
are not taught how to quickly build up new expertise and which (working) conditions are beneficial in this respect. Yet, development in other areas is virtually the
only way of avoiding one-sided 'over-specialization'. Especially in professional
domains where switching to another area is necessitated by company-related circumstances, reorganizations or market changes, all those whose development is too
one-sided, with all their acquired specific expertise in a single area, will be left aside.
BvdH

References and further reading

Atkinson, J. (1984) 'Manpower strategies for flexible organizations', *Personnel Management*
16: 28–31.
Howard, A. (ed.) (1995). *The Changing Nature of Work*, San Francisco: Jossey-Bass.
Stoker, J. I. and Van der Heijden, B. I. J. M. (forthcoming). 'Self-perceptions of employees
and supervisors and their consequences for competence development', *Journal of Career
Development*.

Employee assistance programme (EAP)

The EAP is a recent development and extension of employee counselling, aiming to help 'troubled' employees in a no-blame, confidential, expert and (usually) no-cost manner to handle personal problems affecting their work performance. Its origins are US alcoholism and (latterly) substance abuse programmes, dating from the 1950s. Appearing in Britain from about 1980, EAPs have spread from larger international companies to most parts of the public and private sectors (less so small and medium-sized companies), covering up to 10 per cent of all employees.

The range of employee problems handled within an EAP is wide, including:

- accidents
- HIV/AIDS
- alcohol abuse
- disability
- discipline
- drug abuse
- family problems
- gambling
- gender issues
- indebtedness
- job change
- physical fitness
- racial harassment
- work-related stress
- supervisory style
- violence.

Unlike traditional counselling, the EAP is closely woven into the system of the organization, and attempts to solve corporate as well as personal problems. Its distinctive features are:

1. Stress awareness surveys leading to stress elimination and education programmes for all staff.
2. Training for supervisors and union stewards in defining, identifying and confronting 'troubled' employees.
3. An agreed protocol for no-blame referral (including self-referral) to the EAP.
4. An agreed protocol for acceptance in the EAP, progress and exit, including linkages with other professional agencies and the firm's disciplinary system.
5. Regular confidential programme evaluation managerially and professionally.

Employee assistance programmes use short-term counselling at the individual level, provided by professionally trained psychologists, in most cases working for an independent contractor-provider, externally to the firm, although some in-house programmes exist. A typical duration of counselling would be some months part-time, after which the employee would have learned to cope with the problem to such an extent that it no longer affected his or her job performance. There is no attempt at deep or prolonged psychotherapy, and should this prove necessary, the employee would withdraw from the EAP and seek separate full-time professional help.

In many ways, EAPs do not rest easily with strategic human resource management roles. Employee counselling has in the past been associated with the 'hated welfare role' a low status activity and as disputed 'turf' with occupational health. The validity and cost-effectiveness of employee assistance programmes are hard to demonstrate objectively: British applications seem to show consistent absenteeism reductions, but the causality is debatable. Employee assistance programmes are not a primary method of stress removal, but a tertiary intervention, inculcating coping mechanisms. Managers may view EAPs as a malingerers' charter, exploiting disciplinary procedures and the employee's duty of best endeavours.

Professional psychologists express doubts that a therapeutic technique based on humanistic principles is being used to solve the performance problems of capitalistic economic enterprise As the counselling industry matures, quality standards are under pressure, as new insurance company owner-providers cut costs, reduce services and market EAPs as utilitarian employee benefits.

Employee assistance programmes in the first decade of the 2000s potentially represent more than a diagnostic tool or safety valve. If integrated into the problem-solving and learning mechanisms of an organization, they can contribute towards a cultural change from a blame-centred environment to a more open and transformative work ethos. **JBe**

References and further reading

Berridge, J. (1999) 'Employee assistance programmes and stress counselling: at a crossroads?', in C. Feltham (ed.) *Controversies in Psychotherapy and Counselling*, London: Sage.

Berridge, J., Cooper, C. L. and Highley-Marchington, C. (1997) *Employee Assistance Programmes and Workplace Counselling*, Chichester: Wiley.

Carroll, M. and Walton, M. (eds) (1997) *Handbook of Counselling in Organizations*, London: Sage.

Cunningham, G. (1994) *Effective Employee Assistance Programs: A Guide for EAP Counselors and Managers*, Thousand Oaks, CA: Sage.

Employee attitude surveys

Attitude surveys are a highly structured and formalized means of enabling upward communication in organizations. They can serve a number of functions and although the most immediately obvious use is to give an indicator of overall employee satisfaction, they may also enable organizations to assess the effectiveness of particular changes as well as point the way towards future improvements in work processes or employee relations procedures. Organizations may choose to use surveys at a time of particular change, such as a merger, to assess the mood of employees, although it is common for large organizations to conduct such surveys annually or every two years. The advantage of repeating surveys is that changes can be tracked over time. The major advantage that surveys have over other means of assessing employee opinion is that responses can be (and normally are) given anonymously.

It is important to consider the purpose of conducting such surveys. If over time it is recognized by employees that little action is taken in response to survey findings, then they may have a damaging effect on employee morale, and be perceived as a waste of time or worse a deliberate deception on the part of management. The Advisory, Conciliation and Arbitration Service (ACAS) offers the following advice, 'an opinion survey will raise the expectation of employees. The exercise can generate considerable goodwill to the employer, but only if the results of the survey are freely communicated and acted upon. If expectations are ignored, the survey may well be counterproductive' (ACAS, undated: 14). Additionally, it is worth considering that carrying out surveys requires specialist knowledge, and surveys may be most effective where organizations use external expertise to manage this process. **KM**

References and further reading

Advisory, Conciliation and Arbitration Service (ACAS) (undated) 'Labour turnover', ACAS leaflet no. 4.

Arnold, J., Cooper, C. L. and Robertson, I. T. (1995) *Work Psychology*, London: Pitman, ch. 9.

Beaumont, P. B. (1993) *Human Resource Management: Key Concepts and Skills*, London: Sage, ch. 7.

Hyman, J. and Mason, B. (1995) *Managing Employee Involvement and Participation*, London: Sage, ch. 5.

Munro-Faure, L. (2000) 'How to conduct an employee survey', *People Management*, 6(11): 58–9.

Employee benefits

An organization's reward package can be made up of various elements, financial and non-financial. Employee benefits refer to rewards that are additional to wages or salaries but which have a value to the employee. They are sometimes referred to as 'fringe benefits' or 'perks', but can be a substantial part of the reward package, particularly for higher paid employees, for whom there may be tax and status advantages.

There are a wide range of possible benefits. Some of the more common ones are set out below:

- paid holiday (in excess of the statutory minimum of four weeks)
- pensions
- life insurance
- health insurance
- sick pay
- maternity pay and parental leave
- childcare (creches and nurseries)
- subsidized restaurant facilities
- luncheon vouchers
- paid leave for personal business, including medical and dental appointments
- company cars
- mileage allowance
- housing assistance, including subsidized mortgage
- relocation package
- loans
- discounts
- sports and social facilities
- club membership
- fees to professional bodies.

Some employers, particularly in the USA, have developed 'flexible benefits'. Instead of all employees receiving the same package a choice is given, so that people can optimize their benefits to suit their circumstances, lifestyle and tax position. In this way both employer and employee get more value for money from the expenditure on benefits.

Employee benefits can add over 20 per cent to the labour costs of UK employers. Although there has been a general trend upwards, mainly in response to labour market competition, it is likely that companies will examine their costs and benefits more rigorously in future. **MMo**

References and further reading

Armstrong, M. (1996) *Employee Reward*, London: Institute of Personnel and Development, pp. 325–39.

Armstrong, M. and Murlis, H. (1995) *Reward Management*, 3rd edn, London: Kogan Page, pp. 367–85.

Incomes Data Services (IDS) (1998) 'Flexible Benefits', *IDS StudyPlus*, 652, July.

Smith, I. (2000) 'Benefits', in G. White and J. Drucker (eds) *Reward Management: A Critical Text*, London: Routledge.

Employee development assistance programmes (EDAPs)

The Ford Motor Company at Halewood (Liverpool) plant has become the role model for other organizations regarding the provision of assistance to employees for their development. Ford's model could be regarded as the design of a programme that affected attitudes to learning and generated a more highly skilled workforce which was fundamental to the company's survival in a highly competitive economic market.

Although Ford's EDAP came out of a complex, yet dynamic background, it represents only one amongst a host of other initiatives, nevertheless it includes many potential advantages, the characteristics of which are that the EDAP scheme is:

- part of a collective bargaining between the Ford Motor Company and its trade unions
- reinforced by a system of decision making and resource allocation to the programme
- tripartite collaboration with hourly paid and staff unions and the company
- heavily devolved of decision making to local EDAP committee, each with a local employee development advisor. This gives considerable scope for local autonomy and flexibility
- administered within a corporate context which acts as a basis for the creation and maintenance of development systems for all employees
- open-ended in that it does not require standardization or the outcome to be qualification based.

One of the outstanding innovations of the Ford EDAP scheme is that the committee can commission new or tailor-made courses to be held on site alongside existing courses. All courses are flexible so as to be accessible to those employees who work in a shift pattern. The take-up of the programme *after* the first year was 20 per cent of the workforce which was four times greater that the initial take-up.

When the programme was being created a questionnaire was circulated to just over 10 000 employees of whom 6146 responded. Eighty-five per cent of these respondents stated that if they embarked on any learning, they would require 'preparatory' or introductory courses to enable them to take full advantage of the EDAP. It is worth noting that 70 per cent of the employees replied that they would like to learn a completely new topic.

However, Ford's EDAP provides for all 49 000 employees throughout the UK, 72 per cent of whom left school at the minimum school-leaving age. Any employee can draw up to £200.00 pr annum for education, training, health and lifestyle pursuits. There is an enormous range of subjects selected year on year, though fitness programmes and lifestyle have become increasingly popular. Ford's EDAP innovation was initiated because of the substantial deficience in skills and qualifications. Other organizations have followed Ford's example, although there are considerable variations in the amounts allocated to employees, the range and type of subjects offered, the control and monitoring of financial assistance and the qualification output. Many organizations have been forced into offering financial assistance because of the antipathetic culture to learning that necessitated immediate examination of their training and development strategies. In geographical locations where there are acute skills' shortages, EDAP schemes have been essential to enable employees to develop in these skills. At the same time, it enables the employees to acquire additional 'marketable' skills in some areas where job opportunities are at the minimum, for example, in volatile organizations where mergers and acquisitions are rapidly taking place. Also many organizations are providing EDAP's to encourage employees to get National Vocational Qualifications and, in some instances, the programmes are linked to training credits. Sometimes the employees are given vouchers to use at the local college or university where courses have been updated to meet specific demands in the locality. **SR**

References and further reading

Houghham, J., Thomas, J. and Sisson, K. (1991) 'Ford's EDAP scheme: a roundtable discussion', *Human Resource Management Journal* 1(3): 77–91.

Moore, R., Smith, B. and Longbottom, S. (1994) research paper, EDAPs' TU research unit, Ruskin College, Oxford.

Stevens, B. (1992) *Social Partnership: at Ford*, Involvement and Participation series, Spring/May, no. 613: 12–14.

Employee involvement

Employee involvement (EI) refers to a wide range of management owned initiatives which range in scope from: (1) providing basic *information* to employees (e.g. via a corporate newspaper), to (2) other more involved forms of *communication* (e.g. regular briefings), through the use of (3) *consultation* processes where employees have a level of input into decision-making, to (4) initiatives which offer *co-determination* (e.g. via upward problem-solving) and, ultimately, (5) even *control* (e.g. self-managing teams). These five stages represent what Marchington and Wilkinson (2000: 343) have called the 'ladder' or 'escalator' of participation. What each stage has in common with the others is that it represents a departure from a traditional Taylorist view that division of labour is the key to organizational effectiveness and efficiency. Instead of workers merely being 'machine minders' carrying out repetitive and fragmented jobs, under EI, they are actively encouraged to provide solutions, or at the very least are kept aware of changes which may affect them (Wilkinson, 1998). This difference is enough to suggest that although there have been different forms and patterns of worker participation in the past, EI represents a novel form of participation.

This change in the context of contemporary industrial relations can be couched in the rhetoric of a new knowledge economy, with firms now having to make use of intellectual capital, in the form of their workers, in order to remain competitive. Accordingly, EI schemes complement the idea that people represent the only source of sustainable competitive advantage. Hyman and Mason (1995: 60) write that, 'EI [employee involvement] is an essential component of any move towards HRM'. Setting aside for a moment this rather upbeat and encouraging message, it is important to be aware that increased participation (or the *claim* that workers have a greater degree of participation) does not by itself guarantee greater autonomy, self-management or genuine power. This may be particularly true where EI is explicitly intended to 'replace' a trade union. EI schemes are management owned and their primary concern is to realize organizational goals, unlike unions which offer a basis for negotiation, consultation and bargaining on behalf of their members. Even if we are talking of the top of the participation ladder, some writers have criticized the 'tyranny of teams' (Sinclair, 1992), suggesting these represent a stronger, more insidious form of control (Barker, 1993) than the traditional methods under a system of division of labour.

Another consideration to keep in mind is that much of what determines the success or failure of a scheme depends on one's perspective and also on the particular context. To this extent it is perhaps meaningless to talk of EI, or a form of EI, being a good or bad thing. We would first have to ask, for whom? A comprehensive answer to this would go beyond a simplistic worker–manager dichotomy, but consider different levels of the organization and different departments and functions as well as other stakeholders, such as shareholders. Second, we would need to assess an EI initiative in terms of an organization's industrial and historical contexts. Ultimately, a sophisticated assessment of the nature of EI as a form of participation is likely to rely on understanding the nature of the employment relationship, which is 'built upon both conflict and co-operation' (Marchington and Wilkinson, 2000: 359). **KM and AW**

References and further reading

Barker, J. (1993) 'Tightening the iron cage: concertive control in self-managing teams', *Administrative Science Quarterly* 38: 408–37.

Hyman, J. and Mason, B. (1995) *Managing Employee Involvement and Participation*, London: Sage.

Marchington, M., Goodman, J., Wilkinson, A. and Ackers, P. (1992) *New Developments in Employee Involvement*, Employment Department Report, series no. 2.

Marchington, M. and Wilkinson A. (2000) 'Direct participation' in S. Bach and K. Sisson (eds), *Personnel Management*, Oxford: Blackwell.

Sinclair, A. (1992) 'The tyranny of a team ideology', *Organization Studies* 13(4): 611–26.

Wilkinson, A. J. (1998) 'Empowerment: theory and practice', *Personnel Review* 27(1): 40–56.

Employee relations

'Employee relations' is the contemporary term for the field of study which analyses how the employment relationship between employers and employees is organized and practised. Traditionally, study of the employment relationship focused on regulation of the wage–work bargain between employers and organized labour (trade unions) in the labour market. Up to the late 1980s, this field was generically known as *industrial relations*. The focus of interest in industrial relations during the 1960s and 1970s was on the institutions of job regulation. In Britain, the study of industrial relations concentrated on the analysis of trade unions, collective bargaining and strikes, and the field relied heavily on data drawn from male manual employment in private manufacturing industry. It was a period when unions had relatively high levels of membership density, strong bargaining power and employers were frequently on the defensive. This was because of high employment, generated by Keynesian demand management economic policies, which resulted in shortages of skilled labour and a union movement that was often militant and well organized at plant and factory levels.

In the last decade or so, the typography of employment and the framework of public policy in Britain have both changed radically. There have been substantial job losses in manufacturing, falling union membership and a move towards service sector employment, while public policy has shifted towards supply-side economic initiatives and strong legal constraints on union organization and industrial action. Unemployment has risen and there has been a resurgence of managerial authority in organizations and creation of innovative human resources management strategies aimed at integrating employees in the enterprises where they work.

The term *employee relations* takes account of these contextual, corporate and organizational changes. It reflects more diverse employment patterns including female, high-tech and knowledge workers, reduced levels of union membership and more sophisticated personnel management strategies, often focused on individuals in non-union firms. Employee relations sometimes implies a managerial frame of reference, where the employment relationship is analysed from a predominantly managerial perspective, so as to provide practical guidance on how the wage–work bargain is to be most effectively managed.

For this reason, some commentators prefer the term *employment relations*. While taking note of the changes outlined above, those using it identify the field as one that examines the range and diversity of employment relationships now existing in contemporary Britain, including the public sector. But they have no prescriptive preferences as to what the best pattern of employment regulation is. **DF**

References and further reading

Farnham, D. (2000) *Employee Relations in Context*, London: Chartered Institute of Personnel and Development.

Flanders, A. (1970) *Management and Unions*, London: Faber and Faber.

Gennard, J. and Judge, G. (1999) *Employee Relations*, London: Chartered Institute of Personnel and Development.

Hollinshead, G., Nicholls, P. and Tailby, S. (1999) *Employee Relations*, London: Prentice Hall.

Salamon, M. (2000) *Industrial Relations*, London: Prentice Hall.

Employee resourcing

In the UK the terms 'employee' and 'employment resourcing' are most commonly used to delineate a specific area of human resource management work. The terms have long been used as the title for one of the examination papers set by the Chartered Institute of Personnel and Development (CIPD) which has sustained their use in practitioner and academic circles.

At base, resourcing is about managing the flow of people into, through and out of organizations. Resourcing specialists are thus principally concerned with ensuring that their organizations are properly staffed with suitable people at the times and in the places that they are required. The main areas of activity are as follows:

- human resource planning
- work/job design
- recruitment
- selection
- induction/orientation
- performance management
- absence management
- limiting voluntary turnover
- managing dismissals and retirements.

There is a degree of overlap with other specialist HR fields such as reward management and training and development which share, at least in part, many of the same objectives. Some have argued that career management is better characterized as a resourcing activity than a development activity because it is principally concerned with the flow of individuals from job to job within an organization (e.g. Pinnington and Edwards, 2000; Iles, 2001).

Central to employee resourcing is the management of an organization's relationship with its labour markets. More effort and resources need to be devoted when labour markets are tight than when staff of the required calibre are in plentiful supply. Historically resourcing activities have thus tended to move up and down organizational agendas depending on prevailing economic conditions. In recent years most attention has been focused on flexible resourcing options, organizations looking to move away from their traditional reliance on workers who are employed on full-time permanent contracts of employment. Different forms of contractual relationship have become more common, including part-time and casual working, temporary employment, subcontracting, annual hours arrangements, term time working and irregular shift patterns. The main aim is to resource the organization more efficiently so that staff are only present and being paid when they are most needed. Such arrangements also have the advantage of allowing employers to tap into sources of labour supply which might not otherwise be available to them. **ST**

References and further reading

Corbridge, M. and Pilbeam, S. (1998) *Employment Resourcing*, London: Financial Times Pitman Publishing.

Iles, P. (2001) 'Employee resourcing', in J. Storey (ed.) *Human Resource Management: A Critical Text*, London: Thomson Learning.

Marchington, M. and Wilkinson, A. (2000) *Core Personnel and Development*, part 3, London: CIPD.

Pinnington, A. and Edwards, T. (2000) *Introduction to Human Resource Management*, Oxford: Oxford University Press, ch. 5.

Taylor, S. (1998) *Employee Resourcing*, London: CIPD.

Employee share schemes

Governments since the 1980s have encouraged employee share ownership through various systems of tax relief, some more complex than others. Around 2 million employees take part in 1800 Inland Revenue approved schemes. Currently, shares can be provided through save as you earn (SAYE) share option schemes, employee share option plan (ESOP) or a corporate personal equity plan (PEP). All these schemes can be complex and liable to sudden change, so up-to-date information is essential. The strategic aim is to build the employee's financial participation in the organization, thereby increasing involvement and helping to persuade the employee not to move elsewhere.

Save as you earn share option schemes allow employees to be given options to buy shares in their company on a specified future date at the share price ruling at the start of the contract (often at a discounted price). Employees enter a savings scheme for three, five or seven years, using the proceeds to purchase the shares. For example, an employee who contracts to save for five years at £50 a month may have around £3500 with which to purchase shares. The option price could be, say, 350p which means 1000 shares can be purchased. However, in the five years the shares could have risen to 600p so the employee, on exercising the option, has shares worth £6000, a profit of £2500.

The standard *ESOP* involves the organization setting up an employee benefit trust linked to a share participation scheme. The trust then either borrows money or receives contributions from the company with which to purchase shares from the company to distribute to employees, including directors. The main functions of ESOPs are to promote a perceived identity of interest between recipient employees and the organization, rather than to secure immediate changes in employee behaviour.

A *single company PEP* provides tax advantages for employees in approved profit-sharing or SAYE schemes with a reduced or eliminated capital gains tax.

Alternative share schemes can be introduced for directors, including restricted share schemes and bonuses paid in shares, all of which have specific, constantly changing tax applications.

In November 1999, the Chancellor of the Exchequer announced proposals for a new type of all-employee scheme to be introduced in 2000–2001. This involved tax relief arrangements on up to £3000 of free shares awarded on the basis of performance and other proposals on what were called 'partnership' and 'matching' shares, curently known as 'BOGOF' (buy one, get one free). All such shares would be free of income tax, National Insurance Contributions and capital gains tax if held for five years. **JSk**

References and further reading

Armstrong, M. (1999) *Employee Reward*, London: CIPD.

Income Data Services (IDS) (1999) *All Employee Share Scheme*, Study 680, December.

Pendleton, A., Wilson, N. and Wright, M. (1998) 'The perception and effects of share ownership: empirical evidence from employee buy-outs', *British Journal of Industrial Relations* 36(1): 99–124.

White, G. and Drucker, J. (2000) *Reward Management*, London: Routledge.

Employee welfare

Employee welfare can be defined as:

> any activity (material or intangible) undertaken and funded by an employer, intended for the benefit of employees collectively or individually, in order to off-set a disadvatage, remedy a deficiency, bestow a benefit on the employee or her/his family and thereby influence their potential organisational contribution.

Three main strands may be identified within welfare:

1. *Legalistic-reactive*: stemming from social as well as health and safety legislation, requiring employers to ensure employees' physical safety and health (occupational health; safety officers etc.).
2. *Corporate conscience*: often based on the moral or religious convictions of owners, who sought to replicate these in their enterprises (as at Bourneville, Port Sunlight or Saltaire).
3. *Corporate paternalism*: an early version of corporate culture, seeking to create a corporate identity around a utilitarian consensus of the enterprise (as at Marks and Spencer, John Lewis Partnership, or more tough-mindedly at Ford or Procter and Gamble).

Personnel management and employee welfare have been closely linked at many periods, and the Industrial Welfare Society (1913) was one of the forerunners of the Institute of Personnel and Development (IPD). The origins of welfare were in the nineteenth century (owners' philanthropy) and it was statutorily encouraged in the two World Wars. It withered after 1945 with the 'welfare' state, yet in more demanding business climates and shrinking public health and social security provisions from the 1980s onward, employees again expressed welfare needs, – even if relabelled 'employee benefits' rather than welfare.

These new forms of material help (sometimes co-funded) included personalized life insurance, medical plans, crèches, vacation and after-school programmes for children, eldercare, subscriptions to recreational and cultural facilities, on-site health centres, credit unions or investment clubs – the range is almost endless. Mental health and counselling programmes have acquired a new prominence, especially in relation to stress. Occupational health departments are recovering their former status, with sophisticated health screening, monitoring and enhancement programmes.

Nonetheless, criticisms persist of such innovations as inappropriate and patronizing in ethnically and religiously diverse labour markets, as representing a new form of social control or as unnecessary for educated and informed employees who have multimedia access to information and assistance. Academics see welfare as intellectually incoherent, and lacking recognized professional standards. Stockholders may argue that welfare is not needed, agreeing with Friedman that welfare is tantamount to theft: suitable salary levels permit people to choose for themselves, and employers' provisions may be inefficient and even a restriction on the freedom of the individual. Stockholders may also feel that companies should concentrate on their core businesses and not be distracted into secondary activities benefiting the marginal rather than the key contributors.

So a strategic human resource (HR) function may wish to distance itself from its former hated welfare image (Torrington and Hall, 1997). Meanwhile, it is probably fair to say that HR remains uncertain if not sceptical about its continuing welfare role. **JBe**

References and further reading

Barry, N. (1999) *Welfare*, 2nd edn, Buckingham: Open University Press.
Eggert, M. (1990) 'Welfare at work', in A. Cowling and C. Mailer (eds) *Managing Human Resources*, London: Edward Arnold.
Goss, D. (1994) *Principles of Human Resource Management*, London: Routledge, ch. 7.
Martin, A. (1967) *Welfare in Britain*, London: Batsford.
Torrington, D. and Hall, L. (1997) *Personnel Management*, Hemel Hempstead: Prentice Hall.

Employers' associations

Salamon (1998: 28) defines employers' associations as 'any organisation whose membership is composed of employers and whose purposes include the regulation of relations between employers and their employees or trade unions'. They are voluntary federations of business organizations operating in similar fields. The size of these organizations varies greatly. Some are large with many members and considerable incomes, e.g. the Engineering Employers Federation or the National Farmers Union, whilst others are of a far more modest proportion. The distinction between employers' associations and trade associations is that employers' associations are involved in the management of the employee relations of their members.

According to the Certification Officer's Report (1999–2000) there are 100 employers associations listed in their records and a further 100 that have chosen to remain unlisted. Further to this the Certification Officer admits that there may be others of which his office is unaware. The reason for this lack of certainty lies in the fact that there is no compulsion on associations to be listed and no benefit to them if they do. A further reason is that employers' associations chose to maintain a very low media profile obscuring the importance of employer behaviour in shaping industrial relations. The variation in trade union government, density, strike propensities, structure, workplace organization and industrial democracy, is caused by the differences in the collective bargaining structure. The reasons for this variation in collective bargaining structures, it is argued, is the way in which employers organize. The difficulty in understanding employers associations is compounded by the lack of academic study in this important area This lack of study appears to result from the associations' own wishes to remain outside of the public domain and researchers ongoing disinterest.

The earliest employers' associations pre-date trade unions and were formed for the purpose of the regulation of trade and prices. Many more were founded at the end of the nineteenth century as a response to increased union organization. Around the turn of the nineteenth to the twentieth century employers' associations shaped the collective bargaining structures in the UK so that they designed a system of industrial relations that suited themselves. These arrangements have persisted in tact until very recent times.

The **Donovan Report** (1968) was very critical of employers associations claiming that they were at best a sham, at worst a positive hindrance to orderly collective bargaining. This criticism stemmed from the lack of maintenance of the collective bargaining structures that the employers associations had presided over, resulting in the rise of informal and uncontrolled collective bargaining at the factory level. Post-1968 many have adopted new roles.

The functions of employers' associations are fivefold:

- pay bargaining
- bargaining over conditions of employment
- disputes procedures
- advisory services
- pressure group activities.

It is argued that their role in collective bargaining has diminished and that advisory services have increased in importance. However, there is no single pattern that explains how each association seeks to service its members. The actuality of each employers' association seems to be determined by several factors including the wishes of the membership and the business structure of the trade in which they are involved.

Most employers' associations tend to be run by committees; some of them elect their committee members, some co-opt and some do both. Co-option is used by some employers' associations to give 'balance', to prevent domination by large companies. Decision-making is centralized and often occurs through informal channels where very large firms can have disproportionate influence. Decisions are usually attempted via a consensus and policy tends to be that affordable by the members who are least able to pay (or else they would simply leave). When balloting occurs votes are usually apportioned by numbers of employees, payroll size or dues paid to the association and consequently can give much more sway to large companies. The government in employers' associations is not characterised by the term 'participatory democracy'. However, due to their 'open door' nature there is little evidence that the government structure of employers' associations leads to association officials acting against their members' wishes.

The situation of employers' associations is not without problems. Many organizations (especially the very large and the very small) prefer not to join. Small organizations often only join when they get into difficulties, e.g. a tribunal case. Many small employers follow agreements but do not join. With the increase in the sophistication of the personnel function in many organizations the advice services of employers' associations become redundant. There is the problem associated with employer solidarity. To be effective employers' association solidarity is needed. But is this likely given the wide range of conflicting interests and the fact that many members will be in direct competition? There are continuing examples of solidarity disintegrating in the event of an industrial dispute, e.g. the bakers, the road hauliers and the engineering companies.

Although heavily criticized, employers' associations remain largely unstudied. Their future is not likely to be without difficulty especially with the increasing number of very large companies choosing to be unfederated. However, for a considerable number of businesses, employers' associations provide valued services and a focal point for managers in those businesses. There appears to be a need for people in organizations who share similar environments and concerns to seek affiliation so that problems can be considered and novel solutions generated. Perhaps this explains why Brown (1981) asserts that there is no mood among members to leave.
PH

References and further reading
Brown, W. (1981) *The Changing Contours of British Industrial Relations*, Oxford: Blackwell.
Certification Office for Trade Unions and Employers' Associations, *Annual Report of the Certification Officer*, London: Crown copyright.
Clegg, H. (1979) *The Changing System of Industrial Relations in Great Britain*, Oxford: Blackwell.
Salamon, M. (1998) *Industrial Relations: Theory and Practice*, 3rd edn, London: Prentice Hall.

Employment Appeal Tribunal

The Employment Appeal Tribunal (EAT) was set up in 1975 and sits in St James' Square in London. Like the employment tribunals, it has a tripartite structure with lay member involvement, but is chaired by a High Court judge.

The EAT's principal business is to hear appeals from employment tribunals, but only on specified grounds. The most common ground is that the tribunal misdirected itself in law or misapplied the law, for example, by defining a constructive dismissal on the basis of whether the employer acted unreasonably instead of whether or not the employer fundamentally breached the contract of employment.

Appeals also lie to the EAT if the decision of the tribunal is unsupported by the evidence, but not, in general, on a question of fact. Thus, a tribunal's conclusion that an employee was taking part in a strike or that an 'undertaking' had been transferred within the meaning of the Transfer of Undertakings (Protection of Employment) Regulations 1981 would normally be unassailable.

There is, however, a third ground of appeal, which is that the tribunal's decision was perverse, in the sense that no tribunal, properly directed, could have reached such a conclusion. The Court of Appeal, in a 1986 case, took the view that a decision would be perverse only if 'one can say in effect, "My goodness, that was certainly wrong"' as opposed merely to disagreeing with it. Whilst this ground of appeal has been criticised, it continues to provide a basis for reversing tribunal decisions, and it has been pointed out that without such a ground, there would be a much weaker argument for the presence of lay members.

Employment tribunals are bound to follow rulings of the EAT: further appeal on points of law is to the Court of Appeal and thence to the House of Lords. **JE**

References and further reading
Browne-Wilkinson, J. (1982) 'The role of the Employment Appeal Tribunal in the 1980s', *Industrial Law Journal* 11: 69.
Neale v. *Hereford & Worcester County Council* [1986] IRLR 168.
Vicary v. *British Telecom plc* [1999] IRLR 680.
Wood, J. (1990) 'The Employment Appeal Tribunal as it enters the 1990s', *Industrial Law Journal* 19: 133.

Employment relationship

In contemporary societies, the employment relationship has been conceptualized in several different ways. Each one is associated with a particular approach to employment regulation. One approach to capitalist economies, well established in neo-liberal economics, sees employment as a market transaction, like any other. The employer, as a property owner, buys or 'hires' employees in the labour market. Two individuals agree a price and what work will be done for this. In this view, employer rights are paramount. The main problem with this conceptualization is that it does not acknowledge the long-term and open-ended character of the employment relationship. Indeed, it conflates this with a commercial contract, such as hiring a builder to repair your roof. There are several consequences. First, because the employer still has to determine what actual work the employee will do on a day-to-day basis, this is a recipe for authoritarian *unitarist* relations at work, which may spread into the rest of society, including the home. Second, the employer does not acknowledge the dependence of the employee or his social responsibility towards him. In a real individualized labour market, the bargain is usually highly asymmetrical, with the employer much more powerful than the average employee. Writ large at a societal level, this conception spells low wages, long hours and job insecurity for the poorer, less skilled sections of society.

Employment relations has long recognized that employers hire human potential, rather than just 'buying labour'; and that this potential has to be realized by effective human resource management. Following the French sociologist, Durkheim, this means that the employment relationship has both economic and social aspects. As such, it contains an ethical or moral element beyond just the honouring of the contract. The employer has a duty of care and there are rights and responsibilities on both sides, justifying the use of terms like trust, loyalty and commitment. In short, this is a relatively long-term and open-ended human relationship. Even within a neo-liberal state regime, large or small employers may voluntarily develop their own socialized version of the employment relationship. One instance would be co-operative systems, like Mondragon in Spain or in Italy. Another would be small or medium-sized family firms, as in Germany. Welfare capitalism or *paternalism* occurs where the employer acknowledges his or her social responsibilities and the social nature of the employment relationship. On the economic side, this may be linked to a HRM argument (also used at a societal level by social market regimes) that employee skills are the major source of competitive advantage. Hence, long-term investment through good wages and conditions, training, employee participation and welfare provision will create a high-quality and productive labour force. There are several problems with the voluntary model, whatever the blend of enlightened self-interest and charitable goodwill. First, it has always been a minority pursuit among employers, often as a union-avoidance strategy. Second, it is authoritarian and discretionary, treating the employee as a child without rights. Third, it appears to be in decline under the assault of short-term, free-market capitalism. **PA**

References and further reading

Ackers, P. (2001) 'Employment ethics', in T. Redman and A. Wilkinson (eds) *Contemporary Human Resource Management*, London: FT Prentice Hall.
Anthony, P. D. (1986) *The Foundations of Management*, London: Tavistock.
Edwards, P. (1995) 'Introduction: the employment relationship', in P. Edwards (ed.) *Industrial Relations*, Oxford: Blackwell.
Herriot, P. (2001) *The Employment Relationship: A Psychological Perspective*, London: Routledge.
Hutton, W. (1995) *The State We're In*, London: Cape.
Nolan, P. (1983) 'The labour market', in G. Bain (ed.) *Industrial Relations in Britain*, Oxford: Blackwell.
Sennett, R. (1998) *The Corrosion of Character: The Personal Consequences of Work in the New Capitalism*, London: Norton.

Employment tribunals

Employment tribunals have come a long way since 1964 when they were first set up to hear appeals from industrial training levies under the Industrial Training Act. During the 1970s and 1980s the bulk of their work consisted of unfair dismissal claims but by 1998/99 these accounted for only 37 034 of the 91 913 tribunal applications (Employment Tribunal Service, Annual Report). Almost 80 different kinds of claims can now be brought before employment tribunals, including sex, race and disability discrimination, equal pay, redundancy payments, working time and breach of contract.

Employment tribunal claims are normally heard by a legally qualified chairman (a barrister or solicitor of at least seven years' standing) and two lay members, one from either side of industry. Their role is to input their industrial relations experience into the decision-making, although since 1993 certain classes of case may be heard by a chairperson sitting alone.

In comparison with the civil courts, employment tribunals continue to be speedy and cheap, in line with their original objectives. Legal representation is not required, there are no court fees to be paid and costs are awarded against the unsuccessful party only on rare occasions. Outside London, the target figure of 85 per cent of cases reaching a first hearing within 26 weeks is not only achieved, but frequently exceeded. Employment tribunals are also comparatively informal, although evidence is given on oath and is subject to cross-examination by the opposing side. Whilst tribunals must remain impartial and bias-free, they are encouraged to assist unrepresented parties and explicitly entitled to adopt an inquisitorial stance in cases where the parties do not volunteer the relevant evidence. Decisions, which can be by a majority, are often given orally on the day, but even in such cases, a written decision will follow. Appeals lie to the Employment Appeal Tribunal on points of law (see **Employment Appeal Tribunal**).

Currently, a new arbitral option for unfair dismissal cases is being developed under the auspices of the **Advisory, Conciliation and Arbitration Service** (ACAS) (see separate entry). **JE**

References and further reading

Corby, S. (1999) 'Resolving employment disputes: lessons from Great Britain?', *New Zealand Journal of Industrial Relations* 23(3): 153.

MacMillan, J. K. (1999) 'Employment tribunals: philosophies and practicalities', *Industrial Law Journal* 28(1): 33.

McKee, J. (1986) 'A personal view of the work of industrial tribunals', *Modern Law Review*, 49: 314.

Resolving Employment Rights Disputes (1994) Cm. 2707.

Empowerment

This term became fashionable in the 1980s and continues to be used today. It has been associated with concepts such as human resource management, **total quality management**, business process re-engineering and the **learning organization** (see separate entries). Although the term is new it has many similarities with ideas of **employee involvement** (see separate entry) and its roots can be seen as extending back to the 1920s and the **human relations approach** (see separate entry).

In essence empowerment is concerned with providing opportunities and structures as well as a new culture, so employees can contribute to the organization. The onus is on employers to 'empower' employees. It is individualist rather than collectivist in orientation, i.e. based on individual workers or work groups but not on larger groups such as trade unions. It encourages direct involvement in work practices rather than indirect and thus is distinct from financial and representative participation.

It is assumed that workers have the opportunity to contribute to organizational success and as they are closer to the work situation they may be able to suggest improvements which management would be unable to by virtue of their position in the hierarchy. Empowerment would also increase job satisfaction and reduce turnover as workers feel more committed to organizational goals. In addition, as workers are empowaered this reduces the need for complex and indeed dysfunctional systems of control hence increasing efficiency.

It clearly fits with the 'voluntarist' tradition which left managers and workers (in practice reflecting power structures usually the former) to decide on a suitable approach for the organization. Empowerment can also be seen as different to the 1970s quality of working life (QWL) movement which emphasized labour issues such as job satisfaction, absenteeism and labour turnover. In contrast empowerment emphasizes more direct business considerations, such as quality, flexibility and productivity. It is management who empowers employees and the initiatives have tended to cover direct workforce involvement over a relatively small number of issues connected with the production process or service delivery, with the rationale that highly committed and empowered staff were more likely to engage in a 'beyond contract' effort, i.e. beyond the normal call of duty. It has not, however, extended to significant power-sharing or participation in higher-level strategic decisions. There has tended to be little union negotiation concerning the principle of the initiative with design and planning excluding union involvement. In practice, however, issues arising out of the implementation of empowerment often become industrial relations matters.

Empowerment is a flexible or even elastic term. Different forms of empowerment have been identified:

- information sharing, e.g. more and better communication
- upward problem solving, e.g. suggestion schemes
- task autonomy, e.g. teams having autonomy
- attitudinal shaping, e.g. change in values/attitudes if not structure
- self-management, e.g. control over recruitment, absence, etc. **AW**

References and further reading

Bowen, D. and Lawler, E. E. (1992) 'The empowerment of service workers: why how and when?' *Sloan Management Review* 33(3), Spring: 31–9.

Conger, J. and Kanungo, R. (1988) 'The empowerment process: integrating theory and practice', *Academy of Management Review* 13(3): 471–82.

Cunningham, I., Hyman, J. and Baldry, C. (1996) 'Empowerment: the power to do what?', *Industrial Relations Journal* 27(2): 143–54.

Foy, N. (1994) *Empowering People at Work*, London: Gower.

Lashley, C. (1997) *Empowering Service Excellence: Beyond the Quick Fix*, London: Cassell.

Semler, R. (1989) 'Managing without managers', *Harvard Business Review*, September–October: 76–84.

Simons, R. (1995) 'Control in an age of empowerment', *Harvard Business Review*, March–April: 80–8.

Wilkinson, A. (1998a) 'Empowerment', in M. Poole and M. Warner (eds) *International Encyclopaedia of Business and Management Handbook of Human Resource Management*, London: Thomson Learning.

Wilkinson, A. (1998b) 'Empowerment: theory and practice', *Personnel Review* 27(1): 40–56.

Equal opportunities

Equal opportunities, part of a wider societal movement towards social inclusion and human rights, has been on the employment agenda in the UK since the 1970s, both for governments through legal, social and fiscal policy and for organizations through the introduction of equal opportunities policies and practices. It is based on the recognition that certain groups experience disadvantage and inequality in the workplace and wider labour market, and seeks to eliminate it. The primary vehicle for achieving equality is anti-discrimination legislation, which currently covers sex, race, disability and criminal conviction, and is likely to encompass age in the future. The recent human rights legislation may also have implications. The arguments for equal opportunities are those of social justice, penalty avoidance and human capital optimization (the business case). Whilst these are best treated as mutually supportive rather than alternatives, it is likely that in practice the business case argument will be the most persuasive.

At the organizational level, equal opportunities is about the elimination of unlawful discrimination and the introduction of measures to remove the effects of earlier disadvantage. A good-practice model suggests a systematic process of policy formulation, audit of the existing situation, action planning and implementation, monitoring and policy review. Some equal opportunities policies have been criticized for their ineffectiveness, so it is important that they not only provide a framework for and lead to action but also have top level commitment and accountability. An organizational audit will highlight areas of concern and priority from which to develop an implementation programme and this could encompass any or all aspects of personnel practice. The equal opportunities specialist or personnel practitioner has a key role to play in the promotion and implementation of equal opportunities, although the balance of power within organizations may limit this influence. Guidance on both legal compliance and the development of good employment practice is available from a number of sources, notably the Equal Opportunities Commission, Commission for Racial Equality and the Disability Rights Commission, the Chartered Institute of Personnel and Development and employers interest groups such as the Employers' Forum on Age.

The extent to which equality of opportunity exists in the workplace is debated at length. Progress in terms of the introduction of equal opportunities policies and practices has been made and case studies from the public and private sectors are extensively documented. However, the continued existence of pay discrimination and occupational segregation suggests that substantial changes in the representation and distribution of certain disadvantaged groups is still a long way from being achieved. **SS**

References and further reading

Dickens, L. (1999) 'Beyond the business case: a three pronged approach to equality action', *Human Resource Management Journal* 9(1): 5–19.

Equal Opportunities Review (1999) 'Fair's fair: achieving equal opportunities at Halifax plc', *Equal Opportunities Review* 94, November–December: 21–30.

Equal Opportunities Review (2001) 'The impact of the Human Rights Act on equality and discrimination law', *Equal Opportunities Review*, 95, January–February: 21–30.

Lawrence, E. (2000) 'Equal opportunities officers and managing equality changes', *Personnel Review* 29(3): 381–402.

Welch, J. (2000) 'Mental block', *People Management*, 20 January: 30–5.

Equal Opportunities Commission

The Equal Opportunities Commission (EOC) was established under the Sex Discrimination Act (SDA) 1975 to tackle sex discrimination and promote equality between men and women. It is funded by the government but is nominally independent of it. The commissioners are public appointees chosen by the government or nominated by the Confederation of British Industry and the Trades Union Congress.

The statutory duties of the EOC are to work towards the elimination of discrimination, to promote equality of opportunity and to keep the working of the legislation under review through proposing reform. It has the power to advise or assist people with individual complaints of discrimination, harassment or abuse, to conduct formal investigations of organizations and to take enforcement action against discriminatory advertising and where there is pressure and instruction to discriminate. The number of individuals that are able to receive legal representation from the EOC is constrained by resources to around 100 each year but many thousands more potential claimants do receive advice and guidance. An important (statutory) criterion for legal support is where the case raises a point of principle which will impact on discrimination legislation and the EOC has taken full advantage of European Union law to establish and expand specific principles. Its investigative powers can be used in a particular organization or area of employment but it cannot instigate proceedings directly against an employer suspected of unlawful discrimination. Where the formal investigation reveals discrimination, the EOC can issue a Non-Discrimination Notice (NDN), ordering the cessation of a particular act and the revision of policies and practices. The NDN is therefore potentially an effective way of dealing with institutional discrimination at a structural level. In reality, the EOC has found its investigative powers increasingly curtailed and the preferred approach now with employers is a voluntary one. Guidance and advice is provided not just through the EOC's statutory *Code of Practice* but also through numerous studies and reports on all aspects of the legislation and good practice from the avoidance of sex-typing jobs to maintaining work–life balance for men and women.

Gender inequality is still in evidence in the UK, and the EOC is committed to using its statutory authority to advise the government on legislative reform as well as seeking an extension of its investigative powers. It has also been suggested that in the light of the incorporation of the European Convention of Human Rights, the EOC should merge with the Commission for Racial Equality and the newly established Disability Rights Commission to form a single Human Rights Commission. **SS**

References and further reading

Equal Opportunities Commission (1985) *Code of Practice: For the Elimination of Discrimination on the Grounds of Sex and Marriage and the Promotion of Equality of Opportunity in Employment*, London: HMSO.

Equal Opportunities Commission (1998) *Equality in the 21st Century: A New Approach*, Manchester: EOC.

Townshend-Smith, R. J. (1998) *Discrimination Law: Text, Cases and Materials*, London: Cavendish.

Also visit the EOC's web site at http://www.eoc.org.uk

Equal opportunities (EO) monitoring

Equal opportunities monitoring is a procedure that enables organizations to keep a check on the outcomes of job applications from minority groups, such as women, ethnics, blacks and disabled. Clearly, for this procedure to be worthwhile, the organization must recruit in sufficiently large numbers and sufficiently regularly. It is generally, therefore, used in larger organizations, especially those that are scrutinized by the government for their record on equal opportunities. The police and the fire brigade are examples of this type of organization.

Equal opportunities monitoring involves collecting relevant biographical information from prospective job applicants. Typically, information is collected in the following categories:

- ethnic origin (e.g. white, Afro-Caribbean, Indian, etc.)
- gender
- age
- nationality and disability (e.g. blind, deaf, wheelchair user).

This information is generally collected by the human resource management (HRM) or personnel department and the information is typically kept separate from the candidate's job application to attempt to reduce the effects of bias. At regular periods, usually annually, the HRM department will produce a statistical summary of the progress of minority applicants in comparison with majority applicants (usually white, able-bodied men). This enables the organization to judge whether being a member of a minority group affects the chances of being selected for a job in the company. Equal opportunities monitoring can also be carried out on internal selection, in order to monitor the progress of those minorities who are selected for posts. For example, Bland *et al.* (1999), using statistics from the EO monitoring procedures in UK police forces, report that ethnic minority officers were difficult to retain (being more likely than white officers to resign or be dismissed), and had more difficulty achieving promotion to Inspector and in gaining access to certain specialist departments such as traffic and the Criminal Investigation Department (CID).

To be truly effective, EO monitoring needs to be supported by positive actions, whereby organizations attempt to improve the position of minority groups by acting on the information that EO monitoring provides. Such action might include funding research to identify the reasons for, say, the poor retention of ethnic minorities, or targeting recruitment efforts at minority groups by, for example, advertising in media most likely to be read or seen by minority groups. **PD**

References and further reading

Davidson, M. J. (1989) 'Restructuring women's employment in British Petroleum', in R. Pearson and D. Ellias (eds) *Women's Employment and Multinationals in Europe*, London: Macmillan.

Department of Employment (1988) *Labour Force Survey*, London: HMSO.

Ellis, S. and Dick, P. (2000) *Introduction to Organizational Behaviour*, London: McGraw-Hill.

Ethics

Business ethics is concerned with reflection on the nature and place of morality in business, the identification of the moral dimension, and the application of ethical principles and values in decision-making and practice. The ethical dimension is particularly pertinent to human resource management (HRM) because of the extent to which individuals and their lives are effected by the way they are managed in the employment context.

At the first level, ethical sensitivity is needed to identify the ethical component of decision-making – does the issue have an ethical dimension? At the second level, ethical reasoning, one needs to identify appropriate frameworks to aid ethical decision-making. There are four key axes that tend to distinguish between these frameworks. Let us take two examples, the electronic surveillance of staff and the use of child labour, to explain these differences.

The first axis distinguishes between essentialist and consequentialist reasoning. Consequentialist reasoning, one branch of which is utilitarianism, focuses on the consequences, and the ethical outcomes. If overall there is a net gain in utility, then the activity may be accepted. So, if surveillance led to benefits to the organization in the identification of wrongdoers, which outweighed the infringement of privacy, or if allowing some level of child labour alongside some educational support meant the children would not be forced into prostitution and poverty, then this activity may be accepted. On the other hand, essentialists would focus on whether the act was right in itself, and may argue that due to the infringement of basic rights such as privacy, and human rights which preclude child labour, then these activities would be viewed as unethical.

The second axis distinguishes moral relativism from absolutism. An absolutist may argue that child labour is unethical in all circumstances, whereas a relativist may take into account cultural norms, assuming that moral and ethical standards vary from country to country.

The third axis distinguishes between ethical reasoning which focuses on the content of decision-making – do the decisions or practices accord with fundamental rights for example – and those which focus on the way decisions are made and process issues. Stakeholder approaches to ethics are concerned with the involvement of employees over decisions which affect them – so, for example, what do the employees think about the electronic surveillance, was it brought in with their consultation, what do they think about child labour, how far are they and the children themselves involved in decisions about how work is done, how much freedom do they have in the decision-making?

The fourth axis distinguishes between ethics in the actor and ethics in the action. Virtue ethics is an example of the former, which sees virtue as something that one develops as a habit over a lifetime, whereas Kantian approaches set up rules by which an action can be judged, rules such as 'treat all people as ends in themselves not just as means to an end'. **DW**

References and further reading

Mabey, C., Salaman, G. and Storey, J. (eds) (1998) *Strategic Human Resource management*: *A Reader*, London: Sage, chs 1 and 2.

Legge, K. (1998) 'Is HRM ethical? Can HRM be ethical?', in M. Parker (ed.) *Ethics and Organizations*, London: Sage.

Vallance, E. (1995) *Business Ethics at Work*, Cambridge: Cambridge University Press.

Winstanley, D. and Woodall, J. (eds) (2000) *Ethical Issues in Contemporary Human Resource Management*, Basingstoke: Macmillan.

Winstanley, D., Woodall, J. and Heery, E. (1996) 'Business ethics and human resource management', *Personnel Review* 25(4), October: 187–94.

European Works Councils

The European Works Council Directive was approved by the Council of Ministers in September 1994 under the Maastricht Agreement from which the previous Conservative government had opted out in the UK but to which the incoming Labour government immediately opted in. The Directive requires companies with more than 1000 employees, and at least 150 employees in each of two or more member states, to set up a European Works Council (EWC) or some other European-level information and consultation procedure. On 15 December 1997, the Council adopted a 'mini-Directive' extending the Directive's provisions to the UK. The final draft regulations implementing the Directive in the UK, entitled *The Transnational Information and Consultation of Employees Regulations*, were laid before Parliament in mid-December 1999 and came into force on 15 January 2000. The cut-off date for completing voluntary agreements, known as Article 13 agreements, and so gaining exemption from the Directive's obligations was 15 December 1999. Article 13 agreements have been subject to some employers attempting to marginalize the role of trade union representative, for example, by putting forward management appointees as representatives.

The Directive seeks to ensure that employees in large and medium-sized multinational employers are informed and consulted about the organizations in which they work. The Directive has been seen as one the most far-reaching and important developments in European industrial relations on the one hand, and as far too weak to make any substantial effect on the other. On the positive side EWCs have been seen as an opportunity for management to communicate corporate strategy, to permit discussion of change, to encourage international contact, to facilitate employee identification with the company, build a 'European' culture and to enhance management–union partnerships. Trade unions and employee representatives, in turn, gain access to useful company information to facilitate collective bargaining.

Trade union criticisms have centred on the capacity of EWCs to effectively influence managerial prerogative in multinational companies. Recent research reports some employers paying mere lip service to their EWCs – for example, announcing major plant closures within days of an EWC meeting at which there was no discussion of

such issues (Stirling and Fitzgerald, 2001). Criticism from employers has been that EWCs have not added any value to their pre-existing employee involvement practices but have merely added another layer to the communication process. Other concerns have been expressed in relation to the expense involved, the dangers of raising employee expectations and the potential to foster transnational trade unionism. Fledgling EWCs face a number of challenges to their effectiveness. They are being introduced in a very competitive and fast-changing marketplace with continuous organizational restructuring involving mergers, acquisitions, joint ventures and divestments giving rise to problems of continuity for EWCs. European Works Council delegates also face difficulties in setting up effective communication and reporting-back systems to inform those who they represent about issues arising in discussions.
TR

References and further reading
Cressey, P. (1998) 'European works councils in practice', *Human Resource Management Journal* 8(1): 67–79.
Stirling, J. and Fitzgerald, I. (2001) 'European works councils: representing workers on the periphery', *Employee Relations* 23(1): 13–25.
Wedderburn, Lord (1997) 'Consultation and collective bargaining in Europe: success or ideology', *Industrial Law Journal* 26(1): 27–40.
Weston, S. and Lucio, M. (1998) 'In and beyond works councils: the limits and possibilities for trade union influence', *Employee Relations* 20(6): 551–64.
Wills, J. (1999) 'European works councils in British firms', *Human Resource Management Journal*, 9(4): 19–38.

Excellence movement

By the 1980s some authors such as Peters and Waterman (1982) were arguing that bureaucracy alone was ineffective in dealing with the management of people and processes. They cited authors such as Bennis (1968) and Toffler (1980) who were advocating 'adhocracy' in order to deal 'with all the new issues that either fall between bureaucratic cracks or span so many levels in the bureaucracy that its not clear who should be doing what' (Peters and Waterman, 1986: 121). By contrast their idea of 'excellent' organizations were seen as fluid organizations:

> The concept of organizational fluidity, therefore, is not new. What is new is that the excellent companies seem to know how to make good use of it. Whether it's their rich ways of communicating informally or their special ways of using ad hoc devices, such as task forces, the excellent companies get quick action just because their organizations are fluid. (Peters and Waterman, 1986: 121)

Between 1982 and 1990, *In Search of Excellence* (Peters and Waterman, 1982) had sold over 5 million copies worldwide. The two best known 'excellence' books, Peters and Waterman's *In Search of Excellence* (1982) and Peters and Austin's *A Passion for Excellence* (1985) were followed by other best selling books that included *Thriving on Chaos*: *Handbook for the Management Revolution* (Peters, 1987), *Liberation Management*: *Necessary Disorganization for the Nanosecond Nineties* (Peters, 1992), and a range of other media publications such as journals and videos. This excellence debate was enhanced further by arguments for innovation and entrepreneurship (Kanter, 1983; 1989).

The central strategic idea of the early work was the famous McKinsey 7-S Framework which served to demonstrate the interconnectedness of structure, strategy, skills, staff, style and systems revolving around a central concept of shared values. The investigations of Peters and Waterman led them to challenge the rational or bureaucratic/machine model of management functions by advocating eight principles of excellent organizations:

1. A bias for action: a preference for doing something – anything – rather than sending a question through cycles and cycles of analyses and committee reports.
2. Staying close to the customer – learning his or her preferences and catering to them.
3. Autonomy and entrepreneurship – breaking the corporation into small companies and encouraging them to think independently and competitively.
4. Productivity through people – creating in all employees the awareness that their best efforts are essential and that they will share in the rewards of the company's success.
5. Hands-on, value driven – insisting that executives keep in touch with the firm's essential business.
6. Stick to the knitting – remaining with the business the company knows best.
7. Simple form, lean staff – few administrative layers, few people at the upper levels.
8. Simultaneous loose–tight properties – fostering a climate where there is dedication to the central values of the company combined with tolerance for all employees who accept those values.

These eight principles provided an attack on 'traditional' management, by which they meant:

- the rational model of classical management
- the human relations theories
- more recent contingency theories.

As a result they argued that management needed to focus on customers, involve themselves in constant innovation, and regard employees as a resource rather than a cost. This required effective leadership. Other books that reflected the need to develop strong cultures were Bolman and Deal's (1991) *Reframing Organizations: Artistry, Choice and Leadership*, and Deal and Kennedy's (1988) *Corporate Cultures: The Rites and Rituals of Corporate Life*.

Why was the excellence movement so successful? One argument is that such populist literature simply provides busy managers with a short cut to many complicated issues which, from an academic's viewpoint, are highly contentious and need to be researched and debated (Guest, 1992). On the other hand, it would seem that a common thread running through all of the work could define the excellence movement. Thus despite a variety of authors and some of the redirected ideas of the later books the common theme of the human side of enterprise is evident. Indeed, it is not difficult to put forward a compelling case that despite its weaknesses in methodology its strength is the movement's ability to distil half a century of theoretical debate challenging the worst attributes of Fordism. **JG**

References and further reading
Bennis, W. (1968) 'The tempoary society', in W. G. Bennis and P. Slater (eds) *The Temporary Society*, New York: Harper and Row.
Bolman, L. G. and Deal, T. E. (1991) *Reframing Organizations: Artistry, Choice and Leadership*, San Francisco: Jossey-Bass.
Deal, T. and Kennedy, A., (1988) *Corporate Cultures: The Rites and Rituals of Corporate Life*, Harmondsworth: Penguin.
Guest, D. (1992) 'Right enough to be dangerously wrong', in G. Salaman (ed.) *Human Resource Strategies*, Buckingham: Open University Press.
Kanter, R. M. (1983) *The Change Masters: Innovation and Entrepreneurship in the American Corporation*, New York: Simon and Schuster.
Kanter, R. M. (1989) *When Giants Learn to Dance*, New York: Simon and Schuster.
Peters, T. (1987) *Thriving on Chaos: Handbook for the Management Revolution*, New York: HarperCollins.
Peters, T. (1992) *Liberation Management: Necessary Disorganization for the Nanosecond Nineties*, New York: Ballantine.

Peters, T. and Austin, N. (1985) *A Passion for Excellence: The Leadership Difference*, New York: Random House.

Peters, T. J. and Waterman, R. H. Jr (1982) *In Search of Excellence: Lessons from America's Best-Run Companies*, New York: Harper and Row

Peters, T. J. and Waterman, R. H. Jr (1986) *In Search of Excellence: Lessons from America's Best-Run Companies*, reprint, New York: Warner Books.

Toffler, A. (1980) *The Third Wave*, New York: Morrow.

Exit interviews

These are formal interviews carried out with employees who have resigned voluntarily before they leave. The main purpose of holding an exit interview is to establish the reasons for the resignation. These can then be recorded and used as the basis for the development of staff turnover reduction programmes. More generally, exit interviews provide the opportunity to discuss aspects of an organization's management with more frankness and honesty than is often possible during employment. Of particular value in this respect are the insights that can be gained from exit interviews into matters such as individual management styles, divisive personality clashes, mistrust of senior managers or dissatisfaction with specific policies and practices – issues which people often feel unable to bring to the attention of managers while they remain part and parcel of the organization. Exit interview questions can be either unstructured (i.e. permitting the resignee to range widely and generally in expressing their views) or structured (i.e. covering clearly defined areas such as pay, development opportunities, relationships with managers and colleagues etc.).

Some commentators have played down the usefulness of exit interviews as a means of gaining honest information, arguing that people tend to remain guarded in what they are prepared to say after resigning because of the need to secure good references in the future. It follows that care must be taken in organizing interviews of this kind in order to maximize their effectiveness from an organization's point of view. Interviews should not be carried out by the resignee's immediate line manager, should not take place on the last day of work and should only proceed once assurances of confidentiality have been given. Probably the best approach is to focus questions on ways in which the organization's management practices could be improved in the future. **ST**

References and further reading

Cundift, V. (1993) 'How to conduct an exit interview', *Employee Relations Law Journal* 19(1): 159–73.

Feldman, D. C. and Klaas, B. (1999) 'The impact of exit questionnaire procedures on departing employees' self-disclosure', *Journal of Managerial Issues* 11(1): 13–26.

Finn, W. (1999) 'Avoiding the revolving door', *Director*, January: 18–19.

Taylor, S. (1998) *Employee Resourcing*, London: IPD, pp. 235–8.

Expatriation

The term 'expatriation' in the general dictionary usage refers to the process of an individual moving to live in a different country. In the management literature the term has come to be applied to the process by which individuals, and often their family, are sent by their employer to work in another country for a period of a year or more, with the intention of returning to their home country within a finite period – usually two or three, but sometimes a much as five, years. Of course, there are many other options in international transfers: from video-conferencing and virtual teams, through short-term assignments to permanent relocation, taking in international commuting and frequent travelling along the way. There is also a growth in awareness of those who find their own jobs abroad. However, the research still focuses largely on the traditional expatriate.

Reasons for the use of expatriation vary from new business start-up to filling a gap in local capabilities to management development, though co-ordination and control of the subordinates is often a key purpose. Expatriates have generally been home country nationals but there is an increase in third country nationals (TCNs), reflecting the distinction between different staffing approaches taken by the multinational corporations. Expatriates are expensive – costing the organization perhaps three times as much similar jobs at home – and therefore their management becomes critical. The expatriate cycle (selection, preparation, adaptation to the new environment, evaluation and reward, repatriation) is not always well handled. organizations have a tendency to concentrate on the financial package and to pay less attention to the more important strategic management issues of fitting their expatriation policies to the organization's overall objectives. **CB**

References and further reading

Black, J. S., Gregersen, H. B., Mendenhall, M. E. and Stroh, L. K. (1999) *Globalizing People Through International Assignments*, Reading, MA: Addison-Wesley.

Brewster, C. (1991) *The Management of Expatriates*, London: Kogan Page.

Dowling, P. J., Schuler, R. S. and Welch, D. (1994) *International Dimensions of Human Resource Management*, 2nd edn, Belmont, CA: Wadsworth.

Mendenhall, M., Dunbar, E. and Oddou, G. (1987) 'Expatriate selection, training and career pathing', *Human Resource Management* 26(3): 331–45.

Scullion, H. and Brewster, C. (2001) 'The management of expatriates: lessons from Europe?', *Journal of World Business* (forthcoming).

Experiential learning

One of the most important concepts of learning to emerge in the late 1980s and 1990s is that of *experiential learning*. Based on the idea that learning does not just happen in formal settings, such as when we attend a course, the fundamental premise of experiential learning is that we learn all the time from our experiences of life. The most famous proponent of experiential learning is David Kolb. In his concept, learning is thought of as a four-stage cyclical process, as illustrated in the experiential learning cycle figure.

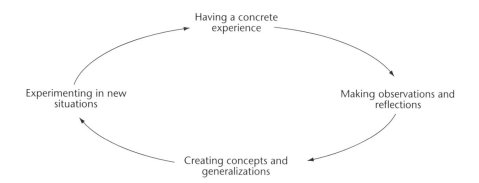

Figure 1: **The experiential learning cycle**
Source: adapted from Kolb (1984)

Briefly, in this model the learning process begins with the experiencing of some event or situation. We then move on to engage in reflective thinking (about what happened, possible reasons, explanations, looking for patterns, similarities and differences, reviewing what happened, etc.). The third stage is that we draw upon other sources of information to bring an external perspective to bear on the situation, conceptualizing about the main issues, formulating an explanation, coming up with alternatives, making judgements and drawing conclusions. The fourth stage is to experiment, actively seeking out opportunities to pursue alternative courses of action, planning and testing things out, changing our approach and behaviour in the future. This takes us into another learning cycle, and so on.

A business example might be a meeting at work. At the meeting, you are sure that a proposal you have to make will find favour with the rest of the participants. The meeting goes badly and your proposal is rejected. Your *experience* at the meeting forms the first part of the learning cycle. After the meeting, you go and get a cup of coffee, sit down and *reflect* on what happened. A colleague who is usually supportive was particularly negative about your proposal. People complained that the meeting was rushed and they did not have time to think. All these things and others are running through your head. You then start to think about how things could have been different. You have read somewhere about the importance of gauging support before a meeting and making sure people have plenty of time to think and prepare before pushing for a decision (*conceptualizing and generalizing*). There is another meeting scheduled next week. You use the time to do something different (*experimenting*): you put out a position paper well before the meeting and you sound out key people beforehand. Your approach at the meeting is different and this time the proposal goes through. By moving through the learning cycle, you have learned many valuable things about the way meetings work, about other people and about yourself.

Kolb's theory was developed in the USA. Peter Honey, Alan Mumford and others have done similar work in the UK. A useful extension to this theory is that of *learning styles*. Here, the theory is that we have a preferred style of learning (activist, reflector, theorist, pragmatist), which corresponds to the stages of the learning cycle (see the experiential learning cycle and learning styles figure). Self-check questionnaires are available that can help people determine their 'learning style'. **LS**

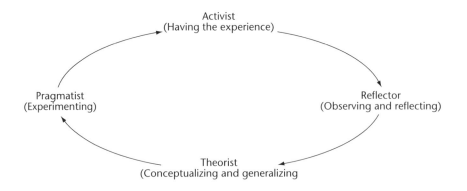

Figure 2: The experiential learning cycle and learning styles
Source: adapted from Kolb (1984) and Honey and Mumford (1992)

References and further reading

Gupta, A. and Misra, L. (2000) 'The value of experiential learning by organizations: evidence from international joint ventures', *Journal of Financial Research* 23(1): 77.

Hobbs, P. (2000) 'The university of life', *People Management* 6(17): 49–50.

Honey, P. and Mumford, A (1992) *Manual of Learning Styles*, Maidenhead: Honey.

Kolb, D. (1984) *Experiential Learning*, Englewood Cliffs, NJ: Prentice-Hall.

F

Family-friendly policies/firms

The closer integration of work and family responsibilities is becoming an increasingly important consideration for organizations and one that receives strong endorsement from the government. The concept of family-friendly policies is part of the wider equal opportunities agenda and a natural extension to the positive action proposals on working arrangements outlined in the Equal Opportunities Commission's *Code of Practice* (1985). In recent years the development of family-friendly schemes has been reinforced by a growing concern for work–life balance. Whereas family-friendly policies have been mainly designed to accommodate working mothers through the provision of flexible working practices, work–life policies are intended to benefit everyone. The main drivers for the introduction of family-friendly policies and practices have been business related: the need to increase flexibility in order to remain competitive and the need to retain skilled staff, particularly women with small children. Measures have received additional impetus through European Union Directives on working time, part-time working and parental leave, and the Employment Relations Act (1999). In some cases practices have developed informally, in response to specific employee requests for more flexibility.

The term 'family friendly' covers a wide range of practices across hours and place of work, leave entitlement and employee assistance. Policies relating to employees' hours and place of work include job-share, part-time or term-time working, 'v time' (reduced hours for a fixed period only), flexitime, homeworking and teleworking. Family-friendly leave entitlement encompasses domestic or parental leave and career breaks. The provision of workplace nurseries, financial support and information for childcare, enhanced maternity pay and, more recently, help with dependent or eldercare assists employees with their caring responsibilities. Although increasing numbers of organizations are developing family-friendly or work–life policies and notable examples of good practice are Littlewoods, Lloyds TSB, Glaxo Wellcome UK and BT, barriers to the introduction of such policies still exist. These constraints may be structural, cultural or stem from an inability to see the business benefit. Even where a policy exists, the prevailing culture and conditions may not facilitate its implementation and there is evidence that the take-up of some arrangements is low and for the most part utilized by women. Human resource specialists therefore have a key role to play in both demonstrating a strong business case to senior management and also in ensuring a supportive workplace culture. **SS**

References and further reading

Bevan, S., Dench, S., Tamkin, P. and Cummings, J. (1999) *Family-friendly Employment*: The *business case,* DfEE research report, RR136, London: DfEE.

Cooper, C. (2000) 'Work–life balance', *People Management,* 11 May: 34–6.

Cousey, M. (2000) *Getting the Right Work–Life Balance,* London: CIPD.

Equal Opportunities Commission (1985) *Code of Practice*: *For the Elimination of Discrimination on the Grounds of Sex and Marriage and the Promotion of Equality of Opportunity in Employment,* London: HMSO.

Lewis, S. and Lewis, J. (1996) *The Work-Family Challenge*: *Rethinking employment,* London: Sage.

Rayman, P., Bailyn, L., Dickert, J., Carre, F., Harvey, M., Krim, R. and Read, R. (1999) 'Designing organisational solutions to integrate work and life', *Women in Management* 14(5): 164–76.

Flexibility

Flexibility has become firmly embedded in the lexicon of management and political and public policy spheres, receiving considerable attention, promotion and pejorative use, with its connotations of adaptability and dynamism and cure for organizational ills. A key aspect concerns enhancing labour flexibilities to lower costs and increase responsiveness and equipment utilization, impacting on a variety of human resource management areas. Such ideas were popularized by work highlighting a new trend in manufacturing towards the 'flexible firm', strategically reorganizing to gain various flexibilities:

1. Functional flexibility, via blurring job demarcations and multiskilling, both horizontally (same level skills) and vertically (higher or lower level skills).
2. Numerical flexibility, by easier movements in and out of firms and 'atypical' work.
3. Financial flexibility, with more individualized, variable and performance-linked remuneration.

These occurred within a core-periphery model of the firm. Core employees with key (and scarce) skills, status, security and careers were supplemented by an easily adjustable 'buffer' of peripheral workers with less skilled and secure jobs.

Flexible work practices and flexible firms are uneven in their extent, pace, causality and nature:

1. Many changes stem from service-sector expansion.
2. Flexibility is evident in earlier literature and practices.
3. Ad hoc and expedient introduction is common.
4. Employer behaviour and employment divisions are oversimplified and misleading. The roles, significance and conditions of different work groups varies and peripheral, not core, workers can be central to organizations.
5. Some deregulation reduces flexibility. Easier 'hire and fire' (enhancing numerical flexibility) weakens pressures to invest, for example, in equipment and training (limiting functional flexibility) to compete by a short-term, low labour cost (with overtime, cost reduction) response.
6. Some rigidities increase flexibility. Limiting 'hire and fire' (restricting numerical flexibility) encourages investment in equipment and training (increasing functional flexibility) to compete by a long-term, adaptable workforce (with retraining, multiskilling, productivity enhancement) response. **CR**

References and further reading

Atkinson, J. (1984) *Manning for Uncertainty*: *Some Emerging UK Work Patterns,* Brighton: Institute of Manpower Studies.

Brewster, C., Hegewisch, A. and Mayne, L. (1994) 'Flexible working practices: the controversy and the evidence', in C. Brewster and A. Hegewisch (eds) *Policy and Practice in European Human Resource Management,* London: Routledge.

Cully, M., Woodland, S., O'Reilly, A. and Dix, G. (1999) *Britain at Work*, London: Routledge.
Millward, N., Forth, J. and Bryson, A. (1999) *All Change At Work?* London: Routledge.
National Economic Development Office (NEDO) (1986) *Changing Working Patterns: How Companies Achieve Flexibility to Meet New Needs*, London: NEDO.
Pollert, A. (ed.) (1991) *Farewell to Flexibility?* Oxford: Blackwell.

Flexibility, numerical/temporal

This type of flexibility can be defined as an ability to adjust numbers employed (numerical) and/or hours worked (temporal) in line with fluctuations in demand. It is associated with the use and growth of certain categories of worker, the most important of which are generally considered to be temporary employees and part-time employees. Certain other types of workers and working are also sometimes considered under the same heading: these include the self-employed, subcontractors, freelance workers, teleworkers, overtime, shift work, annual hours contracts and so on. In fact, difficulties in delineating this conception of flexibility mean that it is often defined in a negative sense. It is thus taken to include all forms of employment that are 'non-standard': those, in other words, that are not full-time, permanent and based on a formal contract of employment.

At issue is whether the development of these forms of flexibility represents part of a current fundamental restructuring of work and employment. In the UK, for example, while the use of temporary workers has shown a marked increase, the growth in part-time employment can be seen as the continuation of a much more long-term trend.

Important difference of opinion also exist over whether these developments should be seen as being advantageous from the employee's point of view. Some commentators would argue that new patterns of employment represent attempts by employees – particularly women – to achieve a better balance between work and other aspects of their lives; others, that new forms of flexibility should be interpreted as the creation by employers of a low-paid 'insecure' workforce which received little in the way of training and development. These differences of opinion arise in part from the problem of definition: under the heading of numerical/temporal flexibility comes too wide a range of practices, undertaken for too wide a range of reasons, for it to be very useful from a conceptual or from a managerial point of view. **SP**

References and further reading

Cully, M., Woodland, S., O'Reilly, A. and Dix, G. (1999) *Britain at Work: As Depicted by the 1998 Workplace Employee Relations Survey*, London: Routledge, chs 3, 4, 7, 8 and 10.
Felstead, A. and Jewson, N. (eds) (1999) *Global Trends in Flexible Labour*, London: Macmillan.
Gregg, P. and Wadsworth, J. (eds) (1999) *The State of Working Britain*, Manchester: Manchester University Press, chs 6 and 7.
Procter, S. and Ackroyd, S. (2000) 'Flexibility', in T. Redman and A. Wilkinson (eds) *Human Resource Management: Theory and Practice*, London: Addison-Wesley.
Sennett, R. (1998) *The Corrosion of Character: The Personal Consequences of Work in the New Capitalism*, London: Norton.
Standing, G. (1999) *Global Labour Flexibility*, London: Macmillan.

Flexible benefits

Flexible benefits are a formalized system that permits individual employees to influence the make-up of their pay and benefits package so that they may select certain items and reject others to match their personal requirements. Each year, the company provides a menu of benefits which indicates the cost in points or cash terms and each employee is told the value of their own individual benefits 'plan', usually based on their job or grade. They then choose the benefits they require, although the choice is often constrained by the company insistence on minimum requirements on items such as holiday entitlement or life assurance. If there is any difference between their benefit choice and their 'plan value' then an adjustment is made through an increase or decrease in their basic salary.

This arrangement allows employees to sacrifice certain benefits, such as a proportion of their holiday or their company car, and take other benefits that might fit their current lifestyle, such as childcare or additional medical cover. Older employees may wish to enhance their pension at the expense of salary or holiday while younger employees may be willing to reduce their pension contributions in exchange for a more expensive company car. Changes in the benefit choice are restricted to once a year except where the employee's personal circumstance changes radically, such as being widowed. The employee can also gain from the reduced prices for items such as childcare and supermarket vouchers plus the remnants of tax advantages on company cars.

For employers, the main advantage is that the benefits cost is fixed for that year and that it is possible to add benefits to the menu without actually incurring any costs. It is also an attractive recruitment and retention aid and goes some way towards diffusing the status difficulties associated with company car levels. Just as important, it reinforces the cultural elements of flexibility in the workplace which usually go hand in hand with the introduction in the scheme.

Administration is certainly costly in the year of introduction but experience seems to indicate that this substantially reduces as only a proportion of employees actually 'flex' their benefits and few change each year. Despite these advantages, only around 100 UK organizations have introduced formalised schemes. **JS**

References and further reading
Arkin, A. (1997) 'Mutually inclusive', *People Management*, 20 March: 32–4.
Smith, I. (2000) 'Flexible plans for pay and benefits', in R. Thorpe, and G. Homan (eds) *Strategic Reward Systems*, London: Financial Times Prentice Hall.
Stredwick, J. and Ellis, S. (1998) *Flexible Working Practices*, London: IPD.
Tane, L. D. (1992) 'Benefits that bend', *Financial Executive* 8(2): 35–40.

Flexible specialization

Flexible specialization involves a comprehensive history of political, economic, social and technological developments combined with manufacturing, product and market changes and 'regimes of regulation'. It has key tenets:

1. There is choice in technological change. At systemic 'industrial divides' outcomes were not due to technological necessity, but historical contingencies and political processes, with prior openness afterwards obscured as dominant forms were presented as 'natural' and 'inevitable'. The first 'divide' at the end of the nineteenth century led to the dominance of mass production ad Fordism, whose crisis from the 1960s led to the 'second divide' opening up.
2. Mass product markets fragmented and differentiated, with demand for changing, high quality goods. Flexible technologies and general-purpose machines operated by craft and multiskilled employees allowed rapid switching within fluid markets.
3. High trust relations with management developed with higher wages from value-added products and more satisfying jobs with skills, initiative and differentiated tasks.
4. Micro-regulation prevented technological stagnation and cost-cutting, and encouraged co-operation.

Such flexible specialization occurred via small firms in spatially agglomerated industrial districts, networks of interdependent and co-operatively competing units in areas specialized in the production of a range of related goods and services. An alternative route was via large firms internally decentralizing into looser federations of semi-autonomous units, or collaborating more closely with local supplier networks in longer-term relationships.

There are difficulties with flexible specialization:

1. It became increasingly problematic with revisions and 'stretching' to include mixed, 'hybrid' production forms.
2. The nature, elements and composition, as well as the spread and dominance of these forms of production, remain debated and contested.
3. Its portrayal of employment relations is naive. Small firms can be highly capricious, while large firms can remain alienating, and also squeeze suppliers, which in turn exploit their labour. **CR**

References and further reading

Piore, M. and Sable, C. (1984) *The Second Industrial Divide*: *Possibilities for Prosperity*, New York: Basic Books.

Rowley, C. (1994) 'The illusion of flexible specialisation: the domesticware sector of the ceramics industry', *New Technology, Work and Employment* 9(2): 127–39.

Rowley, C. (1996) 'Flexible specialisation: comparative dimensions and evidence from the tile industry', *New Technology, Work and Employment* 11(2): 125–36.

Sable, C. (1982) *Work and Politics*: *The Division of Labour in Industry*, Cambridge: Cambridge University Press.

Sable, C. (1989) 'Flexible Specialisation and the Re-Emergence of Regional Economies', in P. Hirst and J. Zeitlin (eds) *Reversing Industrial Decline?* Oxford: Berg.

Sable, C. and Zeitlin, J. (1985) 'Historical Alternatives to Mass Production: Politics, Markets and Technology in 19th Century Industrialisation', *Past and Present*, 108: 133–76.

Fordism

Fordism takes its name from the pioneering developments of Henry Ford, who brought together and expanded existing practices. It involves a rigid form of mechanized organization of large-scale, integrated mass production of standard consumer goods by special purpose machinery on continuously moving assembly lines. These were operated by semi-skilled or unskilled labour with task fragmentation, machine-pacing and labour discipline. Mass markets were developed through such production, high wages and low pricing. A 'regime of regulation' related production to consumption based on the management of the macro-economy and welfare state. This was seen as a dominant paradigm and universal recipe, spreading from the USA. A 'crisis' of Fordism was identified in the 1960s as stability was undermined with a decline in Keynesian demand management and regulation combined with external and internal shocks, such a product market saturation, volatility and fragmentation with less acceptance of mass-produced goods and demand for customized and quality products. This led to experiments as flexible technologies allowed more sophisticated goods manufactured in smaller batches, with commensurate shifts in organization. For some this was a move towards 'neo-Fordism', eliminating Fordism's imperfections and reformulating it while retaining its basic tenets of managerial controls and discipline of the assembly line and work tasks to allow the flexible mass production of a fixed number of variants of a single product. For others it was a move towards the different ideas of flexible specialisation.

Fordism has been criticized:

1. Economies were never truly totally Fordist as it had more limited fields of application.
2. Even within large firms a variety of production systems existed, depending on markets, while not all firms manufactured one product on long assembly lines or were integrated.

3. Small firms remained important, not least in producing specialized equipment, components and assembly of component semi-manufacture.
4. Its exploitative employment relations produced alienation, conflict and poor employment relations. **CR**

References and further reading
Aglietta, M. (1979) *A Theory of Capitalist Regulation*, London: New Left Review.
Coriot, B. (1980) 'The restructuring of the assembly line', *Capital and Class* 10(1): 60–72.
Dohse, K., Jurgens, U. and Malsch, T. (1985) 'From Fordism to Toyotism?', *Politics and Society* 14(2): 128–38.
Lipietz, A. (1987) *Mirages and Miracles: The Crisis of Global Fordism*, London: Verso.
Murray, F. (1983) 'The decentralisation of production: the decline of the mass-collective worker', *Capital and Class* 19(1): 20–30.
Roobeck, A. (1987) 'The Crisis of Fordism and the Rise of a New Technological Paradigm', *Futures*, April: 12–16.
Tolliday, S. and Zeitlin, J. (eds) (1987) *The Automobile Industry and its Workers: Between Fordism and Flexibility*, Cambridge: Polity Press.

G

Gainsharing

There is sometimes a concern expressed by managers that payment schemes that reward employees on an individual basis, such as performance-related pay, operate to the detriment of teamworking arrangements. One method used to address the problem is to introduce a system of team pay, another is to operate an organization-wide bonus scheme. Gainsharing is one such scheme as it allows, 'employees to share in the financial gains made by a company as a result of its improved performance' (Armstrong, 1996: 315).

Gainsharing differs from profit sharing schemes in that profits may be affected by many external factors such as interest rates, increased raw material costs, depreciation or loan repayments. Profits therefore often bear no resemblance to actual productivity gains. A gainsharing scheme recognizes this by rewarding employees for their efforts towards increasing their performance. It also helps establish a link between the achievement of company objectives and increased reward.

Armstrong describes the following gainsharing schemes:

- The Scanlon plan – this links labour costs to a proportion of total sales. If labour costs fall below a set ratio in relation to sales, the savings are shared between the company and the employees on the basis of a pre-established formula.
- The Rucker plan – also linked to labour costs but factors into the calculation of sales the costs of materials and supplies. This is supposed to provide a clearer indication of 'value added'.
- Improshare – a proprietary plan which uses a work measurement formula (an established standard of hours needed to produce a certain level of output) and distributes any savings between the organization and employees that result in increased production in fewer than expected hours.
- Value added – this is calculated by using sales, less the costs of materials and other purchased services, to establish the overall increase in productivity. Again, gains are shared between the organization and employees based on an agreed split.

Non-financial advantages are claimed for gainsharing, including employee commitment to organizational goals, employee ownership of the production processes, increased communication between the company stakeholders to reinforce involvement and the acceptance of the philosophy of continuous improvement. **MMo**

References and further reading
Armstrong, M. (1996) *Employee Reward*, London: Institute of Personnel and Development.
Graham, M. and Welbourne, T. (1999) 'Gainsharing and women's and men's relative pay satisfaction', *Journal of Organizational Behavior* 20(7), December: 1027–42.
Welbourne, T. and Gomez Mejia, L. (1995) 'Gainsharing: a critical review and a future research agenda', *Journal of Management* 21(3): 559–609.

Garden leave

It has become common for the contracts of senior managers and executives, in particular, to contain provision for lengthy periods of notice and a prohibition against working for others during the currency of the contract. Should such staff resign or be dismissed they would normally receive their salary for the notice period (often referred to inaccurately as 'wages in lieu of notice') but not be required – or indeed permitted – to come into work. For the duration of the notice period they are then said to be on 'garden leave', a reference to the fact they may have little choice but to spend their time digging the garden.

The reason for this sort of arrangement is that companies can thereby protect their confidential information without having to rely on more problematic restraint clauses (see **Non-compete clauses**). Employees who have given notice of resignation or been given notice of dismissal are neatly removed from access to confidential information within their own organization and are also unable to pass such information on to a competitor for anything up to six or even 12 months, by which time it may be out of date or in the public domain.

This practice does, of course, call into question whether or not employers are under a duty to provide their employees with work, or simply to pay wages or salary. The traditional view is that there is no duty to provide work unless employees are on piecework, dependent on commission or need the work to maintain their skills or reputation. Thus, in a recent case involving a senior dealer from William Hill, the court held that in view of his unique and specific post, his skills required frequent exercise and his employers were obliged to provide him with work during the notice period. Since they had not done so, they were not entitled to an injunction restraining him from working for a competitor during that period. **JE**

References and further reading
Evening Standard v. *Henderson* [1987] IRLR 64.
GFI Group Inc v. *Eaglestone* (1994) 490 IRLB 2.
Keenan, D. (1997), *Smith and Keenan's Advanced Business Law*, 10th edn, London: Pitman Publishing, pp. 171–2.
Provident Financial v. *Hayward* [1989] IRLR 84.
William Hill v. *Tucker* [1998] IRLR 313.

Glass ceiling

The 'glass ceiling' is a term that is used to describe the fact that while women (and other minority groups) are able to see the career opportunities that should be available to them in any given organization in which they work, they are prevented from accessing those opportunities by barriers in the workplace that operate in subtle and non-obvious ways.

There is a huge amount of research that has examined the 'glass ceiling', focusing particularly on women. One key focus has been on the role that organizational culture plays in impeding the progress of women employees. It has been suggested that many organizational cultures reflect the interests and beliefs of the white male majority, making it difficult for women to be seen as competent in some roles (Robinson and McIllwee, 1991), impeding their ability to communicate effectively (Riley, 1983) and preventing them from accessing informal social networks

(Crompton and Jones, 1984). Research also suggests that women are typecast into certain roles, such as those that mirror their domestic roles as carers, cleaners and mothers (Labour Market Trends, 1996).

Research also suggests that women themselves self-handicap in organizations because of the effects of sex-role socialization – the self-expectations that we develop as children under the influence of society's expectations of boys v. girls. Women, for instance, appear to attribute their success at work more to good luck than to their own ability and are less likely to promote themselves in ways that might facilitate their career progression. This may be because being 'assertive' in these ways is a characteristic associated more with men than with women, and women who act in gender-atypical ways may be judged harshly.

Finally, because women tend to be the primary caregivers in families with children, many leave work for a period of time to have and raise children, and on their return, find that they are out of touch with what is going on in the organization, and may not find it easy to re-engage with work in ways that might help their future prospects.

In an attempt to address some of these issues, organizations have introduced a number of schemes including mentoring (where an employee has a more senior staff member designated to help them and facilitate their career development), actively encouraging women returners through the provision of crèches and other childcare schemes, and the introduction of flexible working patterns, such as part-time work and job share. **PD**

References and further reading
Crompton, R. and Jones, M. (1984) *White-Collar Proletariat*, London: Macmillan.

Davidson, M. J. and Cooper, C. L. (1984) *Shattering the Glass Ceiling*: *The Woman Manager*, London: Paul Chapman Publishing.

Labour Market Trends (1996) 'Women in the labour market. Results from the Spring', *Labour Force Survey*, March.

Riley, P. A. (1983), 'A structurationist account of political culture', *Administrative Science Quarterly* 28: 414–37.

Robinson. J. G. and McIllwee, J. S. (1991) 'Men, women, and the culture of engineering', *Sociological Quarterly* 32(3): 403–21.

Globalization

The term 'globalization' can be taken as referring to a process whereby traditional, local (i.e. regional or national) boundaries are transcended or rendered obsolete. Although there is some debate as to whether globalization as a phenomenon is actually happening, it is perhaps easiest to think of globalization as a summary term, encompassing references to widespread change in several arenas such as politics, international relations, the world's economic systems and business and management. Some specific examples of such change might be:

- the rise of global financial markets
- the development of worldwide communications technology (such as the Internet)
- political unification and transnational organizations (such as the European Union, the North Atlantic Treaty Organization)
- transnational regulatory agreements (General Agreement on Tariffs and Trade).

From a business and management perspective, each of these examples could also be viewed as signalling opportunities and challenges for contemporary organizations.

Confusion can arise as to whether globalization is itself a driver of change, or whether it is merely a description of multiple changes in different contexts. Each example above could be thought of as evidence of globalization (a manifestation), or a consequence of globalization (an effect) or a driver of globalization (a cause), or a mix of these. Complexity and confusion about causal processes is itself a character-istic of the phenomenon, and also a pointer to a key theme that because no single process (or institution) can be identified as a cause, correspondingly, no single insti-tution can exercise sovereignty. In other words, 'no one is in charge'. Allied to this is the idea that globalization results in a shrinking of the social world, or space time compression. The sociologist Anthony Giddens (1990: 64) defines globalization as 'the intensification of world wide social relations which link distant localities in such a way that local happenings are shaped by events occurring many miles away and vice versa'.

Another key theme is that globalization will affect national or local cultures. Two contrasting theories (convergence theory and divergence theory) address this. Con-vergence theory holds that as national boundaries are eroded in the political, tech-nological and business arenas, so too local differences in culture will be eroded, with the end result being one 'global' culture. Divergence theory maintains the opposite, namely that cultural diversity will persist or even be reinforced by the rejection of superficial commonality. Each view has implications for human resource manage-ment (HRM) in so far as HRM concerns the management of culture.

There are limitations with the definitional framework as given above. For example, it often goes unchallenged that there is an ideological aspect to globalization. It may result in a form of cultural imperialism, with an agenda set by the Northern hemi-sphere nations. Giddens has memorably referred to this as being less like 'global vil-lage', and more like 'global pillage'. Writers such as Baumann have been quick to point to problems with any utopian construction of globalization. Whereas the removal of established boundaries and compression of space–time may offer unprecedented opportunity for personal growth, it is likely this privilege will be denied the poor, i.e. the majority of the world's citizens. Also, that globalization is a complex term and not easy to locate or define makes it susceptible to use as a rhetoric to justify otherwise unacceptable change, such as restructuring, delayering or the relocation of manufacturing plants at short notice. **KM**

References and further reading

Baumann, Z. (1999) *Globalization: The Human Consequences*, Cambridge: Polity Press.
Giddens, A. (1990) *The Consequences of Modernity*, Cambridge: Polity Press.
Hoogvelt, A. (1997) *Globalisation and the Postcolonial World: The New Political Economy of Devel-opment*, London: Macmillan.
Lawrence, P. (1999) *Issues in European Business*, London: Macmillan.
Legge, K. (1995) *Human Resource Management: Rhetorics and Realities*, London: Macmillan.

Globalization and human resource management

Debate continues concerning the exact meaning and newness of the term 'globaliza-tion' and its human resource management (HRM) impacts. One aspect is globalization's perceived power in weakening and overriding national HRM systems, thus adding to earlier debates concerning convergence around common practices. Is this happening? The short answer is both 'yes' and 'no'. More macro-level factors (structure, technology) may converge, while more micro-level elements (people's behaviour in organizations) may not. Likewise, globalization may have varied impacts on different levels of HRM system structure. The issue of the globalization of HRM systems then becomes more a matter of degree, what aspects and how much.

Barriers to globalized HRM remain, not least those of a cultural, institutional and structural nature. So-called 'cultural distance' has long been used extensively as a critical explanatory factor and can be applied to HRM. A country's particular culture (i.e. rules, values and norms) may well restrict the transfer and operation of certain HRM practices. Also important is the degree of the practice's 'institutionalization' at recipient units at twin levels (Kostova, 1999). First, the 'implementation' level, simply following formal rules with objective behaviour and actions. At a deeper level is 'internalization', attained when employees have commitment to, satisfaction with and psychological ownership of, the practice. Thus, gaps between practices adopted and mindsets reflects a lack of internalisation, representing failure to infuse the practice with values. It may be easier to implement, but much more difficult to internalize, certain practices, to get people to fully accept and approve them. Likewise, institutional factors such as the state and trade unions impact on globalized HRM. The area of globalization and HRM will retain its high profile. A key issue is to move beyond broad-brush portrayals. We need to disaggregate and distinguish what aspects of HRM may be globalizing from those remaining distinct and their level of acceptance. **CR**

References and further reading

Becker, B. and Gerhart, B. (1996) 'The impact of human resource management on organizational performance: progress and prospects', *Academy of Management Journal* 39(4): 779–89.

Kostova, T. (1999) 'Transnational transfer of strategic organizational practices: a contextual perspective', *Academy of Management Review* 24(2): 308–24.

Leisink, P. (ed.) (1999) *Globalization and Labour Relations*, Cheltenham: Edward Elgar.

Rowley, C. and Benson, J. (eds) (2000) *Globalisation and Labour in the Asia Pacific Region*, London: Cass.

Graphology

The practice of making inferences about a person's character or state of mind from a sample of their handwriting. It is claimed that graphology is a technique that can be used to good effect in personnel selection as a means of predicting likely job performance. In the UK it is very rare for graphology to be used as a selection method, although a small minority of employers have reportedly shown interest in its possibilities. In a number of European countries, notably France and Belgium, its use is a good deal more widespread, especially among smaller employers.

Several academic studies have been carried out to establish whether or not graphology has any predictive validity. Others have simply focused on the ability of professional graphologists to make accurate judgements about the personalities of individuals who have submitted samples of their handwriting. While different graphologists tend to reach similar judgements about the same samples, studies have persistently found that they are unable to make useful deductions about the major personality traits beyond those that would be evident to many lay people (e.g. artistic handwriting indicating an artistically inclined individual). The studies have suggested that a good deal more useful information can be gained from reading the content of handwriting samples than from studying the style in which words are actually written. A robust theoretical case for the use of graphology in personnel selection is thus yet to be made. **ST**

References and further reading

Ben-Shakhar, G. (1989) 'Non-conventional methods in personnel selection', in P. Herriot (ed.) *Assessment and Selection in organisations*, Chichester: Wiley.

Cooper, D. and Robertson, I. (1995) *The Psychology of Personnel Selection*, London: Routledge, pp. 137–40.

North, S. J. (1994) 'Employers turn to handwriting tests', *Personnel Today*, December: 25–8.

Smith, M., Gregg, M. and Andrews, D. (1989) *Selection and Assessment: A New Appraisal*, London: Pitman, pp. 86–8.

Greenfield sites

Interest in human resource management on greenfield sites first emerged in the USA in the 1970s under the guise of the 'new plant' approach. This stressed high-involvement practices such as self-managed work teams, skill-based pay and a strong commitment to selection and training. In the UK in the 1980s, as 'human resource management' (HRM) as a distinct, individualist approach to the management of the employment relationship developed, it was argued that managers on greenfield, as opposed to brownfield, sites would be better able to introduce such practices. Human resource (HR) policies and practices typically found on a small number of greenfield sites appear compatible with the mutuality assumptions of high-commitment HRM. The greenfield situation supposedly gives managers advantages from starting with a congruent total system.

Initially, the definition of a greenfield site emphasized its furbishment and a location separate from existing plants of a parent company. Later definitions focused on the distinction between a new and a greenfield plant by virtue of an attempt to introduce a new approach to managing employees based on a new management philosophy which is a 'break with the past'. Thus, an old philosophy on a new location would not count as a greenfield site, whereas a new philosophy on an old location would.

Recent research suggests that the optimism expressed by advocates of the greenfield approach is overstated. Difficulties have been found in both creating and maintaining a new management philosophy, and in its replication in further site openings where the 'new' approach is believed to be both successful and universal. Problems include:

- employee expectations
- managers not being prepared for consolidation after an initial frenzied start-up period
- coping with adverse product market fluctuations.

Even with the advantage of a *tabula rasa* managers prepared to make a break with their past and introduce a new management philosophy are not able to sustain this approach; greenfield sites can turn brown. In such situations managers committed to the new philosophy experience difficulties in recognising its weakness and with adopting another approach. The common response to browning is to repackage and restate the original greenfield philosophy to often sceptical employees. **JL and JH**

References and further reading

Guest, D. and Hoque, K. (1994) 'Employee relations in non-union greenfield sites: the good, the bad and the ugly', *Human Resource Management Journal* 5(1): 1–14.
Gunnigle, P. (1994) 'Collectivism and the management of industrial relations in greenfield sites', *Human Resource Management Journal* 5(2): 105–34.
Lawler, E. (1990) 'The new plant revolution revisited' *Organisational Dynamics* 10(2): 5–14.
Leopold, J. W. and Baird, M. (eds) (2001) 'Managing human resources on greenfield sites', special issue of *Personnel Review* 30(2).
Leopold, J. W. and Hallier, J. (1997) 'Start-up and ageing in greenfield sites', *Human Resource Management Journal* 7(2): 72–88.
Leopold, J. W. and Hallier, J. (1999) 'Managing the employment relationship on greenfield sites in Australia and New Zealand', *International Journal of Human Resource Management* 10(4): 716–36.

Grievance

In essence a grievance is a formal complaint by made by an employee about treatment received from his or her employing organization. A more comprehensive definition, which although old is nevertheless timely, is given by the International Labour Organization (ILO, 1965) as, with respect to conditions of employment where a situation appears contrary to the provisions of collective agreements, the individual contract, works rules, laws or regulations or custom and practice. As used in Great Britain, grievance can be a notoriously unspecific term that embraces both collective and individual issues, which reflects the idea that the line between a grievance (individual) and dispute (collective) can sometimes be a blurred one. There is remarkably little published research in the UK on grievance or grievance handling, the vast majority of work having emanated from North American sources. However, the word has a very different meaning in the USA, where it is reserved for formal complaints of alleged violations of agreements or contracts. Since American agreements are legally binding, the matter is almost always handled through arbitration or in a labour court.

In Great Britain an issue is normally handled through an organization's own grievance procedure, the necessity for which was acknowledged as long ago as 1972, in the Department of Employment's Industrial Relations Code of Practice (DoE, 1972). However, this was somewhat unspecific in terms of guidelines for constructing adequate procedures and the Advisory, Conciliation and Arbitration Service (ACAS, 2000) has issued a code of a code of practice that covers both disciplinary and grievance procedures. It is normally recommended that attempts to resolve a grievance should commence with informal discussion between the employee and his or her immediate superior. Only if this fails to produce an acceptable solution (to the employee) should the matter then progress to a formal hearing held at a higher level in the organization. If this fails to produce a solution, hearings can potentially take place at even higher levels, the only limit being the number of levels in the organization's hierarchy. As a final step in some organizations, there is a facility for the case to be brought before an independent, external arbiter. Notwithstanding these provisions there is of course, no guarantee that an employee will receive an impartial hearing. Indeed, there is some evidence that managers can be highly defensive in handling employee complaints about their conduct. Nevertheless, without a procedure through which employees can seek redress, it would be much more difficult to ensure that matters are not handled in an arbitrary way. **DRo**

References and further reading

Advisory, Conciliation and Arbitration Service (ACAS) (2000) *Code of Practice on Disciplinary and Grievance Procedures*, London: Advisory, Conciliation and Arbitration Service.

Department of Employment (DoE) (1972) *Industrial Relations Code of Practice*, London: HMSO.

Hook, C., Rollinson, D. J., Foot, M. and Handley, J. (1996) 'Supervisor and manager styles in handling discipline and grievance: part one – comparing styles in handling discipline and grievance', *Personnel Review* 25(3): 2–34.

Internationl Labour Organization (ILO) (1965) *Examination of Grievances and Communications within the Undertaking*, International Conference Report no. 7, Geneva: ILO, pp. 7–9.

Rollinson, D. (2000) 'Supervisor and manager approaches to handling discipline and grievance: a follow-up study', *Personnel Review* 29(6): 743–64.

Rollinson, D., Hook, C., Foot, M. and Handley, J. (1996) 'Supervisor and manager styles in handling discipline and grievance: part two – approaches to handling discipline and grievance', *Personnel Review* 25(4): 38–55.

Halo and horns

The 'halo' and 'horns' effects are frequently cited as being a common weakness in the processes of selection and formal performance appraisal. The terms refer to a situation in which, for whatever reason, the interviewer (or appraiser) rates a job applicant (or appraisee) either over-generously or over-harshly across a range of separate assessment criteria. The halo and horns effects are also identified as being significant in the literature on assessment centres. An example of the halo effect would be that of an interviewer rating a candidate's performance highly on appearance, job knowledge, motivation and relevant experience, when the performance was really only strong on one of these different factors. The horns effect is the opposite. Here the candidate is marked down across the range of assessment criteria despite being weak in only one area. Undoubtedly in some cases such judgements are reached quite deliberately in order to ensure, for example, that the interviewer's preferred candidate is offered the job or in order to reduce the promotion chances of a disliked subordinate. However, research indicates that the effects can also very easily occur unintentionally, despite genuine efforts on the part of interviewers or appraisers to be fair and objective in their judgements.

In the context of the selection interview, the halo effect is said to be particularly common – although often working indirectly. What happens here is that the interviewer, having decided early on that they are well disposed towards a particular candidate, cannot help but convey this during the interview through body language, general enthusiasm and a positive questioning style. Hence, although the questions asked of each candidate are identical, the preferred candidate performs with greater confidence and builds up a stronger rapport with the interviewer. Studies which indicate the presence of halo effects like this are used in the debate about the extent to which the effectiveness of selection interviews is compromised by subjectivity and poor validity. **ST**

References and further reading

Anderson, N. and Shackleton, V. (1993) *Successful Selection Interviewing*, Oxford: Blackwell, ch. 3.
Arkin, A. (1998) 'A suitable old boy?', *People Management* April: 28–33.
Cooper, W. (1981) 'Ubiquitous halo' *Psychological Bulletin* 90: 218–44.
Dougherty, T. W. and Turban, D. B. (1999) 'Behavioral confirmation of interviewer expectations', in R. Eder and M. Harris (eds) *The Employment Interview Handbook*, London: Sage.

'Hard' and 'soft' human resource management

Part of the justification for the claim that human resource management (HRM) is a new and better way of managing people at work is that it offers employers the opportunity to gain commitment from their employees. On this view employees are seen not as a cost, but rather as an investment and potential source of competitive advantage. 'Soft' HRM could be characterized by an emphasis on gaining commitment, managing culture and investing in employee development. Simply put, it can be thought of as human resource management with the emphasis on the 'human', and has its roots in the human-relations school (Storey, 1989).

The claim that HRM is a new and better way of managing 'the human resource' is also partly based on the idea that HRM is integrated with business strategy. This may entail the need to maximize efficiency and profit, and minimize cost of labour. 'Hard' HRM could be characterized by an emphasis on quantifiable business metrics, such as efficiency and unit labour cost. Simply put, it can be thought of as human resource management with emphasis on the 'resource', and is based on the personnel planning approach, which treats management of 'the human resource' as akin to management of any other economic factor (Storey, 1989).

The claim that HRM depends on employee commitment and the claim that HRM needs to be integrated with business strategy do not have to be in conflict. Indeed, one argument for pursuing both is that business strategy can only be realized where employees' potential is maximized. Employees may offer the only sustainable source of competitive advantage, as they cannot be copied, unlike products, buildings and technology. Also, many new forms of work rely more now on intellectual labour and so-called knowledge workers. This may make traditional control mechanisms obsolete. Employees cannot be observed or timed and measured in the same way because their work is too complex. They need to be motivated as well as trusted by management, so control must be based on commitment not compliance. Nonetheless, there is a need to recognize potential conflict between these two claims of HRM, or confusion can result. A specific example may help illustrate this.

Introducing a scheme such as job sharing could encourage greater commitment, by offering employees more flexible ways of working and such a practice would thereby qualify as 'HRM'. By way of contrast, the ability for employers to hire and fire at will could help minimize labour costs and improve efficiency. This ability could be evidence of human resource policy integrated with business strategy (where for example an organization was pursuing a strategy of cost leadership) and would therefore also qualify as 'HRM'. Yet hiring and firing at short notice would be likely to lead to a dissatisfied workforce and prevent an employer gaining employee commitment. If we label the first measure an example of 'soft' HRM and the second 'hard' HRM this may help to resolve such an obvious paradox, but precise definition of HRM remains problematic. **KM**

References and further reading

Beardwell, I. and Holden, L. (2000) *Human Resource Management: A Contemporary Perspective*, 3rd edn, London: Pitman.

Marchington, M. and Wilkinson, A. (2000) *Core Personnel and Development*, London: CIPD

Storey, J. (1989) *New Perspectives on Human Resource Management*, London: Routledge.

Storey, J. (ed.) (1995) *Human Resource Management: A Critical Text*, London: Thomson Learning.

Harmonization

In most organizations there has been historical differences between manual workers, non-manual workers and management. This has been manifested in many ways such as:

- pay structures – weekly pay for manual workers (wages) and monthly pay for non-manual workers (salary)
- employment contracts
- holiday entitlements
- bonus or incentive schemes – payment by results schemes for manual workers, performance-related pay for non manual workers
- financial benefits for non-manual workers–company car, health insurance, company loans etc.
- separate canteen facilities, toilets, entrances.

As a response to various pressures, both internal and external to the organization, more companies have decided to introduce the same terms and conditions of employment for all their employees through the process of harmonization. This is sometimes referred to as single status arrangements, which emphasizes the breaking down of the traditional barriers.

The pressures that have precipitated this change include:

- the introduction of new technologies which have de-skilled some white-collar occupations and up-skilled some blue-collar occupations.
- the need for employee flexibility, especially in flatter, leaner organizations.
- the need for a responsive workforce by empowerment or decision-making arrangements
- cost reductions in personnel administration as running separate arrangements is more costly and time-consuming to administer.
- fostering ideals of whole corporate culture, commitment and motivation.
- legislation in the areas of equal pay between the sexes and for work of equal value, equal rights for part-time workers and holiday entitlement.
- feminization of the white-collar workforce.

Roberts (1990) notes that ideas of morality and egalitarianism have little to do with the harmonization process and it is introduced into organizations purely because of the business need. **MMo**

References and further reading

Arthurs, A. (1985) 'Towards single status?', *Journal of General Management*, Autumn: 16–28.

Price, L. and Price, R. (1994) ' Change and continuity in the status divide?' in K. Sisson (ed.) *Personnel Management*, 2nd edn, Oxford: Blackwell.

Roberts, C. (1990) *Harmonization: Whys and Wherefores*, London: Institute of Personnel Management.

Rowlinson, M., Hassard, J. and Forrester, P. (1991) 'Who wants harmonization – image and reality in single status working', *Personnel Review*, 20(5): 27–33.

Hawthorne experiments

The Hawthorne experiments (see also **Human relations approach**) at the Western Electric Company in America are perhaps the most famous of all social science research experiments of the twentieth century, grounded within the human relations and quality of working life (QWL) movement (Mayo, 1933; Roethlisberger and Dickson, 1939). The initial idea was to prove that employee output and productivity would increase by the use of more light in the workplace (factories had traditionally relied on natural daylight to illuminate the workplace). As the bias of such claims came from a light-bulb manufacturer (Western Electric Company), they were suspect to say the least. In response the Western Electric Company embarked upon a more extensive research programme which lasted for almost eight consecutive years, headed by George Elton Mayo, a professor at Harvard Business School.

The Hawthorne experiments aimed to show a positive impact on organizational performance and profitability by paying attention to the welfare needs of workers and work groups. The four main experiments were as follows (see Rose, 1988, and Buchanan and Huczynski, 1997, for a more analytical assessment):

1. *The Illumination Experiments* (*1924–27*): the objective was to examine whether output increased with changes in light and illumination in the workplace. Employees were split into two population groups for comparison, and the intensity of light varied. However, the researchers did not find any correlation between increased output and more light. Indeed, production in one test increased when the lighting declined.

This led the researchers to conclude that light variation was probably only one minor factor that could affect employee output levels, and other experiments were devised.

2. *The Relay Assembly Room Experiments* (*1927–33*): six employees (all women) were chosen and separated from the main workforce and subject to closer study. They assembled electric relay switches that comprised of 35 components, worked a 48-hour week (six days) and had no work breaks. This regime was systematically altered, and changes in employees output observed.

After introducing a new 'employee benefit', such as rest periods or shorter working hours, output nearly always increased. The researchers felt that these changes were partly explained by the workers attitudes to the group.

3. *The Interview Programme* (*1928–30*): in trying to establish a link between the psychological and physiological conditions for workers on the one hand, and increased productivity on the other hand, the researchers embarked on an extensive interview programme to obtain employee views concerning supervision. Around 20 000 interviews were conducted.

From this stage the researchers discovered two important findings. One was that the dynamics of informal group interaction among workers was used to control (even restrict) output. The second finding was that issues external to the organization were also important influences on group behaviour, such as social and family concerns. These findings led to another stage in the experiments, work observation.

4. *The Bank Wiring Room Observations* (*1931–32*): 14 workers (all men) were divided into three teams. Each team included three workers and one supervisor, and two inspectors who rotated between all three teams. The daily work activities and interactions between teams were then observed.

The findings revealed that additional subgroups emerged across the teams, each with their own informal group leader. It also revealed that workers develop their own values and norms. Thus what represented a 'fair level output' was ostensibly a function of workers' (informal) control. This protected employees against management attempts to increase the pace of work or make employees redundant. In short, informal group interaction produced a twin effect: it stopped group members from working too fast or too slow according to their own (informal) value judgements, and it protected group members from outside interference, especially managerial intrusion (Roethlisberger and Dickson, 1964).

All in all the Hawthorne experiments were extensive, impressive and far-reaching. They etched a distinctive human relations approach to the management of 'people' by exploring social rather than purely economic needs. However there is also a great deal of controversy surrounding these experiments (see Sykes, 1965; Rose, 1988). For example, workers who were separated from the main factory for the purposes of study were in receipt of 'special treatment'. In other words, the researcher–respondent relationship may have been the cause of increased morale, output or productivity. Indeed, this is now known within social science research as the Hawthorne effect: 'the tendency of people being observed as part of a research effort, to behave differently than they would otherwise' (Buchanan and Huczynski, 1997: 183). **TD**

References and further reading

Buchanan, D. and Huczynski, A. (1997) *Organisational Behaviour*, 3rd edn, London: Prentice Hall, ch. 7.

Mayo, E. (1933) *The Human Problems of an Industrial Civilization*, New York: Macmillan.

Roethlisberger, F. and Dickson, W. (1939) *Management and the Worker*, Boston, MA: Harvard University Press.

Roethlisberger, F. and Dickson, W. (1964) *Management and the Worker*, New York: Wiley.

Rose, M. (1988) *Industrial Behaviour*, 2nd edn, Harmondsworth: Penguin.

Sykes, A. (1965) 'Economic interest and the Hawthorne researchers', *Human Relations* 57.

Headhunters

Executive search consultants or 'headhunters' are a specialized method of recruitment. Headhunters do not advertise positions openly, but approach directly potentially suitable candidates who may not be actively seeking a job change. They are used more in private sector, typically only for very senior or specialized appointments. This is because there may be only a very few appropriate candidates, although in some cases they may be used to protect confidentiality of the employer. This is the most expensive method of recruitment (the consultant will typically charge 30 per cent of the appointee's first year's salary on appointment). The ethics of this approach to recruitment have been questioned since it involves direct 'poaching' of staff, and it may be discriminatory against non-traditional groups depending on the methods and networks adopted by the headhunter – identifying potential candidates should be based on research rather than on known contacts only. There is also the concern that consultants may subsequently headhunt the same candidate for another client, or may headhunt staff of the client company for a different client at a later date. As with any consultant, care should be taken in selecting a headhunter and agreeing the terms of contract. **JB**

References and further reading

Arkin, A. (1999) 'Who's Byting' (Internet exectutive search), *People Management* 5(21), 28 October: 58–62.

Ball, D., Britton, C. and Wright, M. (1999) 'Talking Heads', *People Management* 5(1), 14 January: 42–4.

Fowler, A. (1991) 'How to use executive search', *Personnel Management Plus*, January: 20–1.

Fowler, A. (1994) 'How to select an external consultant', *Personnel Management Plus*, February: 26–7.

Industrial Relations Service (1991) 'Executive Recruitment – a case for using your headhunter? 1: main findings and usage', Industrial Relations Review and Report, Recruitment and Development Report, no. 24, December.

Industrial Relations Service (1992) 'Using Executive Search', Industrial Relations Review and Report, Recruitment and Development Report, no. 26, February.

Health and Safety at Work Act

The Health and Safety at Work Act 1974 forms the core of Britain's statutory framework relating to the prevention of work-related illness and injury. The Act imposes broad general duties of care on a range of actors, for example, employers, controllers of premises used for work activities, employees and those who supply articles or substances for use at work. In the case of employers the duties imposed under sections 2 and 3 of the Act encompass obligations relating to the preparation and implementation of health and safety policies, the consulting of union appointed safety representatives, the establishment of safety committees and the taking of action to ensure, so far as is reasonably practicable, the health and safety of employees and others who may be affected by the conduct of their undertaking. The provisions of the Act are supported by a host of other 'relevant statutory provisions' embodied in other statues, notably the Factories Act 1961 and the Offices, Shops and Railway Premises Act 1963, and regulations made under these statues, as well as the Act itself. They are also supported by approved codes of practice which provide more detailed guidance on their requirements.

Inspectors employed by the Health and Safety Executive and local authorities enforce the statutory provisions. These inspectors can serve prohibition notices in situations where there is a serious risk of personal injury which instruct a person to cease carrying out certain specified activities and also improvement notices that require those on whom they are served to remedy any perceived contraventions of their statutory duties. In addition, prosecutions may be initiated. Such prosecutions can give rise to fines and in certain circumstances, to imprisonment. Much debate has taken place about the adequacy of the statutory framework put in place by the 1974 Act. **PJ**

References and further readings

Dawson, S., Willman, P., Bamford, M. and Clinton, A. (1988) *Safety at Work: The Limits of Self-Regulation*, Cambridge: Cambridge University Press.

James, P. (1992) 'Reforming British health and safety law: a framework for discussion', *Industrial Law Journal* 21(2): 83–105.

James, P and Walters, D. (1999) *Regulating Health and Safety: The Way Forward*, London: Institute of Employment Rights.

Nichols, T. (1990) 'Industrial safety in Britain and the 1974 Health and Safety at Work Act', *International Journal of the Sociology of Law*, 18: 317–42.

Wright, F. B. (1997) *Law of Health and Safety at Work*, London: Sweet and Maxwell.

Health and safety committees

Health and safety committees are joint consultative bodies comprising of employer and worker representatives. Such committees can operate at different organizational levels. For example, they can operate within individual departments and on a site-wide basis, as well as at higher levels within an organization. There is evidence to show that workplaces that possess health and safety committees have lower accident rates than those that do not. However, the effectiveness of committees has also been found to vary considerably as a result of a variety of factors, including the degree of management support provided, membership size, the way in which meetings are organized and conducted, the extent to which the membership is trade union based and the broader climate of management–worker relationships. Safety representatives appointed by unions under the Safety Representatives and Safety Committees Regulations 1977 can request an employer to establish a committee. Findings from the 1998 Workplace Employee Relations Survey indicate that 26 per cent of workplaces with 25 or more employees had health and safety committees and that 13 per cent of them had consultative committees which dealt with health and safety matters alongside other issues. **PJ**

References and further readings

Bryce, G. and Manga, P. (1985) 'The effectiveness of health and safety committees', *Relations Industrielles*, 40(2): 257–81.

Cully, M., Woodland, S., O'Reilly, A. and Dix, S. (1999) *Britain at Work: As Depicted by the 1998 Workplace Employee Relations Survey*, London: Routledge.

Health and Safety Commission (1996) *Safety Representatives and Safety Committees*, 3rd edn, Norwich: HSE Books.

Nichols, T. (1997) *The Sociology of Industrial Injury,* London: Mansell, ch.7.

Reilly, B., Paci, P. and Holl, P. (1995) 'Unions, safety committees and workplace injuries', *British Journal of Industrial Relations*, 33(2): 275–88.

Walters, D. and Gourlay, S. (1990) *Statutory Employee Involvement in Health and Safety at the Workplace: A Report of the Implementation and Effectiveness of the Safety Representatives and Safety Committees Regulations 1977*, London: Health and Safety Executive.

High-flyers

All employees, being the prime asset of the organization, deserve investment in their career by their organization. However, high-flyers are those with high potential for fast progress, perceived as a special asset and capable of making a unique contribution to the future of the organization. Thus they are expected to be worth having higher attention and resources dedicated specifically to them. Derr, Jones and Toomey (1988) look at high-flyers as a scarce resource, and because of the demographic reduction in workforce numbers, including managerial layers, suggest that organizations will look for more ways of developing future leaders.

London and Stumpf (1982) suggested an organizational career management two-part model, especially designed for high-flyers. The first stage marks the identification of high-flyers at the beginning of their careers, while the second refers to an accelerated path for those under the programme. Such a development programme provides the high-flyer with a unique opportunity and wider options for fast development, but might also create pressure and stress for the individual. Another problem is that by identify a handful of high-flyers, all the rest are implicitly being phased out from high-potential career paths, and these form the majority of employees and managers. This can cause demoralization for those excluded.

Recent developments, however, question the necessity of specifically designated high-flyer programmes, due to an unpredictable workplace, and constant structural changes (Peiperl and Baruch, 1997). Trends under way in the 1990s indicate that entrepreneurship competencies and less control and exercising power in bureaucratic systems will be required from the twenty-first century high-flyer. In a boundaryless organization, a boundaryless career is called for. **YB**

References and further reading

Derr, C. B., Jones, C. and Toomey, E. L. (1988) 'Managing high-potential employees: curent practices in 33 US corporations', *Human Resource Management* 27(3): 273–90.
London, M. and Stumpf, S. A. (1982) *Managing Careers*, Reading, MA: Addison-Wesley.
Peiperl, M. A. and Baruch, Y. (1997) 'Back to square zero: the post-corporate career', *Organization Dynamics* 25(4) Spring: 7–22.

Human capital theory

Human capital can be defined most simply as the skills a person has acquired from a period spent in education and training, or as a result of experience. The emphasis is placed on the *acquisition* of skills as distinct from a person's natural ability. As some initial investment has to be undertaken in order to develop skills, the creation of human capital can be analysed in a way analogous to the formation of fixed capital, and hence it is an application of standard capital theory.

Capital can be defined as a *stock* of assets that produces a *flow* of benefits over a period of time. All capital formation requires investment, i.e. costs are incurred in the present in order to yield future returns. In the same way, human capital investment incurs an initial investment or capital cost in the form of the costs of education and training courses (direct costs) and foregone income and output (indirect costs). The flow of benefits, or returns, is the increased productivity of workers over their working lives, resulting in higher output and lifetime earnings. Using standard capital theory techniques, this suggests that there are two equivalent approaches to measuring a worker's human capital. The first is that it is the cost of the initial investment in education and training. The second is that human capital is the discounted present value of the increase in earnings (or output) due to education and training over a working life. In equilibrium, the two should be equal as investment is profitable up to the point where the present value of returns is equal to the cost of the capital outlay. In practice, however, they may not be the same, in which case the present value approach is the preferred measure.

An alternative to measuring human capital in present value terms is to measure the rate of return to the initial investment, i.e. determining the (internal) rate of return that equates the present value of future returns with the capital cost. Estimates in the region of a personal rate of return to higher education of 12–20 per cent (UK government economists' estimates are even higher) have been used to support the shift from grants to loans to finance students in UK universities.

The principles of human capital theory were developed by the economists Gary Becker, Jacob Mincer and Theodore Schultz (the University of Chicago) in the late 1950s and early 1960s, although the initial ideas can be traced back at least to Adam Smith's *Wealth of Nations* (1776). The approach has been widely used in the analysis of labour market issues, and indeed, is probably now regarded as one of the standard tools of a labour market analyst. Applications are legion and include:

- explanations of wage differentials and the distribution of income
- contributions to the understanding of why firms train their employees and the types of training that will be provided
- the planning of education provision in developing countries
- explanations of, and providing a rationale for, personnel policies such as those designed to reduce turnover
- the understanding of why some countries grow faster than others.

In the application of human capital theory to training, a useful distinction introduced by Becker is that between training in *firm-specific* skills and *general* skills. As the former are specific to individual firms, it will be in each firm's interest not only to invest in their workers, but they will also be willing to reduce turnover, for example by sharing the training costs and the returns. General skills, however, are more problematic as they are skills that are of use to all firms. The onus will therefore be on individual workers to acquire these skills at their own expense. Many people, however, are unable to finance such training, either because they lack family resources or because financial markets are unwilling to finance human capital formation – unlike physical capital, human capital offers no collateral. This suggests that there is a strong rationale for the public finance and/or provision of general education and training on economic efficiency grounds as well as for the more familiar equity reasons. **SJ**

References and further reading

Hitt, M., Bierman, A., Shimizu, L. and Kochhar, R. (2001) 'Direct and moderating effects of human capital on strategy and performance in professional service firms', *Academy of Management Journal* 44(1): 13–30.

Johansen, K., Ringdal, K. and Thoring, T.A. (2001) 'Firm profitability, regional unemployment and human capital in wage determination', *Applied Economics*, 33(1): 113–25.

Stevens, M. (1999) 'Human capital theory and UK vocational training policy, *Oxford Review of Economic Policies* 15(1): 16–20.

Human relations approach

The human relations approach is one that emphasizes 'people, their feelings and attitudes' (Buchanan and Huczynski, 1997). Key policies include delegating authority, promoting trust and designing jobs that satisfy employees' needs and wants. This approach contrasts with theories of organizational behaviour that emphasize a system of hierarchical control, a division of labour and the separation of management and workers, as promoted by Fredrick Taylor's scientific management.

Human relations has informed management practice since the 1920 and 1930s. In Britain early studies of industrial psychology (Myers, 1929) were concerned with employee fatigue, boredom and long hours of work. During the inter-war years two agencies were established to advise on the psychological and physiological impact of workers' health and industrial efficiency – the Industrial Fatigue Research Board (IRFB) and the National Institute of Industrial Psychology (NIIP). By reducing weekly hours, it was found that output and productivity increased. However, the greatest influence on human relations was the Hawthorne experiments at the Western Electric Company in America (Mayo, 1933; Roethlisberger and Dickson, 1939). The major contribution of this research is the emphasis on 'group behaviour' which led management to consider the 'social' rather than purely 'economic' aspects of work motivation.

Rose (1988) comments that a significant contribution from the human relations camp is the analysis of 'face-to-face relationships' at workplace level. However, Rose (1988) also suggests one major flaw is that these relationships become the 'centre of attention', leading to a (mis)conception that group behaviour can be improved by management intervention alone. Moreover, human relations scholars often ignore the impact of other factors which influence group dynamics, such as technology, the role of trade unions and notions of a collective identity among workers themselves (Child, 1969; Buchanan and Huczynski, 1997). For Fox (1985), the theoretical base of the human relations approach supports a unitarist ideology through the image of a unified team: 'by means of suitably generous personnel polices they [managers] may wean their employees' loyalties away from union attachments' (Fox, 1985: 374). (See also **Hawthorne experiments**.) **TD**

References and further reading

Braverman, H. (1974) *Labour and Monopoly Capitalism*, New York: Monthly Review Press.
Buchanan, D. and Huczynski, A. (1997) *Organisational Behaviour*, 3rd edn, Harlow: Prentice Hall, ch. 7.
Child, J. (1969) *British Management Thought*, London: Allen and Urwin.
Fox, A. (1985) *Man Mis-Management*, London: Hutchinson.
Mayo, E. (1933) *The Human Problems of an Industrial Civilization*, New York: Macmillan.
Myers, C. (ed.) (1929) *Industrial Psychology*, London: Butterworth.
Roethlisberger, F. and Dickson, W. (1939) *Management and the Worker*, Boston, MA: Harvard University Press.
Rose, M. (1988) *Industrial Behaviour*, 2nd edn, Harmondsworth: Penguin.

Human resource development

Human resource development (HRD) is a critical organizational process in any enterprise. It is also a wide-ranging area of practice and of study extending beyond the world of business organizations. It has a complex interdisciplinary base, and has developed differentially across countries, workplaces and in academia. Within organizations, HRD involves the integration of learning and development processes, operations and relationships. Its most powerful strategic outcomes are to do with enhanced organizational effectiveness and sustainability. At the individual level, they are to do with improved personal competence, adaptability and employability.

Many argue that HRD is distinct from 'training' or 'employee development'. For them, 'training' is a short-term, operational activity, while 'employee development' gives too narrow a scope to the developmental process. Human resource development, on the other hand, involves the strategically focused management of learning across the organization for the longer term. It can extend to external stakeholders also in order to ensure that the organization's strategies are realised. Yet there is no consensus here. Some 'trainers' see themselves as HRD specialists; some with 'HRD' titles are in reality operational training practitioners; some see problematic legal implications involved in extending HRD to non-employees.

The theme of 'integration' signals further disputed territory. In one view, HRD belongs within the wider functional umbrella of human resource management, and should be aligned with other HRM policies and with the organization's strategic goals. In another, HRD has its own unique identity. Thus the mission statement of the UK-based University Forum for HRD refers to the strategic significance of organizational learning as a source of competitive advantage, and describes HRD practitioners as learning architects. Finally, for some the command to 'align with strategy' begs awkward questions: what strategy? Corporate or business unit? Short or long term? Feasible and relevant to organizational needs, or merely any strategy that is formally in place at the time?

During the process of revising national occupational standards for the year 2001 a new term – 'Learning and Development' – replaced the former term, 'Training and Development'. Its emergence there, and in the 2001 revised professional standards of the Chartered Institute of Personnel and Development (where it replaced 'Employee Development'), underlines the importance of continuous learning that is achieved through a wide spectrum of durable processes and activities. The Labour government's focus on 'lifelong learning' and national 'learning' (instead of 'training') targets carries a similar vital message. **RH**

References and further reading

Easterby-Smith, M., Artaujo, L. and Burgoyne, J. (eds) (1999) *Organizational Learning and the Learning Organization: Developments in Theory and Practice*, London: Sage.

Harrison, R. (2000) *People and organisations: Employee Development*, 2nd edn, London: Chartered Institute of Personnel and Development.

Sisson, K. and Storey, J. (2000) *The Realities of Human Resource Management: Managing the Employment Relationship*, Milton Keynes: Open University Press.

Stewart, J. (1999) *Employee Development Practice*, London: Financial Times Pitman Publishing.

Walton, J. (1999) *Strategic Human Resource Development*. London: Financial Times Prentice Hall.

Human resource information systems

A human resource (HR) information system is used to record and analyse information about employees (and sometimes about potential employees and ex-employees too). This can include systems for staff records, recruitment tracking, selection (including electronic scanning of CVs and on-screen testing), time recording, holidays, absence and turnover analysis, equal opportunities monitoring, expert job evaluation systems, wage modelling and benefits administration. Computer-based training may also be part of the HR system and the organization's intranet or e-mail system can be used as an important communication channel for policies, procedures and feedback.

Evidence on the use of HR systems is that these tend to be used to computerize information and speed up operational processes rather than to allow radical change in the roles of HR staff, and that there is still much scope to use HR systems at a more strategic level, enhancing the influence of HR on key decisions.

In designing or purchasing a system, key issues are the facility for flexible enquiries, and integration between systems holding different pieces of information, e.g. absence, sick pay and payroll, or recruitment and equal opportunities monitoring.

Legislation requires protection of data accuracy, access, privacy and security. One response to this is to offer individuals access to their own records, giving them the responsibility to ensure its accuracy. **JB**

References and further reading

Ball, K. (2000) 'Interface value', *People Management* 6(1), 6 January: 40–2.

Cooper, C. (2000) 'Live and Clicking', *People Management* 6(13) 22 June: 50–2.

Finn, W. (2000) 'Screen test', *People Management*, 6(13) 22 June: 38–43.

Industrial Relations Service (1992) 'Implementing computerised infromation systems: a challenge for management' Industrial Relations Review and Report: Employee Development Bulletin, no. 518, August.

Kinnie, N. and Arthurs, A. (1996) '"Personnel specialists" advanced use of information technology – evidence and explanations', *Personnel Review* 25(3): 3–19.

Kossek, E. E., Gash D. C. and Young W. (1994) 'Waiting for innovation in the human resources department: Godot implements a human resource information system', *Human Resource Management* 33(1), Spring: 135–59.

Merrick, N. (2000), 'Learning Zone', *People Management*, 6(13), 22 June: 44–8.

Richards Carpenter, C. (1996) 'Make a difference by doing I.T. better', *People Management*, 2(12), 13 June: 39–40.

Temperton E. (2000) 'How to monitor e-communication', *People Management*, 6(13), 22 June: 54–6.

Human resource management in Asia

The growth in both academic and practitioner interest in human resource management (HRM) in Asia is due to several reasons. There was the success of Asian 'tiger' economies and companies and their inward investment and transplant operations in other countries, while Western enterprises moved into newly industrializing Asian economies. For instance, ideas of Japanese management practices and 'Japanization' with its universalistic, 'best practice' and convergence overtones became popular. Many Asian companies were taken as role models and the perpetual search for the magic ingredient to success came to focus in part on their HRM policies and practices. The grouping of 'Asia' is commonly utilized as its economies are often taken as underpinned by common 'values' on the basis of spatial and seeming cultural proximity.

However, the analysis of HRM in Asia can be problematic. Using such a categorization may present partial views based on limited and stereotypical comparisons. HRM practices remain diverse both across and within its economies. While the traditional practices of Japan and Korea, such as lifetime employment, seniority pay, enterprise unionism, or China, such as the 'iron rice bowl' and 'one big pot', may be noted, even these are not as widespread as often presented and are under stress and change. Other economies, such as Thailand and Malaysia, have very different HRM practices from these and also internally between types of enterprise. Such intra-Asian differences stem from several factors. These include political and socio-economic development as well as culture and institutions. While some common destinations, such as deregulation and liberalization, may be evident, the terrain on which these traverse remains diverse and this impacts on patterns of HRM. Thus, despite spatial closeness and some superficial cultural similarities, HRM in Asia remains variable. Nevertheless, HRM in the region remains a fascinating, important and dynamic area. **CR**

References and further reading

Bamber, G. Park, F. Lee, C. Ross, P. and Broadbent, K. (eds) (2000) *Employment Relations in the Asian-Pacific*, London: Thomson Learning.

Bhopal, M. and Rowley, C. (2000) 'Putting the State(s) Back Into Employee Relations: The Case of Malaysian Electronics', *IERA Conference Proceedings*.

Rowley, C. (ed) (1998) *Human Resource Management in the Asia Pacific Region: Convergence Questioned*, London: Cass.

Rowley, C. and Benson, J. (eds) (2000) *Globalisation and Labour in the Asia Pacific Region*, London: Cass.

Rowley, C. and Benson, J. (2001) 'Convergence and Divergence in Asian HRM', *Conference Paper*.

Verma, A.; Kochan, T. and Lansbury, R. (eds) (1995) *Employment Relations in the Growing Asian Economies*, London: Routledge.

Human resource management in Europe

Human resource management (HRM), which emerged from the USA, is a recent phenomenon in Europe. Its adoption has been relatively slow and varies from one national and regional context to another. The variation of national institutions, business systems and culture has influenced the style and approach of HRM policies and practices across Europe. In Germany for example, the label 'human resource management' has yet to surpass 'personnel management' in terms of popular usage in organizations whereas in the UK the term is virtually ubiquitous.

Research in over 20 European countries (within and outside the European Union) in the Price Waterhouse Cranfield Surveys on Strategic HRM (1990–99) (PWC) indicates an increase in what can be termed human resource (HR) practices and practices associated with HRM. Nearly all countries, for example, show a rise in the use of flexible working practices. Flexibility is on the increase in its 'newer' forms (functional and contractual) and is increasing in its older forms (overtime and part-time working). The growth of flexible working practices is not homogenous across Europe and evidence indicates the strong influence of institutional and ideological factors. These institutional factors include the history and development of employment customs and practices as embodied in national and European Union law. Thus numerical flexibility is more likely to be used in the UK where it is easier to legally dismiss staff than in Sweden, Germany and many other European countries where downsizing practices are highly regulated. A case in point is the recent proposed closure of car plants in the UK by General Motors and Ford instead of closing plants in other parts of Europe. Functional flexibility on the other hand is more efficiently practised in Germany where it is supported by national vocational educational and training systems such as the dual training system. This is evidenced in high productivity levels.

Flexibility also reflects ideological concerns about regulated and deregulated labour markets. Should Europe emulate the American model of low regulation with its reduction in worker protections in terms of employment security? Advocates of this idea claim resulting lower unemployment levels. Should a greater degree of regulation prevail as in Germany, France and Spain although unemployment is much higher than in the USA and the UK? Various UK governments during the 1980s and 1990s have promoted the adoption of the American model although there is much resistance by member states within the European Union who have advocated approaches to long-term unemployment by measures proposed within the Amsterdam Treaty. This is a nod in the direction of more entreprenurialism by starting small and medium-sized businesses backed by training and equal opportunities policies.

There has also been a notable increase in training and development as managers within organizations perceive the need for a more skilled and educated workforce prompted by shortage of employees in crucial areas. This is supported by European policy directives and various national initiatives.

The PWC data also indicates a notable increase in forms of organizational communication including employee participation and involvement schemes, many strongly associated with HR strategies. These are partly used to bind the employee to the organization's goals and values by imbuing high commitment, and also to undermine other forms of communication by independent bodies such as trade unions, some critics maintain. This has been counteracted to some degree by European Union (and existing national) policy on works councils.

Perceptions are that HR practices will continue to be adopted across Europe although not in their purely American form, as many American multinational companies operating in the Europe have come to realize. **LH**

References and further reading
Brewster, C. and Harris, H. (eds) (1999) *International HRM: Contemporary Issues in Europe*, London: Routledge.
Brewster, C. and Hegewisch, A. (eds) (1994) *Policy and Practice in European Human Resource Management*, London: Routledge.
Brewster, C., Mayrhofer, W. and Morley, M. (eds) (2000) *New Challenges for European Human Resource Management*, Basingstoke: Macmillan.
Clark, T. (ed.) (1996) *European Human Resource Management*, Oxford: Blackwell.
Ferner, A. and Hyman, R. (1997) *Industrial Relations in the New Europe*, 2nd edn, Oxford: Blackwell.
Hyman, R. and Ferner, A. (1998) *New Frontiers in European Industrial Relations*, 2nd edn, Oxford: Blackwell.
Leat, M. (1998) *Human Resource Issues of the European Union*, London: Financial Times Pitman Publishing.
Sparrow, P. and Hiltrop, J. (1994) *European Human Resource Management in Transition*, London: Prentice Hall.

Human resource management in Japan

Japanese organizations have always placed great importance on human resources, hence the saying, 'people are a castle'. Historically, group-oriented culture was evident in agricultural villages and employees are encouraged to have a similar group commitment to the organization. A key aspect of the Japanese approach to human resource management (HRM) is based on the internalization of labour markets. One company effectively means one labour market. New graduates are hired from different levels of schools, which lead to promotional ladders, however, different ladders are sometimes set for different genders. On-the-job training, frequent transfers and job rotation help to foster employees' general capacity and skills base. Lifetime employment, seniority/age-based pay system, company welfare, short vacations and information sharing between management and employees are common human resource (HR) policies and practices. Behavioral outcomes are seen as including strong motivation, improved skills, self-managed teamwork, positive organizational commitment, low employee turnover, low absenteeism, few violations of working rules and industrial peace.

The ideas of Japanese management practice were highly valued in the 1980s (see **Japanization**), however the external environment changed in 1990s and the 'Japanese way' failed in terms of economic growth. Globalization of markets and the ageing of human resources brought about a need to restructure the system. There are two views on the way forward for HRM in Japan: one is to induce a market mechanism in labour markets, and the other is to maintain the traditional way of Japanese HRM. The idea of lifetime employment is still supported by many employers and employees. Recruitment of new graduates and in-house training is still a common practice. Japanese business organizations are now trying to survive and to raise the return on investment by restructuring, e.g. flattening, outsourcing, deregulation of rules and diversified patterns of employment are now on the increase. This way leads to more unstable employment. However, companies are also trying to solve some of the problems by the reallocation of human resources under the umbrella of a company group. **YS**

References and further reading
Benson, J. and Deboux, P. (1997) 'HRM in Japanese enterprises: trends and challenges', *Asia Pacific Business Review* 3(4): 62–81.
Kim, B. W. (1992) *Seniority Wage Systems in the Far East*, Aldershot: Avebury.
Sako, M. and Sato, H. (1997) *Japanese Labour and Management in Transition: Diversity, Flexibility and Participation*, London: Routledge.
Sano, Y., Morishima, M. and Seike, A. (eds) (1997) *Frontiers of Japanese Human Resource Practices*, Tokyo: Japan Institute of Labour.
Shimizu, R. (1994) *Japanese Management Features*, Tokyo: Keio University Press.

Human resource management in the USA

The dominant theme in American literature on human resource management (HRM) has been that competitive advantage stems from the quality of labour inputs and the way they are organized and managed. The orthodox position is that new technologies and systems of work organization allow firms to achieve significant improvements in labour productivity if managers can obtain a high level of co-operation from employees. Human resource management has therefore been seen to consist of a combination of policies aimed at eliciting this. Its key elements are identified as teamworking and job enrichment, wider forms of employee involvement such as briefing and problem-solving groups, heavy investments in training, employment security provisions and internal promotion opportunities. During the 1990s firms have increasingly adopted new forms of work organization involving quality circles and total quality management, self-managed work teams, job rotation and the use of managers in a facilitating role. They have also introduced policies of wider employee involvement. However, these changes have also been linked to corporate 'downsizing' and moves towards 'lean production', so that employment security provisions and internal promotion opportunities have been curtailed as firms have reduced staff and made more use of contingent labour.

Human resource management has often been portrayed as a 'win-win' solution to the management of the employment relationship. Proponents argue that owners and managers benefit from the impact of higher labour productivity on market share and profitability. Employees gain more interesting work, better pay, employment security, and training and promotion opportunities. This claim is only partly borne out by research evidence. While workers appear to value opportunities to exercise autonomy and responsibility in their tasks there is little evidence that management shares productivity gains with the workforce. Firms that introduce new forms of work organization are more likely than others to cut jobs and are no more likely than others to raise wages. This raises the question of how the high levels of co-operation required by new systems of working are maintained. Possible explanations include greater intrinsic benefits from work arising from increased autonomy, responsibility and involvement, fear of job loss in the wake of widespread organizational restructuring during the 1990s and reduced expectations of job security, especially among new entrants to the labour market. **TC**

References and further reading
Appalbaum, E. and Blatt, R. (1994) *The New American Workplace,* Ithaca, NY: Cornell University Press.
Cappelli, P., Bassi, L., Katz, H., Knoke, D., Osterman, P. and Useem, M. (1997) *Change at Work,* Oxford: Oxford University Press.
Kochan, T. and Osterman, P. (1994) *The Mutual Gains Enterprise*: *Forging a Winning Partnership among Labor, Management, and Government*, Boston, MA: Harvard Business School Press.
Osterman, P. (1999) *Securing Prosperity. The American Labor Market*: *How It Has Changed and What to Do about It,* Princeton, NJ: Princeton University Press.

Human resource planning

Human resource (HR) planning involves seeking a match between the demand for and supply of people in each of an organization's main job/skill categories. Traditionally, the aim was to anticipate and so avoid HR shortages and surpluses and to minimize the need for ad hoc adjustments. In addition, modern HR planning seeks an alignment of HR policies and practices with the strategic priorities of the organization (Walker, 1990; Bechet and Walker, 1993).

Forecasts of demand may be based on anticipated levels of activity, as reflected in the business plan. Human resource requirements may be forecast subjectively, using managers' estimates based on past experience and consideration of future business plans, or more formally using quantitative workload forecasts or time-series analysis. In practice, forecasting demand tends to combine elements of judgement and quantitative modelling. Supply may be projected following an analysis of wastage, retirement, promotion and of trends in the external labour market. In some organizations, internal supply forecasting involves the development of box-flow models of HR movements, based on Markov or replacement analysis. In such models, the flows into and out of each HR category are modelled, to predict staffing flows and levels. In the UK, this approach is epitomized by the computerized models developed by the then Institute of Manpower Studies at Sussex University (e.g. Bennison and Casson, 1984). A simple do-it-yourself approach to box-flow planning models is explained in Malloch (1988).

Organizations also attempt to plan for staff succession in key management and technical or professional positions. Succession planning involves identifying potential successors for key positions from within the organization. Information may be collected on those candidates who are available to fill specific positions immediately, or in a specified time frame. Linked to a forward-looking development programme, such an approach can be useful in helping to make sure that future needs are properly anticipated and met.

On the basis of demand and supply forecasts, a human resource management strategic plan can be drawn up, designed to reconcile demand and supply in each of the main job or skill categories. Such a plan shows how the matching of demand and supply of labour is to be achieved: by recruitment, internal development, redundancies or transfers. How this is achieved will have implications for HR policies, including training and development programmes, performance appraisal and remuneration. It is vital that the planning exercise feeds into action plans for each of the key HR functions. In the past, HR planners have often been accused of drawing up sophisticated human resource plans, which are then largely ignored. It is vital that HR planning is used as a tool to aid decision-making, and for this to occur it must involve line managers in the collection and analysis of data, and the production of analyses which inform HR decisions. The emphasis should be on interpretability and involvement, rather than necessarily on the pursuit of forecasting sophistication for its own sake.

However, human resource planning techniques are not used universally, and many managers question the utility of detailed forecasts in an uncertain environment. Certainly, managers' interest in human resource planning has varied over the years, as the problems faced by organizations have changed (Smith and Bartholomew, 1988). 'Manpower' planning was thus a topic of great interest in the 1960s and 1970s in the UK, when labour shortages and then restructuring were on the agenda, and the later 1980s saw a resurgence of interest, this time in 'human resource' planning, not least because of the projected shortages of young people due to the so-called 'demographic time bomb' (see, for example: Bell, 1989). From today's point of view, it is sometimes argued that such a planning approach may pose problems for organizations faced with rapid change and the need to adapt quickly, since the process concentrates on the current job, rather than on future skills needs. Using this argument, HR planning appears more suited to stable bureaucracies, rather than to the flexible, fast-changing organization.

In recent years, human resource planning has begun to place less emphasis on detailed matching of supply and demand and sophisticated quantitative forecasting techniques. Greater attention has instead been given to changes in the external environment and their implications for the organization, to the HR implications of corporate and business strategies, and to human resource development. The aim has been to move away from the abstract mathematical planning approaches of the past, which often sought to generate detailed quantitative forecasts of supply and demand over the long term, towards a more relevant approach which focuses on short-and medium-term HR decision-making, perhaps concentrating on key issues facing the organization at any one time (e.g. Walker, 1990; Rothwell, 1995). The focus of HR planning is now on identifying the HR implications of business scenarios, and the aim is to assist in the execution of corporate strategies (Bechet and Walker, 1993). Arguments over terminology may be considered arcane, but this shift towards a more qualitative approach is for many what distinguishes traditional 'manpower planning' from what we now call 'human resource planning'. **ES**

References and further reading

Bechet, T. P. and Walker, J. W. (1993) 'Aligning staffing with business strategy', *Human Resource Planning* 16(2): 1–16.

Bell, D. (1989) 'Why manpower planning is back in vogue', *Personnel Management*, July: 40–3.

Bennison, M. and Casson, J. (1984) *The Manpower Planning Handbook*, Maidenhead: McGraw-Hill.

Malloch, H. (1988) 'Evaluating strategies on a cost-based manpower planning model', *Personnel Review* 17(3): 22–8.

Rothwell, S. (1995) 'Human resource planning', in J. Storey, (ed.) *Human Resource Management: A Critical Text*, London: Routledge.

Smith, A. R. and Bartholomew, D. J. (1988) 'Manpower planning in the UK: an historical review', *Journal of the Operational Research Society* 39(3): 235–48.

Walker, W. (1990) 'Human resource planning, 1990s style', *Human Resource Planning* 13(4): 229–40.

Incentive pay

Incentive pay can be in many different forms, containing variations within each type. Some of the most common are:

- Piecework schemes, in which employees are paid for the number of items they produce, with pay being proportional to output.
- Work-measured schemes, in which a bonus is added to an employee's basic rate of pay upon reaching a given target.
- Measured daywork, which ties pay to long-term, previously-agreed, levels of performance.
- Gainsharing, in which employees share in the financial gains and efficiency savings made by the company.
- Team bonuses which are paid to a team or department which achieves its targets.
- Multi-factor schemes which take more than one measure of performance in order to calculate bonuses. This enables the scheme to encompass a wider range of business objectives, such as teamworking, response times, quality and customer service, as well as short-term financial and productivity goals.

Incentive schemes can be designed to achieve specific and changing business objectives. The aim is to measure those aspects of performance which are important to the organization and over which the employee has a reasonable amount of control. These schemes can help focus employees' efforts on long-term business priorities or on short-term targets. In some cases they play a part in recruiting and retaining staff.

All incentive schemes incur costs in setting them up and running them, so it is essential that the expected benefits and better performance will outweigh the greater costs. Problems may arise where employees seek to exploit weaknesses in a scheme in order to maximize their earnings or ignore important aspects of their work in order to concentrate solely on those targets which are rewarded. **AA**

References and further reading
Armstrong, M. and Murlis, H. (1998) *Reward Management*, 4th edn, London: Kogan Page.
Bloom, M. C. and Milkovich, G. T. (1998) 'Relationships among risk, incentive pay, and organizational performance', *Academy of Management Journal* 41: pp. 283–97.
Cannell, M. and Wood, S. (1992) *Incentive Pay*, London: Institute of Personnel Management.
Incomes Data Services (IDS) (1999) 'Bonus schemes', IDS Studies, 665, March.
White, G. and Drucker, J. (2000) *Reward Management: A Critical Text*, London: Routledge.

Incomes policy

Incomes policies are introduced by governments in order to control rising wages and salaries and thereby help restrain inflationary pay rises. During times of national emergency, particularly wartime, where overriding national interest can be invoked, incomes policies have had some impact. At other times the goals of such policies are rarely achieved, except in the very short term.

All incomes policies contain an element of rough justice. Those who have just had a pay rise will be content, whilst those who have missed the cut-off may feel unfairly treated. More sophisticated policies attempt to include some flexibility, allowing pay rises for exceptional circumstances. These circumstances have to be carefully defined to prevent them becoming a reason for everyone to be treated as an exception.

Equity provides one reason for exceptional treatment. The lowest paid are particularly vulnerable to a wage freeze and therefore exceptions may be made on the grounds that wage levels are too low to maintain a reasonable standard of living. Another case for exceptions can be where there is widespread recognition that the pay of a certain group of workers has fallen out of line with the level of pay for similar work and needs 'in the national interest' to be improved. However, public support may erode quickly if a particularly powerful group of workers breaches the pay norm or where other incomes, such as fees and dividends, evade control.

Exceptional treatment may also be justified on economic grounds. An incomes policy, whilst seeking to restrain pay, must take account of wider economic goals and the need for a thriving, growing economy. It needs to allow pay rises where they are necessary to attract and retain workers or as an incentive to improve productivity.

In Britain several attempts at an incomes policy were made between the 1940s and 1970s. Since then direct control of pay rises has been abandoned, partly because pay rises have ceased to be seen as the major reason for economic problems and partly on ideological grounds. During the 1980s free-market ideas became the dominant ideology in many industrial countries and this philosophy is not consistent with government control of pay in the private sector. **AA**

References and further reading

Clegg, H. (1971) *How to Run an Incomes Policy and Why We Made Such a Mess of the Last One*, London: Heinemann Educational Books.

Clegg, H. (1982) 'Reflections on incomes policy and the public sector in Britain', *Labour and Society* 7: 3–12.

Fallick, J. L. and Elliott, R. F. (eds) (1981) *Incomes Policies, Inflation and Relative Pay*, London: Allen and Unwin.

Individualism

As the 1980s and 1990s unfolded the rather static notion of relatively stable 'types' of employment relations gave way to the idea that a crucial dynamic was under way entailing a wholesale shift from collectivist arrangements (union-negotiated standard terms and conditions) to more individually tailored ones (individual target setting, evaluation and reward). Individualism and collectivism are thus terms used to capture management style in employee relations (Purcell, 1987).

Individualism in industrial relations involves managers asserting the individual nature of the contractual relationship between employer and employee enshrined in eighteenth-century labour law (Lukes, 1973) rather than managing with trade unions. In terms of specific human resource (HR) policies individualism is used to refer to such features as individualized appraisal, individual accountability and a general departure from common standardized rules agreed with trade unions. The increased use of such policies is taken to represent the individualization of employment. Marchington and Parker (1990) pointed out that individualization might not mean just decollectivization and a shift to differentiated employment terms and conditions but could also entail an investment approach to employees.

After initially nuancing Fox's (1974) analysis of 'unitarism' and 'pluralism', Purcell (1987), Purcell and Sisson (1983) and Purcell and Ahlstrand (1994) outlined various combinations of individualism and collectivism in employment policies and practices. Likewise, others have attempted to clarify the multiple manifestations of individual and collective practices across the interrelated domains of industrial relations, work organization and personnel policies (Storey and Bacon, 1993) suggesting managers may simultaneously pursue individualism in work design and personnel procedures while maintaining collective relations with trade unions. (See also **Collectivism**.) **NB**

References and further reading

Bacon, N. and Storey, J. (2000) 'New employee relations strategies in Britain: Towards individualism or partnership?', *British Journal of Industrial Relations* 38(3): 407–27.

Evans, S. and Hudson, M. (1993) 'From collective bargaining to personal contracts: the case studies in port transport and electricity supplies', *Industrial Relations Journal* 25: 305–14.

Flanders, A. (1970) *Management and Unions*: *The Theory and Reform of Industrial Relations*, London: Faber.

Fox, A. (1974) *Beyond Contract*: *Work, Power and Trust Relations,* London: Faber and Faber.

Kessler, I. and Purcell, J. (1995) 'Individualism and collectivism in theory and practice: management style and the design of pay systems', in P. Edwards (ed.) *Industrial Relations*: *Theory and Practice in Britain*, Oxford: Blackwell.

Lukes, S. (1973) *Individualism*, Oxford: Blackwell.

Marchington, M. and Parker, P. (1990) *Changing Patterns of Employee Relations,* Hemel Hempstead: Harvester Wheatsheaf.

Purcell, J. (1987) 'Mapping management styles in employee relations', *Journal of Management Studies* 24: 533–48.

Purcell, J. (1991) 'The rediscovery of management prerogative: the management of labour relations in the 1980s', *Oxford Review of Economic Policy* 7: 33–43.

Purcell, J. and Ahlstrand, B. (1994) *Human Resource Management in the Multi-Divisional Company*, Oxford: Oxford University Press.

Purcell, J. and Sisson, K. (1983) 'Strategies and practice in the management of industrial relations', in G. Bain (ed.) *Industrial Relations in Britain*: *Past Trends and Future Prospects*, Oxford: Blackwell.

Storey, J. and Bacon, N. (1993) 'Individualism and collectivism: into the 1990s', *International Journal of Human Resource Management* 4: 665–84.

Induction

The word 'induction' is derived from the Latin word 'inductus', which means 'led in'. In human resource management terms, *induction* is the term we use to describe the initial introduction of a new employee to an organization, or an existing employee into a part of the organization that is new to him or her.

The purpose of induction is twofold. First, it introduces new people to their workplace, colleagues, job, aims and objectives of the organizations and to systems and procedures. Second, it should be the start the learning process by helping them to begin to understand and interact with the organization's culture, values and norms of behaviour.

Induction can be both formal and informal. Whether or not an organization has an induction policy, new employees will still be 'inducted' by the very fact of their arrival at, and their initial period in, their new jobs. So in a sense, induction of some sort or other is unavoidable when organizations take on new staff. However, most organizations try to ensure that the entry of staff into their new environment is a positive one, by organizing introductions and initial instruction and, possibly, also a formal induction course. In this latter case, organizations usually gather groups of new starters together and run courses of one or two days duration, or even longer, either periodically or when demand exists. Induction courses usually consist of a mixture of events, some designed to impart information about the organization, its products or services, and its values and intentions, and some designed to promote the formation of interpersonal relationships and networks that will benefit the new employees in the time ahead. Some activities may be included that aim to develop specific skills and competences. Better designs will make sure that the learning is learner-centred, and encourage the start of a self-development process.

Induction programmes consisting of formal and informal methods can last for up to six months, with regular checks of progress and achievement throughout. The process can be enhanced by the use of mentors, who can act as counsellors and role models for new recruits.

Of course, such provision is expensive. However, research has shown that new employees are at high risk of leaving in the early stages of their employment, the so-called '*induction crisis*'. The potential for sound induction policies and procedures to make an impact on costs by reducing unnecessary staff wastage and avoiding expensive repeat recruitment and selection activities. **LS**

References and further reading

Anakwe, P. and Greenhaus, J. (1999) 'Effective socialization of employees', *Journal of Managerial Issues* 11(3): 315–27.

Fowler, A. (1999) *Induction*, London: IPD.

Klein, H. and Weaver, N. (2000) 'The effectiveness of an organizational level orientation training programme in the socialization of new hires', *Personnel Psychology* 53(1): 47–67.

Skeats, J. (1991) *Successful Induction*, London: Kogan Page.

Industrial conflict

The popular conception of industrial conflict is to equate it with industrial action, and strikes in particular. Sociological interpretations of the term typically adopt a broader view, taking into account both organized (or collective) and unorganized (or individual) expressions of conflict at work (e.g. Edwards and Scullion, 1982). Therefore conflict might be expressed not only through industrial action, but also through lockouts, union derecognition, the incidence of grievance, disciplinary and employment tribunal cases, absenteeism, labour turnover, sabotage and theft at work, poor morale and motivation, confrontational management behaviour, bullying and harassment. Narrow definitions of industrial conflict suggest that there is a growing consensus in the workplace, in light of the substantial decline in strike activity in the 1980s and 1990s. Broader definitions of conflict, however, indicate a shift from collective to individual expressions of it, rather than a decline in conflict per se; and the increased incidence of industrial tribunal cases (renamed employment tribunals in 1998) can be cited in support of this (Blyton and Turnbull, 1998: 157).

Another dimension of these broader approaches is the need to focus upon the causes of such varied expressions of conflict, and whether conflict at work is relatively exceptional or more deeply rooted within capitalist society. Managerial interpretations often suggest that conflict at work is negative and irrational, and convey it as a problem to be solved. Clearly, industrial action, absenteeism, sabotage and theft at work, poor motivation and high labour turnover do pose problems for management which it cannot afford to ignore. However, managerial interpretations commonly deny the perception of workers involved in conflict at work, and indeed collective or individual expressions of conflict may be perceived by employees as positive and meaningful resistance to an oppressive work regime (Hyman, 1989). Therefore, widely used in both everyday and academic debates, the concept of industrial conflict may mean different things in different contexts, and it may conceal a number of important assumptions which it would be better to make explicit. (See also **Strikes**.) **DB**

References and further reading
Blyton, P. and Turnbull, P. (1998) *The Dynamics of Employee Relations*, 2nd edn, London: Macmillan, ch. 10.
Cully, M., Woodland, S., O'Reilly, A. and Dix, G. (1999) *Britain at Work*: *As Depicted by the 1998 Workplace Employee Relations Survey*, London: Routledge, pp. 124–36, 245.
Edwards, P. K. (1992) 'Industrial conflict: themes and issues in recent research', *British Journal of Industrial Relations* 30(3): 361–404.
Edwards, P. K. and Scullion, H. (1982) *The Social Organisation of Industrial Conflict*, Oxford: Blackwell.
Hyman, R. (1989) *The Political Economy of Industrial Relations*: *Theory and Practice in a Cold Climate*, London: Macmillan, ch. 4.
Labour Research Department (2000) 'See you in court, say unions', *Labour Research* 89(2): 17–18.

Injunctions

An injunction is an order of the court forbidding a particular action or ordering that it shall cease, for example, unlawful strike action or solicitation of a former employer's customers in breach of a valid restraint clause (see **Non-compete clauses**). As an 'equitable' legal remedy, however, it is discretionary and will be granted only where damages would not adequately remedy the injured party. In fact, because legal actions tend to take so long to come to trial, what is normally sought by the employer is an 'interim' or 'interlocutory' injunction, which has the effect of maintaining the status quo until the full trial takes place.

In order to obtain an interim injunction, the employer, as the plaintiff, has to show that the claim is not frivolous or vexatious and that there is a serious issue to be tried. The court then considers the 'balance of convenience' before making the order and this normally means weighing up whether, if the injunction is not granted, the employer will be adequately compensated by damages if successful at the eventual trial. In practice, the granting of an interlocutory injunction in the context of strike action generally means that the case proceeds no further.

On the basis that contracts of employment should not be enforced against the wishes of the parties to it, an employee facing a wrongful dismissal should not be able to obtain an injunction to prohibit the dismissal, but only damages in compensation. However, from time to time injunctions have been granted to prevent a dismissal taking place other than in accordance with the contractual disciplinary procedure. In such cases the crucial question is usually whether the relationship of mutual trust and confidence remains, in the sense that if an injunction were to be granted, a workable situation would arise. This might be so, for example, where the employee remained suspended whilst the proper procedure was carried out. **JE**

References and further reading
American Cyanamid Co v. *Ethicon* [1975] 1 All ER 504.
Jones v. *Lee* [1980] ICR 310.
Peace v. *City of Edinburgh Council* [1999] IRLR 417.
Robb v. *London Borough of Hammersmith & Fulham* [1991] IRLR 73.
Wadcock v. *London Borough of Brent* [1990] IRLR 223.

Institutional theory and human resource management

Institutional theory and approaches are an important supplement to others, such as convergence, contingency and culture, which have been usefully applied to the human resource management (HRM) area. Institutional theory argues that traditional values and practices, such as HRM, are embedded in a country's social and economic institutions. It is argued that we cannot examine separate aspects of a system without locating it in its specific societal context. Thus, the success of economies is not attributable simply to cultural forces, such as a strong 'work ethic' and 'discipline'. Rather, institutional factors can be seen as influential. For example, in Japan government support through various agencies, such as the Ministry of International Trade and Industry, substantial enterprise training and consultative practices, underpinned economic success. Likewise, Korea's economic development was fostered not just by so-called 'Asian values', but institutional elements such as the creation, development, direction, control and availability of a skilled workforce, finance, markets and enterprises. Human resource management differences can be explained by variables such as educational and training systems and the nature of business organizations and structure. Therefore, culture on its own is not enough, it needs to be rooted in the social and economic structure of a given society.

Institutional theory has been criticized. First, it tends to present a static view of a national industrial 'order' and 'league' and there is little account of how change comes about. Therefore, how are the shifting competitiveness rankings of countries be explained? Second, it fails to sufficiently recognize that divergent and contradictory ranges of practices may well exist and continue within one society. Finally, little attention is paid to the state's nature and changing role, a key element in many systems. Nevertheless, institutional theory remains important to balance overly culturalist approaches and insights to explaining particular patterns of HRM and possible convergence or divergence. **CR**

References and further reading

Maurice, M., Sellier, F. and Silvestre, J. J. (1986) *The Social Foundations of Industrial Power*, Cambridge, MA: MIT Press.

Morishima, M. (1995) 'Embedding HRM in a social context', *British Journal of Industrial Relations*, 33(4): 617–40.

Rowley, C. (ed.) (1998) *Human Resource Management in the Asia Pacific Region*: *Convergence Questioned*, London: Cass.

Rowley, C. and Benson, J. (eds) (2000) *Globalisation and Labour in the Asia Pacific Region*, London: Cass.

Integrative bargaining

The term 'integrative bargaining' is used in industrial relations to refer to the sub-process of negotiations where managers and employee representatives engage in joint problem-solving activities (Walton and McKersie, 1965). It requires both sides to exchange information and seek solutions in a co-operative and open-ended manner. This usually occurs on issues where mutual gains or a win-win outcome are possible. For example, where managers seek greater flexibility in the working patterns of employees and unions require increased job security an integrative approach to problem solving may be possible (Kochan and Osterman, 1994). A wide variety of topics may be referred to as integrative bargaining issues for example, training, product quality, employee involvement and customer service (Walton, Cutcher-Gershenfeld and McKersie, 1994: 3). These issues are frequently a part of partnership agreements between managers and trade unions. Integrative bargaining is usefully contrasted with distributive bargaining in which one side benefits at the expense of another in a fixed-sum game (see Burchill, 1999). **NB**

References and further reading

Burchill, F. (1999) 'Walton and McKersie, a behavioural theory of labor negotiations (1965)', *Historical Studies in Industrial Relations* 8: 137–68.

Kochan, T. and Osterman, P. (1994) *The Mutual Gains Enterprise*, Boston, MA: Harvard Business School Press.

Walton, R., Cutcher-Gershenfeld, J. and McKersie, R. (1994) *Strategic Negotiations*, Boston, MA: Harvard Business School Press.

Walton, R. and McKersie, R. (1965) *A Behavioural Theory of Labor Negotiations*, Ithaca, NY: ILR Press.

Interim management

The managerial 'temp' is a comparatively recent development in the UK. The agencies which provide this service usually refer to it as 'interim management' or 'executive leasing', or in the picturesque language of North America, 'head-renting'. This approach to resourcing managers was imported into the UK in the 1980s and, although it has been generally slower to take off here than in other European countries such as Holland, it is said to be growing rapidly.

One of the key advantages claimed for the use of interims is the fact that they can be supplied quickly, within five to 15 days. Some organizations use interims as a stop-gap whilst a more permanent manager is being sought. This takes the time pressure off a search and avoids mistakes being made through undue haste. Interim managers may be used where vacancies suddenly arise due to death, sickness or termination, or where a particular one-off need arises. The latter include mergers, acquisitions, management buyouts, relocations, privatizations and recruitment drives.

Some have argued that a growth in the leasing of managers is a deliberate policy decision of employers to introduce a form of numerical flexibility into a hitherto core group. However, some organizations appear to be using interims instead of management consultants rather than at the expense of permanent managers. Management consultants have been the traditional source of numerical flexibility at the management level in the UK, and we may simply be seeing the substitution of one flexible resource for another. Relative cost may provide one explanation for the increased use of managerial leasing at the expense of consultants, with the average cost of an interim manager being a half to two-thirds lower than the average consultancy fee. Another claimed advantage of interims is that there is less distance between the client and the interim than that between client and consultant. The management consultant's role is more one of an 'off-line adviser' and is seen as providing the user with alternatives. The interim by contrast is more involved, not only in making decisions but also in implementing them.

Compared to permanent managers, interims allow savings on pension, social and termination costs. However, there is a potential downside to the use of interims. They may lack involvement in the client organization's culture. This has the potential to produce a 'not invented here syndrome' and a neglect of cultural issues in decision implementation. There may also be problems of acceptability where permanent employees report to an interim manager, particularly if the interim has to take some tough decisions. Another potential problem is the issue of confidentiality. It could be argued, however, that this issue is no more pronounced for the interim than the consultant or permanent employee and even less so than for the latter group, as any breach of confidentiality could amount to professional suicide for the interim, who needs to maintain a good reputation to ensure future hires. Probably the most serious problem for managerial leasing agencies to overcome is the image of interims as out of work, unemployable managers 'resting' between real jobs. **TR**

References and further reading
Goss, D. and Bridson, J. (1998) 'Understanding interim management', *Human Resource Management Journal* 8(4): 37–50.
Houlder, V. (1997) 'When even the boss is a temp (usage of interim management)', *Financial Times,* 11 August: 8.
Redman, T. and Snape, E. (1992) 'Managers for hire: the use of interim management', *Recruitment Selection and Retention* 2(2): 3–7.
Sasseen, J. (1992) 'Brief encounters management', *International Management* 47(8): 44–6.

Internal labour markets

An organization operates an internal labour market (ILM) when the principal employment policies for all or a significant proportion of its employees are determined by administrative rules and procedures rather than by reference to external market conditions. These procedures may refer to a number of areas including the allocation of employees to jobs, the determination of rates of pay and the training and promotion of workers. The characteristic features of an ILM include:

- limited ports of entry, i.e. points at which the organization recruits
- a well-defined career ladder
- the filling of posts by internal promotion
- pay scales set by job evaluation
- the operation of seniority rules.

In the limit, an ILM becomes a 'job for life' policy. An ILM therefore contrasts with the traditional (neo-classical) model of the employment relationship – the 'hire and fire' model – in which pay and other aspects of employment are determined by the supply and demand for labour in the labour market as a whole. An estimate for the UK put the proportion of employees in an ILM at 46 per cent (Siebert and Addison, 1991).

The main inspiration for the analysis of ILMs came from Doeringer and Piore's (1971) book, *Internal Labor Markets and Manpower Analysis*. In explaining the development of an in-firm labour market, they emphasized the importance a stable demand for the firm's product and a stable technology. This produces employment conditions in which customs develop and social and ethical factors begin to override economic factors in determining employment relations. Similarly, ILMs may also develop in firms where there is strong trade union representation and also in pubic sector organizations that are insulated from market pressures. These explanations of the existence of ILMs stress the non-competitive aspects of labour market behaviour, and thus question the relevance of traditional economic models.

Subsequent analysis has extended the theoretical explanation of ILM. One important contribution, from Osterman (1987), suggests that firms exercise a choice over the use if ILM arrangements. They may in fact choose to employ part of their workforce in the ILM and part in which employment relations are determined by market conditions. Another approach has been to demonstrate that there is no conflict between the traditional cost minimizing – profit maximizing behaviour of firms and the use of ILMs. In fact, an ILM may be an optimum response to particular employment conditions. The main explanations include some of the following:

1. *Firm-specific skills*: high levels of firm-specific skills and high training costs in their acquisition mean that firms are keen to retain employees and to keep down turnover rates. This is particularly important if skills are acquired through on-the-job training.
2. *Information asymmetries*: there is also the problem of employees having a greater knowledge of their jobs than employers do. Consequently, employment contracts will be incomplete and there is the risk that employees will engage in opportunistic behaviour to the detriment of the employers. In response employers offer ILM arrangements in return for co-operation.
3. *Deferred compensation*: ILMs offer deferred compensation through the use of pay scales and promotion based on seniority in order to maintain motivation and encourage the transfer of skills from experienced to less experienced employees.
4. *Efficiency wages*: traditional economic theory of labour markets assumes that there is no link between employee productivity and pay levels. Efficiency wage theory, however, suggests that worker effort rises with pay. Thus firms will be willing to offer pay levels above market rates, a feature of ILMs.

The ILM approach has had a major influence on the analysis of labour market and employment behaviour since 1970. It forms the basis of the dual and (some) segmented labour market theories, in which jobs are divided into 'good' jobs and 'bad' jobs. This in turn is related to the flexible firm approach, with the division between core and periphery workers. **SJ**

References and further reading

Doeringer, P. B. and Piore, M. J. (1971) *Internal Labor Markets and Manpower Analysis,* Lexington, MA: Heath.

Osterman, P. (1987) 'Choice of employment systems in internal labour markets', *Indusrial Relations* 26(1): 46–67.

Siebert, W. S. and Addison, J. T. (1991) 'Internal labour markets: causes and consequences', *Oxford Review of Economic Policy* 7(1): 20–40.

International human resource management

For many people international human resource management (IHRM) is synonymous with expatriate management. However, IHRM covers a far broader spectrum than just the management of expatriates. It involves the worldwide management of people. Although international human resource (IHR) managers undertake the same activities as their domestically based colleagues, the scope and complexity of these tasks is increased as a result of working across national borders. For instance, managing careers in an international organization can involve multiple international moves for home-country, host-country and third-country nationals.

Several other factors will influence the degree to which international and domestic activities of the HR function differ. These include the cultural environment, the nature of international operations and attitudes of senior managers to international operations. The need to work effectively in multicultural environments is a critical issue for international organizations. This is problematic, given the evidence from cross-cultural research that different national cultures often have conflicting views on appropriate management styles and organizational processes. Equally, cultural differences need to be borne in mind when deciding on IHR systems. Can a Western-style appraisal system be implemented throughout the world? How do different cultures view reward? Another critical issue in IHRM is the need to balance the advantages of centralization with the need to be sensitive to local demands – the 'global versus local' dilemma. organizations may run their operations as a set of autonomous units, or they may strive for complete integration, depending on factors such as industry type and strategic objectives. The challenge for the IHR manager is to design and implement human resource policies and practices that reflect these choices. A final key variable in the nature of the IHRM orientation of an organization lies in the mindsets of the senior managers at headquarters. In an organization with an ethnocentric perspective, power and control rest with the home country headquarters. Human resource management practices are based on domestic policies and dispersed throughout the world. In contrast, an organization with a geocentric or 'global' orientation will focus on fostering a 'global mindset' in the minds of managers supported by integrated human resource policies which still permit local flexibility. **HH**

References and further reading

Brewster, C. and Harris, H. (eds) (1999) *International HRM: Contemporary Issues in Europe,* London: Routledge.

Dowling, P. J., Schuler, R. S. and Welch, D. E. (1994) *International Dimensions of Human Resource Management*, Belmont, CA: Waldsworth.

Hofstede, G. (1991) *Cultures and Organizations, Software of the Mind: Intercultural Cooperation and its Importance for Survival*, London: McGraw-Hill.

Stroh, L. K. and Caligiuri, P. M. (1998) 'Strategic human resources: a new source for competitive advantage in the global arena', *International Journal of Human Resource Management* 9(1): 1–17.

Trompenaars, F. (1993) *Riding the Waves of Culture*, London: Nicholas Brealey.

International Labour Organization

Following the conclusion of the First World War, the International Labour Organization (ILO) was established as an organization dedicated to securing basic worker rights across the world. Four prime objectives lay behind its establishment:

1. *Humanitarian*: to protect workers and their families from exploitation.
2. *Political*: to prevent revolutionary action in individual countries through establishing a platform of worker rights.
3. *Economic*: universal social reform which raise labour costs would be less likely to meet resistance within any individual state.
4. *Social justice*: this was a highly relevant factor following the end of hostilities and its inclusion was believed to contribute to potential future international harmony.

The ILO is now a specialized agency of the United Nations, which principally seeks to fulfil its humanitarian aims by establishing international labour standards. Since the end of the Second World War broader civil rights and extended social policy issues have also been incorporated into the range of standards. The principal standards are *conventions* and *recommendations*. Conventions are basically international treaties ratified by ILO member states, of which there are 175. A small number of conventions are recognized as fundamental human rights for people at work. These include rights to:

- free association
- freedom of organization
- collective bargaining
- abolition of forced labour
- equality of opportunity and treatment
- more recently, the elimination of child labour.

Recommendations are non-binding guidelines established to assist national policy and practice. To date some 180 conventions and have been ratified and 185 recommendations published. The ILO also publishes codes of conduct, resolutions and declarations. Whilst designed to have 'a normative effect' they are not included in the system of international labour standards.

The ILO consists of *three* principal bodies, the Conference, the Governing Body and the International Labour Office. The Conference meets annually with each member state represented by autonomous delegates representing government, employers and workers. It is the Conference that agrees the labour standards, as well electing the Governing Body. This body acts as the executive council which decides ILO's policies for submission to the Conference. The permanent secretariat of the ILO is provided by the International Labour Office, which is based in Geneva.

The International Labour Office also acts as a valuable source of training, statistics provision and practical help across the broad spectrum of employment and social policy. Its research publications, often commissioned by the independent research faculty of the ILO, the *International Institute of Labour Studies* (IILS), are of particular relevance to policy-makers and to academics. The ILO also publishes the *International Labour Review* on a quarterly basis.

The ILO has been highly active in bringing the world's attention to issues of labour abuse or injustice. Recent campaigns against social exclusion, migrant labour abuse and child labour have received massive publicity. Nevertheless, there are problems. Developed countries contribute substantially to the ILO and, arguably, influence its direction in protection of their interests, which may not necessarily coincide with those of developing countries. There has been a protracted debate on the issue of child labour in this context. It has been argued that it is not straightforward to match universal standards against individual state institutions, laws and practices. Further, the substantive levels of standards are not easy to establish and can be set at too low a level to exert any meaningful effect. There are limited sanctions against transgressors.

Whilst the ILO has been criticized for its bureaucracy and caution, in a world where global enterprise and its attendant focus on comparative labour costs have become established features of economic life, its fundamental role in protecting the most vulnerable is unlikely to diminish. **JHy**

References and further reading
Banplain, R. and Engels, C. (eds) (1998) *Comparative Labour Law and Industrial Relations in Industrialized Market Economies*, The Hague: Kluwer Law International.

International Labour Review, available from ILO Publications, International Labour Office, CH-1211 Geneva 22.

Internet recruiting

Internet recruiting is the process whereby employers advertise positions and solicit applications using the Internet. At the most basic level it simply involves including on an organization's own web site details of current vacancies. In many cases these are simply web-based versions of advertisements that have also been placed in newspapers or journals. It is also possible for employers to pay a fee in order to advertise jobs on a specialist job seekers' web site or virtual recruitment agency. Internet recruiting has most to offer employers in the following circumstances:

- where large numbers of applications are wanted (e.g. where there are dozens of similar vacancies being advertised at the same time)
- where the organization is confident that the majority of its target audience has access to the Internet
- where alternative methods of recruitment are particularly costly (e.g. where expensive large numbers of recruitment brochures would otherwise have to be printed).

A feature of Internet recruiting is the potential it gives for job seekers to arrange for their e-mail numbers to appear on mailing lists drawn up by agents or careers services. This allows employers to target people with the desired qualifications far more directly and inexpensively than is possible using other recruitment methods. Other possibilities include the use of video and audio clips to enhance the content of a recruitment advertisement, and the presence of interactive features to help potential applicants determine whether or not they might be suitable candidates.

One area in which use of the Internet fits all three of the criteria identified above, and has thus developed quickly, is graduate recruitment. Many of the largest firms now focus their activity on this medium, reducing greatly the number of paper publications they need to print, while reaching greater numbers of students. A number also now request that application forms are submitted via the Internet which allows for speedy, electronic shortlisting. In the early, years, however, survey evidence suggests that employers see Internet recruitment as being supplementary to more traditional approaches rather than replacing them altogether. **ST**

References and further reading
Jenner, S. and Taylor, S. (2000) *Recruiting, Retaining and Developing Graduate Talent*, London: Financial Times Management, ch. 2.

Krechowiecka, I. (1999) 'Net that first job from your armchair', *Guardian*, 5 June: R8.

Rothstein, H. R. (1999) 'Recruitment and selection: benchmarking at the millennium', in A. I. Kraut and A. K. Korman (eds) *Evolving Practices in Human Resource Management*: *Responses to a Changing World of Work*, San Francisco: Jossey-Bass.

Interviews and interviewing

There are several distinct types of interview that are carried out regularly by human resource staff, each having rather different requirements. The main examples are selection interviews, disciplinary interviews, performance appraisal interviews and interviews in which feedback is given on performance in a developmental setting. Of these the most common, for generalist human resource managers, is the selection interview.

Interviews are used almost universally in employee selection, being considered indispensable by all employers. They have had something of a bad press from researchers who have investigated their typical predictive validity, numerous studies suggesting that alternative methods have more to offer in terms of their ability to forecast future work performance accurately. Their continued use can be accounted for on the grounds that they fulfil several other functions well: they are relatively inexpensive, are expected and accepted by potential employees, readily give the opportunity for a two-way exchange of views and provide for the possibility of negotiation over terms and conditions.

A second stream of research has focused on common problems with typical interviews conducted by poorly trained or experienced interviewers. These include the halo and horns effects, the similar-to-me effect and stereotyping. In all three examples interviewers make unduly positive or negative assumptions about interviewees. The temporal-extention effect occurs when interviewers falsely infer behaviour during an interview to reflect that which is typical of the interviewee in less contrived situations. An important distinction can be made between unstructured (or typical) interviews and those which are structured. In the case of the latter questions are determined in advance with direct reference to a person specification for the role concerned. All candidates are then asked the same questions and are marked on their responses. Structuring has been found to increase predictive validity markedly. Two types of question are particularly associated with structured interviews. Hypothetical questions involve asking candidates how they would react or what they would do in a particular set of circumstances. Behavioural questions, by contrast, focus on the candidate's past life and involve the interviewer seeking hard evidence of a match between the attributes of candidates and those required in the job for which they are applying. **ST**

References and further reading

Anderson, N. and Shackleton, V. (1993) *Successful Selection Interviewing*, Oxford: Blackwell.
Buckley, M. R. and Eder, R.W. (1995) 'The interview: expecting a quick decision?', in G. Ferris and R. Buckley (eds) *Human Resources Management: Perspectives, Context, Functions and Outcomes*, London: Prentice Hall.
Cook, M. (1995) *Personnel Selection and Productivity*, 2nd edn, Chichester: Wiley.
Cooper, D. and Robertson, I. (1995) *The Psychology of Personnel Selection*, London: Routledge.
Eder, R. W. and Harris, M. M. (eds) (1999) *The Employment Interview Handbook*, 2nd edn, London: Sage.
Herriot, P. (1989) 'The selection interview', in P. Herriot (ed.) *Assessment and Selection in organisations*, Chichester: Wiley.

Investors in People (IIP)

Investors in People was introduced by the government in 1990 as a result of the White Paper, *Employment for the 1990s*. It is a national standard, currently administered by **Training and Enterprise Councils** (TECs) (see separate entry). Its four main principles are that the organization:

1. Makes a public commitment from the top to develop people in order to achieve business objectives.

2. Regularly reviews the training and development needs of people.
3. Takes action to train and develop people on recruitment and throughout their employment.
4. Evaluates the investment in training and development to improve future effectiveness.

The standard is monitored by Investors in People UK (IIP UK), an organization licensed by the Department of Education and Employment (DfEE) to oversee its promotion and development throughout UK organisations. The IIP initiative aims to develop organizations by linking training and development with strategy, in the belief that there is a correlation between people and business development. It is based on the assumption that there is best human resource management practice which can be applied to all organizations.

The standard was developed by undertaking research into successful organizations from all economic sectors to elicit best practice in people development.

Organizations undertaking the IIP process register a commitment with their local TEC. Consultants approved by the TEC audit them against the standard and then work with them to close the gaps identified. The process usually involves the development of business and training plans, human resource (HR) policies such as appraisal and communications strategies. Financial assistance with training is usually offered. Evidence that the organization is an Investor in People is assessed against the standard and, once approved, the award is made. Recognized Investors in People may display the logo for three years before being reassessed.

Debate on IIP has revolved around the difficulties in defining best practice (and best employers), the assumed link between HR practise and business performance and the application and relevance of the standard to all organizations, irrespective of size and sector. In its early years, IIP recognitions were dominated by larger companies and the relevance of the standard to smaller and public sector organizations has had to be addressed. Likewise, only whole organizations or autonomous units were initially eligible but, now, subsidiaries and departments may apply for the award. Management of the process, in the hands of the TECs, has also been contentious. It has been argued that, being target led, the TECs have encouraged and worked with those organizations most likely to succeed, while those organizations in most need of HR development have been ignored.

Despite considerable debate, the standard remains and appears to be growing in popularity. It has become a well-known and respected kitemark, giving recognition to quality standards in people development. The latest version of the standard, less prescriptive and with more emphasis on outcomes than process, has been published in April 2000. Up-to-date figures on commitments and recognitions are maintained by IIP UK. **AS**

References and further reading

Alberga, T., Tyson, S. and Parsons, D. (1995) 'Research report on best practice in people', *Report for Investors in People UK Bedford*, Cranfield: Cranfield School of Management.

Alberga, T., Tyson, S. and Parsons, D. (1997) 'An evaluation of the Investors in People standard', *Human Resource Management Journal* 7(2): 47–60.

Down, S. and Smith, D. (1998) 'It pays to be nice to people: IIP the search for measurable benefits', *Personnel Review* 27(2): 143–55.

Hillage, J. and Moralee, J. (1996) 'The return on investors', *Institute of Employment Studies and DfEE Report no 314*, University of Sussex.

Ram, M. (2000) 'IIP in small firms: case study evidence from the business services sector', *Personnel Review* 21(1): 69–91.

Smith, A. J., Boocock, J. G., Loan-Clarke, J. and Whittaker, J. (2000) 'IIP and SMEs: awareness, benefits and barriers', Business School, Loughborough University Working Paper.

Web site at http://www.iipuk.co.uk/whatsnew/draft.htm

Japanization

Japanization became a focus of debate from the late 1970s as large-scale inward investment of transplant manufacturing from Japan, especially automobiles and electronics, grew in North America and Western Europe, intensifying competitive pressures in these markets. Whereas much of the early debate on Japanization focused on the cultural traits of Japanese society and issues about the feasibility of transferring group-orientated employee relations to the individualistic West, later debate focused on the economic success of Japanese management methods of production and the control of labour, and what Western managers had to learn from this. Much of this focus was upon a new industrial relationship with labour and trade unions, involving no-strike agreements, and non-recognition of established unions in the greenfield sites of the transplants. The intense hostility towards organized labour by the Conservative government of the 1980s and early 1990s encouraged the spread of anti-trade union attitudes amongst management, and Japanization was seen as part of this process.

Three distinct approaches to understanding the nature of Japanization can be identified.

1. A structural approach, where the significance of Japanization is seen in its impact on indigenous firms. This ranges from direct impact, such as transplants controlling suppliers, through mediated impact, where indigenous firms seek to imitate some aspects of Japanese management methods, to full Japanization, where firms seek to emulate the Japanese.
2. A process approach, where Japanization is seen as a spatial concentration of production designed to secure managerial control over the firm's environment. This would include local communities, suppliers and the marginalization or elimination of trade unions. This hegemony is identified as being promoted by global competition and is seen in its most advanced form in the automobile industry.
3. A 'supermarket' approach, the extent to which indigenous industry adopts some of a cluster of managerial techniques focused on securing flexibility of labour and 'lean production'. These techniques include *kaizen* (continuous improvement), *kanban* (just in time production), *ringisei* (team-building), TQM (total quality management) and SPC (statistical process control). Many of these techniques are identified with W. E. Deming, an American who introduced these (Western) methods to the Japanese in the 1950s. **SC**

References and further reading

Ackroyd, S., Burrell, G., Hughes, M. and Whitaker, A. (1988) 'The Japanisation of British industry', *Industrial Relations Journal* 19(1).

Crowther, S. and Garrahan, P. (1988) 'Invitation to Sunderland: corporate power and the local economy', *Industrial Relations Journal* 19(1).

Elgar, T. and Smith, C. (eds) (1994) *Global Japanisation*, London: Routledge.

Job analysis

A systematic process which involves analysing the content and nature of jobs in an organization. The approach provides a foundation on which to build a range of human resource (HR) practices in HR planning, recruitment and selection, training and development, and performance management and remuneration. The outcome of a job analysis exercise is an objective summary of the tasks and duties that make up the job, the methods and processes used to undertake these, the nature of relationships that have to be established and the outputs associated with the job. The analysis can then be used to develop job descriptions, personnel specifications, training needs analyses and/or job evaluation scores. Several methods are used to carry out job analysis, some a good deal more sophisticated than others. The principal alternative approaches are interviews with job holders and colleagues, observation of job holders at work and the use of commercially produced job analysis questionnaires. The latter can now be lengthy and very thorough, requiring those who undertake job analysis exercises to attend formal training in their use. Many systems are also fully computerized, permitting direct inputting of data and the instant production of detailed summary documents.

The major problem with job analysis is the fact that it is 'job based' rather than 'person based', the key unit of analysis being the job. The underlying assumption is that organizations can be usefully defined as comprising a structure of clearly defined jobs into which people are slotted and through which they achieve promotions. While such thinking is appropriate in certain types of organization, it is increasingly inappropriate elsewhere. Where greater flexibility is necessary and possible, there is a need to base recruitment, development and remuneration practices around people and their individual contributions rather than the jobs in which they are employed. In such organizations job analysis has little to offer and may act to restrict the development of flexible thinking on the part of managers and staff. **ST**

References and further reading

Greuter, M. A. and Algera, J. A. (1989) 'Criterion development and job analysis', in P. Herriot (ed.) *Assessment and Selection in organisations*, Chichester: Wiley.

Livy, B. (1988) 'Job analysis, description and specification', in B. Livy (ed.) *Corporate Personnel Management*, London: Pitman.

Parker, S. and Wall, T. (1998) *Job and Work Design: Organizing Work to Promote Well-Being and Effectiveness*, London: Sage.

Pearn, M. and Kandola, R. (1993) *Job Analysis: A Manager's Guide*, London: IPD.

Roberts, G. (1998) *Recruitment and Selection: A Competency Approach*, London: IPD, ch. 6.

Sanchez, J. I. and Levine, E. L. (1999) 'Is job analysis dead, misunderstood, or both? New forms of work analysis and design', in A. I. Kraut and A. K. Korman (eds) *Evolving Practices in Human Resource Management*, San Francisco: Jossey-Bass.

Stokes, R. (1987) 'Defining the job and specifying the ideal candidate', in S. Haper (ed.) *Personnel Management Handbook*, Aldershot: Gower.

Job description

A written document in which the major duties associated with a particular job are briefly summarized. Job descriptions also typically include information on reporting lines, areas of responsibility and the principal outcomes or outputs that the job holder is expected to achieve. Job descriptions are used as the basis for the development of personnel specifications and are frequently sent to individual job applicants to help them prepare for the selection process. They may also be incorporated into individual contracts of employment as a means of establishing clearly what is expected by an organization of its employees. Where used in this way employers are well advised to include a term which requires a degree of flexibility, so that employees do not perceive their roles to be wholly fixed and unchanging. Where this is not done job descriptions can serve to restrict employer's freedom to reorganize duties, reporting lines and/or working locations. Moreover, without built-in flexibility, job descriptions become dated quickly necessitating frequent updating on the part of managers or human resource (HR) staff.

There has been a move away from issuing job descriptions that are entirely descriptive (i.e. which simply describe the tasks which the job holder is required to perform) towards a greater focus on accountability. Hence, the items on the job description are phrased in terms of what the job holder is expected to achieve in the role, rather than simply being a digest of tasks to be undertaken. Aside from permitting greater flexibility, the focus on accountability is intended to send important messages about organizational expectations and criteria on which success will be judged right from the start of an individual's employment. Taken to its logical conclusion, the result of this development is to replace job descriptions with competency profiles, hence merging together the job description and personnel specification. **ST**

References and further reading

Fine, S. and Getkate, M. (1995) *Benchmark Tasks for Job Analysis*, Hillsdale, NJ: Lawrence Erlbaum.

Ghorpade, J. (1988) *Job Analysis: A Handbook for the Human Resource Director*, Englewood Cliffs, NJ: Prentice Hall.

Industrial Relations Services (1996) 'Policy and practice in recruitment: an IRS survey', *Employee Development Bulletin* 81, September.

Job evaluation

Job evaluation is a technique that systematically compares jobs with each other to produce a rank order on which pay differentials can be based. Typically only some occupational groups are covered. There are normally different schemes for such categories as manual, non-manual, professional and managerial staff. In some countries employers have placed all employees in the same scheme, so that the pay of men and women may be determined using the same criteria.

Employers will normally have some of the following objectives in seeking to introduce job evaluation:

- establish a rational pay structure
- create pay relationships between jobs which are perceived as fair by employees
- reduce the number of pay grievances and disputes
- provide a basis for settling the pay rate of new or changed jobs
- provide pay information in a form which enables meaningful comparisons with other organizations.

The main aim of job evaluation is to provide an acceptable rationale for determining the pay of existing hierarchies of jobs and for slotting in new ones. It may be implemented unilaterally or with varying degrees of participation by the workforce. Acceptability, consensus and the maintenance of traditional hierarchical structures are normally the goal of such schemes.

Job evaluation schemes do not directly determine rates of pay. The rate for the job or the salary market for a job grade is influenced by a number of factors outside the scope of most schemes. Often, the pay determinants and indeed hierarchies are linked to external market pay rates, the relative bargaining strengths of the negotiating bodies and traditional patterns of pay differentials between jobs. Job evaluation is concerned with relationships, not absolutes. **AA**

References and further reading

Armstrong, M. and Bacon, A. (1995) *The Job Evaluation Handbook*, London: CIPD.

Armstrong, M. and Murlis, H. (1994) *Reward Management*, 3rd edn, London: IPM, chs 9 and 10.

Kerr, C. and Fisher, L. H. (1977) 'Effects of environment and administration on job evaluation', in C. Kerr (ed.), *Labor Markets and Wage Determination*, Berkeley, CA: California University Press.

Lawler, E. E. (1986) 'What's wrong with point-factor job evaluation', *Compensation and Benefits Review* 18: 20–8.

Welbourne T. M. and Trevor C. O. (2000) 'The roles of department and position power in job evaluation', *Academy of Management Journal* 43: 761–71.

Job redesign

Marchington and Wilkinson (2000: 352) identify five broad types of job redesign: job rotation, job enlargement, job enrichment, autonomous work groups and team-working. The first two of these are referred to as horizontal redesign – the number and variety of tasks performed at the same skill level, while the latter two as vertical, i.e. more responsibility (of skills, decision-making, etc.) The basis for each of these can be seen in Hackman and Oldham's (1976) *job characteristics model* (JCM). This has been extremely influential as a guide for managers seeking to redesign, or design jobs. In the JCM, Hackman and Oldham identify five 'core job characteristics' (Arnold, Cooper and Robertson, 1995: 394–9):

- skill variety (SV), that is the range of skills needed to perform the task
- task identity (TI), the meaning of the workers task and the extent to which they can see it as producing a unified, identifiable outcome
- task significance (TS), the importance of the work to others
- autonomy (Au), the amount of freedom and discretion the worker has
- feedback from the job (Fb), the extent to which the job itself provides the worker with knowledge of the results of their work activities.

Hackman and Oldham suggest that influencing these characteristics can influence, *motivation*, through 'experienced meaningfulness of the work' (SV + TI + TS), *job satisfaction* through 'experienced responsibility for work outcomes (Au) and *effectiveness* through 'knowledge of results and activities' (Fb). Arnold, Cooper and Robinson offer a detailed outline and criticism of this model.

Wilson (1999: 13) defines job redesign as, 'any attempt to alter jobs with the intent of increasing the quality of work experience and productivity'. This definition makes it easy to see the parallel between job redesign and the quality of working life (QWL) movement in the 1970s. The two are closely associated, though whilst the term QWL is now dated, job redesign is still very much in vogue. As is the case with QWL, there have been criticisms of attempts to introduce job redesign. It can be seen as a shallow attempt to get more from workers without introducing significant change (Blacker and Brown, 1980). As a management-owned initiative, the emphasis has shifted from reducing alienation to one where the aim is competitive advantage. It is perhaps questionable as to whether the motives for redesign can ever genuinely be to 'improve the quality of work experience'. This may at best be a secondary outcome to the goal of improved productivity. Nonetheless, some organizations claim to have profited as a result of job redesign, notably the Volvo sub-assembly plant at Kalmar, where as a result of autonomous group working, the number of man hours per car was radically reduced (Buchanan, 1994). Job redesign has also been used to try to reduce absenteeism (e.g. Saab at Malmo, see Buchanan, 1994), which it could be argued would be a benefit to both organization (where presumably productivity would increase) and employee (where presumably lower absence is indicative of less dissatisfaction). **KM and AW**

References and further reading
Arnold, J., Cooper, C. L. and Robertson, I. T. (1995) *Work Psychology*: *Understanding Human Behaviour in the Workplace*, London: Pitman.
Blacker, F. H. and Brown, C. A. (1978) *Job Redesign and Management Control*, London: Saxon House.
Buchanan, D. A. (1994) 'Principles and practice in work design', in K. Sisson (ed.) *Personnel Management*: *A Comprehensive Guide to Theory and Practice in Britain*, Oxford: Blackwell.
Hackman, J. and Oldham, G. R. (1976) 'Motivation through the design of work: test of a theory', *Organizational Behavior and Human Performance* 16: 250–79.
Marchington, M. (1992) *Managing the Team*, Oxford: Blackwell, ch. 6.
Marchington, M. and Wilkinson A. (2000) *Core Personnel and Development*, London: CIPD.
Wilson, F. (1999) *Organizational Behaviour*: *A Critical Introduction*, Oxford: Oxford University Press.

Job rotation

Job rotation is the most straightforward form of job redesign, which involves employees' being moved from one job to another which requires a similar level (normally low) of skill. Typically there will be a range of jobs which fall into this category, and employees may be set to work for a short period on each moving from one to the next in a cycle – hence 'rotation'. For example, on an assembly line in a confectionery factory, different 'rotatable' jobs might be:

- removing bars which get stuck on the rollers
- 'shelling' (unwrapping) defective bars for recycling
- packaging bars/moving boxes for delivery
- carrying out an inventory of health and safety checks
- conducting 'spot' quality control checks on randomly selected bars – for temperature, shape, etc.
- moving between different product assembly lines.

The reasoning behind such rotation is that it alleviates employee boredom and provides some variety, as well as potentially allowing for the learning of new skills. It should be seen from the list of tasks above that a criticism of job rotation could be that this 'variety' merely consists in swapping one boring job for another. Additionally, it is important to recognise that organizations are not merely environments defined by the type and efficiency of work undertaken, but that also they are places where people communicate and interact. This more cultural interpretation illustrates one way in which rotation can be harmful, as it can break up informal teams or communication networks. Equally, depending on the type of reward scheme utilised, rotation may harm employee prospects of gaining bonuses. With an incentive linked to volume of output, constantly working at one thing may mean employees are actually more productive. To the extent that enforced rotation can potentially damage morale or adversely affect employee's pay, it may also be a symptom of 'paternalism', that is a sign that the organization or managers act as though 'they know best'. **KM**

References and further reading
Beardwell, I. and Holden, L. (1995) *Human Resource Management*: *A Contemporary Perspective*, London: Pitman.
Cheraskin, L. and Campian, M. (1996) 'Study clarifies job-rotation benefits', *Personnel Journal* 75(11): 31–6.
Marchington, M. and Wilkinson, A. (2000) *Core Personnel and Development*, London: CIPD.
Stiles-De, S. (1996) 'The new story about job rotation', *Academy of Management Executive* 10(1): 86–8.

Job satisfaction

One of the major aims of human resource management interventions, at least in theory, is the maximization of job satisfaction on the part of a workforce. Such approaches have long been associated with the human relations school of management thought, the expectation being that job satisfaction is positively correlated with organizational effectiveness. The term 'job satisfaction' can be defined in different ways. Some researchers have focused on general satisfaction measured globally, while others look at different forms of satisfaction (e.g. pay, levels of motivation, relationships with supervisors and colleagues, satisfaction with the organization, etc). Another division is between those who see job satisfaction as being essentially an affective phenomenon (i.e. a positive emotional state) and those who see it more in terms of a rational judgement made by an individual with an awareness of their alternative job choices. In the human resource management literature the achievement of a high level of job satisfaction is seen as desirable from an organization's perspective because of its apparent effect on effort, commitment, absence, staff turnover rates and work performance. Some also see it as a means of reducing the propensity to join trade unions and hence of hindering the development of adversarial industrial relations. Studies have tended to find little by way of a direct link between satisfaction and individual job performance, but have confirmed that there is an indirect effect. In particular there is good evidence of a relationship between high job satisfaction and high levels of 'organisational citizenship behaviour' whereby individuals take on tasks or work longer hours than is strictly required contractually.

An interesting alternative perspective has been developed by organizational psychologists who claim that the propensity to be satisfied with a job can be seen as equivalent to a personality trait. It follows that some people are generally more satisfied than others, that the organizational environment is of limited significance in determining job satisfaction and that the best means of predicting whether or not someone will be satisfied in a job is to establish the extent to which they have been satisfied in previous roles. Effective personnel selection may thus be as important, if not more important, than subsequent management initiatives in determining the extent of satisfaction in a workplace. **ST**

References and further reading
Bussing, A. (1998) 'Motivation and satisfaction' in M. Poole and M. Warner (eds) *The Handbook of Human Resource Management*, London: Thomson Learning.
Locke, E. A. (1976) 'The nature and causes of job satisfaction', in M. Dunnette (ed.) *Handbook of Industrial and organisational Psychology*, Skokie, IL: Rand McNally.
Makin, P., Cooper, C. and Cox, C. (1996) *Organizations and the Psychological Contract*, Leicester: BPS Books, ch. 2.
McKenna, E. (1994) *Business Psychology and organisational Behaviour: A Student's Handbook*, Hove: Psychology Press, ch. 6.
Organ, D. W. (1990) 'The subtle significance of job satisfaction', *Clinical Laboratory Management Review* 4. Also in R. Katz (ed.) *The Human Side of Managing Technological Innovation*, Oxford: Oxford University Press.
Walton, R. E. (1991) 'From control to commitment in the workplace', in J. Gabarro (ed.) *Managing People and Organizations*, Cambridge, MA: Harvard Business School.

Just-in-time (JIT)

Just-in-time may sound like a popular song but it is actually a term from operations management. In the 1980s the Japanese economy went from strength to strength and Japanese manufacturing industry in particular began to secure a greater share of international markets for consumer goods (cars, televisions, videos, etc.). Western manufacturers became concerned and many of them made expeditions to Japan to learn the secrets of Japanese manufacturing methods. Japanese manufacturing methods became increasingly popular in the West, particularly in the USA and Europe. The term 'lean manufacturing' came to be used to describe the new approach to manufacturing in the West. The impact of 'lean manufacturing' in Japan was one of the main reasons for the introduction of business process re-engineering in the West in the early 1990s.

Just-in-time was one of the main features of the new Japanese manufacturing philosophy. Basically, it consists of a 'belief' that stocks or inventories are not only undesirable but unnecessary. Consequently manufacturers set out to strip inventory out of their manufacturing systems as far as possible. It was in this sense that manufacturing became 'lean'. Inventory was seen as costly and a waste of resources. Manufacturers reorganized their production facilities to eliminate inventory along with any other non-value adding aspect of the manufacturing process. In future, raw materials or components were to be delivered by suppliers 'just-in-time' to be used in the production process and not held in stock. Production systems were reorganized and suppliers were placed under great pressure to upgrade their delivery systems in accordance with the demands of the JIT system. The effect of JIT, therefore, was to create increased pressure for performance improvement throughout the whole manufacturing supply chain.

Some companies were more successful than others of course. The automotive industry was particularly advanced in using JIT methods. Nissan, for example, required some suppliers to make deliveries three times per day. Not only that, but the components were to be delivered to the precise point in the assembly line where they were needed.

Just-in-time methods mean that companies are much more vulnerable to delivery problems in the supply chain. To ensure reliable supplies, therefore, contracts contain penalty clauses for late deliveries. Volkswagen had a manufacturing plant in Mexico where suppliers were fined $5000 per minute if the assembly line had to stop as a result of a late delivery of components.

The introduction of JIT methods also had significant implications for the finance and purchasing functions which had previously been geared to manufacturing for inventory. For the human resource management function, JIT has also led to major culture change and retraining programmes in companies where JIT methods have been introduced. Just-in-time principles have also been taken up by companies outside the manufacturing sector. **JBr**

References and further reading

Bicheno, J. (2000) *Cause and Effect JIT: The Essentials of Lean Manufacturing*, Buckingham: Picsie Press.

Bragg, S. M. (2000) *Just-In-Time Accounting: How to Decrease Costs and Increase Efficiency*, Chichester: Wiley.

Cheng, T. C. E. and Podolsky, S. (2000) *Just-In-Time Manufacturing: an introduction*, Lancaster: Kluwer Academic.

Hutchins, D. (2000) *Just In Time*, Aldershot: Gower.

L

Labour law

'Labour law' is the term given to law covering both the individual contractual relationship between employer and worker and that of the employer with the workforce collectively, i.e. trade union law. Until comparatively recently the relationships were governed by the principles of laissez-faire and voluntarism respectively in that it was felt that the parties themselves could sort out their own agreements and relationships without the interference of the state. This all changed with the Conservative government which introduced a series of statutes throughout the 1980s designed to curb the powers of unions. In the 1980s and 1990s there has been a continuous outpouring of legislation governing the employment relationship, much of which is dictated by membership of the European Union. The Labour government's decision to 'opt-in' to the Social Chapter also required amendments to the law.

Much of the statute law has been consolidated so that the majority of individual protection rights can be found in the Employment Rights Act 1996, while the key statute governing collective issues is the Trade Union and Labour Relations (Consolidation) Act 1992. Since joining the European Union there has been a considerable input to British law as a result of European Directives on a wide range of matters including sex discrimination, equal pay, working time, maternity and parental rights, and consultation in relation to redundancies, business transfers and acquisitions.

Apart from statutes and European Directives, there is a large body of case law, study of which is essential to understand how the law is applied in different situations. It is also important to appreciate that the primary relationship between employer and worker is based on an agreement and therefore there are many aspects of contract law which underpin the way the law is interpreted and applied. **AB**

References and further reading
Selwyn, N. (2000) *Selwyn's Law of Employment*, London: Butterworths
Web site at http://www.danielbarnett.co.uk
Wiley, B. (2000) *Employment Law in Context*, London: Financial Times Prentice Hall, ch. 1.

Labour market

A market refers to any actual or potential relationship between buyers and sellers of a product or service. The 'labour market' is the term economists give to the buying and selling of labour services. It is a shorthand term to cover a wide variety of employment related issues. These range from the overall level of employment and unemployment, and the average level of earnings at the macro level, to the details of the employment contract, wage differentials and effects of unionization at the microeconomic level.

The standard neo-classical analysis of labour markets regards workers as individuals who freely exchange their labour services with employers in return for wages and salaries. As work is regarded as having disutility, wages compensate for the time spent at work. Consequently, wages have to rise to increase the supply of labour (the supply function). On the other side, employers hire labour because of the contribution it makes to profit, with the wage employers willing to pay falling as employment rises (the demand function). In a freely working labour market, wages and employment levels are determined by the interaction of the overall market supplies and demands (the intersection of the supply and demand functions). No employer or employee, or organization representing them, has an ability to influence the demand or supply conditions and hence wages or employment levels. In other words, the labour market acts as an impersonal mechanism for allocating labour to the most highly valued (i.e. most profitable) uses. Changes in supply or demand conditions bring about the automatic reallocation of labour from one use to another, with the wage level acting as the 'price' signal. For example, a rise in the demand for labour in a particular industry will increase the wage in that industry relative to others, giving rise to a net inflow of labour to meet the industry's demand.

The neo-classical model has a number of applications and implications. For instance, it provides an explanation for the structure of earnings, the most widely used one being human capital theory – the earnings of skilled workers are higher than those of the unskilled because they have to be compensated for the time spent in education and training. Moreover, the approach suggests that intervention by the public authorities (e.g. minimum wage and health and safety regulations) and other non-competitive elements (trade unions and employers organizations) in the labour market reduce the efficiency with which it operates. This reduces overall economic efficiency and may raise the level of unemployment.

While this textbook free-market view offers a useful starting point for the analysis of labour markets, few economists accept it as adequate characterization of actual labour markets. A lack of labour mobility between occupations and geographical areas for example means that the wage/price signals do not necessarily work, or if they do, labour markets are slow to adjust. Perhaps more importantly, market failure may be an inherent aspect of labour markets. These arise due to *information* problems, with wages sending the wrong signals between employers and employees and the result being that the market does not adjust in the textbook fashion. One example of this is the theory of efficiency wages, according to which employers increase wages above market levels in order to motivate employees. In circumstances where efficiency wages are paid, unemployment will not bring about the normal market adjustment in which the excess supply of labour is eliminated by a reduction in wages. Employers will be unwilling to cut wages in case it demotivates existing workers. Another possibility is when unemployed workers offer themselves for work at wages lower than the market rate. The effect is to send a signal to potential employers that they are of lower quality, which reduces their chances of securing employment. Again, the market mechanism by which labour market adjustments are brought about through wage changes does not operate and the excess supply persists.

A final aspect of the non-competitive elements present in labour markets worth noting is the existence of internal labour markets (ILMs), where employment decisions are determined within firms without reference to the external labour market conditions. According to some explanations, ILMs arise because of the problems of devising contracts to cover all aspects of the employment relationship. Consequently, rules and procedures are substituted for the market mechanism. In other theories, such as the segmented labour markets approach, the labour market is in fact made up of a series of separate markets between which there is little mobility. One example of this is the dual labour market approach, with the labour market divided into two broad types of market. One comprises the internal labour market of 'good' jobs, with above market rates of pay, well-defined career paths and training. The other consists of a secondary labour market of 'bad' jobs with little security, high turnover rates, and pay and employment determined by the normal market mechanism. There is little or no mobility from the secondary to the primary market and workers once allocated to the secondary market remain disadvantaged. This view is closely related to the core–periphery approach.

In sum, the conventional economics approach to labour markets emphasizes supply and demand factors as important, treating labour in the same way as oranges or apples. Although this provides some useful insights into the way employers and employees interact, it fails to account for the inherent market failures likely in the labour market. **SJ**

References and further reading

Kilponen, J., Mayes, D. and Vilniunen, J. (2000) 'Labour market flexibility in the Euro area', *European Business Journal* 12(2): 100–8.
Mayhew, K. (2000) 'The assessment: labour markets and welfare', *Oxford Review of Economic Policy* 16(1): 1–20.
Rubery, J. and Wilkinson, F. (1994) *Employer Strategy and the Labour Market*, Oxford: Oxford University Press.

Labour mobility

Labour mobility takes two main forms – occupational mobility and geographical mobility. Occupational mobility refers to the movement of workers from one occupation to another. Geographical mobility is the movement of workers from one area or region to another, and includes migration between countries. Clearly movements of labour can take any combination of occupational or geographical mobility, ranging from a change in employer but in the same occupation and region, to a change in occupation and region.

Mobility is of crucial importance to the operation of labour markets since it determines how supply responds to changes in wages which in turn act as price signals to indicate the relative strengths of demand for workers in different industries, occupations and regions. Where labour is mobile conventional economic theory predicts that the market mechanism operates effectively, allocating labour to its most efficient and highly valued uses. Thus labour responds to market signals, switching occupations or areas as required. Consequently, much of the discussion of the efficiency of the market mechanism in the labour market hinges on the issue of how mobile labour is.

Generally, it is accepted that in the long run labour is more mobile than in the short run. An overall impediment to labour mobility is the existence of information and search costs, i.e. workers may not know what is going on in other parts of the labour market, or it may be too costly to find out. More specifically, occupational mobility is affected by the costs involved in training or retraining, which include time costs and the loss of current earnings as well as monetary outlays. For an individual some of these costs may be insurmountable, although for the market as a whole, mobility is affected by the occupational choices of new entrants as well as existing workers changing occupations. Geographical mobility is affected by social and family ties to an area, the costs of search, and the costs of moving. In the UK much has been made of the housing market as a barrier to mobility. The housing factors include the differences in house prices between London and the South East region and other parts of the UK, and the decline in the private rented housing sector.

The impediments to mobility suggest that in some circumstances labour markets respond rather sluggishly to market signals. The effect this produces is that regional and structural unemployment can coexist alongside labour market shortages. In other words, there may be a mismatch of workers between regions and between occupations. This clearly has implications for government policy, for example, with regard to depressed regions and training and retraining. However, it may be argued that limitations on mobility can be beneficial. For example a firm may be more willing to train its workers in general skills that enhance productivity if it knows that they will not leave after a short period in search of higher pay from other employers.

Labour immobility also plays an important role in segmented labour markets theory. According to this approach, labour markets are divided into two main sectors, a primary labour market of 'good' jobs and a secondary labour market of 'bad' jobs. Workers are allocated to one or other market mainly according to their educational and social background. Mobility from the secondary to the primary sector is highly restricted. The theory is widely used to explain labour market discrimination and inequality. **SJ**

References and further reading

Elias, P. (1994) 'Job-related training, trade union membership and labour mobility', *Oxford Economic Papers* 46(4): 563–79.

Laughland, J. (1998) 'Don't bank on mobility', *European*, May, p. 7.

Schettkat, R. (1997) 'Employment protection and labour mobility in Europe', *International Review of Applied Economics* 11(1): 105–21.

Labour process theory

The desire to undertake meaningful, intelligent labour is characteristic of human beings, it provides the manifestation of the creative impulse that distinguishes humans from animals. As humans we create through purposive action; our labour. Our ability to transcend 'what is' with 'what can be' transforms our world and ourselves with it. In this conception of labour the relationship of people to their environment is simple and natural. The impulse to labour is mediated simply by a relationship between the work itself, the object of the work, and the tools that facilitate the work. This 'natural' relationship between humans and the natural world is altered by the development of the capitalist system.

For Marxists, history is punctuated and defined by the succession of dominant modes of production, that is, the economic structure of society. The dominant mode of production provides the basis upon which 'the character of the social, political and spiritual processes of life' (Marx, 1971:1) are determined. That is the nature of the economic structure of society provides the basis upon which the very nature of the whole of society is built. A fundamental element of the 'mode of production' is what Marxists term the 'relations of production', and under capitalism this is characterized by the ownership of the means of production (factories, capital and so on) by capitalists, and hence the legal separation of workers from the means of production. Capitalism is distinguished by the purchase and sale of labour power. The purpose of labour becomes the expansion of a unit of capital belonging to somebody else, the employer.

This separation from the means of production disrupts the natural processes of labour. Workers, who depend upon labour as an expression of their humanity are separated from the fruits of their labour, they become alienated from it. The removal of control of workers over their labour results in a qualitative change in the nature of work, work becomes a degrading and dehumanizing activity. The essential nature of labour as a free, creative endeavour is lost. Under capitalism work becomes coercion – forced labour.

Thus the study of the process of labour, the labour process, is central to the Marxist study of society in general, and the nature of work in particular. Labour process theory provides a radical set of tools for the analysis of organizational developments that are rooted in the causal connection between the requirements of the capitalist mode of production and the means of managerial control. The nature of the labour process will tend to reinforce capital's dual requirements, neutralize worker resistance to control and increase the productive output of labour. In effect capital needs to ensure that purchased labour power is transformed into productive labour.

Braverman's (1974) distinctive contribution to the study of the labour process is in his analysis of the labour process under a form of capitalism that he terms 'monopoly capitalism'. In this context the labour process is characterized by:

- the separation of the shopfloor from the design of work
- the fragmentation of work into meaningless segments
- the redistribution of tasks leading to labour cheapening
- the transformation of work organization to the Taylorist approach (Littler, 1982: 25).

Significant criticisms have been made of Braverman's approach, the most significant of which are the following:

1. Labour is characterized as monolithic, the disruption in the 'natural' processes of labour is assumed to result in a universal resistance to work under capitalist control. This broad approach fails to account for the effect that workers, as active subjects, can exert on the shaping of the labour process under varying circumstances.
2. The shaping of the labour process is characterized as a functionally determined activity, consciously design by a coherent capitalist class. As Littler (1982: 28) describes 'a single, overall trend – an imperative of control' rather than an iterative process in which employers determine a variety of approaches in response to specific circumstances.
3. That Taylorism represents a coherent and consistent model for capitalist control of the labour process. **NC-A**

References and further reading

Braverman, H. (1974) *Labour and Monopoly Capital*, New York: Monthly Review Press.
Littler, C. R. (1982) *The Development of the Labour Process in Capitalist Societies*, Aldershot: Gower.
Marx, K. (1971) *A Contribution to the Critique of Political Economy*, London: Lawrence and Wishart.
Reed, M. (1990) 'The labour process perspective on management organisation: a critique and reformulation', in J. Hassard and D. Pym, *The Theory and Philosophy of organizations*, London: Routledge.
Sewell, G. (1998) 'The discipline of teams: the control of team-based industrial work through electronic and peer surveillance', *Administrative Science Quarterly* 43(2): 397.

Labour turnover

Labour turnover refers to the number of workers leaving a firm over a specified period of time. Generally it includes voluntary quits, with workers being replaced, as well as redundancies or lay-offs in which the total number of employees in the firm is reduced. The turnover rate is sometimes known as the separation rate and can be divided into employment to employment movements and employment to unemployment movements.

Leaving aside the need to reduce total employment, there are several good reasons why a firm should be concerned about its turnover rate. When employing a new worker all firms will incur fixed costs that cannot be recovered once the firm has taken steps to hire the workers. These include the costs of recruitment and selection before an appointment is made, and the costs of induction and training once the new employee has begun work. The value of the worker's productivity therefore needs to exceed these initial costs if they are to be amortized and the worker is to make a positive contribution to the firm's profit. Thus in order to ensure these fixed costs are covered, the period of employment period has to be sufficiently long and therefore it is in the firm's interests to take steps to retain the worker. There are other reasons for ensuring that turnover rates are not excessive. The first is that workers who have been with the firm some time will have firm-specific capital invested in them, either as a result of training or simply from work experience. This raises their productivity in, and thus their value to, the firm. These workers cannot be replace by recruiting new employees on the open market, and the firm will incur additional human capital investment costs during the time it takes for any new workers to acquire the requisite experience and skills. A second reason is that high turnover rates are likely to have a detrimental effect on the morale and thus the productivity of other employees.

As a result of turnover costs firms adopt numerous personnel policies to reduce the turnover rate. Many of these are often associated with internal labour markets (ILMs) such as a well-defined career structure, seniority pay and, at the limit, lifetime employment. Turnover reduction also figures as a possible explanation of efficiency wages, i.e. when workers are paid at a rate above the market level. The justification is that the increased wage bill is less than any turnover costs that would have been incurred.

One interesting empirical finding is that turnover rates are lower in firms where there are trade unions. Some authors explain this by the voice effects of unions, that is, unions provide a channel through which employees can voice their grievances to which firms can respond more effectively. Other explanations are possible, however. For example, it may be the result of higher pay for unionized workers, or because unions are able to resist workforce reductions.

Most studies show that turnover rates are highest for younger and older workers, and also the unskilled. Perhaps with the exception of the young, who have a higher degree of mobility, these findings are broadly consistent with the fixed-cost and firm-specific human capital explanations of turnover reduction. The costs of replacing these workers are lowest, particularly for the unskilled. With older workers there is the loss of specific human capital, but for employees with a lengthy job tenure the fixed costs will have been recouped. There may also be an optimal age structure and thus rate of turnover of employees, with older workers being replaced by younger ones. Indeed, it is likely that a firm will want to retain a balance of ages to maintain productivity and to facilitate the transmission of specific skills from older to younger employees. **SJ**

References and further reading
Hom, P. and Griffeth, R. (1995) *Employee Turnover*, Cincinnati, OH: South Western College Publishing.

Lee, T. W., Mitchell, T. R., Wise, L. and Fireman, S. (1996) 'An unfolding model of voluntary employee turnover', *Academy of Management Journal* 39: 5–36.

Mobley, W. H. (1982) *Employee Turnover: Causes, Consequences and Control*, Reading, MA: Addison-Wesley.

Morrell, K., Loan-Clarke, J. and Wilkinson, A. (2001) 'Unweaving leaving: the use of models in the management of employee turnover', *International Journal of Management Reviews* 3(3): 219–44.

Price (1977) *The Study of Turnover*, Ames, IA: Iowa State University Press.

Lateral moves to create cross-functional experience

Lateral moves to create cross-functional experience represent the new direction of career in organizations. They are on the increase, and it seems the trend will continue. These may be seen as elementary career planning and management practices which most organizations with human resource management systems need to apply. The flattering of organization was one of the flagships of the 1990s' gurus. Delayering and **downsizing** (see separate entry) followed, with the loss of traditional hierarchy based ladders for managers to climb up. When there are fewer hierarchy levels and horizontal communication is a key to success, people will no longer have the option of fast upwards progress. A slow paced climb to the top, perhaps in the Japanese style, became quite typical in Western organizations. Organizations need to clearly indicate that such a route reflects career success rather than failure, and this would be a shift from the past norm, which perceived 'climbing up' only as a career success. People should be advised that career advance is not along the traditional upward movements.

Some of these lateral movements may form, in part, approaches of developing new ventures, secondments and cross-functional moves. Edgar Schein (1978) presented the spiral move across function, but that too was part of upward progress. Lateral moves will characterize the career path of the future manager, while job rotations and role changes will be frequent for the rank-and-file workforce (Baruch, 1999). Relevant examples of this trend can be found when insurance agents and bank clerks are being moved to direct marketing jobs. **YB**

References and further reading

Baruch, Y. (1999) 'Integrated career systems for the 2000s', *International Journal of Manpower* 20(7): 432–57.

Schein, E. H. (1978) *Career Dynamics*: *Matching Individual and Organizational Needs*, Reading, MA: Addison-Wesley.

Leadership

There is no definitive construct for the term 'leadership'. Most, however, imply a relationship with motivation. It can also be suggested that most definitions of leadership suggest that the ability to get others to follow or willingly comply is essential. This minimal definition suggests that the ability to communicate effectively and to build effective relationships with others is a critical ability to be developed by aspiring leaders.

Essential distinction between leadership and management is the extent to which leadership seeks to influence interpersonal behaviour. At the very least, leadership can be described as a process by which it is possible to inspire others. By contrast managers are generally defined by organizational requirements such as their ability to meet objectives and to solve short-term problems.

In modern organizations it is generally regarded that leadership qualities are displayed through key functions such as developing and executing the vision and mission of the organization, planning change and informing policy.

An example of these characteristics is demonstrated through the concept of action-centred leadership in the work of John Adair. In this approach the leader most address three areas of need: to achieve the *task*, to maintain the *team* and to develop the *individual*'s needs. This is sometimes referred to as a functional approach to leadership. For example, the *task functions* require the leader to achieve the objectives of the group, allocate resources, organize duties and responsibilities, control quality, manage performance and review progress. *Team functions* require the leader to maintain morale and build the team spirit, maintain the cohesiveness of the group, set the standards and maintaining discipline and establish effective communication. Finally, *individual functions* involve the leader's requirement to address the needs of individual members, dealing with personal problems, giving praise and reconciling conflicts, and finally developing the potential of each individual.

Research carried out into the behavioural aspects off leadership essentially through the Ohio State leadership studies, suggests that behaviours fall within two broad groups. The first is consideration and the second is a *structure*. Consideration refers to the ability of leaders to establish trust and mutual respect, develop people and demonstrating concern, and consideration for subordinates. Structure, on the other hand, indicates the extent to which leaders are equipped to structure group interactions towards the achievement of formed goals.

Further research carried out into leadership style has suggested that leadership is highly influenced by attitudes (see **Theory X and Theory Y**), and by cultural characteristics as demonstrated by William Ouchi's (1981) Theory Z.

There are three broad classifications of leadership style: authoritarian-autocratic, democratic and laissez-faire. Various writers such as McGregor, Likert, Blake and Mouton, have all demonstrated the importance of participative leadership behaviour. But this may also have been, to some extent, influenced by factors external to the organization such as an increasingly well-educated and well-informed public, changes to the values and expectations of society, the demands by organizations for increased technical knowledge, pressures for social responsibility and, finally, by government legislation. Other researchers, such as Tannenbaum and Schmidt, suggested that contextual factors would determine the way a leader would need to deal with subordinates. These factors include the type of organization, the effectiveness of the group, the degree of difficulty related to the task, and pressures of time. Other factors identified by Tannenbaum and Schmidt are personality characteristics of subordinates, and the manager's behavioural characteristics. The *personality characteristics* of subordinates include such things as their level of maturity and ability to act independently, their readiness to assume responsibility for decision-making, the extent to which they can tolerate ambiguity, the extent to which they value the task, whether they have the knowledge and experience to deal with problems and their ability to involve themselves in learning activities. The *leader's behavioural characteristics* would include his or her value system, and the extent of the leader's confidence in subordinate to carry out the task.

The contingency model of leadership suggests that no single style of leadership is appropriate for all situations. Although there are various approaches contained within this model, Vroom and Yetton (1973) are useful in drawing attention to the leader as decision-maker. The first aspect of this approach is that the *decision-making characteristics*, they argue, are determined by the leader's ability to apply rationality to the decision-making process and, in so doing, influence group performance. The second aspect, *decision acceptance*, refers to the motivation and commitment of group or team members when they implement the decision. They argue that seven rules enable managers to develop the most appropriate leadership style in a given situation. The first three rules protect the quality of the decision. For example:

1. Is the quality requirement such that one solution is likely to be more rational than another?
2. Is there sufficient information to make high-quality decision?
3. Is the problem structured?

The other four rules protect the acceptance of decisions. Thus:

4. Is acceptance of the decision by subordinates critical to effective implementation?
5. If you were able to make the decision yourself, is it reasonably certain that subordinates would accept it?
6. Do subordinate share the organizational goals to be obtained in solving the problems?
7. Is conflict among subordinates likely with preferred solutions?

Effectively, Vroom and Yetton argue that these rules indicate decision styles the leader should either adopt or avoid in a given situation. By using a decision tree it is possible to apply the rules to a given situation. This work was later refined by of Vroom and Jago.

Finally, *transactional leadership* and *transformational leadership* have become popular definitions that refer to the exercise of legitimate authority in hierarchical organizations (*transactional leadership*) in which the leader is involved in an exchange, or transaction, between the pursuit of goals, objectives, and work tasks and the conferment of rewards and punishments. A transactional approach can therefore be regarded as a simple psychological contract based on a minimal exchange of tasks for rewards. *Transformational leadership*, by contrast, reflects the needs to develop a charismatic or inspirational qualities in order to energized commitment. This is more in keeping with the ability to be either entrepreneurial or intrepreneurial. **JG**

References and further reading
Adair, J. (1979) *Action-Centred Leadership*, Aldershot: Gower.
Adair, J. (1986) *Effective Teambuilding*, Aldershot: Gower.
Dirks, K. T. (2000) 'Trust in leadership and team performance', *Journal of Applied Psychology* 85(6): 1004–11.
Ouchi, W. G. (1981) *Theory Z: How American Business Can Meet the Japanese Challenge*, Reading, MA: Addison-Wesley.
Tannenbaum, R. and Schmidt, W. H. (1973) 'How to choose a leadership pattern', *Harvard Business Review*, May–June: 162–75, 178–80.
Vroom, V. H. and Yetton, P. W. (1973) *Leadership and Decision-Making*, Pittsburgh, PA: University of Pittsburgh Press.
Waldman, D., Ramirez, G., House, R. and Puranam, P. (2001) 'Does Leadership Matter?', *Academy of Management Journal* 44(1): 134–58.

Learning organization

It is assumed that organizations need to enhance knowledge and learning where they face uncertain, changing or ambiguous market conditions (Moinegeon and Edmundson, 1996). Senge (1990) has argued that there will only be two kinds organization: those which fail and learning organizations which have the ability to learn and react more quickly than their competitors to a changing market environment. Senge proposes five key components of a learning organization:

- personal mastery
- shared vision
- team learning
- mental models
- system thinking.

As Easterby-Smith (1997) identifies, there are differing views about the concepts of the learning organization (LO) and organizational learning (OL). He suggests that the LO is concerned with expanding the organization's capacity to learn, whereas OL is concerned with understanding learning within organizational contexts. Thus the former is active and prescriptive, while the latter is analytic and descriptive.

A key issue is the extent to which a learning organization is something more than the sum of learning by individuals within it. A key distinction used in the literature is between levels of learning. Single-loop learning exists when individuals are only able to make corrective responses to organizational problems. Double-loop learning exists when problems are reframed and new ways of doing things are introduced. Triple-loop learning exists when organizational members collectively and continuously produce new structures and strategies for learning as an inherent part of organizational life.

The learning organization is often presented as consistent with policies such as empowerment but some critics suggest this does not take into account power and political issues in the organization. **JL-C**

References and further reading

Argyris, C. and Schön, D. (1978) *Organizational Learning: A Theory of Action Perspective*, Reading, MA: Addison-Wesley.

Easterby-Smith, M., Snell, R. and Gherardi, S. (1998) 'Organizational learning: diverging communities of practice?', *Management Learning* 29(3): 259–72.

Easterby-Smith, M. (1997) 'Disciplines of the learning organisation: contributions and critiques, *Human Relations* 50(9): 1085–113.

Moingeon B. and Edmondson A. (eds) (1996) *Organizational Learning and Competitive Advantage*, London: Sage.

Senge, P. (1990) *The Fifth Discipline: The Art and Practice of the Learning Organization*, New York: and Doubleday.

Snell R. and Chak A. M. K. (1998) 'The learning organisation: learning and empowerment for whom?', *Management Learning* 29(3): 337–64.

Lockouts

Employers may pre-empt a strike by excluding workers from the premises or, when strikes do occur, they may refuse to allow the strikers to return to work. Employers usually take such action in an attempt to impose a reduction in pay or conditions, and this is often linked to plans to break or prevent effective union organization. These situations are known as lockouts. Employers may also take on other workers during a strike, plan to retain the employment of these *strike-breakers* after the strike and therefore dismiss the strikers. Those dismissed in this way are effectively locked out, and will probably continue to picket the affected workplace. Lockouts have sometimes occurred when workers have attempted to establish union recognition or to resist derecognition. However, there could be some decline in such disputes as a result of the 1999 Employment Relations Act, partly because it introduces the possibility of legal intervention when the parties cannot resolve union recognition disputes, and partly because it places some new restrictions upon the power of employers to dismiss strikers (Labour Research Department, 1999).

When lockouts occur, disputes are usually bitter and protracted, causing considerable hardship to those workers *locked out*. In such circumstances these workers are likely to attempt to organize support within the wider labour movement, and fund-raising, media campaigns and secondary picketing are typical features of this. However, these are the kinds of activities from which the Trades Union Congress and the national leadership of most unions have distanced themselves in the late 1980s and 1990s. As a result, local trade unionists and their *unofficial* supporters have often been left to fend for themselves in such protracted disputes. Apart from accounts of particular disputes which became lockouts (e.g. Dromey and Taylor, 1978; Saundry and Turnbull, 1996), most of the relevant literature addresses the broader questions of industrial conflict and strikes. (See also **Industrial conflict** and **Strikes**.) **DB**

References and further reading

Blyton, P. and Turnbull, P. (1998) *The Dynamics of Employee Relations*, Basingstoke: Macmillan, ch. 10.

Dromey, J. and Taylor, G. (1978) *Grunwick: the Workers' Story*, London: Lawrence and Wishart.

Hyman, R. (1989) *Strikes*, 4th edn, London: Macmillan.

Labour Research Department (1998) *The Law at Work*, London: LRD Publications, pp. 80–2, 92.

Labour Research Department (1999) *The Employment Relations Act 1999 – a Guide for Trade Unionists*, London: LRD Publications.

Saundry, R. and Turnbull. P. (1996) 'Melee on the Mersey: contracts, competition and labour relations on the docks', *Industrial Relations Journal* 27(4): 275–88.

Management by objectives

Management by objectives (MBO) refers to a system of goal-setting and appraisal. It can be used specifically to assist employee development – where managers assess performance in terms of ability to meet agreed performance targets (objectives) and subsequently assess development needs as well as agreeing future targets. More often it is used to refer more generally to a process of assessing progress towards identified business goals. Advocates of MBO such as Peter Drucker stress that it has advantages over other systems for appraisal, because it refers to performance rather than personality and it enables both managers and their subordinates to see clearly what is expected. Achievement of business goals should be easier as, 'all contribute towards a common goal [and] all pull in the same direction' (Drucker, 1968: 119). To this extent, the objectives set should follow one favoured acronym of management consultants – SMART. Objectives should be Specific, Measurable, Attainable, Realistic and Timed. In addition it is important to consider these three key stages.

1. Objectives need to be agreed and understood equally.
2. Results should be reviewed in terms of these objectives. Where objectives have not been met improvement areas need to be identified and acted upon.
3. New objectives need to be agreed.

There is some empirical support for the success of MBO systems (Vecchio, 2000: 100), although critics of MBO would suggest it has inherent weaknesses. First, many crucial goals or objectives may not be measurable and may change over time. The organizations themselves may be changing (Harrison, 1997: 209). Also, MBO may be based on an unrealistic picture of how business strategy is developed or ultimately achieved. Strategy may be enacted (Weick, 1988) and emergent rather than formally laid down. Researchers such as Henry Mintzberg (1975) emphasize that ritual, negotiation, subjective assessment and 'word of mouth' influence decision-making by managers, rather than explicitly rational targets which could become a mere paper exercise. In any case, most researchers would see it as unrealistic to expect an MBO system to work at all times in all situations. Vecchio (2000: 101) has pointed out that because the very term MBO arouses suspicion, an MBO system may need to be called something else to avoid people's preconceptions, e.g. START (Set Targets And Reach Them) or GAP (Goal Acceptance Programme). **KM**

References and further reading
Drucker, P. F. (1968) *The Practice of Management*, London: Heinemann, ch 11.
Harrison, R. (1997) *Employee Development*, London: IPD.
Koontz, H., O'Donnel, C. and Weihrich, H. (1980) *Management*, London: McGraw-Hill, ch 7.
Mintzberg, H. (1975) 'The manager's job: folklore and fact', *Harvard Business Review*, July–August: 49–61.
Vecchio, R. P. (2000) *Organizational Behavior Core Concepts*, London: Dryden, pp. 98–101.
Weick, K. E. (1988) 'Enacted sensemaking in crisis situations', *Journal of Management Studies* 25: 305–17.

Management Charter Initiative (MCI)

The Handy (1987) and Constable and McCormick (1987) reports identified that, in comparison with international counterparts, UK managers had low levels of management education. These highly influential reports gave rise to a significant impetus to both increase the provision of management education and to overhaul it. The new approach was concerned with widening access to education and qualifications beyond the purely academic. In the wake of these reports, the MCI was founded under the chairmanship of Sir Bob Reid (ex Post Office).

The MCI is an employer-led body which, through consultation with industry, designs and develops national management standards. The standards, which have been designed, tested and recently reissued, specify what competencies a manager should have at different levels. Standards are published for supervisory, junior and middle managers (Levels 3, 4 and 5) and there are related NVQ qualifications. Senior management standards also exist but there is no equivalent NVQ qualification. The MCI has now published additional standards to the generic ones, for example in Quality and Energy, and specialist standards for managers in small business.

With Tom Cannon as its Chief Executive, the MCI now has as its mission 'to shape and promote management development, particularly competence based management development, for the benefit of both organisations and individuals' (MCI web site). In 1998 it joined forces with the Small Firms Enterprise Development Initiative (SFEDI) to form the National Training organization for Management and Enterprise (METO).

The MCI approach to management development has been concerned with work-based development of competence. It designed a system of assessment, Crediting Competence, which entailed the development of individual portfolios. Managers would gather competence evidence against the standards. The system requires portfolios to be assessed by internal company assessors and, externally, through an MCI-approved regional centre. The system is supported by training courses and learning materials.

The MCI publishes a range of materials associated with the standards and NVQs. It runs workshops for assessors and verifiers and mounts national conferences for both consultation and dissemination of policy issues.

The approach to management education promoted by the MCI has attracted considerable criticism, particularly from the academic community. Crediting Competence has been seen as non-developmental since it allows managers to gain credit for something they currently do, rather than develop knowledge and skill. Additionally, many managers who were attracted to the scheme by its practical focus found that it was bureaucratic and unwieldy. Employers too, who should have been the most enthusiastic, found the approach time-consuming and costly.

Despite concerns regarding the qualification system, the MCI continues to heighten awareness of the importance of raising management education levels and has established itself with industry, academe and government in this regard. **ASm**

References and further reading

Boddy, D., Paton, R. and MacDonald, S. (1995) 'Competence-based management awards in higher education', *Management Learning* 26(2): 179–92.

Constable, J. and McCormick, R. (1987) 'The making of British managers', BIM/CBI Report.

Frank, E. (1991) 'The UK's Management Charter Initiative: The first three years', *Journal of European Industrial Training* 17(1): 9–11.

Handy, C. (1987) 'The making of managers', MSC/NEDO/BIM Report.

Hayes, J., Rose-Quirie, A. and Allenson, C. (2000) 'Senior managers' perception of the competencies they require for effective performance: implications for training and development', *Personnel Review* 29(1): 92–105.

Loan-Clarke, J. (1996) 'The Management Charter Initiative: a catalogue of management standards/NVQs', *Journal of Management Development* 15(6): 4–17.

Management Charter Initiative (MCI), Russell Square House, 10–12 Russell Square, London WC1B 5BZ.

Mullins, L. J. (1996) *Management and Organisational Behaviour*, London: Pitman.

Web site at http://www.management.charter.initiative.org.uk/

Management consultancy

It has been observed that the use of management consultants to advise on human resource management issues has increased rapidly in recent years. Management consultancy covers the whole range of management issues from strategy and information technology to human resource management. In simple terms, management consultancy is the provision of help whereby the consultant is not directly responsible for carrying out the task but for assisting those who are. Consultancy has traditionally been taken to mean the engagement of outside help, but with the rise of internal consultancy in many organizations this definition has become blurred. The services of management consultancy firms are also many and varied. These can range from the provision of proprietary products such as job evaluation schemes or absence management procedures, to the provision of ongoing advice to senior managers on a range of management issues.

Consultancy firms vary too. There are large consultancy firms, sometimes part of huge accountancy practices who offer a range of management specialisms; small 'boutique' consultancies that provide a limited range of 'niche' services; larger specialized firms who offer a particular range of services, such as advice on pay and benefits; and independent consultants, often sole traders, whose services depend very much on the individual skills and experience of the owner.

There are differences in the style of consultancy. Style can range from the 'expert' mode, which is highly prescriptive. Consultants literally tell the organization what the problem is and how to resolve it. At the opposite end of the spectrum, there is process consulting. This approach is based on the premise that the only people who can solve a problem are those who 'own' the problem. The consultant as an outsider can only help those whose problem it is, and he or she does this by acting as a facilitator of change.

The main areas of human resource (HR) consulting are:

- general advice on HR
- advice on specific HR issues
- the development of HR systems (for example, performance management)
- the development of HR processes (for example, communication)
- delivery of training and development interventions
- recruitment and selection services
- introducing and maintaining benchmarking facilities.

When introduced properly into an organization, management consultancy can add real value in many different ways. However, the quality and standards of consultancy firms and the services they offer vary greatly, and the cost of consultancy can be high. It takes knowledge and skill on the part of both the consultants and the commissioning parties to initiate and develop an effective consultancy project. **LS**

References and further reading

Armstrong, M. (1994) *Using the HR Consultant*, London: IPM.
Kubr, M. (1996) *Management Consulting: A Guide to the Profession,* Geneva: ILO.
Wickham, P. A. (1999) *Management Consulting*, London: Financial Times Management.

Management development

> Management development within a single company context refers to activities which gather together numbers of managers from an organisation in order to 'learn'. (Patching, 1999: 1)

There is a view that single company management development programmes are a powerful form of organizational development as they provide opportunity for a shared learning experience which can change beliefs and behaviours to impact positively, one hopes, upon performance. However, management development may also be an individual learning activity which seeks to broaden and grow the management capacity and potential of the person.

Management development, rather than management education or training, has become the more commonly used term to define any activity which, in the broadest sense, adds value to management capability. It is part of the process of organizational development. Training (i.e. skills enhancement) may be one aspect of development, and education (i.e. knowledge acquisition) another. 'Development' is the overarching term which encompasses the growth of managers' skills, knowledge, attitudes and experience in pursuit of career and organizational goals. It is job and organization related.

Activities which management development encompasses may be very wide-ranging. A formal course or programme of courses is one of the commonest forms of management development which may immediately come to mind upon mention of the term. However, its all-embracing nature means that any planned learning activity which enhances managers and their work is a form of development. Networking, mentoring (or being mentored), coaching (or being coached), self-guided learning and project work are only some of the items which may form a list of management development activities.

Management development became a significant activity for companies and individuals in the latter part of the twentieth century. In the late 1980s, the Constable McCormick (1987) and Handy (1987) reports identified that British management lagged behind international counterparts in the level of management education attained. Influential bodies such as the Confederation of British Industry strongly recommended that the provision of management development, including accredited courses at undergraduate, postgraduate and post-experience levels, should be increased in order to improve the management stock and the country's ability to compete. Successive governments have supported the view that there is a link between development and economic growth as evidenced in the Competitiveness White Papers of the 1990s. Despite the fact that evaluating such a link is difficult, the variety of provision is growing, the degree of seriousness with which it is taken by companies, individuals and government support agencies is growing and the market for management development is buoyant. **ASm**

References and further reading

Constable, J. and McCormick, R. (1987) 'The making of British managers', BIM/CBI Report.
Handy, C. (1987) 'The making of managers', MSC/NEDO/BIM Report.

Holman, D. (2000) 'Contemporary models of management education in the UK', *Management Learning* 31(2): 197–217.

Kessells, J. and Harrison, R. (1998) 'External consistency: the key to success in management development programmes?', *Management Learning* 29(1): 39–68.

Patching, K. (1999) *Management and Organisation Development*, Basingstoke: Macmillan.

Winterton, J. and Winterton, R. (1997) 'Does management development add value?', *British Journal of Management* 8: 565–76.

Woodall, J. (1999) 'Corporate support for work based management development', *Human Resource Management Journal* 10(1): 18–32.

Management education

Most organizations wish to develop their managers in recognition that a capable management cadre, as key decision-makers, can make a real difference in the attainment of organizational goals. This is usually referred to as *management development.* Management development comes in a variety of different forms; a distinction has been drawn traditionally between *management education* and *management training*. Management education has focused on management knowledge and understanding, whilst management training has concentrated mainly on the development of managerial skills. However, in recent times, this distinction has become blurred. As we know, managers can develop both informally and formally, and methods can range from sponsored business school education to planned experience, team-building and secondments. Recent interest in this field has focused on the development of *learning* managers (managers who continuously learn and develop) rather than *learned* ones (those who have knowledge, possibly gained in the past). Therefore, we see an emerging model of *management development* as a combination of *management education* (focusing on knowledge and understanding), *management training* (focusing on skills and competence) and *management self-development* (focusing on the emphasis on the individual manager to continually learn and develop). Here, we shall concentrate on management education, although this entry should be read in conjunction with those relating to **management development** and **management self-development**.

Until fairly recently, management education has been the preserve of universities and higher education institutions in the UK. Management qualifications have traditionally been gained through formal academic means (the MBA – Master of Business Administration – is a prime example of this). For experienced managers, management education tends to be delivered at postgraduate level. The most common qualifications are the Certificate in Management Studies (CMS), broadly aimed at developing 'junior' managers, the Diploma in Management Studies (DMS) aimed at developing 'middle' managers and the MBA, which targets those with a career in 'senior' management in mind. We have also seen an expansion in undergraduate courses in business studies and/or management. These courses usually aim to give inexperienced people a basic grounding in business and management before they enter the world of work. On completion, many of these graduates become trainees on accelerated management programmes in organizations. Business schools have proliferated in the 1990s in the UK. Distance learning methods are becoming more popular, as students struggle to balance their studies with busy work and home lives. The Open University, a famous provider of distance learning programmes, is one of the biggest business schools in the UK.

In recent times, the traditional management education market has come under threat. Driven by the Management Charter Initiative in 1988, alternative approaches to management education have become popular, based on competence and nationally set management standards coupled with work-based assessment (for example, National Vocational Qualifications in management levels 3 to 5). In many cases, these programmes are offered by non-academic organizations, sometimes but not always in partnership with academic accrediting bodies. A key feature of some of the newer approaches is the *accreditation of prior learning*, for example, giving academic credit towards a qualification for work experience or qualifications previously gained in similar fields.

At the moment, these two approaches are developing independently of each other, and both have their critics. Academic management education is accused by some of being elitist and remote from reality. Competence-based management education is accused by others of being ill-informed and too concerned with producing large amounts of paperwork in an attempt to provide 'evidence' of competence. It is a debate that has yet to run its course. **LS**

References and further reading

Engwall, L. and Zamagni, V. (eds) (1998) *Management Education in Historical Perspective*, Manchester: Manchester University Press.

Frazer, M. C. and Chattei J. I. (eds) (1998) *Management Education in Countries in transition*, Basingstoke: Macmillan.

French, R. and Grey, C. (1999) *Rethinking Management Education*, London: Sage.

Prince, C. and Stewart, J. (2000) 'The dynamics of the corporate education market and the role of business schools', *Journal of Management Development* 19: 207–19.

Management self-development

Management self-development has become popular with some organizations as part of their management development strategies in recent years. It is based on the following premise: 'That any effective system for management development must increase the manager's capacity and willingness to take control over, and responsibility for, events – particularly for themselves and their own learning' (Pedler, Burgoyne and Boydell, 1994: 3).

Self-development is a powerful form of personal development. The individual takes prime responsibility for their own development and the decisions about how to achieve it. It is a three-stage approach: learners diagnose their learning needs for themselves, plan to fulfil those needs and assess the effectiveness of their actions. Whilst this is a simple enough concept, it requires a highly developed grasp of the skills and disciplines involved to drive the process by oneself. organizations, therefore, have to invest in up-skilling their people to enable them to engage in effective self-development activity.

Stage 1 activities focus on the setting of management self-development goals. To do this, the individual must make decisions about what it is he or she is trying to achieve. This involves a degree of projection into the future, deciding where he or she wants to go in management terms and the knowledge, skills and attributes he or she will have to develop to achieve the objectives. This will probably involve some life/career diagnosis and planning, and developing a great deal of self-awareness.

Stage 2 focuses on the meeting of management self-development goals. The activities here are unlimited: dependent upon the individual's plan, they can range from increasing knowledge required by one's job and organization to improving one's ability to learn in an effective way.

Stage 3 activities focus on the self-evaluation of the effectiveness of the self-development effort. Did the individual achieve what he or she set out to do? Were the methods used the most appropriate? If those activities were to be repeated, could they be done in a better way?

Management self-development is a useful concept for organizations in fast-moving environments where a more rigid approach to management development might be too slow to support major change. It is not, however, without its critics. Research has shown that in some organizations managers feel disappointed with the level of support they receive from the organization. Other writers allege that organizations use the self-development concept as an excuse for failing to provide adequate manage-ment development provision, pushing the responsibility onto individual managers instead. **LS**

References and further reading

Burgoyne, J. (1999) *Developing Yourself, Your Career and Your Organization*, London: Lemos and Crane.

Megginson, D. and Whitaker, V. (1996) *Cultivating Self-development*, London: IPD.

Pedler, M. and Boydell, T. (1999) *Managing Yourself*, London: Lemos and Crane.

Pedler, M., Burgoyne, J. and Boydell, T. (1994) *A Manager's Guide to Self-Development*, Maidenhead: McGraw-Hill.

Management styles

Developed by Fox (1974) and later Purcell (1993) and Purcell and Ahlstrand (1994), management style refers to the general approach taken by companies towards managing the employment relationship. Management style can be categorized according to the decisions managers make over key elements in the employment relationship – whether employees are a resource to be developed or a cost to be minimized and whether relations with employees are co-operative or adversarial, with or without recognized trade unions.

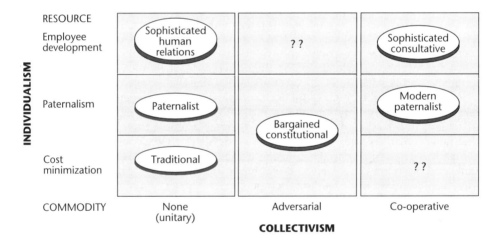

Figure 3: **Classification of management styles**
Source: Purcell and Ahlstrand (1993)

Purcell's recent classification of management style contains six categories, arranged according to companies' approaches to two aspects of human resource management (see figure). At one extreme are *traditionalists* – companies which seek to minimize employment costs. Employees typically receive low pay, minimal training and experience poor working conditions. Managers avoid trade union recognition or mechanisms for employees to voice their opinions, believing that employees and management have the same interests. Examples of this kind of employer are often found among small and medium-sized enterprises, e.g. small textiles firms.

At another extreme are *sophisticated human relations* – companies such as IBM and Marks and Spencer. They minimize distinctions between management and employee interests and therefore avoid recognizing trade unions, but attempt to make employment conditions so attractive that employees feel that their own needs are fulfilled and therefore identify with the company's interests. Mechanisms to achieve this include generous wages and benefits, opportunities for development and internal promotion and employee communication channels.

Two categories of company accept that employees may have different interests and concerns from their employer and recognize trade unions as a mechanism for channelling and managing those views.

The first of these is *bargained constitutionalists* – companies whose major aim is to gain control and stability over workers' efforts. To achieve this, they resolve conflictual issues such as pay levels or grievances through hotly negotiated systems and procedures involving union representatives. Ford is one example.

The second, *sophisticated consultationists,* emphasize joint problem-solving and listening to employees' concerns to build constructive relationships, using union channels and bodies such as works committees to regulate the employment relationship. Several of the giant chemical companies like BP Amoco and ICI take this kind of partnership approach.

Perhaps the most important category of management styles derives not from Purcell and Ahlstrand's work, but from Fox (1974). This is the *standard moderns*. They differ from all other company types since they exhibit no consistent management style. Managers react to changing business conditions, so employees will be offered training and pay rises when business is good but will be made redundant quickly when times are bad.

Surveys (Marginson, Edwards and Martin, 1988) have shown that many British companies are *standard moderns*. How valid therefore is the classification, if large numbers of companies do not have a preferred management style? Companies may also seek to minimize costs and secure employee commitment simultaneously, so the binary division between objectives may not be appropriate. Finally, managers may apply different styles within the same organization, distinguishing between paternalistic policies for managers and a traditional style for manual employees, or between paternalistic approaches to managing 'core' employees and cost-minimization attempts for the 'peripheral' workforce. **AC**

References and further reading

Fox, A. (1974) *Beyond Contract*: *Work, Power and Trust Relations*, London: Faber.

Kessler, I. and Purcell, J. (1995) 'Individualism and collectivism in theory and practice: management style and the design of pay systems', in P. Edwards (ed.) *Industrial Relations*: *Theory and Practice in Britain*, Oxford: Blackwell.

Legge, K. (1995) 'Styles of managing the employment relationship', in K. Legge, *Human Resource Management*: *Rhetorics and Realities*, Basingstoke: Macmillan.

Marginson, P., Edwards, P. and Martin, R. (1998) *Beyond the Workplace*: *Managing Industrial Relations in Multi-Establishment Enterprises*, Oxford: Blackwell.

Purcell, J. (1993) 'Mapping management style in employee relations', *Journal of Management Studies* 24(5): 533–48.

Purcell, J. and Ahlstrand, B. (1993) *Strategy and Style in Employee Relations*, Oxford: Oxford University Press.

Purcell, J. and Ahlstrand, B. (1994) *Human Resource Management in the Multi-Divisional Company*, Oxford: Oxford University Press.

Managing change

Although the model for managing change originated with the discipline of organizational development (OD) in the late 1960s the implicit recognition of organizational change emerged with contingency theory between 1961 and 1970 (see **Contingency approach**). The distinctive metaphor of change as a journey, implicit in most of the change management literature, emerged from Kurt Lewin's concept of force field analysis. This particular focus was concerned with helping clients to understand the dynamics of the change process. This individual focus was later enhanced by the ideas of group and organizational change implicit in the work of contingency theorists.

The original focus was concerned with the *individual*. Intervention strategies were originally dominated by *behaviour modification* theory, the purpose of which was to increase the frequency of desired behaviours and decrease the frequencies of undesired behaviours. Later examples of managing change at the individual level include *Gestalt psychology*, Kohb's model of individual change through *learning interventions* and *management development* which also provides a perspectives on individual change focused on 'experience learning'.

At the organizational level a greater depth was provided by a sociological concern to explain the nature of change. Much of this debate was informed by the late nineteenth-century writings of Comte, Durkheim and Marx whose contributions to the analysis of social change have influenced the management literature. Whilst the notion of evolutionary development runs through all of these accounts, their explanations are very different. Comte's theory suggested that change was 'evolutionary' and based on stages of maturity. Durkheim gave rise to the functionalist view of change which became predominant in the OD literature of the 1960s and 1970s through the organic metaphor and open systems analysis. This is developed further by more recent quality management programmes in which inputs, outputs and internal processes become the focus for managing change. The ideas of Marx have given rise to critiques which challenge the unitarist assumptions of many programmed approaches to change.

A central element common to all planned change programmes is described by Chin and Benne (1976: 22) as 'the conscious utilization and application of knowledge as an instrument or tool for modifying patterns and institutions of practice'. Planned change interventions are therefore extremely varied but they fall under three broad headings. These are:

- *rational-empirical* interventions such as political interventions giving rise to new governmental policies
- *normative-re-educative* interventions which involve organizational and group change and are usually provided by OD consultants, change agents and trainers
- *power-coercive* interventions which range from industrial relations strategies, protests, the use of political institutions and legislation.

We can trace the roots of *normative–re-educative* interventions from the Hawthorne experiments onwards. Studies of anomie and alienation eventually gave rise to a neo-human relations focus on the quality of working life. However, the list of well-known change interventions includes:

- participative management and the management grid in the 1960s
- personal development in the 1970s
- organizational culture, total quality management (TQM) and buisness process re-engineering (BPR) in the 1980s
- human resource development in the 1990s
- the more recent focus on organizational learning.

Recent debates have questioned the assumptions that underlie the planned change model. The concept of managing strategic change has been transformed in relation to the economic climate. Up to the mid-1960s competition was limited to local and national borders. By the late 1960s and1970s many companies diversified to enhance future growth. By the 1980s the excellence movement popularized organizational culture a the vehicle to manage change. Peters and Waterman (1982) popularized the McKinsey 7-S Framework which served to demonstrate the interconnectedness of structure, strategy, skills, staff, style and systems revolving around a central concept of shared values.

During the late 1980s and 1990s globalization and political upheavals in former communist countries have contributed to a volatile marketplace. During the 1980s and 1990s the idea of managing change has become part of the received wisdom of managing turbulent environments. Since the late 1980s there have been various challenges to the older approaches of planned change. For example, one problem is presented consistently in the critiques of the management of change literature. This is the limitation of the rational model of change which views change as a series of strategic episodes in which each element of change has a specific beginning and a finite end. This has led to the accusation that change management has been overly concerned with the mechanics of change at the expense of the historical, processual and contextual issues that inform the underlying dynamics of the organization. The most notable critiques have been Pettigrew (1985), Dawson (1994) and Pettigrew and Whipp (1993). The emerging alternative to planned change models has been dubbed as either the 'emergent change model' (Burnes, 1996a) or 'processual change' (Dawson, 1994). The critiques suggest that change should not be treated as a series of linear events but as a complex, temporal, iterative and non-linear patchwork of unfolding processes. Dawson and Palmer (1995), for example, noted in their study of TQM programmes that unforeseen critical events during the change process could serve to impede, hasten or redirect the route to change. **JG**

References and further reading

Bate, P. (1995) *Strategies for Cultural Change*, Oxford: Butterworth-Heinemann.

Beckhard, R. (1969) *Organisation Development: Strategies and Models*, Reading, MA: Addison-Wesley.

Burnes, B. (1996a) *Managing Change*, 2nd edn, London: Pitman.

Burnes, B. (1996b) 'No such thing as a "one best way" to manage organizational change', *Management Decision* 34(10): 11–18.

Carnall, C. (1995) *Managing Change in Organizations*, Hemel Hempstead: Prentice Hall.

Chin, R. and Benne, K. (1976) 'General strategies for affecting changes in human systems', in W. Bennis, K. Benne, R. Chin and K. Carey (eds) *The Planning of Change*, 3rd edn, New York: Rinehart and Winston.

Dawson, P. (1994) *Organizational Change: A Processual Approach*, London: Paul Chapman Publishing.

Dawson, P. and Palmer, G. (1995) *Quality Management*, Melbourne: Longman.

French, W. L. and Bell, C. H. (1995) *Organization Development: Behavioral Science Interventions for Organization Improvement*, 5th edn, London: Prentice Hall International.

Peters, T. J. and Waterman, R. H. Jr (1982) *In Search of Excellence: Lessons from America's Best-Run Companies*, New York: Harper and Row.

Pettigrew, A. (1985) *The Awakening Giant, Continuity and Change in ICI*, Oxford: Blackwell.

Pettigrew, A. and Whipp, R. (1993) 'Understanding the environment', in C. Mabey and B. Mayon-White (eds) *Managing Change*, London: Paul Chapman Publishing/Open University.

Tichy, N. M. (1983) *Managing Strategic Change: Technical, Political and Cultural Dynamics*, New York: Wiley.

Managing diversity

Managing diversity in employment relates to the realization of the potential of each individual member of the workforce. It is based on the belief that people should be valued for their difference and that by recognizing and utilizing that difference, organizations can improve performance. The term 'diversity' originated in the USA in the 1980s and the concept has spread significantly in America since then. The term is less widespread in the UK but is becoming increasingly used either alongside or instead of the related concept of equal opportunities. Factors which have contributed to this shift in emphasis from equality to diversity not only include changing social and political agendas and demographic profiles but also a growing interest in business ethics and, most importantly, the recognition of the link between diversity and competitiveness in a global economy. In this context the definition of diversity extends beyond gender and race to embrace such things as differences in age, ethnicity, religious beliefs, physical ability, sexual orientation, values, education, economic status and geographical origin.

There is still much inconsistency in the way the terms 'equality' and 'diversity' are used and in the way the latter is defined. However it is possible to identify some underlying differences in the two approaches. Managing diversity, which is business-needs focused, is about working with and benefiting from individual differences in a proactive way and using culture as a vehicle. It is seen as the responsibility of all managers. This is in contrast to equal opportunities, which tends to be legally driven and focuses on the removal of discrimination and the assimilation of disadvantaged groups through setting targets and changing practices and procedures, often in a reactive way. Responsibility for equal opportunities rests with the personnel department.

Managing diversity is sometimes presented as an evolutionary step in the implementation of equal opportunities but nonetheless requiring a systematic approach. The starting point is strategic direction from top management and a clear commitment that diversity matters, followed by an organizational audit of the current situation, the development and implementation of some policy options and continual review and evaluation. As with equal opportunities the importance of embedding it in all human resource management procedures is critical and the centrality of understanding and valuing difference puts a strong focus on training and personal development. Whilst organizational case studies report positive benefits from managing diversity, the precise relationship between a diverse workforce and increased effectiveness needs further examination. **SS**

References and further reading

Equal Opportunities Review (2000) 'Embracing diversity at North Yorkshire Fire and Rescue Service', *Equal Opportunities Review*, May–June: 16–23.

Hicks-Clarke, D. and Iles, P. (2000) 'Climate for diversity and its effects on career and organizational attitudes and perceptions', *Personnel Review*, 29(3): 324–45.

Institute of Personnel and Development (IPD) (1999) *Managing Diversity: Evidence from Case Studies*, London: IPD.

Kirton, G. and Greene, A.-M. (2000) *The Dynamics of Managing Diversity: A Critical Approach*, Oxford: Butterworth-Heinemann.

Liff, S. (1999) 'Diversity and equal opportunities: room for a constructive compromise', *Human Resource Management Journal* 9(1): 65–75.

Maternity rights

Many employers, especially large organizations, give generous contractual leave and encourage employees to return by offering a staged return with gradually increasing hours.

There are minimum statutory rights governing maternity pay and leave, which have been introduced as a result of European Directive 92/85. The most recent rules are to be found in the Maternity and Parental Leave Regulations 1999. These provide that all women, regardless of length of service or number of hours per week worked, are entitled to 18 weeks ordinary maternity leave (OML). This OML will commence on the date which the employee notifies to her employer as the date on which she intends to take her period of absence from work in exercise of her right to maternity leave. (This cannot be before the beginning of the eleventh week before the week the child is expected to be born – the EWC).

Employees who have completed one year's continuous employment by the eleventh week before the EWC are entitled to additional maternity leave which ends 29 weeks after childbirth.

There are detailed rules concerning notice to be given by the employee. The employer may also ask an employee who is entitled to additional leave to confirm that she intends to return to work.

An employee who takes OML is entitled to the benefits of the terms and conditions of her employment *except* remuneration, including matters connected with her employment whether or not they arise under her contract of employment, that would have applied if she had not been absent. She, in turn, is bound by any obligations arising under those terms and conditions which are not inconsistent with her right to be absent from work during OML, such as her implied obligation of good faith.

As regards remuneration, the Secretary of State may make regulations as to what is, or is not, to be treated as coming within the term. Currently the Regulations provide that 'only sums payable to an employee by way of wages or salary' are to be so treated.

The Employment Rights Act gives pregnant women the right to time off for ante-natal appointments and if a pregnant woman is treated unfairly she may argue that this is unlawful sex discrimination. **AB**

References and further reading
Hammond Suddards Edge (2000) *Maternity Rights*, 2nd edn, Legal Essentials Series, London: CIPD. Web site at http://www2.dti.gov.uk/er/maternity.htm

Mediation

From unitary perspectives mediation may be viewed as irrelevant, in contrast to pluralist type approaches. Mediation in the area of human resource management (HRM) may be seen as an assisted continuation of negotiation and related to conflict. It is an interventionist process involving an independent and neutral third party helping parties to resolve differences and come to some agreement. It is more proactive than conciliation as mediators may suggest their own, non-binding, proposals for a settlement, which the parties may accept, reject or vary. However, in practice the dividing line is thin and often blurs. The process of mediation may be similar to conciliation or it may be more formal and similar to arbitration, except with no final binding award. This distinction is reinforced in the UK publicly funded system as mediators are drawn from a list of the Advisory, Conciliation and Arbitration Service (ACAS) arbitrators, who are on the whole academics. In 1999–2000 ACAS completed 595 advisory mediation projects (17 per cent involved collective bargaining arrangements, 13 per cent rewards and 28 per cent communications, consultation and employee involvement).

There are several issues around mediation. Calling for mediation can be seen as a sign of weakness and undermining authority. Varied amounts of 'compulsion', removing some of the parties' freedom, could be used as it avoids giving third parties power to resolve issues on uncongenial terms. Mediation provides 'public relations' aspects, being used to shift some 'blame' and responsibility for settlements. Yet, reliance on mediation can become 'addictive', it can 'chill' processes such as negotiation, making earlier settlement less likely. Nevertheless, mediation forces the sides to re-examine cases, making some movement possible, while mediators approach issues with fresh minds and can also bring their own suggestions and proposals for resolutions. The area of mediation will remain an important one for HRM. **CR**

References and further reading
Advisory, Conciliation and Arbitration Service (ACAS), Annual Reports, London: ACAS.
Margerison, C. and Leary, M. (1975) *Industrial Conflict: The Mediator's Role*, Bradford: Resource Development Associates.
Salaman, M. (2000) *Industrial Relations: Theory and Practice*, London: Pearson.

Mentoring

Mentoring has many different forms, but the most common is encapsulated in the definition provided by Mullen and Noe (1999: 234): 'A mentoring relationship is a one to one relationship between a more experienced member (the mentor) and a less experienced member (the protégé) of the same organization or profession.' The mentoring relationship can provide the protégé with a number of career-related benefits, such as coaching or being put forward for desirable positions, and also psychosocial benefits such as emotional support and friendship (Kram, 1985). It can also be beneficial for the mentor – for example by keeping him or her in touch with new ideas/techniques, and by developing his or her staff development skills. There can also be organizational benefits, many of which arise as a consequence of benefits to the mentor and protégé. For example, newcomers may learn their roles more quickly and information may flow better within an organization. Indeed, many organizations run formal mentoring schemes, where certain categories of staff (e.g. graduate recruits) are assigned a mentor from amongst the fairly or very senior members. However, mentoring can also happen informally, where mentor and protégé find each other and run the relationship in ways that suit them. Most mentoring relationships have a limited life of a few years at most, but can nevertheless have a very powerful influence on the participants.

Mentoring has rapidly become a very popular form of staff development. There are many people who attest to its usefulness. It is sometimes used as a way of increasing the opportunities and achievements of members of disadvantaged groups, such as ethnic minorities and those with very limited educational achievements. Research suggests that people who have received mentoring tend to enjoy more promotions and higher salaries than those who have not. However, there is very little systematic evidence that mentoring (especially formal mentoring) actually causes positive outcomes, and there is often a suspicion that people who would have been successful anyway are the ones who are able to find effective mentors. There are also some risks – for example, mentors may abuse their power, or organizations may find attempts at culture change are frustrated by mentors passing on 'old' ideas to protégés. Formal mentoring is probably more likely to succeed if both mentors and protégés receive some training, there are clear goals to the scheme which cannot easily be achieved by other means, participants are volunteers, and mentors are rewarded for performing their role properly. **JA**

References and further reading

Chao, G. T., Walz, P. M. and Gardner, P. D. (1992) 'Formal and informal mentorships: a comparison of mentoring functions and contrast with non mentored counterparts', *Personnel Psychology* 45: 619–36.

Clutterbuck, D. (1992) *Everyone Needs a Mentor*, London: Institute of Personnel Management.

Gibb, S. (1999) 'The usefulness of theory: A case study in evaluating formal mentoring schemes', *Human Relations* 52: 1055–75.

Kram, K. E. (1985) *Mentoring at Work: Developmental Relationships in Organizational Life*, Glenview, Ill: Scott Foresman and Co.

Mullen, E. and Noe, R. A. (1999) 'The mentoring information exchange: when do mentors seek information from their proteges?', *Journal of Organizational Behavior* 20: 233–42.

Ragins, B. R. and Cotton, J. L. (1999) 'Mentor functions and outcomes: a comparison of men and women in formal and informal mentoring relationships', *Journal of Applied Psychology* 84: 529–50.

Scandura, T. (1998) 'Dysfunctional mentoring relationships and outcomes', *Journal of Management* 24: 449–67.

Misconduct

For many organizations, the management of discipline can be problematic and time-consuming, and dismissals for misconduct generate a substantial proportion of unfair dismissal claims.

Certain types of misconduct such as theft, fighting, falsifying time sheets/expenses, drinking or taking unauthorized absence tend to be generic. Others, such as leaving keys in a vehicle (in the case of a van delivery service) or physically restraining a child (in the case of a nursery) are more context specific and may therefore require the organization in question to spell out clearly what is, and what is not, acceptable.

Most organizations except the very smallest now have formal disciplinary procedures which provide for the progressive handling of conduct issues via oral and written warnings (information about these must be included in the statutory statement of terms and conditions of employment). An informal, counselling approach is, however, increasingly utilized before moving into the formal stages of the procedure.

When drawing up disciplinary procedures it is important to specify what behaviour constitutes misconduct as well as how matters of discipline will be handled. It may also be prudent to indicate which stage of the procedure will be triggered by a particular act of misconduct, especially in the case of gross misconduct, which normally leads to dismissal for a first offence.

Suspected misconduct should be investigated thoroughly and a disciplinary hearing held at which the employee has the right to be represented. Accurate minutes are advisable and employees should be clearly warned what the likely outcome of a repetition of the behaviour will be.

If an employee is dismissed for misconduct and makes an unfair dismissal claim, the employer will not be required to prove that the employee was actually guilty of the particular offence. However, in judging the reasonableness of the dismissal, the tribunal will generally take into account whether:

- the disciplinary procedure was followed
- the employee was made aware of the allegations and given an opportunity to respond to them
- the decision to dismiss was made after considering the employee's response, length of service and any mitigating factors
- there was consistency in the application of sanctions
- the employee was permitted to appeal to a higher level of management. **JE**

References and further reading

Advisory, Conciliation and Arbitration Service (ACAS) (2000) 'Disiplinary and grievance procedures', *Code of Practice 1*, Norwich: The Stationary Office.
British Home Stores v. *Burchell* [1978] IRLR 397.
Earnshaw, J., Goodman, J., Harrison, R. and Marchington, M. (1998) *Industrial Tribunals, Workplace Disciplinary Procedures and Employment Practice*, Employment Relations Research Series, no 2, DTI.
Employment Rights Act (1996) Section 1, (requirements of statement of terms and conditions) London: HMSO.

Mission statement

A mission statement describes the long-term purpose of the organization, the range of products or services offered, the markets and customer or client needs to be met.

A mission should be thought of as the strategic aim of the organization with the mission statement identifying the organizational goals. In addition the mission statement often includes references to corporate philosophy. A well-designed organization is likely to have a written mission statement that serves as the focal point of the organization's strategy. This in turn will inform the priorities of departments or functional areas.

There are two central aspects to be identified in the construction of a mission statement. The first is designed to identify *corporate purpose*, or the *raison d'être* of the organization. This should enable the organization's members to judge the extent to which the organization is successfully pursuing its aim. A second aspect defined by a mission statement should be the *corporate strategy* or the actions required to achieve the organization's purpose. However, it is possible to add a third and more recently recommended consideration. This is concerned with the organization's *corporate conduct*. This aspect may refer to ethical policy in such areas as: the disclosure of information, the environment, equality of opportunity, marketing policy, industrial democracy and experiments on animals. Corporate conduct is therefore designed to indicate how actions and strategies are managed in a legally and socially desirable manner. Corporate conduct also applies to how the organization intends to treat its stakeholders – its shareholders, customers, suppliers, employees and the public. The mission should state how the company intends to serve each of them.

There are various synonyms that stand for a mission statement – corporate purpose, goal, aim, objectives and corporate plan – that can be found in management textbooks. These are often ill-defined and are often used interchangeably. Confusion of these synonyms will hinder the development of corporate objectives leading to ineffective strategic decisions. Defining the mission can provide a valuable starting point for envisioning what the organization should look like and how it should operate. If people have conflicting views about the mission then the resolution of these views becomes a critical action that will mobilize and direct energy to design and achieve the objectives required.

A major argument against mission statements is that they are often little more than platitudes. Many are banal when they simply aspire to 'be the leader in the field'. This usually occurs when they fail to communicate an imaginative vision. Equally, if a mission statement fails to capture the organization's objectives thus enabling the development of measurable performance indicators then it will also be meaningless. **JG**

References and further reading

Argenti, J. (1993) *Your Organization: What Is It for?* London: McGraw-Hill.
Bart, C. (2000) 'A comparison of mission statements and their rationales in innovative and non-innovative firms', *International Journal of Technology Management* 16(1): 64–77.
Cummings, T. G. and Worley, C. G. (1997) *Organisational Development and Change*, Cincinnati, OH: South Western College Publishing.
Morris, R. J. (1996) 'Developing a mission for a diversified company', *Long Range Planning* 29(1): 103–15.

Models of human resource management

Definition of the term 'human resource management' (HRM) is problematic. The extent to which there is no one way of actually 'doing' HRM makes it problematic to talk of HRM per se. A wide variety of management initiatives can fall under the banner of HRM and some of these may be mutually exclusive. For example, some HRM initiatives place emphasis on managing culture, communication and leadership striving for high employee commitment, whilst other HRM initiatives may entail widespread use of numerical flexibility and delayering or downsizing. Additionally, it can be unclear how closely the actual effects of HRM initiatives relate to descriptions of these initiatives, in other words whether the reality of HRM can match the rhetoric. In addition to these definitional and contextual complexities, we need to be aware that there are various interest groups, each with a stake or vested interest in 'HRM'. One way of making sense of this confusion is to look for conceptual frameworks (or models) which outline a particular version or interpretation of HRM. This can make it easier to organize thoughts about planned or actual HR initiatives consistently. A number of different interpretations and models of HRM are offered below.

The Harvard model

Developed by Beer and colleagues at the university of Harvard in the 1980s, this is perhaps the best known model of HRM. This model acknowledges the role of context-specific factors in the choice of HRM policies. These comprise *situational factors* (such as workforce characteristics, business strategy and the labour market) and *stakeholder interests* (such as shareholders, management, unions, employees and government). These influence the way in which *HRM policy choices* (e.g. systems of pay) lead to *HR outcomes* (e.g. commitment) and *long-term consequences* (e.g. organizational effectiveness and individual and societal well-being). An advantage of this model is the degree to which it emphasizes that HR initiatives need to fit the particular industry context, thus allowing for flexibility in terms of the choice of an HR strategy. This sets it apart from other less flexible models, which may have a more 'unitarist' conception of HRM, ignoring the role of different interest groups.

Guest's model
Drawing in part on the Harvard model, David Guest has outlined a framework for assessing the effectiveness of organizations, based on the testing of propositions such as 'strategic integration', 'quality', 'flexibility' and 'commitment'. Although the extent to which these propositions are amenable to testing remains a matter of debate, there is no doubt that his extension of the Harvard model is useful in so far as it gives an example of how fairly abstract notions of 'commitment' and 'organizational effectiveness' might be operationalized, and seen to interrelate. Guest's model of HRM places organizational commitment at its core, and to this extent it is also useful in terms of drawing a clear distinction between HRM and traditional systems of personnel management/industrial relations, which centre more on compliance. Nonetheless, it should be recognized that the belief that high commitment is key to organizational effectiveness remains an assumption which has received little direct empirical support.

Storey's 25-item checklist
This offers a comprehensive way of thinking about the difference between HRM (as an ideal type), and personnel and industrial relations (IR) as a system of management. For each of 25 'dimensions' of management (Storey, 1995: 10), the difference between HRM and personnel and IR is sketched. So, for example, in the dimension of 'conflict handling', for personnel and IR we have 'reach temporary truces', whereas for HRM we have 'manage climate and culture'. Again for the dimension of 'contract', for personnel and IR we have 'careful delineation of written contracts', whereas for HRM we have 'aim to go "beyond contract"'.

The trouble with models of HRM
It can be argued generally that however comprehensive a model may be, it is bound to be an oversimplification of what happens 'in real life', and as such, using a model may distract us from thinking about the inherent complexities involved in managing people. To paraphrase Gareth Morgan, in providing ways of seeing, they also provide us with ways of *not* seeing.

More specifically, it is problematic the extent to which HRM models or theories are 'normative' (how things should be) or 'descriptive' (how things are). One criticism levelled at comparisons between HRM as seen as a new, better way of managing people, and other traditional models such as personnel management (PM) is that they blur this distinction. Models of PM describe or caricature what is actually going on, whereas models of HRM are idealized or 'normative'. Writers such as Legge have argued there is little or no difference between the normative ambitions of PM and HRM.

Finally, other writers such as Tom Keenoy have argued that the term 'human resource management' itself is beset with contradictions and internal tensions, an ambiguous term which can mean anything to anyone. Attempts at definition may be futile or misconceived, and we may need to look at the concept holistically or through metaphor. **KM**

References and further reading
Beer, M., Spector, B., Lawrence, P. R., Mills, D. Q. and Walton, R. E. (1984) *Managing Human Assets*, New York: Free Press.
Beardwell, I. and Holden, L. (1997) *Human Resource Management: A Contemporary Perspective*, London: Pitman.
Keenoy, T. (1999) 'HRM as hologram: a polemic', *Journal of Management Studies* 36(1): 1–23.
Legge, K. (1995) *Human Resource Management: Rhetorics and Realities*, London: Macmillan.
Marchington, M. and Wilkinson, A. (2000) *Core Personnel and Development*, London: IPD.
Morgan, G. (1997) *Images of Organization*, London: Sage.
Storey, J. (ed.) (1995) *Human Resource Management: A Critical Text*, London: Thomson Learning.

Motivation

Defining motivation at work and establishing how managers can best develop it in their employees has long been a major and central topic of research for specialists in the fields of human resource management, organizational behaviour and occupational psychology. It is an area of study characterized by the presence of large numbers of theories, vigorous debates and several distinct traditions. There is no single generally accepted answer to the question of what motivates us at work?

The various theories are usually divided into two types labelled the 'content' and 'process' approaches. The first, associated with authorities such as Abraham Maslow, Frederick Herzberg and David McClelland are needs based. The starting point is the assumption that all humans have definable needs (e.g. money, social life, self-esteem, power, etc.) and that motivation in the workplace follows when these needs are satisfied. The key task for managers is then to create jobs and an organizational context which facilitate the satisfaction of these needs. The alternative tradition (the process approach) is not needs based and thus starts from a rather different set of assumptions. Here motives are neither predefined nor universal, but can be created in the workplace. Hence our actions are less determined by our needs, and more by our responses to the opportunities provided for us at work. The most influential theories here are those which relate to goals, expectancy and equity. From a management perspective these suggest that the most effective ways of sustaining motivation involve the provision of incentives and/or disincentives within a framework which is perceived to be equitable. Process theories of motivation underlie contemporary arguments in favour of performance appraisal systems, incentive payments and employee participation programmes.

A different tradition in thinking about motivation centres on the notion of effective leadership in organizations and stresses its significance rather than the design and structural factors identified above. While it is possible to distinguish between different types of effective leadership style, some of which owe more to the ability to motivate positively than others, it is unwise to ignore the contribution that able individuals can make to the motivation of a team of employees. Arguably this aspect of workplace motivation is becoming increasingly significant as the need grows for organizations to compete more intensely while remaining capable of handling rapid, frequent and unpredictable change. **ST**

References and further reading
Buchanan, D. and Huczynski, A. (1997) *Organizational Behaviour: An Introduction Text*, 3rd edn, London: Prentice Hall, ch 4.
Bussing, A. (1998) 'Motivation and Satisfaction', in M. Poole and M. Warner (eds) *The Handbook of Human Resource Management*, London: Thomson Learning.
Herzberg, F. (1968) 'One more time: how do you motivate employees?', *Harvard Business Review*, January–February: 53–62.
Makin, P., Cooper, C. and Cox, C. (1996) *Organizations and the Psychological Contract*, Leicester: BPS Books, ch. 4.

McKenna, E. (1994) *Business Psychology and Organisational Behaviour: A Student's Handbook*, Hove: Psychology Press, ch. 2.
Steers, R. M., Porter, L. W. and Bigley, G. A. (eds) (1996) *Motivation and Leadership at Work*, 6th edn, London: McGraw Hill.

Multiskilling

Multiskilling is seen as important to organizational success, allowing enhanced utilization of labour and equipment and it is a form of functional flexibility. Multi-skilling includes task integration at two levels: horizontal (tasks formerly undertaken by similarly skilled employees) and vertical (tasks previously done by employees at higher or lower skills). Much of the focus has been on shifts in manufacturing and skilled craft workers with cross-trade working and the idea of the 'multiskilled craftsworker'. This is partly because these groups can be subject to greater trade union representation, more formal agreements, collective bargaining and requiring management negotiation. Many changes in this areas may be relatively shallow, with some blurring at the margins between crafts and the integration of related skills and tasks, such as mechanic-electrician. There has also been some shifts in service sectors and in non-manual areas, where developments in information technology cut across job classifications with electronic equipment designed to input, store, retrieve and transmit information. Other changes have involved less skilled jobs where manage-rial aims have been to operate at lower staffing levels with cover provided by broadening job responsibilities, such as minor maintenance and inspection work undertaken by production operators.

One indication of multiskilling is a declining number of job grades and demarcations within organizations to facilitate greater mobility and transfer across job boundaries. Thus, at Nissan's UK plant one of its 'people principles' was multiskilling, with no job descriptions to encourage flexibility. Yet, the concerns, problems and limits to multiskilling are acute. These range from job losses and work intensification, remuneration and trade union representation to health and safety issues. Critically, multiskilling assumes that adequate training is provided for work-ers to safely and competently undertake a broader range of tasks. This is limited in economies blighted by short-termism, poor investment and weak vocational and education training. **CR**

References and further reading

Atkinson, J. (1984) *Manning For Uncertainty: Some Emerging UK Work Patterns*, London: Institute of Manpower Studies.
Brewster, C., Hegewisch, A. and Mayne, L. (1994) 'Flexible working practices: the controversy and the evidence', in C. Brewster and A. Hegewisch (eds) *Policy and Practice in European Human Resource Management*, London: Routledge.
Cross, M. (1988) 'Changes in working practices in UK manufacturing', Industrial Relations Review and Report, 415: 2–10.
Hendry, C. and Pettigrew, A. (1988) 'Multiskilling in the round', *Personnel Management*, April: 36–43.
National Economic Development Office (NEDO) (1986) *Changing Working Patterns: How Companies Achieve Flexibility to Meet New Needs*, London: NEDO.

Mystery shopping

Some commentators argue that customer service can only be really effectively evalu-ated at the boundary been between customer and organization, and this view has fuelled the growth of mystery shopping as a data-capturing process. Here staff employed by a specialist agency purport to be real shoppers and observe and record their experience of the service encounter. It is now commonly used in banks, travel agencies, insurance companies, supermarkets and parts of the public sector. For example, an element of the Citizens Charter requires the setting of performance indicators on answering telephone calls and letters. Some local authorities evaluate the quality of telephone responses by employing consultants to randomly call the authority and assess the quality of the response.

Mystery shopping is argued to provide a rich source of data that cannot be uncovered by other means, such as customer surveys. Such surveys, although useful for some purposes, are often conducted many months after the service encounter and thus exact service problems are difficult to recollect. Mystery shopping is also seen as being particularly useful in revealing staff performance that causes customers to leave without purchasing. In many service sector organizations a natural consequence of the use of mystery shoppers has been to utilize the data in the performance evaluations of staff. However, mystery shopping, as one could well expect, is not very popular with staff. Employees often question the ethics of introducing shoppers and feel that it represents a distinct lack of managerial trust in them. Thus employees often describe shoppers in terms of 'spies' and 'snoopers' and react with hostility and 'shopper spotting' to their introduction. The introduction of mystery shopping for largely negative reasons of catching staff performing poorly only fuels such reactions. Staff acceptance of mystery shopping can be helped by using the reports to reward staff for good performance rather than punish them for poor performance. Staff who obtain good mystery shopping ratings should be rewarded and recognized, whilst those who obtain poor ones should use the reports as a source of identifying training needs. **TR**

References and further reading

Editorial (1999) 'Mystery shopping's lightweight reputation undeserved', *International Journal of Retail and Distribution Management* 27(2): 114–55.

Leeds, B. (1992) '"Mystery shopping" offers clues to quality service', *Bank Marketing* 24(11): 24–7.

Morrall, K. (1994) 'Mystery shopping tests service and compliance', *Bank Marketing* 26(2): 13–18.

Wilson, A. (1998) 'The use of mystery shopping in the measurement of service delivery', *Service Industries Journal* 18(3): 148–63.

N

National minimum wage

A national minimum wage (NMW) can be introduced in order to prevent the worst cases of worker exploitation. Many industrialized countries have a minimum wage, but only in 1999 was one introduced into the UK. This was set at £3.60 (for those aged 18–21 it was £3.00 an hour), but it has subsequently been increased. In introducing an NMW the British government was seeking to set a rate which would make a substantial difference to the low paid whilst trying to ensure that jobs would not be lost or goods and services become more expensive.

Nearly 10 per cent of the working population benefited from the introduction of the NMW. Of these 1.5 million were women, more than half of whom worked part-time. Other groups most affected were homeworkers, lone parents, ethnic minority workers and 18–20-year-olds.

Initial research findings showed that the NMW did not reduce employment levels or lead to a significant increase in inflation. This was partly because the rate was set at a 'prudent' level and partly because it was introduced at a time of economic growth and prosperity. The impact on pay differentials was found to be minimal (IDS, 2000). Usually, only the very lowest rates in grade structures required adjustment. Employers tended to report that people earning more did not object to those below the minimum getting larger percentage rises.

An NMW is of benefit only if it can be enforced and cannot be evaded by work in the 'informal economy'. In addition the NMW will lose its value if not regularly uprated. In Britain there is no mechanism for automatic changes and it is left to the discretion of the government. **AA**

References and further reading

Burkitt, N., O'Donnell, C. and Patel, B. (1999) 'George Bain and a "mechanistic formula": the purposes and politics of £3.60', *Industrial Relations Journal*, 30(3): 178–84.

DTI web site, National Minimum Wage, at http://www.dti.gov.uk/IR/nmw/index.htm

Edwards, P. and Gilman, M. (1999) 'Pay equity and the national minimum wage: what can theories tell us?', *Human Resource Management Journal*, 9(1): 20–39

Incomes Data Services (IDS) (2000) 'Impact of the minimum wage in 1999/2000', IDS Report 802.

Metcalf, D. (1999) 'The British National Minimum Wage', *British Journal of Industrial Relations*, 37(2): 171–201.

National Targets for Education and Training (NTET, previously known as NETTS)

National Targets for Education and Training were proposed by the Confederation of British Industry (CBI) in 1989 and launched by the government in 1991. The Handy report (1987) having identified the comparatively poorly educated UK workforce, NETTS were seen as a means of addressing the situation. Initially, the target was that, by 1996, 50 per cent of the workforce would be working towards achieving the NVQ award, or units thereof. This has been, in practice, overambitious. First-year targets (1992) were met but there have been subsequent revisions.

In 1994 the targets were that:

- by 1997, 80 per cent young people to achieve National Vocational Qualification (NVQ) Level 2 or equivalent
- training to Level 3 (or equivalent) to be available to all young people who would benefit
- 50 per cent young people to reach NVQ Level 3 (or equivalent) by 2000
- education and training provision should develop self-reliance, flexibility and breadth
- by 1996 all employees should take part in training and development activities as the norm
- by 1996 50 per cent of employees should be aiming towards NVQs, supported by employers
- by 2000 50 per cent of employees should have achieved an NVQ or its equivalent
- by 1996 50 per cent medium and larger organizations should be Investors in People (IIP) recognized.

These targets were to be realized through the Training and Enterprise Councils (TECs) which provide advisory and financial support to individuals and companies engaging in the process. In the future, responsibility will move to the new Learning and Skills Councils (LECs).

Debate around NETTS has focused upon their ambitiousness. In 1997 a review was announced regarding the foundation targets which had stated that, by 2000, 75 per cent of 19-year-olds and 35 per cent of 21-year-olds should have reached specific levels in literacy, numeracy and information technology. The 1997 monitoring revealed that 9.7 per cent of 19-year-olds and 0.4 per cent of 20-year-olds had attained the required level. However, there has been a large increase in the past decade in the number of school leavers entering higher education.

Additionally, there is debate around the appropriateness of IIP for all organizations and NVQs as a credible qualification for individuals. While equivalent qualifications are included in NETT statements, it is NVQs themselves which are more likely to attract TEC funding. These are not, however, uniformly well regarded or felt to be of equivalent value to more traditional academic or professional qualifications. Finally, general awareness of NETTS seems to be fairly limited to policy-making circles and this may be a contributor to the difficulty in their achievement. **ASm**

References and further reading

Handy, C. (1987) 'The making of managers', MSC/NEDO/BIM Report.
Robinson, P. (1997) 'Measure for measure – a critical note on the National Targets for Education and Training and international comparisons of educational attainment', *LSE Discussion Paper*, June 1997, no. 355.
Web site at http://www.dfee.gov.uk/insidedfee/

National Vocational Qualifications

National Vocational Qualifications (NVQs) were introduced in the UK following the report of the Review of Vocational Qualifications Working Group (1986). This group had been asked to consider a new system for accrediting vocational skills. In the UK this approach was driven by the Employment Department (now the Department for Education and Employment – DfEE) and the National Council for Vocational Qualifications (now the Qualifications and Curriculum Authority – QCA). The key intention of NVQs was that they should be based on detailed specifications of occupational competence, in the form of occupational standards, which would apply uniformly across the country. The term 'competence' was used to describe what people could/should do at work. Various lead bodies were created across the different occupational sectors of the economy in order to develop these standards.

It is important to differentiate the term 'competence' from 'competencies' (see a dictionary entry for competence/competencies).

National Vocational Qualifications have been produced at five levels. Levels 1 and 2 tend to concentrate on craft/technical skills, e.g. catering, hairdressing, etc.; Level 3 is meant to denote skills which require supervision of others; Levels 4 and 5 are related to management activity for a given occupational area.

There has been considerable debate regarding the value of NVQs. Criticisms have centred around such issues as:

1. The downgrading of the importance of knowledge within NVQs.
2. The method used for specifying occupational standards.
3. The credibility of the assessment process and the quality of those undertaking assessment.

The uptake of National Vocational Qualifications has varied considerably by sector and by level of qualification. In terms of provision, the further education sector has seen NVQs as an opportunity to expand its activities, whilst the higher education sector has been rather more sceptical. The higher-level NVQs have rather tended to struggle to acquire credibility against more traditional management qualifications.

Overall, whilst the idea of NVQs has clearly been beneficial to numerous individuals it remains debatable whether this form of qualification actually enhances the performance of individuals and contributes to economic success. **JL-C**

References and further reading
Beaumont, G. (1996) *Review of 100 NVQs and SVQs*, London: Department for Education and Employment.
Competence, the journal – all editions.
Hyland, T. (1994) *Competence, Education and NVQs: Dissenting Perspectives*, London: Cassell.
International Journal of Training and Development (1999) 3(2), special edition on competence-based training and development.
Wolf, A. (1995) *Competence-Based Assessment*, Buckingham: Open University Press.

Negotiation

Those of a unitary persuasion may view negotiation as irrelevant, unlike those with pluralist-type perspectives. Negotiation is a process of joint decision-making to reconcile differences. In the human resource management (HRM) area negotiation is different from those is other spheres, for several reasons. For instance, normally there is a continuing relationship between parties and a need to reach working solutions. Negotiation can be an expression of conflict, with recognition of mutual dependence and damage that can be inflicted, with threats and use of sanctions as part of the process. It also impacts on future dealings and settlements. Negotiation is a dynamic and unique process requiring skills and judgement, planning and tactics to secure the maximum from perceived power, inter- and intra-group relationships and conflicts and the overall micro and macro context in which it takes place. There are models of the process within the framework of collective bargaining (Walton and McKersie, 1965), with 'distributive' (or 'zero-sum'), 'integrative' (or 'positive sum') and 'intraorganizational' (within parties) bargaining and 'attitudinal structuring'.

There are some problems with the area of negotiations:

1. Negotiation often does not involve simple, clearly delineated, single or equally important issues, but rather complex packages with trade-offs, counter-offers and time frames explored over long periods and impacting on tactics and future dealings.
2. Concessions, unless made conditionally, can be taken to equate to a 'loss' (in image, prestige) as they are not easily withdrawn and tactically are a reduction of the bargaining zone and limit scope, while encouraging 'stand-offs' in anticipation of further concessions to come.
3. If agreement is not reached, sanctions can be applied but these then may well change the negotiations as parties incur 'costs' which they may then try to recover.

Nevertheless, negotiation remains commonly utilized and a fascinating area in HRM. **CR**

References and further reading
Fowler, A. (1990) *Negotiation Skills and Strategies*, London: IPM.
Gulliver, P. H. (1979) *Disputes and Negotiations*: *A Cross-Cultural Perspective*, New York: Academic Press.
Hiltrop, J. M. and Udall, S. (1995) *The Essence of Negotiation*, London: Prentice Hall.
Salaman, M. (2000) *Industrial Relations*: *Theory and Practice*, London: Pearson.
Walton, R. E. and McKersie, R. B. (1965) *Behavioral Theory of Labor Negotiations*, New York: McGraw-Hill.
Walton, R. E., Cutcher-Gershenfield, J. E. and McKersie, R. B. (1994) *Strategic Negotiations*: *A Theory of Change in Labor-Management Relations*, Boston, MA: Harvard Business School Press.

Neuro-linguistic programming

Neuro-linguistic programming (NLP) has been described as the study of how we structure our experience of the world. Its origins are associated with the work of two Californian academics – Richard Bandler and John Grinder – and the development of NLP reflects their interests – psychology, language, computer programming and successful people. They were concerned to find out what distinguished excellent practitioners, who appeared to have 'magical' skills, from the merely competent.

'Neuro'comes from the Greek word 'neuron', meaning nerve. A key starting point for NLP is that behaviour is the result of neurological processes – from awareness of sensations through our five senses, through thought formation, to decision-taking and motor actions. 'Linguistic', from the Latin for 'language', refers to the representation and shaping of experience through language. 'Programming' picks up the image of the brain as a computer – ideas and thoughts are organized into actions in a way which is largely automatic. It is these 'automatic' programmes which NLP practitioners say can be made explicit, and therefore learnable and available to others, to help them change their behaviours in situations which they experience as problematic. Once we understand that we create our internal world, we realize we can change it

Neuro-linguistic programming works by helping people reframe a situation. There is strong emphasis on recognizing patterns of thought and behaviour which lead to unwanted outcomes and deploying alternative techniques to change the result.

As well as a set of tools and strategies, NLP is based on a philosophy of optimism about human capacity to choose alternative ways of behaving and to change and grow. The philosophy is expressed through a set of 'presuppositions' for which no 'truth' is claimed.

The application of NLP has expanded beyond the fields of psychotherapy to include personal development, education, training, sales and management. In the field of human resource management, relevance of NLP has been claimed for selection (Georges, 1996), training (Weisburgh, 1990; Stuart, 1992; Dastoor, 1993), career counselling and coaching (Dowlen, 1996) and facilitation (Bee and Bee, 1998). Knight (1999) describes how NLP can be used to develop and improve relationships generally in the business context.

Neuro-linguistic programming is not without its critics. Summerfield and van Oudtshoorn (1995) express unease with NLP, deriving both from its origins and its use. Neuro-linguistic programming draws from a wide and complex range of theories about human behaviour but does not itself have a theoretical base. This makes it difficult to subject its claims to empirical examination. Dowlen (1996) summarizes the results of some of the research into evidence for the effectiveness of NLP. It is seen by some to suffer from overenthusiastic packaging and marketing into a quick fix 'grab-bag' of techniques, which ignore ethical implications of their application and can be seen as manipulative. Dowlen's summary of the research into NLP ends with this comment:

> There is a disappointing lack of research evidence on NLP and a clear need for further work if NLP is to achieve wider credibility in the development field. That it is enthusiastically supported by those who practise it is both its strength and its weakness. (Dowlen, 1996: 34) **PM**

References and further reading

Association for Neuro-Linguistic Programming web site at http://www.anlp.org
Bee, F. and Bee, R. (1998) *Facilitation Skills*, London: IPD.
Dastoor, B. (1993) 'Speaking their language', *Training and Development Journal* June: 47(6): 17–20.
Dowlen, A. (1996) 'NLP -help or hype? Investigating the uses of neuro-linguistic programming in management learning', *Career Development International* 1(1): 27–34.
Georges, D. P. (1996) 'Improved employee selection and staffing through meta programmes', *Career Development International* 1(5): 5–9.
Knight, S. (1999) *Introducing NLP*, London: IPD.
Neuro-Linguistic Programming Research Database web site at http://nlp.de/research
NLP Information Centre web site at http://www.nlpinfo.com
Stuart, P. (1992) 'Learning-style theories', *Personnel Journal* 71(9): 91–3.
Summerfield, J. and van Oudtshoorn, L. (1995) *Counselling in the Workplace*, London: IPD.
Weisburgh, M. (1990) 'Using NLP to focus on learners', *Training and Development Journal* 44(11): 21–5.

New public management

New public management (NPM) is an expression used to describe the changes which have occurred in the management of public services since the early 1980s. New public management has its origins in the rejection of traditional 'public administration', a model for public service delivery whereby bureaucrats sought to ensure equitable treatment for taxpayers through the direct, and monopolistic, provision of uniform, tax-financed services. Critics said public administration lacked flexibility, that it was concerned with inputs rather than outputs and was insufficiently customer focused, in sharp contrast to 'excellent' private sector organizations. These criticisms were reinforced by those engaged in a more fundamental attack on the public sector per se and who became known as the New Right. Their views were implemented in the UK between 1979 and 1997 by successive Conservative governments, designed to reduce the size of the public sector and to transform the way it was managed, mainly by importing private sector personnel and management techniques and by subjecting public sector activities to private sector competition. The UK experience both reflected and accelerated a wider international acceptance of the views of the New Right.

Hood (1991: 4–5) states there are seven main 'doctrinal components' of NPM, i.e.:

- hands-on professional management
- explicit standards and measures of performance (involving greater managerial accountability)
- greater emphasis on output controls
- disaggregation of units
- greater competition (involving the move to term contracts and public tendering procedures) designed to reduce costs and improve standards
- adoption of private sector styles of management
- greater discipline and 'parsimony' in resource use (involving cutting costs, reducing demands for more resources and the need to do more with less).

Clark (1996) identifies three component parts to NPM, i.e. marketization (namely, competition), disaggregation (namely, increased central control over policy combined with decentralization of service provision) and incentivization (namely, linking incentives, e.g. performance-related pay, to performance).

In summary, NPM involves an emphasis on four key themes:

- competition
- decentralization
- customer focus
- performance measurement.

However, the transition from 'administration' to 'management' is easy to overstate. Internationally there are clear differences in the adoption of NPM within Europe and between European and non-European countries, and little evidence as to the adoption or relevance of NPM in developing countries. Domestically, its prevalence and impact are also contestable within and across the public services. Consumers are not sovereign and, even if they were, the freedom of managers to respond is considerably constrained, not least by statute, ongoing commitments and overall resource limitations. **JW**

References and further reading
Clark, D. (1996) 'Open government in Britain: discourse and practice', *Public Money and Management* 16(1): 23–30.
Gray, A. and Jenkins, B. (1995) 'From public administration to public management: reassessing a revolution?', *Public Administration* 73(1): 75–99.
Hood, C. (1991) 'A public management for all seasons?', *Public Administration* 69(1): 3–19.
Horton, S. and Farnham, D. (eds) (1999) *Public Management in Britain*, Basingstoke: Macmillan.
Polidano, C. and Hulme, D. (1999) 'Public management reform in developing countries: issues and outcomes', *Public Management* 1(1): 121–32.
Pollitt, C. and Summa, H (1997) 'Trajectories of reform: public management change in four countries', *Public Money and Management* 17(1): 7–18.

New technology

New technology is seen as increasingly important to competitive success and human resource management, not least as it is a key contextual variable. Yet, is there anything 'new' about it? It is often linked to information technology and microelectronic-based computing technologies allowing the capture, storage, manipulation and distribution of information. Such capabilities allow for a wide scope of application, from manufacturing to administrative processes, and also the rapid transfer of information, which provides speed and flexibility. This also allows technology to intervene in the social relations of production, such as supervision, monitoring and surveillance, while it also has potential to be self-diagnostic, requiring less 'creative' labour to rectify faults.

Give such widespread applicability and characteristics, the impacts of new technology are varied:

1. On employment levels. For 'optimists' new technology allows productivity gains and cost reductions which increase demand and jobs and also employment in producing and maintaining technology. For 'pessimists', massive unemployment and the 'workless society' will result from new technology. A more balanced view notes both sides and adjustment costs, such as skills mismatches.
2. Skills and managerial control. Technology for some has an inherent tendency to de-skill work and increase managerial control. For others technology upskills and empowers workers. Yet, technology is less deterministic than this, with other determinants of skill, employee resistance and management approaches important.
3. Health and safety areas. Technology can reduce, but also create, problems, such as those stemming from use of computers.
4. The organization of production. Technology has the potential to change in the factory system as the method of production and control with developments such as teleworking. These bring their own problems in areas such as motivation, isolation, careers and management techniques of supervision.
5. Trade unions. Technology alters occupational and industrial structures and impacts on union organization, coverage and mergers. **CR**

References and further reading

Bamber, G. and Lansbury, D. (1989) *New Technology: International Perspectives On Human Resources And Industrial Relations*, London: Routledge.

Clark, J. (ed.) (1993) *Human Resource Management and Technical Change*, London: Sage.

Daniel, W. (1987) *Workplace Industrial Relations and Technical Change*, London: Pinter.

Policy Studies Institute (PSI) (1990) *The Employment Effects of New Technology in Manufacturing*, London: PSI.

Wilkinson, B. (1983) T*he Shopfloor Politics of New Technology*, London: Heinemann.

No-strike deals

No-strike deals are primarily associated with the Japanese car and consumer electronics companies which have established factories at greenfield sites in Britain particularly since the mid-1980s. These agreements between the employer and a single union sometimes incorporate pendulum arbitration as a compulsory and final stage of a disputes procedure. Not only does this effectively exclude the possibility of industrial action, but it also forces the union (and, in theory, management) to make significant concessions prior to the implementation of the arbitration process. This is because pendulum arbitration is based on the principle that the arbitration panel's decision will either be in favour of the union's claim in full or in favour of management's offer in full, rather than a compromise. More conventional methods of arbitration may be incorporated in no-strike deals, but where they are, they are likely to be compulsory and binding. Such deals also typically lay the foundation for a broad programme of lean production and human resource management initiatives. The Nissan site near Sunderland pioneered such deals in the mid-1980s with its agreement with the Amalgamated Engineering Union.

These deals caused considerable furore and division within the trade union movement in the 1980s, and this debate needs to be seen within the broader industrial relations and political context of this period. The small minority of unions which advocated no-strike deals were arguing for the end of adversarial trade unions strategies, and these unions and many employers – portrayed no-strike deals as representing the future of British industrial relations. Numerically such agreements have not had the impact anticipated by their advocates (Gall, 1993). Nevertheless, they may have played a more important role than the statistics suggest, in sowing divisions within the trade union movement, and encouraging a shift to the right in terms of the adoption of *new realist* perspectives by the dominant sections of the trade union movement. (See also **Single union deals** and **Company unionism**.) **DB**

References and further reading

Bassett, P. (1986) *Strike-Free: New Industrial Relations in Britain*, London: Macmillan.
Blyton, P. and Turnbull, P. (1994) *The Dynamics of Employee Relations*, Macmillan: London, pp. 96–103.
Gall, G. (1993) 'What happened to single union deals?', *Industrial Relations Journal* 24(1): 71–5.
Industrial Relations Review and Report (IRRR) (1992) 'Single union deals in perspective', *Industrial Relations Review and Report*: IRS Employment Trends, no. 523: 7–15.
Lewis, R. (1990) 'Strike free deals and pendulum arbitration', *British Journal of Industrial Relations* 28(1): 32–56.
McIlroy, J. (1995) *Trade Unions in Britain Today*, 2nd edn, Manchester: Manchester University Press, pp. 114–16.

Non-compete clauses

Non-compete clauses aim to prevent employees from entering employment which competes with that of their current, or previous, employer. In principle, contractual clauses which outlaw competition with the current employer are unobjectionable and such conduct would in any case be covered by the employee's implied duty of good faith. However, restrictions on the ability of employees to compete with their former employer need a more cautious approach because in law they are regarded as being in restraint of trade. In consequence, they are contrary to public policy and void unless proved reasonable by the person relying on them.

Restraint clauses which merely stifle competition can never be reasonable: it must be shown that the employer, in using such a clause, is attempting to protect a proprietary interest such as trade secrets (or other confidential information) or customer connections. Hence it would not be unusual to find a restraint clause in the employment contracts of, for example, hairstylists, sales staff or solicitors – individuals who have contact with customers and potentially, influence over them.

Even in such cases, however, the particular clause must not go further than is necessary, in terms of time, geographical area or the trades it forbids, to protect the employer's legitimate interest. Because a clause which is drafted too widely will simply be struck down rather than the court rewriting it so as to make it reasonable, case law has suggested that a non-solicitation clause may be more prudent. This prevents former employees from soliciting customers and avoids guesswork as to the appropriate area from which they should be excluded. Any restraint clause needs careful drafting, however, and legal advice is generally thought to be desirable.

Where a valid restraint clause is breached, the employer can seek damages (which may be hard to quantify) or an injunction to prevent the individual from taking up employment which competes unlawfully. **JE**

References and further reading

Furmston, M. P. (1991) *Cheshire Fifoot and Furmston's The Law of Contract*, 12th edn, London: Butterworths, pp. 396–426.
Herbert Morris Ltd v. *Saxelby* [1916] 1 AC 688.
Keenan, D. (1997) *Smith and Keenan's Advanced Business Law*, 10th edn, London: Pitman, pp. 167–79.
Office Angels Ltd v. *Reiner Thomas and O'Connor* [1991] IRLR 214.
Spencer v. *Marchington* [1988] IRLR 392.
Stenhouse Australia Ltd v. *Phillips* [1974] 1 All ER 117.

Non-financial rewards

For many people money is the main reason for working, but there are many other factors which people take into account when deciding to take or remain in a job.

Various writers on motivation (for example Maslow, 1954; MacGregor, 1960) have identified non-financial influences on people's propensity to work and to improve their performance. A famous study at the Western Electric Company's Hawthorne Works in Chicago concluded that the greatest influence on increased productivity of employees was not so much the organization of work but the fact that they felt special and recognized.

A successful reward system will take account of this and include a mixture of policies and practices to enable an employer to align the reward strategy with the business strategy. Some of the non-financial rewards which have been found to motivate people are:

- *Achievement*: some people have a high need to achieve and therefore working arrangements which allow them to take ownership of their work should produce increased performance levels.
- *Influence*: employees will be positively motivated if they believe that their views and ideas are being actively sought and they are given the opportunity to influence decisions.
- *Personal growth*: people want to develop their skills and competences and therefore should be given learning opportunities and access to relevant training and development.
- *Recognition*: a very important motivator is the need of people to have a high opinion of themselves (self-esteem) and to be recognized by others (prestige). This may be met simply by praise for a task well done or by more public recognition, with awards and status symbols.
- *Responsibility*: individuals are normally motivated by being given increased responsibility. This will lead to recognition and often leads to people who have been given responsibility actively seeking more. **MMo**

References and further reading
Alderfer, C. (1972) *Existence, Relatedness and Growth*, New York: Free Press.
Latham, G. and Locke, E. A. (1979) 'Goal setting: a motivational technique that works', *Organizational Dynamics*, Autumn: 68–80.
Lawler, E. E. (1969) 'Job design and employee motivation', *Personnel Psychology* 22: 426–35.
Maslow, A. (1954) *Motivation and Personality*, New York: Harper and Row.
McGregor, D. (1960) *The Human Side of Enterprise*, New York: McGraw-Hill.
Rose, M. (1998) 'Rewarding with recognition', *Human Resource Management Yearbook*, London: Kogan Page/IPM.

Non-unionism

The 1998 Workplace Employee Relations Survey described the extent of trade unionism in terms of the presence of any union members in workplaces, union density (i.e. the percentage of employees who are union members), union recognition, the coverage of collective bargaining within unionized workplaces and the proportion of union members in workplaces where unions are recognized (Cully *et al.*, 1999: 234–42). A broad interpretation of *non-unionism* might use the same set of factors to define it. However, non-unionism is often used specifically to refer to the denial of union recognition by some employers, and their associated tactics to discourage union membership and activity. Whilst such non-unionism is essentially absent from the public sector, it has grown significantly in the private sector in the 1980s and 1990s. Union recognition has fallen from approximately 65 per cent (1980) to 30 per cent (1998) in private manufacturing and extraction, and from approximately 41 per cent (1980) to 24 per cent (1998) in the private service sector (Cully *et al.*, 1999: 239).

The growth of non-unionism needs to be considered within the context of the political and economic climate of the 1980s and 1990s, the restructuring of the economy, the substantial shift in the balance of power in favour of employers in this period and the promotion of human resource management. Many explicitly anti-union employers make use of cheap labour and extensive numerical labour flexibility, and their organizations are associated with high labour turnover and minimal investment in training (e.g. MacDonald's). Other non-union employers, however, may make significant concessions in terms of pay, conditions and investment in the workforce, thus undermining the case for trade unionism in their organization (e.g. Marks and Spencer – Blyton and Turnbull, 1998: 245–51). These different approaches can be related to hard and soft forms of human resource management, and may be partly explained by different product markets, company size and whether the company is significantly *subsidized* by smaller cheap labour suppliers. (See also **Trade Unions.**) **DB**

References and further reading

Blyton, P. and Turnbull, P. (1998) *The Dynamics of Employee Relations*, 2nd edn, London: Macmillan, pp. 245–51.

Cully, M., Woodland, S., O'Reilly, A. and Dix, G. (1999) *Britain at Work: As depicted by the 1998 Workplace Employee Relations Survey*, London: Routledge, pp. 234–42.

Gall, G. and McKay, S. (1999) 'Developments in union recognition and derecognition in Britain, 1994–98', *British Journal of Industrial Relations* 37(4): 601–14.

Kelly, J. (1998) *Rethinking Industrial Relations*, London: Routledge, pp. 42–51.

Smith, P. and Morton, G. (1993) 'Union exclusion and the de-collectivization of industrial relations in contemporary Britain', *British Journal of Industrial Relations* 31(1): 97–114.

Terry, M. (1999) 'Systems of collective employee representation in non-union firms in the UK', *Industrial Relations Journal* 30(1): 16–30.

o

Occupational accidents

Over one million workers in Britain suffer an accident at work each year. Accidents are therefore a common feature of employment. However, the frequency of their occurrence varies considerably between different sizes of workplaces, types of worker and sectors of industry. In particular, accident rates have been found to be notably higher in smaller workplaces, in 'heavier' industries and among those who are self-employed. Research findings indicate that both individual and organizational factors contribute to the occurrence of accidents. At the same time, the balance of evidence points to the fact that organizational failures, such as poorly designed work systems and equipment, and inadequate supervision and training, generally play a larger role than factors associated with worker personality, cognitive capabilities and attitudes and motivation. More generally, the evidence highlights that the avoidance of accidents requires attention to be paid to a wide variety of possible preventive activities that encompass both 'technical' and 'human' elements. For example, the removal of hazards from the workplace by such means as the ceasing of certain types of activities and the adoption of safer machinery and processes, the supply of protective equipment, and the design of work environments, equipment and processes that are compatible with the physical and psychological characteristics and capabilities of workers. In addition, the effective management of safety is widely seen to encompass the establishment of adequate methods for assessing risks and identifying necessary remedial actions, the provision of appropriate information and training to workers, initiatives to change worker safety perceptions and attitudes, and the putting into place of adequate mechanisms to ensure that organizational rules and procedures are complied with. **PJ**

References and further readings

Dawson, S., Willman, P., Bamford, M. and Clinton, A. (1988) Safety at Work: *The Limits of Self-Regulation*. Cambridge: Cambridge University Press.

Glendon, A. I. and McKenna, E. (1995) *Human Safety and Risk Management*. London: Chapman and Hall.

Health and Safety Commission. (2000) *Health and Safety Statistics 1999/2000*. Norwich: HSE Books.

Nichols, T. (1997) *The Sociology of Industrial Injury*, London: Mansell.

Reason, J. (1990) *Human Error*. Cambridge: Cambridge University Press.

Occupational ill health

In 1995 around 2 million workers considered themselves to have suffered from an illness that had been caused or made worse by work. The most commonly reported of these illnesses were musculoskeletal disorders (1.2 million), stress, depression and anxiety (279 000), other stress-ascribed diseases (254 000), lower respiratory disease (202 000) and deafness, tinnitus or other ear conditions (170 000). Occupational ill health therefore encompasses much more than such 'traditional' industrial diseases as occupational deafness and asthma, pneumoconiosis and asbestosis. As a result, its avoidance can be seen to require attention to not only be paid to the removal and control of the hazardous substances and other factors that give rise to these long-standing forms of work-related harm, but also to those features of the work environment that contribute to the occurrence of musculoskeletal and stress-related conditions. These features include the intensity and speed of work activities, the length and distribution of working time, the design of work tasks and equipment, worker–customer interactions and the relationship that exists between work and domestic responsibilities. In other words, the effective management of occupational health requires organizations to adopt a broad-based approach within which attention is paid to the development of work tasks and activities that embody an appropriate fit with the physical and mental capabilities and domestic obligations of workers. **PJ**

References and further readings

Buckle, P. and Devereux, J. (1999) *Work-Related Neck and Upper Limb Musculoskeletal Disorders*, Luxembourg: Office for Official Publications of the European Communities.
Cooper, C. L. and Williams, S. (1997) *Creating Healthy Work Organisations*, Chichester: Wiley.
Health and Safety Commission (2000) *Health and Safety Statistics 1999/2000*, Norwich: HSE Books.
Humphrey, J. and Smith, P. (1991) *Looking after Corporate Health*, London: Pitman.
Jones, J., Hodgson, J., Clegg, T. and Elliott, R. (1998) *Self-Reported Work-Related Illness*, Norwich: HSE Books.

Organizational climate

The concept of climate can be traced back to Lewin, Lippit and White's (1939) work on experimentally created social climates. The concept was primarily introduced into organizational research by Tagiuri and Litwin (1968). Organizational climate research received less attention from the early 1980s. This can be attributed to the development of research on organizational culture (see **Organizational culture**). Leading organizational climate researchers, e.g. James and Jones (1974), generally consider climate to be a reflection of employees' perceptions of organizational practices. In contrast, organizational culture is often considered to reflect the fundamental assumptions employees hold about their organization (e.g. Schein, 1985).

Organizational climate research has traditionally used positivistic research methods, e.g. employee surveys. In contrast, organizational culture research has generally been considered to be qualitative in its nature, using research methods such as interviews.

Although the two concepts ostensibly have a different focus, as Dennison (1996) has noted, many studies investigate largely similar phenomena, increasingly using similar research methods, yet use different 'labels', sometimes called climate and sometimes called culture. Given this blurring in both the concept and the methods used for execution, Reichers and Schneider (1990) have proposed a greater integration in research on these two concepts.

The late 1990s saw something of a re-emergence of climate research, with a particular emphasis on methodological issues in attempting to clarify the concept, e.g. Sparrow and Gaston (1996). **JL-C**

References and further reading

Denison, D. R. (1996) 'What is the difference between organizational culture and organizational climate? A native's point of view on a decade of paradigm wars', *Academy of Management Review*, 21(3): 619–54.

James, L. and Jones, A. (1974) 'Organizational climate: a review of theory and research', *Psychological Bulletin*, 18: 1096–112.

Lewin, K., Lippit R. and White, R. (1939) 'Patterns of aggressive behaviour in experimentally created social climates', *Journal of Social Psychology*, 10: 271–99.

Patterson, M., Payne, R. and West, M. (1996) 'Collective climates: a test of their sociopsychological significance', *Academy of Management Journal*, 29(6): 1675–91.

Reichers, A. and Schneider, B. (1990) 'Climate and culture: an evolution of constructs', in B. Schneider (ed.) *Organizational Climate and Culture*, San Francisco: Jossey-Bass.

Schein, E. (1985) *Organizational Climate and Leadership*, San Francisco: Jossey-Bass.

Sparrow, P .R. and Gaston, K. (1996) 'Generic climate maps: a strategic application of climate survey data?', *Journal of Organizational Behavior*, 17(6): 679–98.

Taguiri, R. and Litwin, G. (eds.) (1968) *Organizational Climate: Explorations of a Concept*, Boston, MA: Harvard Business School.

Organizational commitment

Commitment replaced satisfaction as the employee attitude most often studied by researchers during the last 15 years or so of the twentieth century. This was mirrored by managers' interest in the same topic, and in particular how to build commitment in an employment climate where a 'job for life' was a thing of the past. organizational commitment has been defined by Mowday, Porter and Steers (1982: 27) as 'the relative strength of an individual's identification with and involvement in an organisation'. The organization concerned is nearly always the employer. So someone who is committed to their employing organization can be expected to agree with its values, feel a sense of loyalty, be willing to exert effort on its behalf, and want to stay in it.

Writers as far back as the mid-twentieth century such as Becker noted that there are many different facets of commitment. More recent research has suggested three components:

- *Affective commitment*: the extent to which a person feels emotionally attached to the organization.
- *Continuance commitment*: the extent to which a person feels that the costs and risks associated with leaving the organization would outweigh the benefits.
- *Normative commitment*: the extent to which a person feels a sense of obligation and duty to the organization.

Almost by definition, people who are more committed are less inclined to try to leave the organization. In the case of affective commitment and to a lesser extent normative commitment, their continued presence is enthusiastic. But continuance commitment can be seen as a mixed blessing because it can reflect simply that the person has no alternative but to stay. Commitment seems to be relatively stable, but can be changed by the extent to which a person's experiences in the organization are positive, particularly concerning the extent to which their work challenges them and the extent to which future career opportunities are available. Commitment is a complex phenomenon. People can feel committed to many constituencies at work such as their work group, department, boss or colleagues, not just the organization as a whole. There can also be tensions between people's commitment to their profession or occupation, and to their employing organization. **JA**

References and further reading

Arnold, J. and Mackenzie Davey, K. (1999) 'Graduates' work experiences as predictors of organisational commitment, intention to leave, and turnover: Which experiences really matter?', *Applied Psychology: An International Review*, 48: 211–38.

Becker, H. (1960) 'Notes on the concept of commitment', *American Journal of Sociology* 66: 32–40.

Coopey, J. and Hartley, J. (1991) 'Reconsidering the case for organisational commitment', *Human Resource Management Journal* 1: 18–32.

Meyer, J. (1997) 'Organisational commitment', in C. Cooper and I. Robertson (eds) *International Review of Industrial and Organizational Psychology* 12: 175–228.

Meyer, J., Allen, N. and Smith, C. (1993) 'Commitment to organizations and occupations: extension and test of a three-component conceptualization', *Journal of Applied Psychology*, 78: 538–51.

Mowday, R., Porter, L. and Steers, R. (1982) *Employee–Organization Linkages*, New York: Academic Press.

Organizational culture

The topic of organizational culture became very popular with managers in the early 1980s. However, this anthropological concept had previously been applied by others to the world of organizations and work. For example, Harrison (1972) had written about organization ideologies.

In many ways this sophisticated concept has been oversimplified. Academic authors such as Schein (1992) suggest that culture exists at a number of levels. They propose that culture, at its deepest level, reflects the underlying assumptions that exist in an organization which are understood and accepted by everyone. They argue that attempts to change culture are often superficial, e.g. changing corporate logos etc. Others have argued that culture is not something that can be created or manipulated by managers, it simply exists within an organization.

Other critics have argued that the notion of a single culture within an organization is much too simplistic. The existence of a number of subcultures, often based around functional areas or different professional groupings has become common (Hampden-Turner, 1990). Therefore, for example in the National Health Service, it could be argued that there are at least two subcultures, e.g. managerial/administrative and clinical.

Despite these comments, numerous books have been produced claiming they can identify how managers should attempt to manipulate and change organizational culture (e.g. Kilman, Saxton and Serpa, 1985). A particularly useful book detailing honest accounts of a range of UK organizations and their attempts to change culture was produced by Williams, Dobson and Walters (1993).

The most recent accounts of culture have tended to split the concept into much smaller components e.g. the idea of a service culture. (See, for example, Harris and Ogbonna 1998.)

Despite attracting substantial research interest there is little substantive evidence indicating that culture management can be controlled and used to enhance organizational performance, e.g. Kotter and Heskett (1992). Nevertheless the concept continues to attract attention and no doubt will continue to do so. **JL-C**

References and further reading

Hampden-Turner, C. (1990) *Corporate Culture: From Vicious to Virtuous Circles*, London: Random Century.

Harris, L. C. and Ogbonna, E. (1998) 'Employee responses to culture change efforts', *Human Resource Management Journal* 8(2): 78–92.

Harrison, R. (1972) 'Understanding your organization's character', *Harvard Business Review*, May–June: 119–28.

Kilmann, R. H., Saxton, M. J. and Serpa, R. (eds) (1985) *Gaining Control of the Corporate Culture*, San Francisco: Jossey-Bass.

Kotter, J. P. and Heskett, J. L. (1992) *Organizational Climate and Culture: New Organizational Approaches*, London: IPM.

Schein, E. H. (1992) *Organizational Culture and Leadership*, 2nd edn, San Francisco: Jossey-Bass.

Williams, A., Dobson, P. and Walters M. (1993) *Changing Culture: New Organizational Approaches*, 2nd edn, London: IPM.

Organizational development

Organizational development (OD) has its roots in behavioural science research which goes back to the 1930s/1940s. The OD movement is based on values/assumptions which reflect the importance of people in organizations. It is assumed that people are central to organizational success, and that most people wish to enhance their capabilities and achieve personal growth.

The key elements of OD reflect an approach to change which is planned and long-range in its focus, and seeks to enhance organizational effectiveness. Historically, OD has sought to achieve this by improving the interrelationships between people in the organization. Organizational development assumes that organizations are systems which consist of interdependent parts.

The types of intervention strategies used will vary depending upon their target group. In relation to individuals, strategies could involve personal development activities, the use of mentors or job secondment in order to broaden the individual's work and personal experience. Team-building activity would target the interpersonal skills and work processes utilized by a number of people who need to work co-operatively. At the organizational level techniques such as surveys and feedback are utilized.

Traditionally, OD change efforts reflected Lewin's (1947) model which identified the need to unfreeze the current state of affairs, to apply an intervention strategy to induce change, and to refreeze the new state of affairs. The role of key change agents, who can be internal or external to the organization, is crucial in facilitating successful change.

Organizational development has been criticized for being too incremental, assuming that employee participation will facilitate change, when it may prove a barrier, and not taking power/political issues into account.

Concepts such as organizational culture, enhancing employee commitment etc now tend to dominate organizational development activity. Consistent with this harder-edged perspective, much greater emphasis is now placed on outcomes rather than processes. **JL-C**

References and further reading

Cummings, T. G. and Worley, C. G. (1993) *Organization Development and Change*, 5th edn, St Paul, MN: West Publishing.

French, L. and Bell, C. H. Jr., (1999) *Organization Development*, 6th edn, Englewood Cliffs, NJ: Prentice-Hall.

Lewin, K. (1947) 'Frontiers in group dynamics: concepts, method and reality in social science', *Human Relations*, 1: 5–41.

Mendelow, A. and Liebowitz, S. J. (1995) 'Difficulties in making O.D. a part of organizational strategy', *Human Resource Planning* 12(4): 317–29.

Smither, R. D., Houston, J. M. and McIntire, S. D. (1996) *Organization Development: Strategies for Changing Environment*, New York: HarperCollins.

Outdoor development

Using the outdoors as a medium for management training has become a popular option for large numbers of organizations in the latter half of the twentieth century. Its benefits can be great and long lasting because the experience is so memorable. However, it is also a form of development which is perhaps more fraught with potential pitfalls than most.

The origins of outdoor development can be traced back to the Second World War when the outdoors was used in officer selection assessment, known as War Office Selection Board (WOSB) tests. These tests, which required creativity, intelligence and interpersonal skills as well as physical fitness and the ability to work in a team, were used purely for assessment purposes rather than development. However, the forces have consistently used the outdoors for more developmental military training in survival and fitness and many outdoor developmental centres will be staffed by ex-forces personnel.

Outdoor development, as accessed by managers today, draws from a variety of areas such as the youth movements of scouting and Duke of Edinburgh awards, outward bound, outdoor education and adventure holidays, such as PGL, and outdoor sports as well as military exercises. All these forms exist in their own right. When used as a tool of organizational development, the outdoor medium can be a powerful form of experiential learning.

As with most forms of management development, providers and their approaches vary enormously. However, as a baseline, outdoor development consists of the requirement to apply skills to tasks which use the outdoors, i.e. they are very different from work tasks, but may require application of work skills. The exercises are challenging and the results of participants actions are usually immediately apparent, thus providing evidence for analysis of performance. In a series of short tasks, management processes can be laid bare. The aim is to learn or improve skills from doing rather than being taught.

It is a broadly held view that the best outdoor development programmes contain considerable time for review with skilled facilitators who will help the group to analyse what went well, and not so well, the effect of individual behaviours, future actions and the relationship with current and potential work situations. There are, however, practitioners who will not conduct reviews, arguing that experience is all.

Positive aspects of outdoor development are that it has the advantage over role play in that participants behave 'normally' albeit in a strange situation; it allows risk-taking in a controlled environment and develops team, leadership, problem-solving and a large range of personal and interpersonal skills. Retention of learning is long term because of the novel experience. Less positively, it can be expensive since it requires intensive, small-group work with well-trained facilitators. Instructors who have moved into this development area from sports or the military may not have appropriate skills in training and facilitation. It requires very careful design to ensure its relevance to individuals and the organization, and needs careful selling both to participants, who may be anxious, and to colleagues not participating who can resent the 'holiday' their peers are 'enjoying'. **ASm**

References and further reading
Bank, J. (1985) *Outdoor Development for Managers*, Aldershot: Gower.
Barrett, J. and Greenaway, R. (1995) *Why Adventure? The Role and Value of Outdoor Adventure in Young People's Personal and Social Development*: *A Review of Research*, The Foundation for Outdoor Adventure.
Krouwel, B. and Goodwill, S. (1994) *Management Development Outdoors*, London: Kogan Page.

Outplacement

Outplacement programmes are provided by employers as a means of providing assistance for staff who are going to be made redundant. At present there is no legal requirement on employers to offer such assistance, although they are expected to allow people under notice of redundancy reasonable time off for job-searching purposes. However, survey evidence suggests that the practice is common, especially in larger organizations. The typical approach involves outplacement consultants being appointed for a number of weeks to carry out this work.

Two distinct areas of outplacement activity can be identified – counselling and practical assistance. In the case of the first, the focus is on helping people to come to terms with their dismissal and the reasons that it is occurring. It involves seeking to help in the development of a constructive and positive outlook. The second comprises the provision of advice about career options, job-search techniques, effective

CV writing, interview skills, training opportunities and financial matters. The practical assistance can either be delivered by means of group-based training courses or through individual consultation. Some outplacement consultants play a more hands-on role in helping people to find jobs by also acting as headhunters.

There are several reasons that explain the willingness of employers to commit resources to outplacement programmes at times when there is little money to spare. Aside from straightforward paternalistic motives, the fact that such advice is appreciated by employees helps to reduce bitterness and may reduce the likelihood of unfair dismissal claims. It also assists those who are not being made redundant to cope with the stress suffered in witnessing the departure of others–an important dimension of effective redundancy management.

There is relatively little UK research evidence on the actual effectiveness of outplacement services. However, the findings of some American researchers suggest that there can be a substantial positive effect for participants in terms of speed in finding new positions and wage levels in their new jobs. It can thus be concluded that the provision of outplacement services is potentially beneficial to employer and employee alike. **ST**

References and further reading

Edwards, P. and Hall, M. (1999) 'Remission possible' *People Management*, July: 44–6.
Incomes Data Services (IDS) (1995) 'Redundancy terms' IDS Study, 586.
Lewis, P. (1993) *The Successful Management of Redundancy*, Oxford: Blackwell.
Stanton, E. S. (1985) 'Outplacement services', in W .R. Tracey (ed.) *Human Resources Management and Development*, New York: Amacom.

Outsourcing

This term refers to situations in which organizations move to subcontract activities which they have hitherto carried out themselves on an in-house basis. While there is nothing at all new in the concept of subcontracting, there is evidence of a growth in outsourcing in recent years. Of particular significance has been the growth of outsourcing activity in the public sector, whereby activities such as catering, security, cleaning, maintenance and areas of administrative work have often been contracted out to private sector service providers. In the private sector the main growth areas have been in contracting out parts of manufacturing processes. Aside from these trends having important general human resource (HR) consequences for organizations, HR specialists have an additional interest in that some of their own activities are also considered appropriate for outsourcing (notably pensions and payroll administration, recruitment and selection and the provision of specialist advice).

A number of different pressures explain the increased incidence of outsourcing:

1. The argument that firms best gain competitive advantage by focusing their efforts on core business activities and distinctive areas of competence.
2. The straightforward cost pressures driving managers to consider whether support functions could be provided more cheaply by an external provider. In addition to lowering the costs (sometimes by locating work in the developing world), many subcontractors also seek to provide a better service, being able to draw on expertise and equipment that is not available to their clients.
3. The attractions of flexibility and leanness. When a non-core activity is outsourced suppliers can readily be changed when they are considered to be performing poorly or charging uncompetitive rates.

A number of HR implications follow from outsourcing in particular and subcontracting more generally. There are, for example, important legal issues to consider when an in-house activity is transferred to a subcontractor. In many cases such situations fall within the purview of transfer of undertakings regulations which restrict management's room for manoeuvre and require consultation with affected worker representatives. Moreover there are a range of issues that are associated with control of the activities concerned. Instead of this occurring through a hierarchical employment relationship, performance levels are regulated through commercial contracts and service-level agreements. There are also implications for job security and work intensification within the outsourced functions. **ST**

References and further reading

Baron, J. N. and Kreps, D. M. (1999) *Strategic Human Resources: Frameworks for General Managers*, Chichester: Wiley, ch. 18.

Capelli, P. (1999) 'Rethinking employment' in R. S. Schuler and S. E. Jackson (eds) *Strategic Human Resource Management*, Oxford: Blackwell.

Colling, T. (2000) 'Personnel management in the extended organization', in S. Bach and K. Sisson (eds) *Personnel Management: A Comprehensive Guide to Theory and Practice*, Oxford: Blackwell.

Mabey, C., Salaman, G. and Storey, J. (1998) *Human Resource Management: A Strategic Introduction*, Oxford: Blackwell, ch. 8.

Merrick, N. (1999) 'Premier Division', *People Management*, August: 38–41.

Stredwick, J. and Ellis, S. (1998) *Flexible Working Practices: Techniques and Innovations*, London: IPD, ch. 7.

Participation

The concept of participation defies any attempt to reduce it to a single definition. Any attempt to make sense of participation, therefore, must begin by analysing those factors, which make participation complex and ambiguous. Thus, the existence of a diverse range of actors and commentators operating in diverse settings and contexts has led to the discussion and implementation of many organizational initiatives, which in different ways claim to enhance participation in decision-making.

Actors

Different groups of commentators have tended to define participation to reflect their own personal agendas. For economists, 'participation' is a descriptive term. From an economist's perspective groups of workers with low rates of participation in employment suffer disproportionately from unemployment. Managers and management consultants, however, have tended to invoke a more extensive definition of participation, which links participation in decision-making to a range of desirable organizational outcomes – improvements in staff morale, improvements in quality, increases in the speed of decision-making and reductions in staff turnover. While accepting that beneficial changes should be sought in systems of workplace decision-making, academic commentators have questioned the methods and values of management consultants, and have argued that the social-democratic potential of participation is reduced by a focus on business matters alone. In a similar way other groups, such as the trade union movement in Britain have argued that discussions of participation envisage a partnership role between management and unions, which may restrict the ability of unions to represent the interests of their members.

Contexts

Differences in legal, political and institutional arrangements influence the nature and conduct of participation.

Concepts

At an elementary level it is possible to distinguish 'direct' and 'indirect' forms of participation. Direct forms of participation, such as those found under **total quality management** (see separate entry) offer workers greater discretion in the tasks they perform. Those initiatives labelled as indirect participation have, in contrast, more of a policy character. It is important to note, however that indirect participation may take many forms such that 'involvement', 'consultation', 'financial participation' and 'collective bargaining' are all forms of indirect participation, yet each suggests different roles and responsibilities for the various actors involved. As in much else in life, therefore, the questions who? what? when? where? why? should be applied to the analysis of participation at work. **DC**

References and further reading

Blumberg, P. (1968) *Industrial Democracy: The Sociology of Participation*, London: Constable.

Clegg, H. (1960) *A New Approach to Industrial Democracy*, Oxford: Blackwell.

Heller, F., Pusic, E., Strauss, G. and Wilpert, B. (1998) *Organizational Participation: Myth and Reality*, Oxford: Oxford University Press.

Marchington, M. and Wilkinson, A. (2000) *Core Personnel and Development*, London: Institute of Personnel and Development, pt 5.

Ramsay, H. (1977) 'Cycles of control', *Sociology* 11(3): 481–506.

Ramsay, H. (1997) 'Fool's gold? European works councils and workplace democracy', *Industrial Relations Journal* 28(4): 314–22.

Paternalism

Paternalism is a common-sense term, widely used by managers and employees, to describe an *employment relationship* in which a company looks after its workers, sometimes in a rather overbearing way, often while denying them a right to join trade unions. Its classical usage applies to the traditional small family firm, where the owner – characteristically a male father-figure – takes a personal interest in the lives of his employees, typically walking round the factory and addressing them by their first names. In addition to this primitive version, academic research has uncovered a sophisticated paternalism, like that found at Cadbury's Bournville and other model employers of the early twentieth century. In these cases, growing company size rendered the face-to-face attention untenable and management replaced this with a set of institutions, such as housing, consultation systems and benefits, which the USA terms 'welfare capitalism'. Often the aim is *unitarist*, to avoid trade unions and win employee loyalty and commitment. In Britain, however, hybrid forms of *pluralist* paternalism developed which combined sophisticated welfare techniques with trade union representation.

Paternalism has often been associated with traditional authority and regarded as an archaic form of management, which would fade away with the forward march of modernity and the rational-legal, bureaucratic organization. To some extent this has happened, so that as many British companies became public limited companies (PLC)s, they lost their original Christian social philosophy, in favour of a more value-free social science approach. Likewise, the emergence of the welfare state after the Second World War, with its universal benefits, caused many large employers to phase out their welfare provision.

It would be wrong, however, to see paternalism purely as a hangover from the past. For companies have been prone to reinvent paternalistic relationships where they did not exist before, as in the large manufacturing and railway companies at the end of the Victorian era. Even today, there is talk of human resource management (HRM) as a new form of paternalism. In so far as HRM is unitarist, and breaks with trade unions, this bears some surface resemblance to primitive paternalism. There is less evidence, however, that modern management is prepared to invest in a long-term employment relationship to the extent that major welfare capitalists did in the past. **PA**

References and further reading

Ackers, P. (1999) 'On paternalism: seven observations on the uses and abuses of the concept in industrial relations, past and present', *Historical Studies in Industrial Relations* 5, Spring: 173–93.

Ackers, P. (2001) 'Paternalism, participation and partnership: rethinking the employment relationship, *Human Relations* 54(3): 375–86.

Ackers, P. and Black, J. (1991) 'Paternalism: an organisation culture in transition', in M. Cross and G. Payne (eds) *Work and the Enterprise Culture*, London: Falmer/BSA.

Greene, A.-M., Ackers, P. and Black, J. (2001) 'Lost narratives? From paternalism to team-working in a lock manufacturing firm', *Economic and Industrial Democracy*. (forthcoming)

Jacoby, S. M. (1997) 'Modern manors: welfare capitalism since the new deal', Princeton, NJ: Princeton University Press. (Reviewed by the author in 1999 in *Historical Studies in Industrial Relations* 8, Autumn: 188–94.)

Joyce, P. (1980) *Work, Society and Politics: The Culture of the Factory in Later Victorian England*, London: Methuen.

Payment by results

Payment by results (PBR) schemes are those in which an individual is rewarded directly for results achieved. This includes piecework, in which workers are paid by the amount produced, measured daywork, where an additional fixed sum or bonus is paid above the basic rate, so long as a prescribed level of performance is achieved, and bonuses directly linked to output, sales or other targets.

Payment by results is based upon a number of assumptions about employee motivation, many of which are unproven or valid only in certain situations. It is assumed that:

- there is a direct link between individual effort and the results achieved
- employees have the opportunity and ability to change their levels of effort
- there is a continuous supply of work and that the method of production is under the control of the employee
- employees want to achieve higher or extra pay
- they are prepared to accept variations in their earnings.

Those in favour of PBR argue that it enhances mangagement control of work without the need for greater supervision, that it gives employees an opportunity to vary their earnings according to individual need and that lower levels of supervision give employees greater discretion on how and when to do their work.

A flourishing literature, often based on detailed case studies, has shown how PBR may work in practice. Employees may use much effort and ingenuity in attempting to manipulate the scheme to their own advantage. Peer group pressure is often exerted to stop colleagues from exceeding an accepted norm. Changes in working practices or technology may be resisted by workers who fear loss of earnings under a new system.

Payment by results is used much less than it was 30 years ago. Over 20 per cent of British employees received PBR at the beginning of the 1990s, but this had fallen progressively to under 15 per cent by the end of that decade. This can be accounted for by a recognition of the above criticisms and by a greater appreciation of the difficulties of identifying individual as opposed to group effort. Other qualities, such as teamwork, responsibility, flexibility, skill and knowledge are seen as more important qualities to reward. **MMo**

References and further reading

Armstrong, M. (1996) *Employee Reward*, London: Institute of Personnel and Development.

Behrend, H. (1959) 'Financial incentives as a system of beliefs', *British Journal of Sociology* 2: 137–47.

Brown, W. (1973) *Piecework Bargaining*, London: Heinemann.

Casey, B., Lakey, J. and White, M. (1992) *Payment Systems: A Look at Current Practice*, Research Series no. 5, Department of Employment: Policy Studies Institute.

Roy, D. (1952) 'Quota restriction and goldbricking in a machine shop', *American Journal of Sociology* 57, March: 427–42.

White, G. and Drucker, J. (2000) *Reward Management: A Critical Text*, London: Routledge.

Peer appraisal

Peer appraisal is the assessment of an employee's performance by their work colleagues. There are three basic types of peer appraisal:

1. Nomination, where each member of a work group is asked to nominate one or more colleagues who are highest on some particular aspect of performance. Nominations for the lowest performers are also sometimes requested and self-nominations are usually excluded.
2. The peer ranking method whereby the employee ranks the other employees from best to worst on one or more dimensions of performance.
3. Standard-rating systems may be used, usually anonymously.

Researchers have generally been supportive of the use of peer appraisal. Peer assessments have been found to be sound in terms of the key psychometric properties of reliability and validity, to be a useful mechanism for differentiating between an employees' effort level and achievement outcomes, and to be effective in focusing on the most relevant abilities and competencies of those being rated. Peer review may be particularly appropriate for specialist professional staff, where only peers may possess the necessary technical expertise to make a credible assessment of performance. Further, professionals feel that they themselves are responsible for maintaining the performance standards of the profession and that performance appraisal by organizational managers may violate the principle of professional autonomy. The close teamwork involved in the work of professionals may also make peer review particularly appropriate here.

Given such favourable reports it is perhaps surprising that peer appraisal is not very widespread. Peer appraisal is much discussed and researched but little used. There are number of possible reasons for this. Some suggest that peer reviews are perceived as amounting to little more than a 'popularity contest' and that this greatly undermines their credibility in the eyes of managers, leading to negative user reactions. Others suggest that peer appraisal may create friction, damage interpersonal relationships, and erode trust amongst peers and is also subject to a friendship bias. For many commentators, this limits the use of peer appraisal to a developmental role at best. **TR**

References and further reading

Druskat, V. and Wolff, S. (1999) 'Effects and timing of developmental peer appraisals in self-managing work groups', *Journal of Applied Psychology* 84(1): 58–69.

Barclay, J. and Harland, L. (1995) 'Peer performance appraisals: the impact of rater competence, rater location, and rating correctability on fairness perceptions', *Group and Organization Management* 20(1): 39–61.

Industrial Relations Service (IRS) (1999) 'New ways to perform appraisal', *IRS Employment Trends* 676: 7–16.

McEvoy, G. and Buller, P. (1987) 'User acceptance of peer appraisals in an industrial setting', *Personnel Psychology* 40(4): 785–97.

Pensions

Pensions may be seen as a form of deferred payment. Occupational pensions are important. About 4.5 million people in the UK receive pensions from private sector occupational pension schemes and about another 8.5 million people of working age have pension rights through such occupational schemes which will become payable in future. There are three main sources of pensions – state, occupational and individual.

The *state* pension scheme is paid for by employers' and employees' contributions to the National Insurance Fund. It is a universal benefit paid to each individual who has made sufficient contribution to the fund during their period of employment. The pension is payable when a person reaches the state pension age, which is currently

65 for men and 60 for women. From 2010 the pension age for women is to change and by 2020 will be 65.

An *occupational* pension is one where normally both employer and employee make contributions. This can promote a positive image of the organization as a benevolent employer and act as an incentive in attracting and retaining employees. It can also help ease the problems of early retirement and redundancy. Occupational pensions may be managed by the company or through commercial fund managers. Pensions are a complex and ever-changing area and, therefore, considerable expertise is needed. Occupational pension schemes receive favourable tax treatment if their rules are approved by the Inland Revenue's Pension Scheme's Office. However, the number of occupational pension schemes is in decline, particularly among smaller employers.

Individual pension schemes are for people who want to make their own arrangements. They allow greater flexibility for mobile employees and lower administrative costs for employers.

Because women have normally had shorter working lives their pensions can be significantly lower than those of men. New legislation for sharing pensions was introduced by the Welfare Reform and Pensions Act 1999. The regulations allow for both private and state additional pensions to be shared by couples divorcing after 1 December 2000. **MMo**

References and further reading

Blake, D. (1995) *Pension Schemes and Pension Funds in the United Kingdom*, Oxford: Oxford University Press.

Casey, B. (1993) *Employers' Choice of Pension Schemes*: *A Report of a Qualitative Study*, London: HMSO.

Incomes Data Services (IDS) (2000) *Pension Scheme Profiles 2000/01*, London: IDS.

Smith, I. (2000) 'Benefits', in G. White and J. Drucker (eds) *Reward Management*: *A Critical Text*, London: Routledge.

Performance appraisal

Performance appraisal, consisting of the review of an employee's performance typically conducted by the immediate line manager, has grown rapidly in the UK over the last decade or so. One key driver of the growth of performance appraisal has been the increasing popularity of the **Investors in People** initiative (see separate entry). For example, the most recent Workplace Employee Relations Surveys (WERS) data finds organizations who are recognized as Investors in People are significantly more likely to have a performance appraisal scheme in use. The spread of performance appraisal has resulted in the inclusion of previously untouched organizations and occupational groups. In particular performance appraisal has moved down the organizational hierarchy to encompass blue-collar, secretarial and administrative staff, and from the private to the public sector. The last decade has seen its introduction in schools, hospitals, universities, local authorities, the civil service, etc. Increasingly, it seems, in line with harmonization policies, all employees in an organization are included in the performance appraisal system. New forms of appraisal have also emerged. We thus now have competency-based appraisal systems, staff appraisal of manager, team-based appraisal, customer appraisals and the so called '360°' systems (see also entries on **peer appraisal**, **upward appraisal**, **customer appraisal** and 360° **appraisal**).

There are a wide range of methods used to conduct performance appraisals, from the simplest of ranking schemes through objective, standard and competency-based systems to complex behaviourally anchored rating schemes. The nature of an organization's appraisal scheme is largely a reflection of managerial beliefs, the amount of resources that it has available to commit, and the expertise it possesses. Thus smaller organizations with limited human resource expertise tend to adopt simpler ranking and rating schemes whilst the more complex and resource consuming systems, such as competency-based and 360° appraisal, are found mainly in larger organizations. Most employers use only one type of appraisal scheme, often a 'hybrid form' of a number of methods and a few companies even provide employees with a choice of methods in how they are appraised. The main reason for organizations using multiple systems of appraisal is the wish to separate out reward and non-reward aspects of appraisal, the customizing of different systems for different occupational groups (e.g. managerial and non-managerial employees) and separate systems for different parts of the organization.

Organizations use performance appraisal for a wide range of different purposes. Surveys commonly report the use of performance appraisal for:

- clarifying and defining performance expectations
- identifying training and development needs
- providing career counselling
- succession planning
- improving individual, team and corporate performance
- facilitating communications and involvement
- allocating financial rewards
- determining promotion
- motivating and controlling employees
- achieving cultural change.

Recent trends suggest that the more judgemental and 'harder' forms of performance appraisal are on the increase and that 'softer' largely developmental approaches are declining. Thus there has been a shift in performance appraisal away from using it for career planning and identifying future potential and increased use of it for improving current performance and allocating rewards. Here the arrival of flatter organizations has given rise to the need to uncouple to some extent performance appraisal and promotion whilst competitive pressures have emphasized the need to incentivise improvements in short-term performance. **TR**

References and further reading

Armstrong, M. and Baron, A. (1998) *Performance Management*, London: IPD.
Grint, K. (1993) 'What's wrong with performance appraisals? A critique and a suggestion', *Human Resource Management* 3(3): 61–77.
Industrial Relations Service (IRS) (1999) 'New ways to perform appraisal', *Employment Trends* 676: 7–16.
Redman, T., Snape, E., Thompson, D. and Ka-ching Yan, F. (2000) 'Performance appraisal in the national health service: a trust hospital study', *Human Resource Management Journal* 10(1): 1–16.
Snape, E., Thompson, D., Ka-ching Yan, F. and Redman, T. (1998) 'Performance appraisal and culture: practice and attitudes in Hong Kong and Great Britain', *International Journal of Human Resource Management* 9(5): 841–61.

Performance management

Performance management, like many human resource management innovations is an American import that has been a major driver in the increased use of performance appraisal by British organizations. Performance management has been defined as systems and attitudes, which help organizations to plan, delegate and assess their operations. Bevan and Thompson (1991) describe a 'textbook' performance management system thus:

- A shared vision of the organization's objectives communicated via a mission statement to all employees.

- Individual performance targets which are related to operating unit and wider organizational objectives.
- Regular formal review of progress towards targets.
- A review process which identifies training and development needs and rewards outcomes.
- An evaluation of the effectiveness of the whole process and its contribution to overall organizational performance to allow changes and improvements to be made.

A principal feature of performance management is thus that it connects the objectives of the organization to a system of work targets for individual employees. In such models of performance management objective setting and formal appraisal are placed at the heart of the approach. The development of performance management systems has had major implications for performance appraisal. A key trend has been away from 'stand-alone' performance appraisal systems and towards individual appraisal becoming part of an integrated performance management system. There is a growing critique of performance management systems:

1. They are seen as adding more pressure to a short-term view amongst British managers, which may well hamper organizational performance over the long term.
2. They are often proffered in a very prescriptive fashion with many writers advocating a single best way for performance management, to the neglect of important variables such as degree of centralization, unionization etc. This is in contrast to the actual practice of performance management in the UK, which is extremely diverse. The real danger is that performance management systems cannot be simply 'borrowed' from one organization and applied in another, as many advocates appear to suggest.
3. They are supposed to be line management 'driven' but case studies of its practices report the motivating forces in organizations as being chief executives and human resource departments with often questionable ownership and commitment from line managers.
4. There is a growing concern that performance management systems, because of their dedicated focus on improving the 'bottom line' have added unduly to the pressures and stresses of work life for many employees. Many systems have been introduced with scant regard for employee welfare.
5. Perhaps more damming is the view that they are ineffective. The main driver of performance management is the improvement of overall organization effectiveness. However, there is little support from various studies that performance management actually improves performance. For example, Bevan and Thompson's survey of performance management in the UK found that there was no relationship between high-performing UK companies (defined as those demonstrating pre-tax profit growth over a five year period) and the operation of a performance management system. **TR**

References and further reading

Armstrong, M. and Baron, M. (1998) 'Out of the tick box. The use of performance management in UK', *People Management* 4(15): 38–41.

Bevan, S. and Thompson, M. (1991) 'Performance management at the crossroads', *Personnel Management*, November: 36–9.

Fletcher, C. and Williams, R. (1992) 'The route to performance management', *Personnel Management,* October: 42–47.

Stivers, B. and Joyce, T. (2000) Building a Balanced Performance Management System, *SAM Advanced Management Journal* 65(1): 22–8.

Taylor, S., Masterson, S. S., Renard, M. K. and Tracy, K. B. (1998) 'Managers' reactions to procedurally just performance management systems', *Academy of Management Journal* 41(5): 568–79.

Performance-related pay

Performance-related pay (PRP) has historically been seen as a way to incentivize white-collar workers. These schemes are said to reward performance, unlike incentive pay schemes that are supposed to stimulate performance .

Armstrong (1996: 239) states that it, 'emerged in the 1980's [*sic*] as the answer to motivating people and developing performance-orientated cultures'. Unlike incentive pay schemes, which some managers believe can be manipulated to the benefit of the workers, PRP schemes are seen as ideal for workers who associate themselves with the corporate goals and culture.

A common form of PRP is that of the annual increment that is linked to an individual's performance. The criteria used to measure performance for this purpose can include such things as attendance, customer care, effort, initiative and time-keeping. However many of these criteria can be perceived as arbitrary and subjective and therefore inherently unfair. It is therefore thought to be more effective for any pay increase to be linked to pre-set and agreed individual targets, although this approach can be problematic at the goal/target/objective-setting stage. Kessler and Purcell (1992) highlight this by noting that there could be inconsistency between managers about which criteria are the most important and that there is an inherent difficulty in setting meaningful objectives for certain workers such as administrative and clerical staff.

This type of pay system can help to maintain employee morale in flatter organizations when it is not always possible to reward good performance with promotion. If set up properly and well administered, it can also support ideals of 'distributive justice', often seen as an important factor in eliciting employee loyalty.

In recent years the British government has sought, not very successfully, to encourage public sector employers to introduce PRP. Unlike in the private sector, employees cannot generate greater profits from which extra pay can be generated and there has been considerable scepticism as to whether such schemes can work (Marsden and Richardson, 1994). **MMo**

References and further reading
Armstrong, M. (1996) *Employee Reward*, London: Institiute of Personnel and Development.
Armstrong, M. and Murlis, H. (1998) *Reward Management*, 4th edn, London: Kogan Page.
Armstrong, M. and Brown, D. (2000) *Paying for Contribution*: *Real Performance-Related Pay Strategies*, London: Kogan Page.
Kessler, I. and Purcell, J. (1992) 'Performance-related pay: objectives and application', *Human Resource Management Journal* 2, Spring: 16–33.
Marsden, D. and Richardson, R. (1994) 'Performing for pay? The effects of 'merit pay' on motivation in a public service', *British Journal of Industrial Relations* 32(2): 243–62.
Rubery, J. (1995) 'Performance-related pay and the prospects for gender equity', *Journal of Management Studies* 32(5): 637–54.

Personal development plans

Personal development plans (PDPs) have become popular in recent years, growing from the same culture which has spawned the learning organization and self-development. Personal development plans are often the documentation emanating from self-development initiatives but, formally, they have been introduced by many organizations seeking to implement an approach to planning skill and career development activities. Although there is not a standard format, PDPs usually comprise a form which an employee will complete as a clear development action plan. The development itself may take many guises from formal training activities to a wider selection of development opportunities such as coaching, project work, action learning, self-study and distance learning to secondments and career moves. The PDP is the individual's responsibility but, in organizations, it is usually supported by the human resource department and/or line management, which may take on a coaching or mentoring role.

Personal development plans are usually developed either as part of the appraisal system, in which case they are likely to apply to all employees, or as a result of a development centre. In the latter case, since development centre activity tends not to be an organizationwide event, PDPs tend to be a management, graduate or high-flyer issue. Management competencies are often used as a framework for their development but the focus they take can vary between organization. For example, some PDPs are job focused and will concentrate upon the current job, maybe the next career move and longer term. This narrowly focused approach will often derive from appraisal. Personal development plans which are broader tend to be person centred primarily and will concentrate upon both life and career issues. This is more the development centre approach.

The degree of organizational intervention in PDPs is variable. There is an argument that tight organizational control over individual issues, involving monitoring procedures, is somewhat against the spirit of self-development and self-managed learning. Agreeing structured forms on development plans with organizational representatives is, it is argued, contrary to the learning organization philosophy. The notion of self-development and PDPs does not fit easily within UK culture (there is an underlying assumption that we are all motivated to learn) and may, therefore, take time to embed. It is recommended that the task of communicating and implementing a PDP approach within an organization should not be underestimated and that participants will need to be enthused and to have both their own interest and that of management supporters maintained. The introduction of PDPs may well be regarded with some suspicion and employees will need to know what these are for, what the benefits are likely to be and whether they are voluntary. Issues of confidentiality and honesty will need to be addressed.

An increasing number of organizations seem to be adopting the PDP approach but there has been little research to evaluate their effectiveness. There is also an assumption that an individual's PDP will align with organizational goals (Pedler, Burgoyne and Boyder, 1988) which may be a little naive. However, the ethos of the learning organization, which implies that individuals and teams are consistently looking for better ways of doing things, may require a formalized approach such as PDP to capture enthusiasm and good ideas. **ASm**

References and further reading

Floodgate, J. F. (1994) 'Personal development plans: the challenge of implementation – a case study', *Journal of European Industrial Training* 18(11): 43–7.

Pedler, M., Burgoyne, J. and Boyder, I. T. (1988) *Applying Self Development in organizations*, London: Prentice Hall International.

Tamkin, P., Baxter, L. and Hirsh, W. (1995) 'PDPs: case studies of practice', *Institute for Employment Studies Report*, 280.

Personnel management

Personnel management is the generally recognized term to describe the organizational processes concerned with the employment and deployment of people in and around the business. To academics, and to some extent to practitioners, it also describes a phase in people management practice that lasted from about 1920 to about 1985: before was welfare, after was human resource management. The change in the 1980s can be attributed to two developments: first was the decline in the assertiveness of British trade unions; second was the emergence in the USA of a concept of human resource management. Previously Americans had used the terms 'labour management' and 'personnel administration', and 'administration' is not a term to set the pulses racing in management circles.

To describe the approximately 60-year phase of personnel management it is easiest to contrast it with human resource management. Personnel management is *workforce centred*, administering a contract for employment. It is directed mainly at the organization's employees: finding and training them, arranging payment, explaining management's expectations and justifying management's actions. The workforce is a resource that is relatively inflexible in comparison with other resources like cash and materials. Although indisputably a management function, personnel is never totally identified with management interests, as it becomes ineffective when not able to understand and express the aspirations and opinions of the workforce, just as sales representatives have to understand and articulate the aspirations of the customers. There is always some degree of being in between the management and the employees, mediating the needs of each to the other.

Human resource management is *resource centred*, administering a contract for performance. It is directed mainly at management needs for human resources (not necessarily employees) to be provided and deployed. Demand rather than supply is the focus of the activity. There is greater emphasis on planning, monitoring and control, rather than on mediation. Problem-solving is undertaken with other members of management on human resource issues rather than directly with employees or their representatives. It is totally identified with management interests, being a general management activity, and is relatively distant from the workforce as a whole, as employee interests can only be enhanced through effective overall management. **DT**

References and further reading
Bach, S. and Sisson, K. (eds) (2000) *Personnel Management*, 3rd edn, Oxford: Blackwell.
Hackett, P. (1991) *The Personnel Department at Work*, London: Institute of Personnel Management.
Hall, L. A. and Torrington, D. P. (1998) *The Human Resource Function: the Dynamics of Change and Development*, London: Financial Times Publishing.
Legge, K. (1995) *Human Resource Management: Rhetorics and Realities*, London: Macmillan Business.
Sisson, K. (ed.) (1994) *Personnel Management*, 2nd edn, Oxford: Blackwell.
Thomason, G. F. (1981) *A Text Book of Personnel Management*, London: Institute of Personnel Management.

Personnel specification

Personnel or person specifications are documents which list the attributes needed to undertake a particular job. They are principally used in the recruitment and selection of staff, but can also provide the basis for a training needs analysis. They are typically quite short documents, the aim being to summarize on a single sheet of paper the key characteristics that an organization is looking for when seeking to fill a vacant post. A common approach is to list separately those attributes which are considered 'essential' and those which are merely 'desirable'. A further subdivision is then made between different types of requirement such as formal qualifications, skills, knowledge, experience and personality attributes. There are two distinct approaches used to compile personnel specifications, although in either case there can be a great deal of variation in the degree to which a formal procedure is used. The first approach involves deriving the characteristics from a written job description. The process thus starts with the key duties undertaken by the job holder. A technique which is often recommended here is the use of a repertory grid, where by each main job task is assessed separately in terms of the attributes required to perform it to the required level of performance. The second approach, sometimes described as being 'competency based', involves focusing on the attributes of the most successful current holders of the job in question. The aim is thus to establish what distinguishes the good from the less good performers and then formally to record these characteristics.

The chief advantage of personnel specifications is the role they play in helping to make a selection process objective. In focusing the minds of individual interviewers and assessors on the key attributes required in a job holder, they play a part in discouraging decision-making based on prejudice, hunch or on factors which are relatively unimportant for the role in question.

The major criticism of the use of personnel specifications, as for job descriptions, is the view that they are unnecessarily bureaucratic. They take time to compile properly, have to be updated regularly to meet the changing needs of an organization, and may thus serve to delay the recruitment of urgently needed new employees. **ST**

References and further reading

Roberts, G. (1997) *Recruitment and Selection: A Competency Approach*, London: IPD.

Smith. M., Gregg, M. and Andrews, D. (1989) *Selection and Assessment: A New Appraisal*, London: Pitman, ch. 3.

Stokes, R. S. (1987) 'Defining the job and specifying the ideal candidate', in S. Harper (ed.) *Personnel Management Handbook*, Aldershot: Gower.

Taylor, S. (1998) *Employee Resourcing*, London: IPD 85–6.

Wood, R. and Payne, T. (1998) *Competency Based Recruitment and Selection: A Practical Guide*, Chichester: Wiley, ch. 2.

PEST(E)/SWOT analysis

These terms are mnemonics (devices to help memory) for two basic conceptual frameworks used in strategy. Although the names may sound daunting to the uninitiated, the output of a simple PEST(E) (the second 'E' has been put in brackets because it is unpronounced. Originally 'ethical/environmental' was not part of the acronym but nowadays many companies (e.g. Xerox) consider ethical/environmental issues alongside economic and political factors. Sometimes this acronym is also known as LEPEST, to indicate consideration of legal implications) or SWOT analysis may be nothing more than a list of ideas or bullet points grouped on a piece of paper or flip chart under headings, the first letter of each heading being recalled by the acronym. So, PEST(E) helps us remember the headings Political, Economic, Social-legal, Technological and Ethical or Environmental, and SWOT helps us remember Strengths, Weaknesses, Opportunities and Threats.

Deciding if and when to use these mnemonics in making business (or personal) decisions is a matter of judgement, though it might help to think of PEST(E) analyses as useful in analysing the external environment, or as an answer to the question, 'What are the wider implications if our organization does X?' SWOT analyses are principally used to assess and evaluate the current state of any of a wide range of things, e.g. product/brand/initiative/department/organization. Strengths and weaknesses are usually thought of in terms of internal properties, so, for example, a product might be high quality (a strength), or a department might have too few staff (a weakness). Opportunities and threats are usually functions of the external environment, so for example, a luxury brand may sell better in times of prosperity (an opportunity), or an organization such as a supermarket may see a competitor open a new store nearby (a threat). It is worth stressing that genuine 'analysis' involves more than reciting acronyms, or superficial 'listing', and it is very rare that SWOT or PEST(E) analyses will be useful if they merely result in a list of 'pointers'. Instead, it is likely they will only be useful if they enable the generation and evaluation of a range of competing ideas about 'what can be done', in response to a specific problem. **KM**

References and further reading

Johnson, G. and Scholes, K. (1997) *Exploring Corporate Strategy*, London: Prentice Hall.

Picketing

When a strike occurs, trade union representatives and union members sometimes organize pickets at the entrances of workplaces which are or might become involved in the particular dispute. Pickets attempt to persuade other workers to join or support the strike, and those approached by them may include any employees who are doing the work of those on strike, suppliers or contractors planning to enter the affected premises and any strikers deciding to return to work during the strike. The civil law in relation to picketing emphasizes peaceful communication and persuasion but, in the 1980s, picketing has been further restricted to locations at or near the workplace at which the strikers are employed (1980 Employment Act as incorporated in the Trade Union and Labour Relations [Consolidation] Act 1992). In addition, the picketing *Code of Practice* (DoE, 1980) provides a *guideline* of a maximum of six pickets at any entrance.

Whilst civil action has been taken against unions to restrict the activities of pickets, the criminal law generally plays a more important role. On the occasions when the police arrest pickets they are usually charged with obstruction and breach of the peace offences, though occasionally – as in the case of the 1984–85 miners' strike – the charges can be much more serious. When strikes are protracted, picketing is usually organized on a larger or more sophisticated scale, and it is in these circumstances that the police are more likely to intervene. However, employers normally prefer a more pragmatic approach and, in light of this, it is relatively unusual for pickets to be arrested. It is also surprising perhaps, particularly in light of media images of strikes and picketing, that the majority of strikes which have taken place in Britain in recent years have not been accompanied by picketing (Millward *et al.*, 1992: 303–4; Kelly 1998: 77–8). **DB**

References and further reading

Department of Employment (DoE) (1980) 'Picketing', *Code of Practice*, London: DoE.
Kelly, J. (1998) *Rethinking Industrial Relations*, London: Routledge, 77–8.
Labour Research Department (1998) *The Law at Work*, London: LRD Publications, pp. 76–7, 81–2.
Marsh, D. (1992) *The New Politics of British Trade Unionism*, London: Macmillan, pp. 101–4.
McIlroy, J. (1985) 'Police and pickets', in H. Beynon (ed.) *Digging Deeper: Issues in the Miners' Strike*, London: Verso.
Millward, N., Stevens, M., Smart, D. and Harves, W. R. (1992) *Workplace Industrial Relations in Transition: the ED/ESRC/PSI/ACAS Surveys*, Aldershot: Dartmouth, pp. 302–13.
Wallington, P. (1985) 'Policing the miners' strike', *Industrial Law Journal* 14: 145–59.

Pluralism

Pluralism is widely used in political theory to describe the diversity of advanced Western societies, composed of many different interest and belief groups. In employment relations, the term is used with similar meaning to describe relationships within the business organization. In direct opposition to *unitarism*, pluralism rejects the model of the company as a unified order, following management leadership. Equally, it resists the Marxist or radical view of the organization as riven by a 'class war' between management and labour. Instead it discerns a plural society, composed of many interest groups, like a microcosm of Britain or America. These groups are often in conflict with each other, so that there is no single focus of loyalty and authority, but rival sources of attachment. Within a large complex organization, such as the National Health Service, these interest groups will include professions, such as doctors, nurses and physiotherapists, each with their own associations. It will include too managers and manual workers, such as porters and cleaners, who belong to the trade union, UNISON. And there will be still others, such as drivers and white-collar workers with their own representative bodies.

The pluralist approach to employment relations focuses on the division between the goals, interests and values of management, which revolve around the need to improve profits or performance, and those of employees, which centre on wages and conditions. In this respect, pluralism expects a measure of conflict at the heart of the employment relations, notwithstanding a degree of shared concern in the long-term success of the organization. Trade unions play a central role here, not in causing conflict, but as a means of expressing conflicts of interest, bringing them to the surface, channelling and resolving them. For, in this view, conflict is a fact of organizational life, which cannot be wished away. The solution instead, is to manage conflict by institutionalizing it, rather as fire-breaks prevent a forest fire engulfing an entire forest. This is done by management recognizing trade unions, forming committees for negotiation and consultation and procedures for disputes, discipline, grievances and redundancy. These create order and predictability, where otherwise conflict might break out in hidden, explosive forms, such as sabotage, wildcat strikes, absenteeism, low productivity and high labour turnover. Pluralism lost favour, as an industrial relations approach, in the 1980s and early 1990s. This was due to the union-led strikes of the previous decade, the anti-union backlash of Thatcherism and the decline in trade union influence that followed. However, a 'neo-pluralism' has revived recently in the form of **Social Partnership** (see separate entry). **PA**

References and further reading

Ackers, P. (2002) Reframing industrial relations: the case for neo-pluralism, *Industrial Relations Journal*. (forthcoming)

Ackers, P. and Payne, J. (1998) 'British trade unions and social partnership: rhetoric, reality and strategy', *International Journal of Industrial Relations* 34(4), December: 473–95.

Fox, A. (1966) 'Industrial sociology and industrial relations', Royal Commission on Trade Unions and Employers Associations, Research Paper 3, London: HMSO.

Fox, A. (1974) *Beyond Contract*: *Work, Power and Trust Relations*, London: Faber.

Fox, A. (1985) *Man Mismanagement*, London: Hutchinson.

Provis, C. (1996) 'Unitarism, pluralism, interests and values', *British Journal of Industrial Relations* 34(4), December: 473–95.

Poaching

One of the problems associated with getting qualified staff to fill the number of vacancies that employers need to fill so that they can compete in turbulent economic and fast-moving markets, is that poaching has become an accepted practice. Though not necessarily agreeing with the principles and tactics that are used to attract people into organizations, most employers have come to recognize that poaching other employers' staff is necessary to obtain the requisite skills and knowledge, that they need for their organization.

Poaching has become more than what has been in the past generally accepted as head hunting. There is more emphasis on targeting employees more directly and within the employing organization's time and in some extreme circumstances within the employing organization's location. In this latter example, the 'poacher' will approach an employee by claiming to be a bona fide supplier or advertiser of a given product and service. In this way, the poacher gains access to the organization and to the specific employee who will be approached and persuaded that he or she may like to consider contacting the poacher's organization.

There are many disadvantages of approaching an employee or by being aggressive in pursuit of getting that employee to work for the 'poacher's organization. Conflict can arise between the competitors and can lead to 'soured' relationships. Where the information technology demand for talent outweighs supply and there is a severe shortage of skills, the Internet is used to scan for prospective candidates, but headhunters are a 'ubiquitous feature of business life where their power is growing' (Garrison-Jenn, 1998: 300). In New York for example headhunters' business rose by 14 per cent during 1999. There are no authenticated statistics available for the UK.

The increasing pressure on companies to have the best person in the job may mean survival in the intense competitive market place, poaching and headhunting has become a profitable business. If it is critical for a company to depend on the skills and knowledge of its workforce, direct mail is also becoming the norm in efforts to attract those people who are not necessarily looking for a job change.

Although direct mail is impersonal and intrusive, even 'unprofessional', some employers state that well-produced, carefully targeted mail campaigns can reach an untapped pool of potential job candidates.

Headhunting and poaching are not illegal practices, though Johnson (2000) refers to some of the practises as using 'dirty tactics' for employers to obtain suitably quali-fied staff. In his article Johnson reports that human resource (HR) professionals are fac-ing a tough battle to hold on to their key people and that 'poaching executives has become the new sport of the global corporation'. It would appear from the various research projects that poaching has become a problem for HR people to address. Addi-tional or different retention packages have to be so designed so as to encourage employees to remain with the company. There is evidence that highlights this problem, which is reflected in employees' willingness to gain experience in different organizations, irrespective of the long-term benefits of the employing organization.

The current emphasis is on short-term financial and status gains over long-term job tenure benefits. This is exacerbated by the uncertainties created by downsizing, mergers and acquisitions where jobs are volatile and likely to cease as a result. Out-sourcing has also created job uncertainty and employees are likely to respond to a job offer if the immediate benefits are worthwhile (in their individual views) or prospects for promotion are likely in the short term. **SR**

References and further reading

Garrison-Jenn, N. (1998) *The Global 200 Executive Recruiters*: *The Essential Guide to the Best Recruiters in the United States, Europe, Asia and Latin America*, San Fransisco: Jossey-Bass.

Johnson, M. (2000) 'Dirty tactics', *HR World Journal* 14, March–April: 16, 18, 21–2.

Lewis, J. (1999) 'A price on their heads' *Personnel Today,* 8 July: 26–7.

Matthew, L. (2000) 'Attracting the head hunters' *Management Today*, December: 84–5, 87.

McCallum, T. (1998) 'The HR professional as head hunter', *HR Professional Journal*, 15(6) December: 30–2.

Woodward, N. M. (2000) 'Direct mail pushes the recruiting envelope', *HR Magazine* 45(5), May: 145, 147–9, 152.

Policies and procedures

Polices and procedures are defined as 'formal, conscious statements' that support organizational goals. Policies and procedures tend to be the official way companies disseminate their policies 'as the *leitmotif* of acceptable practice' (Storey and Sisson, 1993: 6). There is a significant difference between a 'policy' and a 'procedure'.

Policies are written documents that outline defined rules, obligations and expecta-tions for managers and employees. Typically, policy statements cover areas such as discipline, grievance, redundancy, reward, recruitment or promotion. The policy may be a statement of intent, such as 'it is the policy of this company to promote and reward high achievers'.

Procedures outline the details of how to enact a policy. For example, having a pol-icy of 'rewarding high achiever's' would require some guidance on how managers implement the policy, such as the criteria for promotion or how much they can reward an individual. Similarly, a discipline procedure would outline possible sanc-tions, areas of conduct and so on.

The scope and depth of human resource (HR) policies and procedures have been used by researchers as a proxy for management style (McLoughlin and Gourlay, 1994; Purcell and Ahlstrand, 1994). At one extreme, the absence of policies and procedures can indicate a very informal managerial approach, while at the other extreme detailed policies and procedures point to a formalised managerial style. The type and range of policies may also indicate an organization's culture, the extent of 'integration' between different HR polices such as reward, relations or training (Marchington and Wilkinson, 2000).

However, there are many different types of organizations. Thus the reading of a set of polices and procedures as a proxy of management style or the extent of HR integration can be a rather simplistic approach. For example, a small engineering factory will be quite different to a hospital, school or large multinational corporation. Each of these will have their own set of HR polices. organizational structure is therefore an important factor in assessing how policy is translated into procedure. Indeed, actual practices are often very different from policy statements (see also **Custom and practice**). A large corporation may allow plant managers to determine their own set of procedures in accordance with a broad policy objective, while a smaller firm may adhere to detailed procedures for the whole company.

Overall, the use of policies and procedures has increased over the last decade (Cully *et al.*, 1999). Most common are those in the areas of health and safety, discipline, grievance resolution and pay and conditions arrangements. **TD**

References and further reading

Cully, M., O'Reilly, A., Millward, N., Forth, J., Woodland, S., Dix, G. and Bryson, A. (1998) *Britain at Work: As Depicted by the 1998 Workplace Employee Relations Survey*, London: Routledge.

Marchington, M. and Wilkinson, A. (1996) *Core Personnel and Development*, London: IPD.

McLoughlin, I. and Gourlay, S. (1994), *Enterprise without Unions*, Buckingham: Open University Press.

Purcell, J. and Ahlstrand, B. (1994) *Human Resource Management in the Multi-Divisional Company*, Oxford: Oxford University Press.

Storey, J. and Sisson, K. (1993) *Managing Human Resources and Industrial Relations*, Buckingham: Open University Press.

Political funds

Trade unions are legally obliged to establish separate funds for their expenditure on political activities. Most manual unions and many white collar unions have political funds, though not all unions use this money for affiliation to and support of the Labour Party. Where unions have such a fund, a small proportion of members' subscriptions are allocated to it. Union members can *contract out* of paying this *political levy*. Since 1913 it has been a legal requirement that union expenditure on party political affiliation and activity must be made from a distinct political fund. However, the 1984 Trade Union Act meant that for the first time unions had to hold a secret ballot every ten years if they wished to retain their political funds. In addition, this Act widened the definition of *political*, potentially posing a legal challenge to a variety of union campaigns. The provisions of the 1913 and 1984 Acts are now essentially incorporated in the 1992 Trade Union and Labour Relations (Consolidation) Act.

The evident government rationale for the 1984 Trade Union Act was that trade unions needed the intervention of the law to establish more democratic procedures within them, and with such intervention would emerge less politically orientated organizations. However, in the ballots held in the wake of the 1984 Act every union retained its political fund, and most did so with a large majority of votes. In addition, many unions, which were not affiliated to the Labour Party, nor chose to be so, ran successful campaigns to establish new political funds. They feared that, without such funds and in light of the 1984 Act, any of their campaigns which were critical of government policy might now be interpreted by the courts as political, and therefore would be vulnerable to legal challenge. Therefore, contrary to Conservative government intentions, the outcome of the 1984 Act – in relation to political funds – proved to be a considerable success for the trade unions. (See also **Ballots**.) **DB**

References and further reading

Certification Office for Trade Unions and Employers' Associations, *Annual Report of the Certification Officer*, London: Crown copyright.

Labour Research Department (1993) 'What are political funds for?', *Labour Research*, 82: 10, 8–10.

Leopold, J. (1988) 'Moving the status quo: the growth of trade union political funds', *Industrial Relations Journal* 19(1): 286–95.

Leopold, J. (1997) ' Trade unions, political fund ballots and the Labour Party', *British Journal of Industrial Relations* 35(1): 23–38.

Marsh, D. (1992) *The New Politics of British Trade Unionism*, London: Macmillan.

McIlroy, J. (1995) *Trade Unions in Britain Today*, 2nd edn, Manchester: Manchester University Press.

Positive-affirmative action

'Positive action' is the term used to describe measures which take a proactive approach to the removal of disadvantage in employment by providing special support and encouragement to members of particular disadvantaged groups such as women and ethnic minorities. It is based on the recognition that the outlawing of discrimination, by itself, will not change the composition of the workforce or lead to a significant overall improvement in the position of disadvantaged groups in employment. It can be distinguished from positive or reverse discrimination which, in order to redress past discrimination, gives preferential treatment to a member of a disadvantaged group, even though that person may be less qualified. Under domestic law positive discrimination is unlawful except in the areas of women's training and representation on trade union governing bodies. Anti-discrimination literature defines some but by no means all forms of positive action and further guidance is given by the equality commissions. At the same time employers are under no obligation to engage in positive action although they may be strongly encouraged to do so. Practice and terminology varies across countries. In the USA, for example, positive action is laid down in legislation and known as 'affirmative action'.

In practical terms positive action involves monitoring the composition of the workforce, identifying areas of under representation, developing and implementing strategies to deal with under representation and evaluating the outcomes. Strategies fall into two broad areas. The first focuses on the needs of disadvantaged or under represented groups by ensuring they have the training and resources to help them participate. These typically include accelerated development programmes, women only training and flexible employment policies and working patterns. The second focuses on the organizations themselves and the dominant groups within them. The starting point is the development and implementation of an equal opportunities policy and the creation of an equal opportunities culture through awareness training and organizational development. It might also include outreach programmes, the setting of goals or targets to increase the proportion of underrepresented groups in a particular job or career grade and the introduction of contract compliance. There has been much debate about the advantages and disadvantages of positive action and positive discrimination and what part the law should play. It would seem that progress in the future might best be achieved through a combination of both legal and voluntary measures reinforced by government action to address more deep seated social and economic inequalities. **SS**

References and further reading

Agocs, C. and Burr, C. (1996) 'Employment equity, affirmative action and managing diversity: assessing the difference', *International Journal of Manpower* 17(45): 30–45.

Bergman, B. R. (1999) 'The continuing need for affirmative action – the sources and consequences of job segregation', *The Quarterly Review of Economics and Finance* 39(5): 757–68.

Brew, K. and Garavan, T. N. (1995) 'Eliminating inequality: women-only training', *Journal of European Training* 19(2): 13–19.

Welsh, C. (1999) *Acting Positively under the Race Relations Act 1976*, Employment Department, Research Series, 36.

Postmodernism/postmodernity

Originally 'postmodernism' was a term developed within the arts to describe a rejection of the 'modernist' movement, which used unconventional subject matter and experimental techniques. Postmodernism by contrast involves artists revisiting traditional materials or classical styles, although often in a cynical manner, using irony and pastiche. Outside this rather narrow, technical sense, the terms 'postmodern', 'postmodernism' and 'postmodernity' are widely used in a number of academic disciplines such as history, sociology, politics and business and management. In these areas, there are several different ways in which we can interpret them. It is perhaps easiest to think of the term 'postmodern' as being used in either (or both) of two main senses. It can refer to a *philosophical stance* or attitude (which for the sake of clarity I shall label *postmodernism*), or to an *era* (which for the sake of clarity I shall label *postmodernity*).

Postmodernism is a way of thinking about the world, and the nature of truth. It can be seen as questioning what constitutes reality (an ontology) and questioning what constitutes knowledge (an epistemology). It is misleading and paradoxical to call postmodernism a theory, because writers such as Lyotard, Baudrillard, Foucault (each closely associated with postmodernism) reject the idea that there are theories or truths independent of history or an enacted social order. Lyotard (1984) offers as a somewhat cryptic definition of postmodernism that it is 'incredulity towards metanarratives', in other words, disbelieving of wide-ranging belief systems (such as Marxism) or rigid social structures (such as bureaucratic hierarchies). This scepticism goes beyond the claims of political philosophies, or organizational forms however. For example, another key theme is that reality is socially constructed. This means not only that grand systems or structures are suspect, but that what we take to be true depends on the social and historical setting. Thus any truths are partial and local.

There are potential problems for postmodernist thinkers which arise from the nature of this approach. Two key ones are *relativism* and *conservatism*. The problem of relativism can be thought of in this way: if we accept that reality is socially constructed, and that truth is local and partial, then there is no basis for judgement – any and all things may be 'true'. A consequent, related problem is conservatism. Because postmodernism does not offer any scope for judgement, there is no basis for undertaking change.

Postmodernity is a description of a historical period (the present), which is after the epoch known as 'modernity'. The period of modernity can be described as dating from before the Industrial Revolution and ending some time after the Second World War, and can be characterized by the drives of rationality and scientific method. Many have seen the Second World War as evidence of the failures of these forms of (modernist) 'progress', thereby necessitating a rejection of reason and science as means of understanding and explaining the world. Hence the implications of the succession of the period 'modernity' by the period 'postmodernity' are not that some arbitrary date has been passed, but rather that widespread changes in the nature of social order, international politics, global capitalism and business have meant that the perspective of modernity has been invalidated and made redundant.

In the world of business and management, postmodernity is associated with the much heralded demise of bureaucratic organizations and traditional hierarchies, as well as changes in the nature of work and technology, and the impact of globalization. Books such as Kanter's (1989) *When Giants Learn To Dance* emphasize the need for large organizations to be flexible in response to the quickly changing demands of consumer driven mass markets. Charles Handy's books such as *The Empty Raincoat* (1994) deal with the personal consequences of the changing nature of work in organizations and Tom Peters's (1989) *Thriving on Chaos* preaches to those seeking to cope with the demise of established ways of managing organizations. In the field of human resource management (HRM), writers such as Karen Legge and Tom Keenoy have seized on the scope for paradox and disregard for conventional logics in postmodernism to critique HRM, or to attempt to reconcile obvious definitional tensions in the term. **KM**

References and further reading

Appignanesi, R. and Garratt, C. (1999) *Introducing Postmodernism*, Cambridge: Icon Books.
Handy, C. (1994) *The Empty Raincoat*: *Making Sense of the Future*, London: Hutchinson.
Kanter, R. M. (1989) *When Giants Learn to Dance*, New York: Simon and Schuster.
Keenoy, T. (1999) 'HRM as hologram: a polemic', *Journal of Management Studies* 36(1): 1–23.
Legge, K. (1995) *Human Resource Management*: *Rhetorics and Realities*, London: Macmillan.
Lyotard, J.-F. (1984) *The Postmodern Condition*: *A Report on Knowledge*, Manchester: Manchester University Press.
Peters, T. J. (1989) *Thriving On Chaos*, New York: Harper and Row.

Profit-related pay

Profit-related pay refers to any pay scheme which in which a 'cash bonus or payment is made to employees based upon the share price, profits or dividend announcement at the end of the financial year' (Marchington *et al.*, 1992: 11).

Poole and Jenkins (1990) have distinguished four main types of scheme:

- profit sharing with cash rewards
- profit sharing awarding shares in the company
- Save as you earn share option schemes (SAYE)
- executive share options.

There was a major growth in such schemes in the 1990s , which can be attributed partly to tax incentives introduced by the government in order to make them more attractive to companies. The 1998 Workplace Employee Relations Surveys (WERS) data showed that over 40 per cent of employees received profit-related payments or bonuses and that nearly 30 per cent were entitled to SAYE share options (Conyon and Freeman, 2000).

In 2000 the British government proposed changes which would allow firms to give shares tax free. Employees can buy shares out of pre-tax income and firms can match the employee's purchases. Employees who keep the shares for five years in trust will pay no income tax and will pay capital gains tax only on the increase in value.

This approach increases a company's flexibility as pay costs vary with profitability. Proponents claim that these schemes will also foster communication and consultation with employees and develop greater economic democracy (Conyon and Freeman, 2000). In addition it is assumed that the schemes will encourage workers to identify more with the company's owners and therefore make decisions that increase corporate value.

There is little consensus on whether profit-related pay achieves its behavioural objectives. Poole and Jenkins (1990: 96) claim that 'the most important impact of profit sharing is almost certainly to improve organisational identification and commitment and hence, indirectly, to enhance industrial relations performance'. Others are more sceptical (see Baddon *et al.*, 1989). **AA**

References and further reading
Baddon, L., Hunter, L., Hyman, J., Leopold, J. and Ramsay, H. (1989) *People's Capitalism? A Critical Analysis of Profit Sharing and Employee Share Ownership*, London: Routledge.
Conyon, M. J. and Freeman, R. B. (2000) 'Shared modes of compensation and firm performance: UK evidence', NBER Paper, December.
Estrin, S., Perotin, V., Robinson, A. and Wilson, N. (1997) 'Profit sharing in OECD countries: a review of some evidence', *Business Strategy Review* 8(4): 27–32.
Incomes Data Services (IDS) (1998) 'Profit-sharing and share options', IDS Study 641, January.
Poole, M. and Jenkins, G. (1990) *The Impact of Economic Democracy*: *Profit Sharing and Employee Shareholding Schemes*, London: Routledge.
Marchington, M., Goodman, J., Wilkinson, A. and Ackers, P. (1992) 'New developments in employee participation', Employment Department Research Series 2.

Psychological contract

The term 'psychological contract' has been around in the academic literature for many years. However, it has become much more widely used at the end of the twentieth century and the start of the twenty-first. There is no single definition, but the term usually refers to the implicit, unwritten understandings that employees and employers have of what each can expect to give to and receive from the other. So the psychological contract is not a legal contract, but a state of mind. Its main significance lies in the fact that it reflects what people expect to give or receive, and what they feel they have promised or been promised. Hence, when one party perceives that the other party is not delivering their side of the contract, they are likely to feel cheated and wronged. Many writers argue that this leads to more negative reactions than simply not receiving all that one hoped to.

It is helpful to distinguish between relational and transactional psychological contracts. The former refers to a long-term relationship based on mutual trust, loyalty and help in times of trouble. It is said that many employees once saw their employment relationship in this way, but that changing economic conditions towards the end of the twentieth century saw many employers move, without consultation or warning, towards a more transactional contract. This is characterized by a short-term perspective, and a quasi-economic approach where labour is bought and sold as a commodity and usually the buyer can dictate the terms. This change has caused a lot of disillusionment for some.

Much is currently written and said about the psychological contract, especially its violation. It is recognized that violations of the contract do not necessarily lead to disillusionment. For example, if the violation is minor, if the other party tries to rectify it and if it is not seen as their fault that the violation has occurred, consequences may not be severe. People probably have different thresholds for perceiving violation. For example, a committed and motivated employee may see their employer's decision to impose a pay freeze as not contrary to prior commitments, and as necessary in difficult economic circumstances. A less positively inclined person may see it as an unjustified and arbitrary cost-saving measure. **JA**

References and further reading
Herriot, P. and Pemberton, C. (1995) *New Deals*, Chichester: Wiley.
Morrison, E. (1997) 'When employees feel betrayed: A model of how psychological contract violation develops', *Academy of Management Review* 22: 226–56.
Robinson, S. (1996) 'Trust and breach of the psychological contract', *Administrative Science Quarterly* 41: 574–99.
Robinson, S. and Rousseau, D. (1994) 'Violating the psychological contract: not the exception, but the norm', *Journal of Organizational Behavior* 15: 245–59.
Rousseau, D. (1995) *Psychological Contracts in Organizations*, London: Sage.
Rousseau, D. and Tijoriwala, S. (1998) 'Assessing psychological contracts: Issues, alternatives and measures', *Journal of Organizational Behavior* 19: 679–95.

Psychometric testing

Psychometric testing concerns the measurement of people's psychological character-istics. The development of tests is one of the most long-established fields in applied psychology. Broadly, tests are of two types: personality and ability. The former concerns a person's habitual or preferred ways of behaving, thinking or feeling. The latter concerns a person's capacity successfully to complete a task or solve a problem requiring mental (and sometimes physical) effort and skill. Most tests are 'paper and pencil', that is, they come in printed form and require written responses. However, some are different – for example, a test of manual dexterity may require the person taking it to work quickly and accurately with small objects such as pins. Increasingly, tests are available on the Internet as an alternative to paper form.

Psychometric tests are used most often in the workplace as a means of selecting people for jobs. But they are also used in vocational guidance, employment rehabil-itation, and team-building. Personality tests may cover a broad range of characteris-tics, such as extraversion, conscientiousness, emotionality, dominance and so on. Or they may focus on specific characteristics only, such as need for achievement or lead-ership style. Then again, they may assess a person's interests or values. Ability tests usually measure one or more aspect of what is often thought of as intelligence, such as verbal, numerical or spatial reasoning. The last of these concerns the ability to visualize and manipulate shapes in the mind's eye.

Psychometric testing is very popular, and it is important that users are able to eval-uate what is on offer. The better tests have extensive information about how well they predict work performance and how reliable scores on it are. They also have information about how people typically score, which aids interpretation of an indi-vidual's score. The cost of using tests can be high, but the benefits even higher, because used carefully psychometric tests can be good predictors of work perform-ance and therefore useful in selection and guidance. The key is to make sure that a test assesses characteristics that really are relevant to the job(s) concerned. The dis-tribution, administration and interpretation of tests is restricted to those appropri-ately qualified to use them, and in the UK the British Psychological Society regulates this, in association with test producers. **JA**

References and further reading

Anastasi, A. (1988) *Psychological Testing*, 6th edn, New York: Macmillan.
Bartram, D. (1992) *Review of Psychometric Tests for Assessment in Vocational Training*, Leicester: British Psychological Society.
British Psychological Society web site at www.bps.org.uk
Jackson, C. (1996) *Understanding Psychological Testing*, Leicester: British Psychological Society.
Jones, S. (1993) *Psychological Testing for Managers*, London: Piatkus.
Kline, P. (1998) *The New Psychometrics: Science, Psychology, and Measurement*, London: Routledge.

Quality circles

Quality circles (QCs) originated in Japan where they have been widely employed for many years, primarily as a training vehicle and as a means of gaining ideas for improvement from employees at all organizational levels. They were first imported into the USA and Western Europe during the late 1960s and early 1970s in an attempt to emulate Japan's enviable post-war industrial performance. Quality circles, in pure form, are small groups of employees engaged in broadly similar work in the same work unit, who meet together voluntarily, usually for one hour per week or fortnight, in order to identify, analyse and solve work-related problems. They are normally led by members' immediate supervisor, but may be assisted in undertaking their projects, by an organizational facilitator. Quality circle members and leaders are trained in the use of basic quality control tools, such as histograms, check sheets, graphs, Pareto analysis, cause and effect diagrams, scatter diagrams and control charts – sometimes referred to as the QC7. Completed, costed projects are formally presented to management for comment and approval. Once implemented, it is a QC's responsibility to monitor their project's progress, to review activities related to the project and to consider improvements for the future.

In Japan, QC activity is a fully integrated element of organizational life. There, considerable importance is placed on the motivating potential of QC participation, and on its human resource development capacity; for example, the development of leadership qualities and skills, the identification of leadership potential, the acquisition of problem-solving skills and quality control methodologies and the development of team-building and communication skills. By way of contrast, in the West, the operation and achievements of QCs have been the subject of considerable debate, particularly amongst academics. One reason for this is, that when they were first introduced into the West, QCs were hailed as a panacea for almost all industrial ills, primarily by consultants eager to exploit the latest management fad. Over time however, little empirical evidence emerged to substantiate many of the claims made, especially in relation to alleged psychological and behavioural benefits. However, recently, attitudes to QCs have become more positive. This is partly because the early 'hype' has been forgotten, expectations are more realistic and some well-publicized Western organizations have sustained QC programmes over many years. There is also research evidence to suggest that QCs can make a meaningful contribution outside Japan, particularly in organizations wishing to progress towards **total quality**

management (see separate entry). In such organizations QCs can facilitate the development of a systematic problem-solving capability, a focus on continuous improvement and a team ethos. **FH**

References and further reading

Bradley, K. and Hill, S. (1983) 'After Japan: the quality circle transplant and production efficiency', *British Journal of Industrial Relations* 21(3): 291–311.

Dale, B. G. (ed.) (1999) *Managing Quality*, 3rd edn, Oxford: Blackwell.

Hill, F. M. (1993) 'An evaluative study of the attitudinal and performance-related outcomes of quality circle participation, *International Journal of Quality and Reliability Management* 10(4): 28–47.

Hill, F. M. (1996) 'Organisational learning for TQM through quality circles', *TQM Magazine* 8(6): 72–6.

Olberding, S. R. (1998) 'Toyota on competition and quality circles', *Journal for Quality and Participation* 21(2): 52–4.

Quality of working life

The quality of working life (QWL) movement can be seen as the second in three phases of approaches to designing work systems (Buchanan, 1994). The first of these was 'scientific management' (1900–50), the second QWL (1950–80) and the most recent being a concern with 'high performance work systems' (1980–present). These dates are, of course, an approximation, but QWL was particularly popular in the 1960s and 1970s, and can be seen as a response to concerns that when people's jobs were redesigned and made simpler. This was associated with their having negative attitudes towards work, as well as poor mental and physical health. This draws from work in the fields of industrial and organizational psychology (Arnold, Cooper and Robertson, 1995: 392) and in the same way that the rise of the human relations school of management in the 1930s can be seen as an answer to 'scientific management' (Taylorism), QWL represents an alternative approach to the management of employees which is centred more on the worker than on the task. Quality of working life argued for a recognition that as well as the economic cost of labour with which managers are preoccupied, work can have personal costs for employees.

Although job redesign was put forward as a potential method of enhancing QWL, Taylor reported in 1979 that three key factors in the design of most jobs were minimizing skill requirements, maximizing management control and minimizing the time needed to perform a task. Each of these can be seen as driven by economic rather than social concerns. Blacker and Brown (1978) are sceptical about the extent to which QWL was motivated by genuine concern about workers' health. Instead it may have been used in a superficial sense, as a sop to sensibilities, or for public relations or as a means of reconstituting control (Legge, 1995: 169). The QWL movement still has resonance for contemporary management for at least two reasons. First, because it is possible to trace the roots of 'soft' human resource management (HRM) back to the human relations school via QWL, we have one powerful reminder that the claims for HRM as a new way of managing people can be overstated. Second, the research done by writers such as Blacker and Brown (1978), Child (1975) and Fox (1973) documents how it was possible for some organizations to appropriate the language of QWL and use it to reinforce, or disguise, existing relations of power. **KM and AW**

References and further reading

Arnold, J., Cooper, C. L. and Robertson, I. T. (1995) *Work Psychology: Understanding Human Behaviour in the Workplace*, London: Pitman.

Blacker, F. H. and Brown, C. A. (1978) *Job Redesign and Management Control*, London: Saxon House.

Buchanan, D. A. (1994) 'Principles and practice in work design', in K. Sisson (ed.) *Personnel Management: A Comprehensive Guide to Theory and Practice in Britain*, Oxford: Blackwell.

Child, J. (1975) 'Organisation: a choice for man', in J. Child (ed.) *Man and the organisation*, London: Allen and Unwin.

Fox, A. (1973) 'Industrial relations: a social critique of pluralist ideology', in J. Child (ed.) *Man and the organisation*, London: Allen and Unwin.

Legge, K. (1995) *Human Resource Management: Rhetorics and Realities*, London: Macmillan.

Taylor, J. C. (1979) 'Job design criteria twenty years later', in L. E. Davis and J. C. Taylor (eds) *Design of Jobs*, Santa Monica: Goodyear.

Wilson, F. (1999) *Organizational Behaviour: A Critical Introduction*, Oxford: Oxford University Press.

R

Race discrimination

Race discrimination in employment relates to less favourable treatment of an individual on racial grounds, defined in the legislation as 'colour, race, nationality, or ethnic or national origins'. The recruitment and geographical settlement patterns of immigrants in the 1950s and 1960s laid the foundation for the subsequent racial segregation in employment and the current employment distribution and pay position of ethnic minorities in Great Britain confirms the continuing existence of disadvantage and discrimination for this section of the workforce. Whilst there is considerable variation between ethnic groups, ethnic minorities as a whole have lower economic activity rates, higher levels of unemployment and lower average pay than their white counterparts. Furthermore they are disproportionately found amongst semi-skilled and unskilled manual workers.

Until very recently discrimination and racial inequality has been addressed primarily through domestic legislation. European Union (EU) influence on race discrimination has been limited and in stark contrast to its influence on gender discrimination. The principal domestic statute is the Race Relations Act (RRA) 1976 which together with its subsequent amendments outlaws race discrimination in employment except in a limited range of circumstances and makes provision for complaints to be brought before an industrial tribunal. The RRA makes both overt and subtler forms of discrimination illegal through the concepts of direct and indirect discrimination as well as prohibiting victimization. All aspects of employment are covered including recruitment, promotion, training, working conditions and dismissal. Breach of the legislation can be costly as a tribunal can award unlimited compensation, with interest, if discrimination is proved. Guidance for employers on the provisions of the RRA and wider measures to promote racial equality is contained in the Commission for Racial Equality's statutory *Code of Practice* (1984). Although not a legally binding document, breach of the guidelines may be used in evidence in a tribunal. The RRA has recently been strengthened by the Race Relations (Amendment) Act 2000. The new act, which has arisen out of the Stephen Lawrence Enquiry, extends protection against racial discrimination by public authorities and places a new enforceable positive duty on them.

Recent developments in EU legislation are also important. The non-discrimination clause in the Treaty of Amsterdam (1997) provided explicit power for the European Community in the area of race. It remains to be seen if the subsequent Directive on

Race Discrimination (2000), will lead to a more marked European influence in the future. **SS**

References and further reading

Commission for Racial Equality (1984) *Code of Practice: For the Elimination of Racial Discrimination and the Promotion of Equal Opportunity in Employment*, London: HMSO.

Income Data Services (IDS) 'Race discrimination' *IDS Employment Law Handbook*, London: IDS.

Le, P. M. and Kleiner, B. H. (2000) 'A review of current empirical research concerning race discrimination at work', *Equal Opportunities International* 19(67): 98–100.

Monaghan, K. (2000) *Challenging Race Discrimination at Work*, London: Institute of Employment Rights.

Rubenstein, M. (2000) *Discrimination: A Guide to the Relevant Case Law on Race and Sex Discrimination*, London: Industrial Relations Service.

Radicalism

In employment relations terms, Radicals are those on the traditional left who hold a highly critical view of Western capitalist society and business behaviour. They include Marxists, such as the labour process school of industrial sociology. Once more, Alan Fox has done most to define radicalism as an employment frame of reference, and his own work reflects the shift from a 1960s pluralist critique of *unitarism* to a 1970s 'radical pluralism' which accused traditional *pluralism* of defending the economic status quo.

A radical model of the business enterprise regards it as divided by class conflict between two main sides: employers and workers. Accordingly, the 'bosses' exploit their employees, both in terms of the amount of work they expect from them and the wages they are prepared to pay them for it. As a result, employment relations becomes mainly about a zero-sum power conflict between profits, on the one hand, and wages and conditions on the other. In light of this, radicals regard conflict at work as something that is inevitable, continuous and potentially explosive. In contrast to pluralists, they do not believe that conflict can be easily contained, managed or insitutionalized in the interests of all. Rather they anticipate a total power struggle based on a complete clash of interests, linked to wider political divisions in society. Where overt conflict is palpably absent, radicals tend to either search for it 'under the floorboards', in instances of shopfloor misbehaviour, or to explain workers 'false consciousness' as the product of management ideological manipulation. The role of trade unions, for radicals, is to challenge management power and defend workers interests. Sometimes, this battle is described in terms of a 'frontier control', like the trench warfare of the First World War. In this strife, union leaders are expected to remain unrelentingly and uncompromisingly militant, in contrast to the more moderate, collaborative approach advocated by pluralists. Where union leaders deviate from this adversarial role, to work with management, they are regarded as 'class collaborators' who have betrayed the 'rank and file' and contributed to their low level of class consciousness.

Ultimately, radicals hope that capitalism will be overthrown or transformed out of recognition, to be replaced by a new socialist order in which industrial conflict is no longer necessary. Radicalism has number of attractions:

1. It highlights the many injustices of contemporary employment, including overwork and low pay.
2. The radical image of employment conflict comes fairly close to the real situation in certain industries at certain times, such as the British coal industry in the 1920s or parts of the Third World today.
3. Some trade union leaders and activists have found attractive the simple appeal for wages militancy.

Today, however, radicalism is in eclipse. The collapse of the Soviet model and demise of radical socialist politics in the West, has undermined belief in a socialist system that can replace capitalism. In employment relations terms, radicalism has little practical to say to managers and policy-makers. The most obvious current manifestation of radical thinking are the high profile demonstrations against global capitalism and the literature associated with this. **PA**

References and further reading

Ackers, P. (2001) 'Paternalism, participation and partnership: rethinking the employment relationship, *Human Relations* 54(3): 375–86.

Ackers, P. (2002) 'Reframing industrial relations: the case for neo-pluralism', *Industrial Relations Journal*. (forthcoming)

Braverman, H. (1974) *Labour and Monopoly Capitalism*, New York: Basic Books.

Fox, A. (1974) *Beyond Contract: Work, Power and Trust Relations*, London: Faber.

Fox, A. (1985) *Man Mismanagement*, London: Hutchinson.

Hyman, R. (1975) *Industrial Relations: A Marxist Introduction*, London: Macmillan.

Kelly, J. (2000) *Rethinking Industrial Relations*, London: Routledge.

Klein, N. (2000) *No Logo: No Space, No Choice, No Jobs*, London: Flamingo.

Recognition schemes

There are two main types of recognition schemes. The first is a development and updating of the long-established 'suggestion scheme' format, sets out to motivate employees to produce improvements in the way the company operates with particular reference to the employees' own jobs and responsibilities. A philosophy behind encouraging such schemes is that employees who put forward ideas and going to want to see them successfully implemented and will give them their full support. This may not always be the case with all management suggestions.

Key aspects of successful schemes include:

- Encouragement to employees to participate by inculcating the culture of 'kaizen' whereby it is a natural process for employees to think about how the work processes could be improved and it is expected that all employees to make at least one suggestion for improvement a year.
- Training for employees in putting forward their proposals.
- An efficient and well-motivated committee drawn from all levels and activities in the company who will help to sift major ideas and encourage participation in their areas.
- Swiftness in decision-taking, including authorizing supervisors to make instant awards and a guaranteed response rate for all ideas.
- Worthwhile awards, which can include a proportion of the saving and the opportunity to be entered in draws for desired events, sporting and otherwise, holidays or days out.
- Encouragement to teams to apply themselves so that an idea can represent the thinking of a number of people in an area.
- Good publicity on success through company magazines. Recognition may include a platform handshake from the chief executive.
- Campaigns which integrate with company strategy, such as health and safety, quality, environmental issues, waste reduction, etc.

The second type of scheme is where employees who have done something out of the ordinary are recognized by some small award. This may involve 'going beyond the call of duty', such as providing outstanding customer service or reflect admirably the company's purpose and values. In this type of scheme, nomination can be by the manager or employees. In general, the prizes are limited (vouchers up to £150) and organizations concentrate on the value of the recognition process. ICL, for example, have bronze, silver and gold awards. **JSk**

References and further reading
Income Data Services (IDS) (1995) 'Suggestion schemes', IDS Study 573, March.
Income Data Services (IDS) (1999) 'Recognition schemes', Study Plus, Winter.
Stredwick, J. (1997) *Cases in Reward Management*, London: Kogan Page, pp. 266–76.

Recruitment

Recruitment is the process by which organizations attract a pool of candidates from whom to select new staff. It is often characterized as being a positive activity, involving actively marketing an organization to potential employees. Several different methods are used including advertising in newspapers and trade journals, placing notices in job centres, employing agents of one kind or another, attending careers fairs and posting job advertisements on the internet. Survey evidence persistently shows, however, that the most significant single recruitment method is word of mouth. Decisions about which method or combination of methods to use have to be based on the budget available, the number of applicants considered necessary and the current size of the labour market concerned. The rarer the skills being sought, the more sophisticated and costly the recruitment process has to be. A number of legal issues have to be taken into account when recruiting new staff. In particular there is the requirement not to discriminate either directly or indirectly on grounds of sex, marital status, race, ethnicity, national origin, disability or trade union membership/non-membership. Particular care must be therefore taken when considering the wording, design and placing of advertisements.

While it is important to distinguish between the recruitment and selection processes, it must also be remembered that a feature of effective recruitment campaigns is their ability to encourage a degree of self-selection on the part of potential candidates. Where a particular personality type is sought, for example, it makes sense to design recruitment messages which are likely to attract applications from the target group, while discouraging those who do not possess the required characteristics. Conversely it is important to remember that selection processes also fulfil a recruitment role. There remains a need to positively promote the organization as an attractive employer at the selection stage so as to ensure that the strongest candidates choose to take up any jobs that are offered to them. **ST**

References and further reading
Barber, A. E. (1998) *Recruiting Employees*: *Individual and Organizational Perspectives*, London: Sage.
Riggs Fuller, S. and Huber, V. L. (1998) 'Recruitment and selection', in M. Poole and M. Warner (eds) *The Handbook of Human Resource Management*, London: Thomson Learning.
Taylor, S. (1998) *Employee Resourcing*, London: IPD, ch. 6.
Watson, T. (1994) 'Recruitment and selection', in K. Sisson (ed.) *Personnel Management*: *Theory and Practice in Britain*, Oxford: Blackwell.

Recruitment advertising

This is one of the major methods used by employers to attract applicants when vacancies are available. The major publishers of recruitment advertisements are local newspapers, national newspapers and trade/professional journals. However, job recruitment web sites are becoming increasingly significant, while those seeking new graduates are best advised to place advertisements in specialist recruitment directories. Costs vary considerably from one publication to another, there being substantial differences between the rates charged by the various national newspapers. Key decisions to take when in drawing up recruitment advertisements include the elements of the role that are to be stressed, the amount of detailed information to be given and the extent to which elaborate, eye-catching design features are to be incorporated. Studies suggest that advertisements which do not specifically mention pay rates and job location are a great deal less effective than those which do. These should thus be included unless there are good reasons for their exclusion (such as a need for confidentiality). Recruitment advertising agents can play a useful role for employers as providers of expertise and of discounted rates.

An interesting debate concerns the extent to which employers gain by excluding from recruitment advertisements material which is not entirely positive about either the job or the organization. One view holds that the purpose of an advertisement is to maximize the number of good applications. It thus follows that stress should be placed on the positive aspects of working for the organization concerned and that advertisements should actively 'sell' jobs to potential job holders. Critics of this view stress the role played by 'realistic job previews' in determining the subsequent effectiveness of employee performance. According to this perspective, recruitment advertisements should be entirely honest about the role and the organization, so as to ensure that new employees do not join an organization with unrealistic expectations. Because disappointment arising from such situations is a significant cause of employee turnover, it is argued that advertisements which are entirely positive in their messages lead employers to incur unnecessarily high recruitment costs over the long term. **ST**

References and further reading
Courtis, J. (1994) *Recruitment Advertising: Right First Time*, London: IPD.
De Witte, K. (1989) 'Recruiting and advertising', in P. Herriot (ed.) *Assessment and Selection in Organisations*, Chichester: Wiley.
Wanous, J. P. (1992) *Organizational Entry*, Reading, MA: Addison-Wesley, chs 2 and 3.

Recruitment agencies

Recruitment agencies come in many different shapes and forms. At one end of the scale are well-established, highly professional organizations, with genuine expertise. At the other are large numbers of less professional outfits characterized by an overpowering sales culture and with little genuine interest in serving the long-term needs of either employers or employees. At present the recruitment industry is unregulated to any great degree, leaving unwary employers open to sharp practice on the part of some agents. Most of the problems are associated with headhunting organizations which do no more than try to sell organizations to individual candidates and vice versa, before charging the employer a commission equivalent to a percentage of the successful candidate's first annual salary. However, headhunters can provide a useful service in certain circumstances, especially where they are can draw on a network of contacts or make confidential approaches to individuals working for other employers.

Other types of agent include recruitment consultants, who are able to provide a complete recruitment and selection service on a subcontracted basis, and various government and charitable agencies seeking to find positions for people who would otherwise find job-hunting difficult. A fourth variety are temping agencies who provide certain types of staff on a temporary basis and charge an hourly fee. The final category comprises recruitment advertising agencies who are solely concerned with drawing up and placing advertising copy on behalf of their clients. Because of their muscle in the marketplace, they are able to pass on considerable discounts to employers as well as providing expert advice on the design and wording of advertisements.

From an employer's perspective the best approach is to use agents only when they can offer something which other less costly recruitment methods can not. In certain specialist labour markets, where agents have become the accepted means by which job-hunters locate new jobs, organizations have little choice but to employ them. Where such is the case, it is preferable to build up reasonably close relationship with one or two agents so as to foster a high degree of trust and confidence over the long term. **ST**

References and further reading

Courtis, J. (1989) *Recruiting for Profit*, London: IPD.

Littlefield, D. (1999) 'Pooled resources', *People Management*, June: 52–3.

Taylor, S. (1998) *Employee Resourcing*, London: IPD, pp. 107–12.

Whalley, L. and Smith, M. (1998) *Deception in Selection*, Chichester: Wiley.

Redeployment

Redeployment is spatial flexibility. It refers to firms' needs to move their employees to new geographic locations with little, or only minor, change in job content and it is a process which can refer to movements within a plant or business location or between locations in the same firm situated in geographically separate locations, either regionally, nationally or internationally. Redeployment can be considered as a fourth form of labour flexibility along with those of time, function and numbers

There are four reasons why firms want to redeploy their employees:

1. It helps them meet promises of 'no redundancy'. In order to improve their competitive positions firms close some plant, improve other plant, and build some anew. In most cases this reduces the total numbers employed, but new posts are created in new locations. Redundancies for some employees can be avoided if they move to new locations. British Steel is a good example of a firm which has used redeployment in this way.
2. It helps firms deliver service strategies. The essence of a service strategy is that producers and consumers meet at the moment and place of consumption; services cannot neither be stored nor transported. Two important human resource management (HRM) issues of service delivery are therefore the location and timing of employee availability. In some service industries such as local government, health and banking the demand for services is influenced by demographic shifts in the structure (age, sex, socio-economic class) of the population served. Redeployment helps these service industries relocate staff to where they are needed most.
3. Redeployment is an important component of knowledge management. Many craft-based skills (e.g. metalworking) are tacit and informal and have long resisted management attempts to extract, analyse and codify them; and to spread them to other employees by means of a managerially prescribed training package. Where there has been a need for skills to be transfered between employees, some companies have tried to overcome this by placing all the concerned staff in the same location. Centralizing staff in the same location can also ease problems of communication, functional integration and speed up decision-making; these factors can be seen at work in the decision of some of the major car companies (e.g. General Motors) to concentrate new model design teams in one spot.
4. Redeployment is emerging as a theme in globalization. It is a key dimension of IHRM in any multinational enterprise (MNE) which is considering staffing its operations with an expatriate workforce, or one which involves third-country nationals. Some writers have argued that succesful HRM in the MNE requires the integration of managers from diverse cultural backgrounds, and that this can only be achieved by trust based on prolonged face-to-face contact. Redeployment is central to the resolution of this problem.

Implementing redeployment can be costly. Staff are often paid extra in return for their geographic flexibility; these costs can be very expensive in the case of people redeployed internationally. Not all the costs are financial. Staff can become very attached to a particular place of work; physically relocating their work can be emotionally difficult for them. **HM**

References and further reading
Dowling, P. J. (1999) *International Human Resource Management*: *Managing People in a Multi-national Context*, 3rd edn, Cincinnati, OH: South Western College Publishing.
Malloch, H. (1992) 'Hutton Borough Council', in J. Woodall and D. Winstanley (eds) *Case Studies in Human Resource Management*, London: Institute of Personnel Management, pp. 245–51.

Redundancy

Dismissal on grounds of redundancy can occur when either 'the employer has ceased, or intends to cease carrying on the business; or the requirements for employees to carry out work of a particular kind, or to carry it out in a place in which they are employed have ceased or diminished' (Labour Research Department, 1998: 106). Redundancy can be compulsory or voluntary, but in either case employees who are declared redundant may be entitled to a statutory minimum redundancy payment based upon age, number of years service and wages. Failure of employers to justify their case for redundancy, or to select fairly, may lead to unfair dismissal claims at employment tribunals. Initial legislation governing redundancy was introduced in the 1960s, with the decline of traditional industries in particular geographical areas in mind. However, with the dramatic changes in the political and economic climate and technological environment in the 1980s and 1990s, redundancies have become commonplace in most employment sectors.

Redundancies have been particularly severe in the manufacturing and engineering sectors in the 1980s and1990s. It has been estimated that in relation to the British economy as a whole there have been over 4 million redundancies between 1990 and 1995 alone (Labour Force Survey, cited in Blyton and Turnbull, 1998: 56). Not only have redundancies been significant in terms of the decline in the number of trade union members, but also certainly they have become an important factor in persuading unions to make concessions to management, and to reformulate their policies and strategies within a *new realist* perspective. Whilst redundancy can have a severe impact upon those who lose their jobs, it can also cause considerable change to the culture of the workplace in terms of employee commitment and fear. This raises important questions in relation to the promotion of both hard and soft forms of human resource management, the extent of trust in employee relations and the nature of the psychological contract. **DB**

References and further reading
Blyton, P. and Turnbull, P. (1998) *The Dynamics of Employee Relations*, London: Macmillan, ch. 3.
Cappelli, P. (1995) 'Rethinking employment', *British Journal of Industrial Relations* 33(4): 563–602.
Cully, M., Woodland, S., O'Reilly, A. and Dix, G. (1999) *Britain at Work*: *As Depicted by the 1998 Workplace Employee Relations Survey*, London: Routledge, pp. 78–80, 167–70, 202.
Incomes Data Services (IDS) (1999) 'Managing redundancy', IDS Study Plus, Spring.
Labour Research Department (1998) *The Law at Work*, London: LRD Publications, pp. 106–18.
Turnbull, P. (1988) 'Leaner and possibly fitter: the management of redundancy in Britain', *Industrial Relations Journal* 19(3): 201–13.

References

Also known as testimonials, job references are used by employers in the selection process as a means of obtaining information about individual candidates. They can be verbal, but are more usually written by referees who have been nominated for the task by job applicants. Most are managers who the candidate has worked for in the past, but it is not unusual for university tutors, schoolteachers or other acquaintances to be asked to provide character references or general assessments of someone's suitability for a job. While very widely used in recruitment and selection, research evidence suggests that they are most commonly used at the final stages to confirm impressions already gained during interviews or other selection processes. The extent to which they can be seen as being objective in any meaningful sense is questionable as it clearly in the candidate's interest to choose people who can be expected to stress positive aspects of their work performance or general character. It is only in those lines of work where referees and potential employers know one another reasonably well that a reference can be assumed to be a truly objective assessment. References remain, however, a useful means for employers to confirm basic factual information about someone's background (e.g. absence records or college grades). Job references have been the subject of significant legal rulings in recent years. It has thus now been established that employers are under a duty not to write inaccurate or derogatory assessments which may unfairly damage a candidate's job prospects. Refusal to provide a reference for an individual when it is common practice to do so for employees and ex-employees generally can also lead to claims of unfair discrimination.

It has been persuasively argued that there are only two questions that serve any real purpose when included in questionnaires sent to referees. The first is 'do you know of any reason why I should not employ this person', the second is 'would you re-employ this person'. In both cases the aim is to establish whether or not a significant weakness in a candidate exists which has not been picked up during the rest of the selection procedure – the area in which references probably play their most useful role. **ST**

References and further reading
Cook, M. (1995) *Personnel Selection and Productivity*, 2nd edn, Chichester: Wiley, ch. 5.

Cooper, D. and Robertson, I. (1995) *The Psychology of Personnel Selection*, London: Routledge.

Dobson, P. (1989) 'Reference reports', in P. Herriot (ed.) *Assessment and Selection in Organizations*, Chichester: Wiley.

Industrial Relations Services (IRS) (1997) 'The state of selection: an IRS survey', *Employee Development Bulletin* 85, January.

Whalley, L. and Smith, M. (1998) *Deception in Selection*, Chichester: Wiley.

Relocation

Employees are asked or required to relocate in all manner of different ways. On the one hand there is the relatively straightforward situation in which the workplace is moved from one location in a city or region to another. This has implications in terms of commuting costs and times, but does not normally require someone to move house. Second, there are relocations within the UK, which do involve moving house. In such circumstances it is usual to pay some form of expenses, although the size and nature of the package offered will often vary between relocation as existing employees and new starters. Finally there is international relocation or expatriation, which brings with it a range of additional requirements and has become a specialist human resource management activity.

The extent of relocation packages is governed to an extent by Inland Revenue rules which limit the extent to which assistance can be given on a tax free basis. At the time of writing the limit was £8000 – including direct and indirect costs as well as the value of bridging or interest-free loans. The typical package will include allowances to cover the costs associated with seeking new accommodation and then of selling and buying a house. Relocation is a significant and complex issue in the law on employment contracts and redundancy. Unless there is some form of mobility clause in someone's contract the employer has no right to require them to move without their agreement. As a result some form of compensation is normally needed to gain acceptance of a new contractual term. Even where there is a mobility clause, however, care must be taken to apply it reasonably. Requiring people to move across the country at short notice is thus unacceptable in law.

All the above applies equally to expatriate relocation, but here many other factors also have to be taken into account. Much expatriation fails in practice, with people coming home early because they (or their families) are unable to adjust to life in an overseas location. Proper preparation is thus essential, as is the provision of an adequate and attractive remuneration package. Another factor to consider is repatriation at the end of an overseas assignment. Here too problems of readjustment are common and need to be managed sensitively. **ST**

References and further reading

Aikin, O. (1997) *Contracts*, 2nd edn, London: IPD, ch. 30.
Brewster, C. and Harris, H. (1999) *International HRM: Contemporary Issues in Europe*, London: Routledge, Pt 3.
De Cieri, H. and McGaughey, S. L. (1998) 'Relocation', in M. Poole and M. Warner (eds) *The Handbook of Human Resource Management*, London: Thomson Learning.
Gee Publishing (1998) *The Remuneration and Benefits Handbook*, Gee, ch. 7.11, London: Gee Publishing.
Littlefield, D. (1998) 'Going concerns', *People Management*, November: 51–2.
Medenhall, M. and Oddou, G. (1995) 'Expatriation and cultural adaptation', in T. Jackson (ed.) *Cross-Cultural Manager*, London: Butterworth.

Resource-based theory of human resource management

Resource-based theory originates from economic and strategic management literature. It focuses on organizations' capacity to use physical and non-physical resources to gain competitive advantage.

Barney (1991) outlines four criteria to be met in order that an asset is considered a true resource:

1. *Value*: the asset must be sufficiently important and substantial to be genuinely significant to its owner, e.g. the design for a Formula One racing car or an information technology specialist.
2. *Rarity*: the asset must be sufficiently unusual to be distinctive, e.g. the unique taste of whisky from a particular distillery, a production manager who speaks three European languages.
3. *Imperfect imitability*: it must be impossible for competitors to copy the asset exactly, e.g. a hotel which has the most picturesque views of the bay in a coastal resort.
4. *Non-substitutability*: the resource is not replacable by an alternative, e.g. a paediatric nurse cannot be replaced by a cardiac care nurse.

This theory has significant implications for human resource management (HRM). It could draw attention to the importance of HRM practices and outcomes among strategists and chief executives. For example, a reputation for outstanding customer service at Virgin Airlines or First Direct is an asset depending largely on the companies' abilities to harness and use the skills of its employees. Other examples might include a board-level team which functions harmoniously without political infighting, a distinctive organizational culture which enables an organization's employees to acquire and use new knowledge or uniformity in line managers' application of human resource (HR) practices.

Optimistically, one might expect companies to think carefully about how they manage and treat valuable employees rather than viewing them as disposable factors of production. But using resource-based theory of HRM is difficult:

1. Identifying why a company has strengths in an HR process, e.g. teamworking is not easy, since the participants themselves often cannot identify why a practice is successful in their enterprise.
2. Companies find that identifying 'core' employees or 'core competences' is difficult. Moreover, selecting 'core' employees to manage via an array of

sophisticated HRM practices challenges the universalistic prescriptions of 'best practice' theories.

3. Proving connections between using human resources effectively and competitive advantage is challenging. Resource-based theory represents an opportunity to make employers take HRM seriously, but whether it can be translated into practice remains an open question. **AC**

References and further reading

Barney, J. (1991) 'Firm resources and sustained competitive advantage', *Journal of Management*, 17(1): 99–120.

Boxall, P. (1996) 'The strategic HRM debate and the resource-based view of the firm', *Human Resource Management Journal* 6(3): 59–75.

Dyer, L. and Reeves, T. (1995) 'Human resource strategies and firm performance: what do we know and where do we need to go?', *International Journal of Human Resource Management* 6(3): 656–70.

Mueller, F. (1998) 'Human resources as strategic assets: an evolutionary resource-based theory', in C. Mabey, G. Salaman and J. Storey (eds) *Strategic Human Resource Management: A Reader*, London: Open University Press/Sage, pp. 152–69.

Prahalad, C. and Hamel, G. (1990) 'The core competence of the corporation', *Harvard Business Review* 68(3): 79–91.

Purcell, J. (1999) 'High commitment management and the link with contingent workers: implications for strategic human resource management', *Research in Personnel and Human Resources Management* 4: 239–57.

Retirement preparation programmes

This is a career practice directed at the target population of employees approaching retirement age. These programmes can be short, for example, a three-day workshop, taking place a couple of months before retirement (Baruch, 1999). They can also be longer, both in terms of programme time and its spread over wider time span. An investment in this practice indicates high commitment of the organization to its employees. In these programmes the employee is prepared to face the retirement in several dimensions. Much is devoted to financial consideration, understanding the pension conditions and learning tax regulations. However, the better programmes takes into account also the psychological issue of need to readjust to life without work, a transformation that, if not managed, might end in deterioration of health and well-being of people used to full-time hard work. Leisure activities and other ways to fill the time with fulfilling activities form a significant part of such programmes, and in some of them the spouse is invited to take part too.

With the advent of heavy redundancies we witness how fewer people are leaving the workplace at the legal retirement age. Thus traditional pre-retirement programmes might become more rare in the future. The necessity of this practice obviously depends also on the age of the organization and the maturity of its employees. For an established organization with young employees there is no real need for formal institutionalized pre-retirement programmes. If there are only very few due to retire, the issue may best be dealt with by private consultancy that will conduct an internal organizational programme of preparation for retirement, in line with the contemporary approach in outsourcing human resource (HR) functions.

Assuming that large-scale redundancy programmes will still prevail in the near future, the pre-retirement programme may be transformed into a pre-redundancy programme. In this kind of programme, the organization will first prepare the employees for the possibility that 'it could happen to you, too'. Subsequently the focus will move on to what can be done, how an employee in a plateau stage career can be trained to look successfully for a new job in declining industrial sectors. In addition to such a pre-redundancy programme, the same organization will need an after-redundancy programme, to confront the possible 'survivor syndrome' which might affect those who have stayed (Brockner, Tyler and Cooper-Schieder, 1992). Professional use of 'best practice' may combat the survivor syndrome successfully (Baruch and Hind, 1999). **YB**

References and further reading

Baruch, Y. (1999) 'Integrated career systems for the 2000s', *International Journal of Manpower* 20(7): 432–57.

Baruch, Y. and Hind, P. (1999) 'Perpetual motion in organizations: effective management and the impact of the new psychological contracts on "Survivor Syndrome"', *European Journal of Work and Organizational Psychology* 8(2): 295–306.

Brockner, J., Tyler, T. R. and Cooper-Schieder, R. (1992) 'The influence of prior commitment to institution on reactions to perceived unfairness: the higher they are, the harder they fall', *Administrative Science Quarterly* 37: 241–61.

Reward policy

Armstrong (1996: 59) states that a 'Reward strategy defines the intentions of the organisation on how its reward policies and processes should be developed to meet business requirements. Reward strategy is driven by business needs'. He lists the features of an effective reward strategy as:

- based on corporate values and beliefs
- flowing from the business strategy but also contributing to it
- driven by business needs and 'fitting' the business strategy
- aligns organizational and individual competencies
- integrated with other personnel and development strategies
- is congruent with the internal and external environment of the organization – the content of the strategy will be contingent on those environments
- rewards results and behaviour that are consistent with key organizational goals, thus driving and supporting desired behaviour
- linked with business performance, adopting a competitive strategy perspective
- practical and implementable
- been evolved in consultation with key stakeholders (Armstrong, 1996: 60).

This perspective on reward strategy is linked to contingency approaches to human resource management, as opposed to best practice models, as there is an acknowledgement that the strategy has to be flexible. This allows reward to be correlated with the broader business plan, which is essential to allow organizations to remain competitive in constantly changing markets.

A company's reward strategy can also provide symbolic images for employees, in that it can bestow on them status and importance other than that they create themselves directly as a result of their earnings. For example, employee benefits such as company cars, telephones, free health insurance and so on, all create images and messages of how valued the employee is to the organization.

Research has found a lack of consensus on the role of pay in human resource strategies. This may simply reflect the fact that similar pay approaches can be compatible with very different corporate human resource strategies (Schuler, 1992; Kessler, 2001). Kessler (2001: 212) argues that 'any given pay practice can be used in very different ways and for markedly different purposes rather than necessarily being associated with any particular HR model or narrowly defined goal'. **MMo**

References and further reading

Armstrong, M. (1996) *Employee Reward*, London: Institute of Personnel and Development.

Armstrong, M. and Murlis, H. (1994) *Reward Management*, 3rd edn, London: Kogan Page.

Kessler, I. (2001) 'Reward system choices', in J. Storey (ed.) *Human Resource Management: A Critical Text*, London: Thomson Learning, pp. 206–31.

Schuler, R. (1992) 'Strategic human resource management: linking people with the needs of the business', *Organizational Dynamics*, 22: 19–32.

Role plays

As trainers are looking at different ways in which to present their material and to get the message across, and to help create innovative solutions, role play is becoming a popular method. Moreover, during the past five or six years there has been a proliferation of companies who offer the services of professional actors, especially when the topic is sensitive either to the learners' organization or could cause embarrassment to the learners if they acted out the scenario.

Role-playing is a valuable technique for the innovative trainer as it provides the opportunity for action learning, achieves active involvement of participants and the learner is able to 'act out' real-life situations in a non-threatening environment.

Role plays can also be useful to help the trainee appreciate the different viewpoints and is a most effective way to learn providing that the trainees (learners) are comfortable about the environment in which the role plays take place. The trainer (facilitator) should ensure that learners are given amplye opportunity to practise, in a protected environment, different situations that may either be imaginary or real-life circumstances that the learners are likely to face within their own workplace.

The potential uses of role play are most appropriate for management development where participants can practise managerial skills, such as negotiating, communication and influencing skills. Interpersonal skills in a work context can also be practised that explores the different types of behaviour by people at work especially those who manage people.

In principle, role plays take the form of a one act, usually unscripted 'playlet' that involves two or more people taking the role of designated job titles, which relate to a specific organization. One of the most important aspects of role play is that the feedback given to the participants is critiqued sensitively but constructive as some people may feel inhibited by other participants observing the actual role play. However, in addition to one or more 'formal' facilitator feedbacks, all other participants should be given the opportunity to feed back to each other. It is the responsibility of the facilitator to build up an atmosphere of mutually trust and support to enable the role plays to take place without any undue stress to the participants. If the role play is to be video recorded, the participants should be given several practice runs so as to become accustomed to the camera. This is particularly important if a learner has to overcome shyness and for the role play to be meaningful and effective.

Mistakes can be observed and commented upon if recording is played back to the group for feedback where behaviours, mannerisms and abilities to handle the situation can be assessed. In this risk-free environment, participants can learn how to deal with a wide range of circumstances such as aggressive behaviour, handling trade union representatives and learning how to cope under pressure.

Organizations are increasingly turning to role plays and according to Jane Pickard (2000) using professional actors to reduce the possibility of 'hurt feelings' in certain situations such as the scenario where the human resource manager has to advise someone about their 'personal hygiene problem'. **SR**

References and further reading

Bolton, G. and Heathcote, D. (1999) *So You Want to Use Role Play?*, Stoke-on-Trent: Trentham Books.

Harris, A. W. and Myers, G. (1996) *Tools for Valuing Diversity: A Practical Guide to Techniques for Capitalising on Team Diversity*, London: Richard Chang Associates.

Merrick, N. (1998) 'Theatrical treatment: case study Hereford Hospitals NHS Trust', *People Management*, 22 January: 44–66.

Pickard, J. (2000) 'Best supportive actors', *People Management*, 2 March: 48–50.

Turner, D. (1996) *Role Plays: A Sourcebook of Activities for Trainers*, London: Kogan Page.

S

Safety representatives

Safety representatives are appointed by recognized unions under the Safety Representatives and Safety Committees Regulations Regulations 1977. Such representatives are entitled to be consulted by employers on health and safety matters. They also possess a number of other rights and functions. These include, carrying out workplace inspections at least once every three months, conducting investigations into notifiable accidents and other incidents, requesting the establishment of safety committees and receiving paid time of to carry out their functions and undergo training. Representatives are entitled to complain to an employment tribunal if their rights to time off are breached. Inspectors employed by the Health and Safety Executive and local authorities are responsible for enforcing the other provisions of the regulations.

The introduction of the 1977 regulations reflected a long-held and empirically supported belief that systems of worker representation, particularly when trade union based, can make an important contribution to the improvement of health and safety standards. At the same time, the activities and influence of safety representatives has been found to vary widely as a result of such factors as the degree of support provided by both employers and constituents, and the strength and degree of integration of workplace union organization. In addition, as a result of the reduction that has occurred over the 1980s and 1990s in the extent of union recognition, there has been a marked decline in their coverage of workplaces and workers. However, following the introduction of the Health and Safety (Consultation with Employees) Regulations 1996, employers are now also required to consult employees who are not covered by safety representatives. **PJ**

References and further reading

Health and Safety Commission (1996) *Safety Representatives and Safety Committees*, 3rd edn, Norwich: HSE Books.

James, P. and Kyprianou, A. (2000) 'Safety representatives and safety committees in the NHS: a healthy situation?', *Industrial Relations Journal* 31(1): 50–61.

James, P. and Walters, D. (1999) *Regulating Health and Safety at Work: The Way Forward*, London: Institute of Employment Rights, ch. 4.

Kirby, P. (1998) *TUC Survey of Safety Representatives*, London: Trades Union Congress.

Walters, D. and Gourlay, S. (1990) *Statutory Employee Involvement in Health and Safety at the Workplace: A Report of the Implementation and Effectiveness of the Safety Representatives and Safety Committees Regulations 1977*, London: Health and Safety Executive.

Secondments

Secondment is a temporary assignment to another area within the organization, and sometimes even to another associated organization (such as a customer or supplier). It is a period in which the manager acquires a different perspective within the company boundaries or from the outside. A period of time spent in marketing, human resource management or finance can improve the acquaintance of a production manager with organizational processes, help build interrelations with colleagues and increase communication thereafter (Baruch, 1999). At a more advanced level, secondments can be taken outside the organization. Exchange programmes under which managers and executives serve a period of time in another company, sharing knowledge and gaining some insight in return, can provide a win-win situation for both companies involved.

As in other career practices, the stimulus for offering people secondments can be derived from their manager, mentor, or from human resource (HR) counselling and performance appraisal (PA) systems. The possible pitfall of secondment is the need for long-term HR planning and for mutuality, thus making it feasible mostly for large or well-established corporations. There is also a risk of losing successful managers to the company they are seconded to, in addition to the usual risk of benchmarking, where it might be that only one side benefits from the deal. If the practice of satellite firms develops in the West, as in Japan, for example, the use of secondments will expand and the future may see more of this practice in a wider range of organizations. **YB**

References and further reading
Baruch, Y. (1999) 'Integrated career systems for the 2000s', *International Journal of Manpower* 20(7): 432–57.
Evans, J. (1990) 'The short sharp shock approach to secondment', *Personnel Management* 22(1): 57–60.
Hobbs, P. (1988) 'Bringing secondment in from the cold', *Personnel Management* 20(5): 36–9.

Selection

Selection is the process whereby employers determine who from among those who have submitted applications is to be offered a job and who is not. When carried out formally the process starts with a shortlisting stage during which application forms and CVs are screened and a judgement reached about which candidates are to proceed to subsequent rounds of interviews or other selection activities. Of course, much selection is carried out in a less formal, ad hoc manner, through which candidates learn about vacancies through word of mouth and are taken on after a brief meeting with a manager. While the research evidence strongly suggests that the more formal and sophisticated approaches lead to the most satisfactory outcomes, employers inevitably have to balance such considerations with those of cost and the frequent need to fill vacancies as quickly as possible. Where time and resources are available, it is advisable to adopt formal approaches, the aim being to maximize the chances of appointing the best qualified person. All conceptions of good practice in selection recommend starting with a robust personnel specification setting out the attributes or competencies which are essential and desirable in the successful candidate. Subsequent shortlisting criteria, interview questions and selection exercises are then designed with a view to establishing effectively which candidates most closely fit the profile required. In practice there are three distinct means that can be used to determine a match between candidates and required competences:

- asking for evidence through questions at interview and on application forms
- observing behaviour at interview and assessment centres
- through the use of personality and ability tests.

Employee selection is a field which has attracted the interest of academic researchers in large numbers for many years. Numerous problematic issues have thus been identified, researched and debated. These include the validity, reliability and utility of the various alternative selection methods available and the impact of selection processes on candidate perceptions of organizations. Another issue of interest is the balance that needs to be struck between selecting people who share similarities with existing high-performers and those who bring a greater degree of diversity to the organization. Legal and ethical matters relating to unfair discrimination are also issues that need to be taken into account. **ST**

References and further reading

Cook, M. (1995) *Personnel Selection and Productivity*, 2nd edn, Chichester: Wiley.
Cooper, D. and Robertson, I. (1995) *The Psychology of Personnel Selection*, London: Routledge.
Herriot, P. (ed.) (1989) *Assessment and Selection in Organisations*, Chichester: Wiley.
Iles, P. and Salaman, G. (1995) 'Recruitment, selection and assessment', in J. Storey (ed.) *Human Resource Management*: *A Critical Text*, London: Routledge.
Industrial Relations Services (IRS) (1997) 'The state of selection: an IRS survey', *Employee Development Bulletin* 85, January.
Newell, S. and Shackleton, V. (2000) 'Recruitment and Selection', in S. Bach and K. Sisson (eds) *Personnel Management*: *A Comprehensive Guide to Theory and Practice*, Oxford: Blackwell.
Smith, M., Gregg, M. and Andrews, D. (1989) *Selection and Assessment*: *A New Appraisal*, London: Pitman.

Selection methods

The major alternative selection methods are application forms, CVs, selection interviews, job references, ability tests, personality tests, assessment centre exercises and bio-data questionnaires. In some countries methods such as graphology and astrology are reportedly used, but not to any degree in the UK. It is usual for two or more of these tools to be used in combination, the most sophisticated selection exercises employing five or six separate methods.

Research into the relative effectiveness of each technique has been dominated by occupational psychologists who have sought to establish how useful each is as a means of predicting future job performance. Validity studies of this kind involve calculating the extent of any correlation between predictions of job performance at the selection stage and actual subsequent performance ratings. A key finding of this body of research is of relatively low validity scores for references and typical interviews. By contrast the methods found to be the most effective predictors of job performance are ability tests and assessment centres. Validity research also suggests that interviews are more effective when they are properly structured. This means that , questions relate to criteria included in a personnel specification and that the same questions are asked of each candidate.

While the more sophisticated selection methods are the most valid, they are not the most commonly employed. Indeed there appears to something of an inverse relationship between the extent to which a method is used and its known predictive qualities. Various reasons for this finding can be identified:

1. There is the question of cost, the more sophisticated approaches requiring greater commitment of time and resources than the more straight forward methods.
2. There is the question of what candidates expect and are comfortable with.
3. Consideration must be given to the two-way character of a selection interview and its usefulness as a forum both for negotiation and questioning of interviewees by candidates.

For all their weaknesses, therefore, there remain good reasons for continuing to make use of the less sophisticated selection methods. **ST**

References and further reading

Herriot, P. (ed.) (1989) *Assessment and Selection in Organisations*, Chichester: Wiley.

Newell, S. and Shackleton, V. (2000) 'Recruitment and Selection', in S. Bach and K. Sisson (eds) *Personnel Management*: *A Comprehensive Guide to Theory and Practice*, Oxford: Blackwell.

Smith, M., Gregg, M. and Andrews, D. (1989) *Selection and Assessment*: *A New Appraisal*, London: Pitman.

Taylor, S. (1998) *Employee Resourcing*, London: IPD, Pt 4.

Whalley, L. and Smith, M. (1998) *Deception in Selection*, Chichester: Wiley.

Wood, R. and Payne, T. (1998) *Competency Based Recruitment and Selection*: *A Practical Guide*, Chichester: Wiley, ch. 2.

Selection testing

The use of tests in selection has grown over the last 20 years. The main types are ability or attainment tests (e.g. keyboard skills), aptitude tests, tests of intelligence or cognitive skills, and personality tests, which are not strictly 'tests', but measures of preferences and styles. The main reason for using tests is to try to obtain objective information about candidates, to counteract the subjectivity inherent in the interviewing process. Tests are used more in the private sector than the public sector, more by large organizations than small, and mostly for graduate and management posts.

In choosing a test, it is important that selectors are clear about what is to be measured, that this is relevant to job performance, and that the test used is a reliable and valid instrument.

Most controversy is with regard to personality questionnaires, since the links between personality and job performance are tenuous (it is not possible to specify an exact profile of the ideal employee). Candidates may not be entirely honest in their responses and it is important to realise that the outcomes of personality inventories are not objective, but merely subjective assessments by candidates of themselves.

Candidates tend to view tests negatively. Concern has been expressed also about possible discrimination and cultural bias in some tests, and because of such concerns, several Codes of Practice have been produced about how to use them (by the British Psychological Society, the Chartered Iinstitute of Personnel and Development, the Equal Opportunities Commission and the Commisssion for Racial Equality).

These codes suggest that: tests should only be used by trained individuals, (there is a competence based qualification scheme); full information should be given to candidates; confidentiality should be protected; tests should be valid and reliable; representative norms should be used to compare scores against; sensitive feedback should be given to candidates; and employers should monitor tests for their value in selection as well as any possible adverse impact on certain groups. **JB**

References and further reading:

Baker, B. and Cooper, J. (2000) 'Occupational testing and psychometric instruments: an ethical perspective', in D. Winstanley and J. Woodall (eds), 'Ethical Issues in Conetmporary Human Resource Management', MacMillan Business.

Baldry C. and Fletcher, C. (1997) 'The integrity of integrity testing' *Selection and Development Review* 13(1), February.

Dulewicz, V., Fletcher, C. and Toplis, J. (1997) 'Psychological Testing: a manager's guide' CIPD.

Fletcher, C. *et. al.*, (1990) 'Personality tests: the great debate', *Personnel Management*, September.

Fletcher, C. (1998) 'A deciding Factor', *People Management*, 26 November.

MacKay, J. (1993) 'Psychological test matches', *Human Resources*, 10, Summer.

Sternberg, N. (1998) 'Survival of the fit test', *People Management*, 11 December.

Self-appraisal

A technique used in performance management and employee development. It involves asking individual employees formally to rate their own performance, usually against a set of predefined criteria. Self-appraisal can be adopted as a free-standing management technique in its own right, can play a role in a traditional supervisor–subordinate appraisal process or can form part of a broader 360° appraisal exercise. In any of these situations it requires individuals to identify for themselves key strengths and weaknesses with a view to focusing on ways of improving their personal performance. When used as part of a wider appraisal process the opportunity is given to compare self-ratings with the perceptions of others. This permits the identification of 'hidden' strengths and weaknesses of which the individual was hitherto unaware. Self-appraisal can also be seen as a form of employee participation aimed at gaining acceptance of wider appraisal processes and reducing defensiveness in situations where employees are rated by managers. Used in this way the technique turns a formal appraisal into a two-way affair, reducing the extent to which it simply involves one person exercising judgement on another's performance. Self-appraisal is probably most useful as a basis for helping to identify individual development needs. Here it forms part of the process whereby individuals are encouraged to take responsibility for their own training and career development plans.

The major problems with self-appraisal occur when the process is perceived as playing a part in decision-making about remuneration or promotion. In such situations the likelihood of individuals rating their own performance leniently or generously is great, in which case it serves little useful purpose. Research suggests that individuals have the capacity to assess themselves with a high degree of objectivity, but that they are not always inclined to do so. Women are apparently more inclined to accuracy in this respect than men. The tendency to be lenient towards oneself suggests that self-appraisal has rather more to offer in employee development programmes than it does in processes which are essentially evaluative in nature. **ST**

References and further reading

Fletcher, C. (1997) *Appraisal: Routes to Improved Performance*, 2nd edn, London: IPD, pp. 56–9.

Fletcher, C. (1999) 'The implications of research on gender differences in self-assessment and 360 degree appraisal', *Human Resource Management Journal* 9(1): 39–46.

Furnham, A. and Stringfield, P. (1998) 'Congruence in job-performance ratings: a study of 360 degree feedback examining self, manager, peers and consultant ratings', *Human Relations*, 54(4): 517–30.

Ward, P. (1997) *360-Degree Feedback*, London: IPD.

Self-development

Self-development (i.e. by self and of self) involves the individual taking responsibility for and control of his or her learning (Pedler, Burgoyne and Boydell, 1988). Ideally, self-development requires individuals to identify their own learning needs (rather than management telling them), devising means of meeting the needs and carrying out development actions. Self-development is a process involving continuing effort rather than an objective to be achieved, although the process will, no doubt, have objectives and milestones along the journey.

Self-development involves learning related to outcomes. 'Development . . . is the process of becoming increasingly complex, more elaborate and differentiated, by virtue of learning and maturation' (Collin, cited in Beardwell and Holden, 1994: 274). These outcomes relate to the way we think, feel and interpret the world and, if self-development is supported by the employer, will benefit the organization both through learning and development activities, which revolve around work-based projects, and through employee motivation. Self-development should be self-initiated. In fact, Mullins (1996) suggests that furthering one's own development is part of being an effective manager. However, self-development is enhanced by management and organizational support which can help people to spot and use opportunities within the workplace. The role of management is critical to effectiveness here, both to counsel and act as a resource, and to delegate to and support people in their learning. (See also **Learning organization.**)

During the 1990s, there has been considerable emphasis on the notion of learning and development with a particular focus upon both self-responsibility and responsibility within organizations to develop the human resource. Government promotion of initiatives such as Lifelong Learning and Individual Learning Accounts are all related to the concept of individual responsibility for learning and development, that this should be facilitated and supported because the individual's gain is also the organization's gain and ultimately that of the economy.

Self-development processes are, by nature, individual and may involve formal courses, distance learning, computer-based learning undertaken either individually or within groups. Action learning and self-managed learning groups may be engaged as support mechanisms. However, advice given to the would-be self-developer is common: to conduct a self-analysis focusing on key developmental life events and their outcomes as a means of seeking what works and a self-assessment focusing upon current state and future plans. How to assess, plan and monitor is described in a number of key texts referenced below. **ASm**

References and further reading

Beardwell, I. and Holden, L. (1994) *Human Resource Management: A Contemporary Perspective*, London: Pitman.

Boydell, T. (1985) *Management Self Development*, Geneva: International Labour Office.

Cox, C. and Beck, J. (eds) *Management Development: Advances in Practice and Theory*, Chichester: Wiley.

Francis, D. and Woodcock, M. (1996) *The New Unblocked Manager: A Practical Guide to Self Development*, Aldershot: Gower.

Megginsa, D. and Pedler, M. (1991) *Self Development: A Facilitators Guide*, London: McGraw-Hill.

Mullins, L. (1996) *Management and Organisational Behaviour*, London: Pitman.

Pedler, M., Burgoyne, J. and Boydell, T. (1988) *Applying Self Development in Organizations*, London: Prentice Hall International.

Temporal, P. (1984) *Helping Self Development to Happen*, Aldershot: Gower.

See also: *Personnel Review Special Edition* 29(4) published in 2000.

Sex discrimination

Sex discrimination in employment relates to the less favourable treatment of an individual on the basis of sex. The term generally refers to discrimination against women although it can equally apply to men. Recently sexual orientation and transsexuality have also been included in this broad area. Gender inequality over the centuries has resulted in very different employment practices between the sexes, with women typically in low-status and low-skilled occupations, often working part-time. Whilst women's economic activity has increased steadily in the last 50 years, a gender gap in average pay levels and underrepresentation in senior management positions in organizations persist.

Discrimination and gender inequality have been addressed through legislation and European Community law operates along side our own domestic law, influencing and shaping its provisions. The cornerstone is Article 119 of the Treaty of Rome, 1975, which enshrines the principle of equal pay for men and women. Directives, notably those on Equal Pay (1975) and Equal Treatment (1976) are also important. The principal domestic statutes are the Sex Discrimination Act (SDA) 1975, which covers all aspects of employment other than pay and the Equal Pay Act (EqPA) 1970, which deals specifically with pay and benefits. These two pieces of legislation and their subsequent amendments prohibit sex discrimination in employment in all but a limited set of circumstances and make provision for complaints to be brought before an industrial tribunal. Breach of the legislation can be very costly for employers both in time and money, as compensation for sex discrimination (although not remuneration arrears) is unlimited. The SDA makes both overt and subtler forms of bias illegal through the concepts of direct and indirect discrimination as well as outlawing victimization. Practical guidance on its provisions is contained in the Equal Opportunities Commission's statutory *Code of Practice* (1985) which, whilst not imposing legal obligations, must be taken into consideration by an industrial tribunal when reaching a decision. The code also provides guidance to employers on wider measures to promote equality of opportunity. The EqPA provides women (and men) with the right to receive equal pay not only for like work and work rated as equivalent but also for work of equal value. Claims under this latter category are very complicated and often take a long time to reach a conclusion. The continued existence of sex inequality together with the complex legal framework have been put forward as arguments for consolidating and simplifying anti-discrimination legislation. **SS**

References and further reading

Equal Opportunities Commission (1985) *Code of Practice for the elimination of discrimination on the grounds of sex and marriage and the promotion of equality of opportunity in employment*, London: HMSO.

Hite, L. M. (1996) 'Black women managers and administrators: experiences and implications', *Women in Management Review* 11(6): 11–17

Paci, P., Makepeace, G. and Dolton, P. (1995) 'Is pay discrimination against young women a thing of the past? A tale of two cohorts', *International Journal of Manpower* 16(2): 60–5.

Rubenstein, M. (2000) *Discrimination: A Guide to the Relevant Case Law on Race and Sex Discrimination*, London: IRS.

Sexual harassment

The term and interpretation 'sexual harassment' was coined in the 1970s by US radical feminists in order to problematize unwanted male sexual conduct in the workplace. MacKinnon (1979) identified two broad types of sexual harassment: 'condition of work' and 'quid pro quo'. She explained that in condition of work sexual harassment, a woman may be constantly felt or pinched, visually undressed and stared at, surreptitiously kissed, commented upon, manipulated into being found alone and generally taken advantage of at work, but never promised or denied anything explicitly connected with her job. Quid pro quo sexual harassment is defined by a more or less explicit exchange: the woman must comply sexually or forfeit an employment benefit.

Subsequently, sexual harassment has become widely understood as 'unwanted conduct of a sexual nature or conduct based on sex which is offensive to the recipient' (Rubenstein, 1992: 2). In 1985 the first victory in a sexual harassment case (*Porcelli* v. *Strathclyde Regional Council*) was brought under the Sex Discrimination Act (1975). Equally, the Employment Protection (Consolidation) Act (1978) may be used to complain of sexual harassment at work. As sexual harassment is beginning to be accepted as a major health hazard, the Health and Safety at Work Act (1974) may be deployed as a remedy for workplace sexual harassment. As well as the financial implications to organizations of women winning industrial tribunal cases, sexual harassment causes disrupted work, reductions in productivity and quality of work, demoralized staff and financial loss related to increased turnover of staff. As such, organizations have been encouraged to develop sexual harassment policies (Collier, 1995).

Nevertheless, 'sexual harassment' has always been a contentious topic: the *Sun* newspaper, for example, observed that, 'while serious minded union officials . . . are getting their knickers in a twist about sexual harassment at work, the workers themselves say "Carry on groping" . . . "it makes the day more pleasant" ' (22 March 1982, cited in Wise and Stanley, 1987: 34). One reason why the concept of sexual harassment was available for undermining in the 1980s by salacious British tabloid press reporting was the way in which sexual harassment was then frequently presented as 'sexual' conduct. A strong critique of this theorization of sexual harassment was subsequently made by Wise and Stanley (1987), who perceived sexual harassment as conduct in which men use sex in order to maintain power. This argument has been widely accepted.

Yet recent years have seen a rethinking of sexual harassment. Thomas and Kitzinger (1997) said that many women and men have never accepted the interpretation of women's experiences of unwanted male sexual conduct as sexual harassment. Epstein (1997) felt that the word 'sexual' in 'sexual harassment' was problematic, given that it obscures 'sexist harassment'. Kitzinger (1994) said that 'harassment' sounds like something that 'happens'. It is quite hard to interpret the word to mean silences, absences and evasions (e.g. when a lesbian woman is not dismissed from her job because she stayed 'in the closet').

While most sexual harassment research has concentrated upon women victims, men's experiences have recently begun to be explored. Epstein (1997) interviewed gay men who spoke of being harassed by men because of their sexuality, of harassing other men through a presumption of their gay sexuality (harassment which functioned to define the harasser as heterosexual), as well as harassing women to avoid accusations of homosexuality. Lee (2000) analysed heterosexual men's experiences of sexual harassment, revealing that sexual allegations (e.g. rape, incest, poor sexual performance) have a distinctive place in such experiences. The sexual harassment of men in the form of verbal sexual allegations feminizes those men who find such allegations distressing. **DL**

References and further reading

Collier, R. (1995) *Combating Sexual Harassment in the Workplace*, Buckingham: Open University Press.

Epstein, D. (1997) 'Keeping them in their place: hetero/sexist harassment, gender and the enforcement of heterosexuality', in A. Thomas and C. Kitzinger (eds) *Sexual Harassment*, Buckingham: Open University Press.

Kitzinger, C. (1994) 'Anti-lesbian harassment', in C. Brant and Y. L. Too (eds) *Rethinking Sexual Harassment*, London: Pluto.

Lee, D. (2000) 'Hegemonic masculinity and male feminisation: The sexual harassment of men at work', *Journal of Gender Studies* 9(2): 141–55.

MacKinnon, C. (1979) *The Sexual Harassment of Working Women*, New Haven, CT: Yale University Press.

Rubenstein, M. (1992) *Preventing and Remedying Sexual Harassment at Work*: A Resource Manual, London: Eclipse.

Thomas, A. and Kitzinger, C. (eds) (1997) *Sexual Harassment*, Buckingham: Open University Press.

Wise, S. and Stanley, L. (1987) *Georgie Porgie*, London: Pandora.

Shop steward

Shop stewards are workplace union representatives. Elected annually, they typically represent between 10 and 30 union members within the workplace at which they are employed. The shop steward's role is to inform and advise his or her members in relation to pay, conditions and related workplace matters, to represent members both individually and collectively before management, and arguably to provide union members with leadership on key issues. If a dispute results in industrial action, then shop stewards would normally play an important role in organizing this at a workplace level. The day-to-day duties of shop stewards are largely carried out during their paid work time, within the framework of the Advisory, Conciliation and Arbitration Service (ACAS) Code of Practice on time-off for trade union duties (ACAS, 1977). The term *shop steward* is particularly associated with engineering and manufacturing. Whilst white-collar and professional workers' unions have similar workplace representatives, they are usually known as *staff representatives*, *departmental representatives* or simply *union representatives*.

The British shop stewards movement was born in the engineering industry during the First World War. In the 1950s and 1960s era of full employment, the extent and strength of the shop steward movement increased considerably, particularly in respect of local wage bargaining in the private sector. These and related industrial relations issues were addressed in the Donovan Report in 1968. With the considerable fall in union membership in the 1980s and 1990s, and the difficulties created for unions by prolonged high unemployment, extensive legal restrictions in relation to their activities and unsympathetic governments, the power and influence of shop stewards and union representatives declined considerably. However, it is by no means certain that this is a permanent feature of workplace industrial relations, and indeed a significant shift in the economy towards full employment could create considerable improvement in the fortunes of the trade unions. If this does occur, a new version of the shop stewards movement might play an important role in these developments. (See also **Trade Unions**.) **DB**

References and further reading

Advisory, Conciliation and Arbitration Service (ACAS) (1977) 'Time off for trade union duties and activities', *ACAS Code of Practice 3*, London: ACAS.

Cully, M., O'Reilly, A., Millward, N., Forth, J., Woodland, S., Dix, G. and Bryson, A. (1999) *Britain at Work*: *As Depicted by the 1998 Workplace Employee Relations Survey*, London: Routledge, chs 9 and 5.

Darlington, R. (1994) *The Dynamics of Workplace Unionism*, London: Mansell.

Gall, G. (1998) 'The prospect for workplace trade unionism: evaluating Fairbrother's union renewal thesis', *Capital and Class* 66: 149–56.

Godfrey, G. and Marchington, M. (1996) 'Shop Stewards in the 1990s', *Industrial Relations Journal* 27(4): 339–44.

McIlroy, J. (1995) *Trade Unions in Britain Today*, 2nd edn, Manchester: Manchester University Press.

Terry, M. (1995) 'Trade unions: shop stewards and the workplace', in P. Edwards (ed.) *Industrial Relations*: *Theory and Practice in Great Britain*, Oxford: Blackwell.

Sick pay

Sick pay is paid to employees who are absent from work because of illness. It can be a major cost to employers since, although absence rates in many organizations are normally 3 to 4 per cent, they are higher in certain occupations and industries. A Confederation of British Industry survey in 1998 found that the typical employee loses 8.4 days a year due to sickness absence.

In 1983 the British government introduced statutory sick pay, by which an employer paid the employee an amount that they would have previously claimed from the state when sick. The employer reclaims this payment from the national insurance contributions which would normally have been passed on to the government.

Occupational sick pay schemes vary according the amount of benefit payable, the length of entitlement, the period of service required for eligibility and whether or not the employee is paid from the first day of sickness. Some of the more generous schemes may provide full pay for the first six months of sickness, followed by six months at half pay for longer-serving employees.

Traditionally employers have been more likely to pay higher status workers when they are sick. Where manual workers have been paid they have often been in a separate, less generous scheme. These distinctions have diminished in recent years and in many cases disappeared, but there are still employers, particularly in the manufacturing sector, who treat manual workers less favourably. Other groups who are less likely to be covered are new and part-time employees. For example, in retailing, sick pay is often not open to those who work less than about ten hours a week.

A major concern of employers is that sick pay should not be abused and that only those who are genuinely sick should have their claims accepted. Absence rates are monitored to look for unusual patterns. A company doctor or home visits may be employed to check up on staff, and employees interviewed when they return after a period of absence. In some workplaces a culture can develop in which employees perceive that they have an entitlement to a certain number of 'sickies'. **AA**

References and further reading

Confederation of British Industry (CBI) (1998) *Missing Out*: *1998 Absence and Labour Turnover Survey*, CBI, September.
Income Data Services (IDS) (1998) 'Sick pay schemes', IDS Study, 660, December.
Income Data Services (IDS) (1998) 'Managing absence', IDS Study, 645, March.

Single table bargaining

Single table bargaining (STB) is the merger of separate bargaining agents (at plant, divisional or industry level) into one negotiating unit where multi-union recognition remains within an organization (Salamon, 1999).

The 1980s witnessed a shift from centralized (multi-employer) to decentralized (single-employer) bargaining arrangements. Accompanying this shift has been the rise in single table bargaining between separate unions and a single employer (Kinnie, 1990; Gall, 1993). Single table bargaining is more common in public (40 per cent) than private (12 per cent) sector establishments, with the highest concentration of STB arrangements found in electricity, gas and water (Cully *et al.*, 1999: 94). The same research reported that about 26 per cent of all unionized workplaces conduct single table bargaining. This represents about three-fifths of all establishments in Britain where two or more unions are recognized. Around 17 per cent of companies that have multi-union recognition continue to negotiate separately with the different unions. The remainder (57 per cent) have 'consolidated bargaining', which falls short of full single table bargaining.

There are several factors that can be used to explain the rise in single table bargaining (Marginson and Sisson, 1990; Gall, 1993; Salamon, 1999):

- It can help management integrate pay and grading across large and complex organizational structures.
- It is tool to manage a more flexible workforce, where multiskilling and job redesign tends to minimise manual and non-manual demarcation barriers.
- Single table bargaining can be used by employers to prevent 'leapfrogging' in terms of pay negotiations between different unions in one organization.
- Single table bargaining can facilitate the harmonization of terms and conditions between different grades of employees.
- Bargaining with different unions can help management facilitate the introduction of employee participation and involvement schemes.
- For unions, STB can be seen as a pragmatic response to the decline in power and membership.
- Single table bargaining can also help different unions recognize their differences and potentially widen the collective bargaining agenda to include issues beyond pay and terms and conditions.

One of the more difficult issues with STB is the formula and configuration of representation. If this is weighted according to union membership figures, then larger unions may dominate the bargaining agenda. Yet if representation is based on equal share at the bargaining table, then smaller unions could have an influence disproportionate to their membership level in an organization (Salamon, 1999). **TD**

References and further reading

Cully, M., O'Reilly, A., Millward, N., Forth, J., Woodland, S., Dix, G. and Bryson, A. (1998) *Britain at Work*: *As Depicted by the 1998 Workplace Employee Relations Survey*, London: Routledge.
Gall, G. (1993) *Harmony Around a Single Table*, London: Labour Research Department.

Industial Relations Service (IRS) (1990) 'Single table bargaining: a survey', *Employment Trends* 463, May.

Kinnie, N. (1990) 'The decentralisation of industrial relations: recent research considerations', *Personnel Review* 19(3): 30–47.

Marginson, P. and Sisson, K. (1990) 'Single table talk', *Personnel Management*, May: 46–9.

Millward, N., Stevens, M., Smart, D. and Hawes, W. R. (1992) *Workplace Industrial Relations in Transition. The ED/ESRC/PSI/ACAS Surveys*, Aldershot: Dartmouth.

Salamon, M. (1999) 'Collective bargaining', in G. Hollinshead, P. Nicholls and S. Tailby (eds) *Employee Relations*, London: Pitman Publishing.

Single union deals

Sometimes no distinction is made between single union deals and no-strike deals. This can be misleading. No-strike deals, of which the Nissan agreement with the Amalgamated Engineering Union is perhaps the most well known, are single union deals – but most agreements which recognize a single union in a workplace do not incorporate no-strike procedures. The 1998 Workplace Employee Relations Survey reported that 24 per cent of all unionized workplaces had formal single union agreements (Cully *et al.*, 1999: 93), but this fails to clarify the percentage of these which included no strike deals. The same survey also indicates that, of workplaces which recognized only one union, 72 per cent did so through a formal agreement, whilst a significant proportion of single union arrangements were not a deliberate outcome of management policy. No-strike elements apart, the initial arguments of employers in favour of single union deals were focused on the potential to avoid job demarcation disputes, the streamlining of negotiations and the avoidance of *leap-frogging* in respects of pay claims and settlements.

Single union deals per se have not posed great difficulties for trade unions in Britain. Contention has arisen particularly when they have incorporated no-strike procedures, and in turn been linked to an all-embracing package of lean production and human resource management initiatives. It is not surprising, therefore, that unions have given some support to *single table bargaining*, which is based upon joint negotiations in multi-union workplaces (Gall, 1994). In addition, the great wave of union mergers which has occurred in the 1980s and 1990s may encourage a reduction in the number of bargaining units in the workplace, which in turn may contribute to an increasing harmonization of pay and conditions. These developments may play a part in encouraging single table bargaining and single union arrangements that exclude no-strike deals. (See also **No-strike deals** and **Single table bargaining**.) **DB**

References and further reading

Bassett, P. (1986) *Strike-Free*: *New Industrial Relations in Britain*, London: Macmillan.

Cully, M., Woodland, S., O'Reilly, A. and Dix, G. (1999) *Britain at Work*: *As Depicted by the 1998 Workplace Employee Relations Survey*, London: Routledge, 93.

Gall, G. (1993) 'What happened to single union deals?', *Industrial Relations Journal* 24(1): 71–5.

Gall, G. (1994) 'The rise of single table bargaining in Britain', *Employee Relations* 16(4): 62–71.

Industrial Relations Review and Report (IRRR) (1992) 'Single union deals in perspective', *Industrial Relations Review and Report*: *IRS Employment Trends* 523: 7–15.

McIlroy, J. (1995) *Trade Unions in Britain Today*, 2nd edn, Manchester: Manchester University Press, pp. 114–16.

Situational interviewing

Situational interviewing is an approach to questioning used in selection interviewing whereby candidates are given hypothetical situations which might occur and are asked hoe they might respond. Responses should be evaluated by comparison to predetermined 'standard' answers given by existing good performers.

Experimental research has demonstrated the reliability and predictive validity of situational questions over more traditional approaches, although this relies on the interviewers using properly designed realistic 'situations' which are relevant to each post, appropriate questions and scoring standards. However, it is often the case that interviewers just make up hypothetical scenarios and questions and use them unsystematically in interviews.

Whilst the systematic use of situational interviewing can ensure consistency and fairness in selection, in that candidates are presented with the same situations, it has been criticized for its inflexibility, and reducing the role of the interviewer to a mere administrator of standard questions, which can feel like an oral 'test' to the candidate.

The approach is based on the assumption that actual behaviour is consistent with intentions, however there is also a view that candidates are likely to give the response that they think the interviewer wants to hear, and that their actual behaviour in practice may not be in line with their stated intentions. In this respect, behavioural interviewing is argued to be more valid. **JB**

References and further reading

Anderson, N. and Shackleton, V. (1993) *Successful Selection Interviewing*, Oxford: Blackwell.

Barclay, J. (1999) 'Employee selection: a question of structure', *Personnel Review*, 28(1/2): 134–51.

Barclay, J. (2001) 'Improving selection interviews with structure: organisations' use of "behavioural" interviews', *Personnel Review* 30(1): 81–101.

Latham, G. (1997) 'Predicting an applicant's intentions through the situational interview', *Human Resources Professional* 14(2), April–May: 39, 41–2.

Maurer, S. D. (1997) 'The potential of the situational interview: existing research and unresolved issues', *Human Resource Management Review* 7(2), Summer: 185–201.

Taylor, P. J. and O'Driscoll, P. (1995) *Structured Employment Interviewing*, Aldershot: Gower.

Skill-based pay

This is a reward that enhances an employee's base rate pay by paying them for skills and competencies acquired. It emerged from the USA in the 1980s in response to the problem of providing incentives to technical staff who perhaps cannot be easily measured on the criteria which are used in performance-related pay schemes or incentive pay schemes.

An increment is paid to staff who complete a defined skill module or who gain external qualifications. The skills gained have to be linked to the organization's business objectives and the employee must be able to apply these skills to a wider range of jobs or tasks or at a higher level then they were capable of previously.

The advantages of this approach for an organization are:

- It encourages multiskilling and employee flexibility.
- It raises the skills base of an organization.
- It allows the organization to become 'lean'.

The disadvantages are:

- It is costly to introduce and maintain this type of reward system.
- There can be difficulties in accrediting or assessing the acquisition of a particular skill.
- Highly skilled employees may be more difficult to retain.
- There is the danger of 'topping out', whereby employees reach the top of the skills ladder and have nowhere to progress to. This can be overcome by supplementing skill-based pay arrangements with some other scheme such as a profit-related pay scheme.

Drucker (2000) believes that there is a lack of convincing evidence about the extent of skill-based pay in the UK. She argues that it requires a careful analysis of skill needs and a clear commitment to training opportunities: 'The scope for advancement through skills acquisition is likely to be inhibited both by the training budget and by employer willingness to accommodate increased wage costs, unless it is an integral and necessary aspect of organizational change' (Drucker, 2000: 119). **MMo**

References and further reading

Armstrong, M. (1996) *Employee Reward*, London: Institute of Personnel and Development, ch. 18.
Drucker, J. (2000) 'Wage systems', in G. White and J. Drucker, *Reward Management: A Critical Text*, London: Routledge.
Incomes Data Services (IDS) (1992), 'Skill-based pay', IDS Study, 500, February.
Lawler, E. E. (1990) *Strategic Pay*, San Francisco: Jossey-Bass, ch. 9.
Murray, B. and Gerhart, B. (2000) 'Skill-based pay and skill seeking', *Human Resource Management Review* 10(3): 271–87.

Social Charter

The 1957 *Treaty of Rome* is the founding treaty creating the European Economic Community (EEC, now the European Union, EU). The aim was to create a Common Market by bringing down barriers to the free movement of goods. labour, capital and services between member states. The original aim was to achieve the Common Market objectives within 12 years, but progress was slow partly because each proposal needed the unanimous agreement of all member states. To speed up the achievement ot the original objectives, the *Single European Act* was signed by member states in 1987 with the aim of freeing up the movement of goods, people, services and capital between member states by 31 December 1992. This was to be achieved by amending the EEC Treaty to allow member states to adopt certain key measures by qualified majority voting (QMV), i.e. 70 per cent support of member states, rather than unanimous vote.

Whilst most of the 1957 Treaty is about economic harmonization, two chapters are about employment. The *Free Movement of Workers Chapter* establishes the right of EU citizens to live and work anywhere in the union without discrimination. The *Social Chapter* attempts to improve working conditions and the standard of living of workers. It sets out:

- A commitment to harmonization of social conditions between member states so that free trade is conducted on the basis of a level playine field of minimum employment conditions.
- It requires member states to ensure and maintain equal pay for equal work.
- All employment conditions under the Social Chapter, except for health and safety, have the unanimous support of all member states. Health and safety issues could be adopted by QMV.

Slow progress in the social policy area led all member states except the UK to sign the Community Charter of the Fundamental Social Rights of Workers (the *Social Charter*) in 1989. The Charter has no legal force, but aimed to address concerns that social policy was falling behind the development of the single market.

The Social Charter proclaims that a floor of basic common employment rights and objectives should be established across all member states to ensure that:

- The right of free movement in the EU become a reality.
- Workers are paid a sufficient wage to enjoy a decent standard of living.
- Adequate social security protection is provided in all member states.
- basic law on working time, provision of contract, treatment of part time and temporary workers and collective redundancies is improved and harmonized.
- All workers have the right to join or not to join a union, negotiate collective agreements and take collective action, including strike action.

- All workers have access to continuous vocational training throughout their working life.
- Equal treatment and equal opportunities between men and women are developed, particularly to enable men and women to reconcile family and work responsibilities.
- Information and consultation are developed.
- Health and safety protection is improved.
- Young workers are given access to training and fair treatment.
- The elderly are guaranteed a sufficient income.
- Measures are taken to improve the social and professional integration of people with disabilities.

The UK did not sign the Social Charter because of concern that the result would be an obligation to adopt new EU laws which would involve a cost and damage competitiveness. The lack of the UK commitment to the Social Charter did not stop the European Commission proposing new Directives under the 1989 Social Charter Action Programme. In fact the Action Programme was based on articles in the 1957 Treaty of Rome which already covered the UK and did not need the Social Charter to be proposed.

The UK government was further troubled in December 1991 when the heads of state met in Maastricht to agree further political, economic and monetary union. The resulting Maastricht Treaty was implemented in November 1993. As part of the Maastricht proposals, the member states (except the UK) signed a *Social Protocol* to extend the Social Chapter issues which could be introduced by QMV. The UK was strongly against this, but the other states went ahead and agreed to harmonize their employment laws by QMV in five areas: health and safety, working conditions, information and consultation of workers, equal treatment and equal opportunities for men and women, and the integration of persons excluded from the labour market.

The change of government in 1997 removed the UK objections to the Social Charter, and steps have been taken to harmonize UK practice in the social policy area with the rest of Europe. **DK**

References and further reading
Chartered Institute of Personnel and Development, *European Update*, monthly publication from IPD.
Chartered Institute of Personnel and Development, *European Employment Law: The State of Play Checklist*, quarterly publication from IPD.
Leach, R. (1998) *Europe. A Concise Encyclopaedia of the European Union*, London: Profile Books.

Social partnership

The notion of social partnership originates in the co-operative industrial relations of the successful West German and Scandinavian economies of the post-war period. There it involved close collaborative relationships between employers and trade unions at both national and enterprise level, leading to a positive, proactive attitude on both sides to increasing efficiency and productivity, and to low levels of strike activity. This version of *pluralism* was frequently contrasted to the more conflictual and arm-length relations found in British engineering, where management and trade unions regarded each other with suspicion and distrust. In 1975, the abortive Bullock Report on industrial democracy, proposed copying one element of the German model, employee representatives on the company board. Since the advent of European Union Social Chapter, social partnership has taken on a looser meaning, though still referring to the involvement of various interest groups in the formulation of social and employment policy. It has also been associated with the creation of European Works Councils at large, multinational companies.

In Britain, the term is associated with the election of New Labour in 1997 and the re-engagement with continental European social policy, though the Trade Union

Congress had begun using it several years earlier. Here it refers mainly to a close, collaborative relationship between trade unions and management, which focuses on addressing and resolving problems over wages and conditions before they spill over in conflict. Often, it is associated with a strong emphasis on consultation and a downgrading of adversarial bargaining, as in the agreement between Tesco and the Union of Shop Distributive, and Allied Workers (USDAW). Elsewhere, it is linked with promises of job security, as at Blue Circle. Usually, these agreements shift trade union attention away from points of conflict, like wages, to areas of joint interest like training and the quality of working life. They also draw unions into employee involvement schemes, which, in the past, have been used to weaken them or else have been weakened by them. For trade unions, social partnership is seen as an updated, more constructive version of industrial relations pluralism. However, some employers, and at times New Labour, have interpreted it in much more *unitarist* terms, as an extension of 1990s employee involvement. What they have in common, perhaps, is an emphasis on co-operation between management and workers, and a recognition that employees require some channel of representation or collective voice, whether a trade union, a consultative body, or a combination of both. **PA**

References and further reading
Ackers, P. and Payne, J. (1998) 'British trade unions and social partnership: rhetoric, reality and strategy', *International Journal of Human Resource Management* 34(4), December: 473–95.
Ferner, A. and Hyman, R. (eds) (1998) *Changing Industrial Relations in Europe*, Oxford: Blackwell.
Hantrais, L. (2000) *Social Policy in the European Union*, London: Macmillan.
Kelly, J. (1996) 'Union militancy and social partnership', in P. Ackers, C. Smith and P. Smith (eds) *The New Workplace and Trade Unionism*, London: Routledge.
Sparrow, P. and Marchington, M. (1998) *Human Resource Management: The New Agenda*, London: Financial Times Pitman Publishing.
Tailby, S. and Winchester, D. (2000) 'Management and trade unions: towards social partnership', in S. Bach and K. Sisson (eds) *Personnel Management*, 3rd edn, Oxford: Blackwell.

Socialization

Socialization is the process by which individuals learn what is required or expected of them by other individuals, groups, organizations or society as a whole. Socialization happens most obviously and extensively in childhood. But it also applies to adults, especially nowadays when many people live and work in several quite different contexts during their lifetime, and have to learn how to operate in each of them. Some work organizations socialize newcomers quite systematically, taking care to expose them to an appropriate range of experiences and people. Often newcomers stay together as a group for some time (e.g. graduate trainees) and have a clear timetable indicating which assignments they will undertake when, and who will oversee them. This has been termed 'institutionalized socialization' by Van Maanen and Schein (1979) amongst others. Other organizations either deliberately or through neglect leave much more to chance, so that newcomers' experiences are much more haphazard and uncertain. This has been termed 'individualized socialization'.

Georgia Chao and colleagues (1994) have identified the following six content areas of socialization:

1. *Performance proficiency*: learning how to do the tasks required in the job.
2. *People*: establishing good relationships with organizational members.
3. *Politics*: understanding relationships and power relationships in the organization.
4. *Language*: understanding the necessary technical language and jargon.
5. *Goals and values*: learning what the organization is trying to achieve and what the values of its members are.
6. *History*: knowledge of the past of the organization and its members.

Research suggests that institutionalized socialization tends be appreciated by new-comers, and to make them committed but rather conforming, whereas individual-ized socialization tends to make newcomers feel rather neglected and uncommitted, but also innovative because they have had to find their own ways of making sense of the organization. But research can also be criticized for being unclear about just what socialization is. Does it concern how people learn in a detached way what is expected of them, or does it involve behaving in the right ways, or even to *want* to behave in those ways? These can be thought of as different depths of socialization: learning about, learning how and changing self-identity. Top managers tend to want to win 'hearts and minds' but in times of insecure employment many new employees are surely unwilling to offer that. **JA**

References and further reading

Anderson, N. and Thomas, H. (1995) 'Work group socialization', in M. West (ed) *Handbook of Work Groups*, Chichester: Wiley.

Ashforth, B. and Saks, A. (1996) 'Socialization tactics: longitudinal effects on newcomer adjust-ment', *Academy of Management Journal* 39: 149–78.

Chao, G., O'Leary-Kelly, A., Wold, S., Klein, H. and Gardner, P. (1994) 'Organizational socialization: its content and consequences', *Journal of Applied Psychology* 79: 730–43.

Gundry, L. and Rousseau, D. (1994) 'Critical incidents in communicating culture to newcomers: The meaning is the message', *Human Relations* 47: 1063–87.

Morrison, E. (1993) 'Longitudinal study of the effects of information-seeking on newcomer socialization', *Journal of Applied Psychology* 78: 173–83.

Van Maanen, J. and Schein, E. (1979) 'Toward a theory of organizational socialization', *Research in Organizational Behavior* 1: 209–64.

Speak-up schemes

These form a vehicle for upward communication from employees to management. Unlike suggestion schemes, which are mainly to encourage improvements in busi-ness processes, the principal focus of speak-up schemes is on addressing employment relations concerns. Speak-up schemes can be seen as one of a range of systems or devices which are meant to replace trade unions, or to compensate for their absence, and are a feature of some non-unionized workplaces. The underlying justification for having speak-up schemes is that they provide a channel for communicating employee concern, ostensibly in the same way that a trade union offers employees a 'voice'. To this end, it may be that speak-up schemes incorporate formal alternative communication channels (i.e. outside the everyday employee–line manager rela-tionship) with designated managers acting as people to whom employees can address concerns, in the same way that a unionized employee might contact their shop stew-ard (official union representative). Speak-up schemes are unlike formal disciplinary or grievance procedures, whose focus in on the individual employee's relationship with his or her manager or employer. Instead, they have a more generic aspect, encouraging the discussion of issues which affect employees collectively, such as health and safety.

Although such schemes can be a feature of 'model' non-unionized employers, and represent a real desire to improve employment relations, they may not adequately replace the role of trade unions. If we believe employees can have different interests from management, there remains the possibility that where there is a conflict of interests, speak-up schemes will fail employees because they are management owned. **KM**

References and further reading

Marchington, M. and Wilkinson, A. (2000) *Core Personnel and Development*, London: IPD.

Ryan, K. (1996) *The Courageous Messenger: How to Successfully Speak Up at Work*, New York: Jossey-Bass.

Staff associations

During the 1960s and 1970s white-collar staff, including clerical and technical workers, supervisors, managers and professionals increasingly sought collective representation at work. This was reflected in the development of staff associations and specialist trade unions, as such staff were often very reluctant to join the larger unions which represented their subordinates and blue-collar workers. In some cases staff associations grew at the expense of the larger Trades Union Congress (TUC)-affiliated unions. There is also some evidence that staff associations have fared rather better than the TUC-affiliated unions in a period of union membership decline. One explanation for their growth and continued resilience is that white-collar staff may fear that union membership involves disloyalty to the employer and that it brings with it the risk of being drawn into industrial action in support of fellow trade unions in disputes with other employers. In this sense a third party, the trade union, is seen as intruding into the employment relationship and is something that is unwelcome to some white-collar staff who aspire to be treated on an individualized basis. The reluctance to organise collectively may be reduced in the case of an internal staff association with a closer identification with the employing organization and its guarantees of autonomy from external influence.

Staff associations thus tend to be specific to single employers and are found largely in the private sector. The financial services industry, particularly the building society sector, is where staff associations are most common. The independence of staff associations has been criticized and some employers have been seen to encourage them in order to keep out trade unions. Staff associations that are independent of the employer financially and organisationally are provided with a certificate of independence from the **Certification Officer** (see separate entry). Although often criticized as being an ineffective alternative to trade unionism, staff associations can often evolve into more capable representation bodies. There is also some evidence to suggest that some white-collar staff, whilst initially reluctant to joining a trade union, may subsequently come to terms with being a member of a union once they have 'passed through' an intermediate position of being a member of a staff association. The initial experience of collective organisation may thus result in reducing resistance to being a member of a trade union in the future. **TR**

References and further reading

Bryson, C., Jackson, M. and Leopold, J. (1995) 'The impact of self-governing trusts on trades unions and staff associations the NHS', *Industrial Relations Journal* 26(2): 120–33.

Industrial Relations Service (IRS) (1995) 'Staff associations: independent unions or employer-led bodies', *Employment Trends* 575: 6–11.

Swabe, A. and Price, P. (1984) 'Building a permanent association: the development of staff associations in the building societies', *British Journal of Industrial Relations* 22: 195–204.

Strategic choice theory

'Strategic choice theory' refers to a model of industrial relations and human resource management that adds a dynamic component – 'strategic choice' – to earlier analyses. Kochan, McKersie and Cappelli (1984) first developed this perspective, and use the concept to encompass three levels of decision-making: macro or global, the employment relationship and industrial relations system, and the individual workplace. Although their perspective focused on the changing patterns of American employment relations, Kochan, McKersie and Capelli take an interdisciplinary approach and their work has a comparative application.

Kochan, McKersie and Capelli argue that the decisions made by employers, unions and governments at each of the three levels can have effects that are relatively independent. For example, at the macro level an employer decides where to locate its plants; at the employment relationship level it develops a human resources management policy; and at the workplace level it implements individual or group forms of work organization. The emphasis given by the different parties to decisions at various levels tends to change according to circumstances.

The strategic choice model does not dispense with the need for institutional analysis, nor has it been without its critics, who do not accept that strategic choice is a valid concept. Some writers argue that choices made by individual managers or unions are so constrained by their external environment, over which they have little control, that it is not credible to describe the parties as acting 'strategically'. According to Hyman (1987), those who assume that management as a whole has a unified 'strategic choice' are glossing over the complex realities of organizational power. However, the theory has been used to enrich the study of industrial relations by placing greater emphasis than earlier models on the role that is played by employers and managers. **GJB**

References and further reading

Bamber, G. J. and Lansburry, R. D. (eds) (1998) *International and Comparative Employment Relations: A Study of Industrialised Market Economies*, London: Sage/Sydney: Allen and Unwin.

Godard, J. (1997) 'Whither strategic choice: do managerial IR ideologies matter?', *Industrial Relations* 36(2): 206–28.

Hyman, R. (1987) 'Strategy or structure? Capital, labour and control', *Work, Employment and Society* 1(1): 25–53.

Kochan, T. A., Katz, H. C. and McKersie, R. B. (1991) 'Strategic choice and industrial relations theory: an elaboration', *The Future of Industrial Relations: Proceedings of the Second Bargaining Group Conference*, Ithaca, NY: ILR Press.

Kochan, T. A, McKersie, R. and Cappelli, P. (1984) 'Strategic choice and industrial relations theory', *Industrial Relations* 23(1), Winter: 16–39.

Locke, R. M., Kochan, T. A. and Piore, M. (1995) *Employment Relations in a Changing World Economy*, Cambridge, MA: MIT Press.

Locke, R. M., Piore, M. and Kochan, T. A. (1995) 'Reconceptualising comparative industrial relations: lessons from international research', *International Labour Review* 134(2): 139–61.

Thurley, K. and Wood, S. (1983) *Industrial Relations and Management Strategy*, London: Cambridge University Press.

Strategic human resource management

The main characteristic of strategic human resource management (HRM) is its integration with business strategy, the idea being that human resource (HR) policies and practices should support the goals of a business. Academics have proposed different versions of how HRM should fit business strategy which can broadly be divided into best practice and contingency theories.

Taking some examples of contingency theorists first, according to Kochan and Barocci (1985), HR policies should vary according to the stage of the product life-cycle for a business. For example, in terms of staffing, a new business will need to devote much attention to recruitment and selection of new employees, whereas a declining business will be more concerned to implement redundancies and early retirement options. Fombrun, Tichy and Devanna (1984) take a different approach and focus on matching HR policies to the structure of the organization based on the way it generates its products and services. For example, a business with many unrelated products across many subsidiaries and geographic locations will face more complexity in designing reward policies suited to the entire company than a manufacturer producing a single product in a single location. Finally, of the contingency theorists, Schuler and Jackson (1987) base their work on Michael Porter's categorization of business strategies into three basic types of cost minimization, quality and innovation. They argue that a company striving to compete on quality will need to place more emphasis on developing that awareness in employees, perhaps through training, than a company pursuing innovation, which will need to stimulate employees' creativity.

Best practice theorists such as Pfeffer (1994; 1998) and Guest (1987) argue that strategic HRM is composed of a single set of HR policies which will fit all organizations in all circumstances. For Guest, these are the pursuit of quality, innovation and flexibility.

Critics of notions of 'strategic HRM' such as Legge (1995) argue that in practice it exhibits little difference from properly practised personnel management. Furthermore, Purcell and Ahlstrand (1994) question the 'strategic' aspects of HRM since in organizations HR strategies are usually formed in response to business strategies. The debate over whether HRM can become strategic by assuming a proactive role in influencing business decisions rather than a reactive role in responding to them therefore remains unresolved. **AC**

References and further reading

Fombrun, C., Tichy, N. and Devanna, M. (1984) *Strategic Human Resource Management*, New York: Wiley.

Guest, D. (1987) 'Human resource management and industrial relations', *Journal of Management Studies* 24(5): 503–21.

Kochan, K. and Barocci, T. (eds) (1985) *Human Resource Management: Text, Reading and Cases*, Boston, MA: Little, Brown.

Legge, K. (1995) *Human Resource Management: Rhetorics and Realities*, Basingstoke: Macmillan.

Pfeffer, J. (1994) *Competitive Advantage through People: Unleashing the Power of the Workforce*, Boston, MA: Harvard Business School Press.

Pfeffer, J. (1998) *The Human Equation*, Boston, MA: Harvard Business School Press.

Purcell, J. and Ahlstrand, B. (1994) *Human Resource Management in the Multi-Divisional Company*, Oxford: Oxford University Press.

Schuler, R. and Jackson, S. (1987) 'Linking competitive strategies with human resource management practices', *Academy of Management Executive* 1(3): 209–13.

Stress management

Work plays an important role in determining health and well-being. Whilst work can be stimulating and satisfying, it can also be stressful and lead to long-term health problems. Stress has been defined in a variety of ways and is best understood as occurring when the demands made on the individual exceed the resources available in the person or provided by the organization. It is estimated that one in six managers is likely to be absent each year due to stress and one in 13 consult their general practitioner (GP) about stress-related problems.

Under the Health And Safety At Work Act 1974, employers have a duty to ensure that as far as is reasonably practicable that their workplaces are safe and healthy. In 1995, John Walker, a social worker successfully sued his employer for £175 000 when he suffered a second mental breakdown due to excessive workload. This landmark case, (*Walker* v. *Northumberland County Council* 1995) emphasized that organizations need to assess the risk of ill health due to psychosocial, as well as physical hazards in the workplace and highlighted the tough penalties which they might face if they did not meet these responsibilities. Employers are not under any legal duty to prevent ill health caused by stress due to problems outside of work, e.g. financial or domestic matters. But non-work problems can make it hard for people to handle the pressures of their work and their work performance may suffer as a result.

Organizations can seek to reduce stress in three ways. Primary interventions are directed at eliminating or modifying the sources of stress inherent in the working environment. This involves the conduct of some form of diagnostic stress audit or employee survey and then using this information to tailor stress intervention strategies so that they target vulnerable employee groups in an appropriate way. Instruments exist, such as the Occupational Stress Indicator (Cooper, Sloan and

Williams, 1988) which enable companies to benchmark the stress levels and health status against other organizations.

Secondary interventions are directed at increasing awareness, improving the stress resilience of the individual and improving their coping skills to manage stress more effectively. The content of stress management programmes can vary enormously but typically includes training in symptom recognition, basic relaxation methods, time management techniques and cognitive restructuring. Evidence suggests that stress management training can be effective in the short term as reducing the stress–strain relationship, but that the beneficial effects tends to decay over time if action is not taken to address the continuing source of stress itself.

Tertiary interventions are directed at providing remedial help and assistance to those individuals who have suffered or are suffering from stress-related ill health and typically involve employee counselling services.

Stress management activities in the UK tend to be confined to large organizations employing in excess of 500 employees. To be effective an organization needs to develop a stress policy which incorporates all three levels of intervention. **SC**

References and further reading

Cartwright, S. and Cooper, C. L. (1996) *Managing Workplace Stress*, Thousand Oaks, CA and London: Sage.

Cooper, C. L., Liukkonen, P. and Cartwright, S. (1996) *Stress Prevention in the Workplace*: *Assessing the Costs and Benefits to Organizations*, Dublin: European Foundation for the Improvement of Living and Working Conditions.

Cooper, C. L., Sloan, S. and Williams, S. (1988) *The Occupational Stress Indicator*, Windsor: NFER-Nelson.

Kompier, M. and Cooper, C. L. (1999) *Preventing Stress, Improving Productivity*: *European Case Studies in the Workplace*, London and New York: Routledge.

Stretch management

A relatively new approach to performance management, developed in the USA, is the so-called 'stretch management'. Instead of a traditional approach of generating more output by committing more input, corporate America seems to be trying to get more output just by demanding it. Stretch management is being applied in US companies such as Boeing (to drive down costs) and 3M (to improve product innovation). Stretch management involves setting demanding objectives for the organization, the so-called 'stretch' targets. Accounts chronicle its success in achieving major performance improvements in areas such as return of investment, product innovation, productivity and capital utilization. Alcoa, the world's largest aluminium company, provides a good example. Following the appointment of a new chief executive, a large-scale total quality management (TQM) programme was initiated in 1987 and by many standards proved highly successful. However, by 1991 a new strategy emerged due to the chief executive's frustration with the slow pace of TQM. The new strategy demanded intense and focused commitment to 'quantum-leap' rather than continuous improvement management (Kolesar, 1993).

Given its recent introduction it is perhaps too early to write off 'stretch management'. However, its sustainability must be open to question and critics view it simply as one of the latest and most intense forms of 'management by stress'. Indeed, early reports show an especially high casualty rate amongst middle managers, with estimates of between a third and a half of managers being unable to cope. Some companies have now 'softened' their stretch programmes. At General Electric its role is seen as an 'artificial stimulant' for new and more effective ways of working, and employees are not punished for failing to achieve demanding targets. This leads to a particular problem with stretch management: its demotivation potential. The danger is that such a system of performance management which sets truly stretching goals, which employees thus often fail to achieve, results in making high-performing staff feel like losers. In an attempt to get employees to buy into stretch programmes some companies are now linking the achievement of targets to gainsharing programmes. **TR**

References and further reading

Kolesar, P. (1993) 'Vision, values and milestones', *Californian Management Review* 35(3): 133–65.

Seward, G. (1987) 'Revitalizing MBO: the "stretch" dimension', *Management Review* 76(10): 16–19.

Sherman, S. (1995) 'Stretch goals: the dark side of asking for miracles', *Fortune*, November: 231–2.

Tully, S. (1994) 'Stretch targets', *Fortune*, 14 November: 83–90.

Strikes

Strikes are temporary stoppages of work carried out by workers collectively and are usually organized through trade unions. Strikes focus on specific demands, but may sometimes serve as an act of protest. Specific demands may conceal deeper and more complex grievances and discontent. Unlike some countries, there has never been a legal right to strike in Britain. Instead, the 1906 Trades Disputes Act established the principle of trade union immunity from legal action in the event of a strike. In the 1980s and 1990s successive Acts of Parliament have denied such immunity from unions unless they meet a very wide and complex range of requirements when organizing industrial action. The incidence of strikes and other forms of industrial action (e.g. overtime bans and working to rule) has declined very considerably during this period. This has been the case not only in Britain, but also in other countries within which such severe legal restrictions do not apply.

Certainly the legal changes introduced by the Thatcher and Major governments have made industrial action more difficult to organize. Also the ballot requirements may have enabled unions that have secured a ballot in favour of industrial action to win concessions from management without actually implementing the action. However, there is a strong case to say that a more complex set of factors determine the incidence of strike activity (Hyman, 1989; Blyton and Turnbull, 1998: 291–310; Kelly, 1998: 83–107). Important dimensions of strike activity include the number of strikes, their duration, the number of workers involved in them and their incidence in different employment sectors and organizations. It is a mistake to interpret strike activity, however measured, as a simple indicator of the extent of workplace conflict or discontent, since this may be expressed through a wide variety of collective and individual actions. (See also **Picketing**, **Lockouts** and **Industrial conflict**). **DB**

References and further reading

Blyton, P. and Turnbull, P. (1998) *The Dynamics of Employee Relations*, Basingstoke: Macmillan, ch. 10.

Hyman, R. (1989) *Strikes*, 4th edn, London: Macmillan.

Kelly, J. (1998) *Rethinking Industrial Relations*, London: Routledge.

Labour Research Department (1998) *The Law at Work*, London: LRD Publications, ch. 9.

Lyddon, D. (1998) 'Rediscovering the past: recent British strike statistics in historical perspective', *Historical Studies in Industrial Relations* 5: 107–51.

Walsh, J. (1999) 'Minister approves strike action as a *last resort* ', *People Management*, 19 August: 11.

Succession planning

Succession planning refers to the process by which people to fill particular posts in an organization are identified and prepared for it before actually taking it up. This might be on a very individualized basis – that is, one individual is groomed for one particular post, probably a very senior one. Alternatively, succession planning can be a more general activity whereby a large group of individuals are prepared for roles at a certain level in an organization. The number of posts available may be smaller than the number of individuals, which would mean that some element of competition is involved. Sometimes succession planning is carried out without the knowledge of those whose futures are affected by it. This may help to avoid inflated expectations on the part of the chosen and disappointment amongst the unchosen. However, it might be ethically dubious, and it means that people cannot participate in steering their own development.

There has been particular interest in chief executive officer (CEO) succession, especially whether to appoint an insider or an outsider, and whether the new CEO should have a particular functional background. Perhaps predictably, research does not clearly favour one strategy over the other. However, it seems dangerous for staff commitment if insiders are not even considered. It also seems that for many CEOs six or seven years is about the limit before they go 'off the boil' – though there are no doubt exceptions to this, especially those who maintain many external contacts and seek new ideas and directions. In general, the impact of succession planning is likely to be only as good as the techniques used for identifying future organizational needs and individual potential, as well as the strategies for developing individuals. It also needs to be proactive and ongoing, so that sudden departures of key individuals do not have disastrous results. **JA**

References and further reading
Alexander, J. A. and Lee, S. (1996) 'The effects of CEO succession and tenure on failure of rural community hospitals', *Journal of Applied Behavioral Science* 32: 70–88.

Hirsh, W. (1990) *Succession Planning: Current Practices and Future Issues*, Brighton: Institute for Employment Studies.

Kesner, I. F. and Sebora, T. C. (1994) 'Executive succession: past, present and future', *Journal of Management* 20: 327–72.

Sonnenfeld, J. A. and Peiperl, M. (1988) 'Staffing policy as a strategic response: a typology of career systems', *Academy of Management Review* 13: 588–600.

White, M. C., Smith, M. and Barnett, T. (1997) 'CEO succession: overcoming forces of inertia', *Human Relations* 50: 805–28.

Zajac, E. and Westphal, J. D. (1996) 'Who shall succeed? How CEO/board preferences and power affect the choice of new CEOs', *Academy of Management Journal* 39: 64–90.

Suggestion schemes

These are set up by management to encourage the communication of ideas aimed at improving work processes and ultimately organizational effectiveness. Although it is often the case that employees are encouraged to make improvements in the course of their everyday work on an ad hoc basis, suggestion schemes are a more formalized mechanism to invite additional recommendations. It is important to recognize that an effective suggestion procedure will need to be regularly evaluated to ensure it is in line with the strategic and human resource (HR) goals of the organization. Also importantly, such a procedure will not merely invite suggestions, but have four elements or stages:

- Invite suggestions.
- Investigate the feasibility of such suggestions.
- Implement suggestions where possible (and evaluate).
- Recognize and (possibly) reward successful or valuable suggestions.

Some employers incentivize suggestions by offering a financial reward (e.g. for the suggestion of the month, or for *all* serious suggestions) although it is arguable that schemes which are consonant with the HR goal of 'managing culture' will instead focus on recognition or symbolic rewards. The motivation for any suggestions in this case will be intrinsic and evidence of employee's commitment and motivation, though cynics might add that 'symbolic' rewards also have the advantage of being cheaper.

The potential benefits of a well run scheme are obvious. It may lead to improvements in business processes, and cost savings as well as being beneficial to employment relations and organizational culture – where for example greater recognition and two-way communication results in a climate of mutual trust and openness. Such schemes may also be good for an organization's image, and thus attract employees, suppliers and customers. Schemes which fail to actually implement and recognize suggestions (or even to generate suggestions) are likely to be a waste of time and money, and damaging to organizational climate if they are perceived as an example of a management fad or rhetoric. Notable examples of successes in suggestion schemes are a suggestion implemented by Rover to improve fixing of door casings, which saved £380 000 annually, and IBM calculates it saves over £0.5 million annually through its suggestion scheme. **KM**

References and further reading

Beardwell, I. and Holden, L. (1997) *Human Resource Management: A Contemporary Perspective*, London: Pitman, ch 14.

Hyman, J. and Mason, B. (1995) *Managing Employee Involvement and Participation*, London: Sage.

Marchington, M., Goodman, J., Wilkinson, A. and Ackers, P. (1992) *New Developments in Employee Involvement*, London: Employment Department Report.

Marchington, M. and Wilkinson, A. (2000) 'Direct participation', in S. Bach and K. Sisson (eds) *Personnel Management*, Oxford: Blackwell.

Taylorism

Frederick Winslow Taylor and his disciples gave rise to Taylorism, an influential international movement, for example, with impacts ranging from Japanese management practices to industry in communist states. 'Classic' Taylorism revolved around systematic time and motion study, increasing managerial control and the specialisation of work tasks. For Taylor, 'slacking' by workers was the main source of inefficiency. Both labour and management had to be 'guided' in such respects. Thus, he set out to systematize the study of workflow organization by subdividing tasks into their smallest detail to analyse and time them and devise ways to speed up their accomplishment. He studied jobs 'scientifically' and measured workflows to achieve higher productivity. Job techniques could then be redesigned to make maximum use of operatives' skills. A main concept within this was the 'task-idea', based on the principle that management should specify what must be done as individuals would then become more productive and trouble-free.

Taylorism is often used pejoratively and as short hand for capricious management, tight labour control and exploitative employment relations. Taylorism has also been widely criticized:

1. For its individualist assumptions, which gave priority to distinctly individual motivation, rewards and controls in order to break the collective power of work groups.
2. For its time and motion study techniques and financial incentives, which were part of management's definition of what were 'appropriate' workloads and work methods in order to increase managerial control.
3. For its inappropriate 'scientific' label and overly narrow view of work.
4. Its assertion that such practices would create an atmosphere of trust in industry based on a value-neutral approach was dubious and misleading.
5. Its universal, 'one-best-way' approach to management was too simplistic and naive and indeed contradicted by a plethora of examples of varied practices from both within and across sectors and economies. **CR**

References and further reading
Braverman, H. (1974) *Labor and Monopoly Capital: The Degradation of Work in the Twentieth Century*, London: Monthly Review Press.
Kanigel, R. (1997) *The One Best Way: Frederick Winslow Taylor and the Engima of Efficiency*, New York: Viking.

Kelly, J. (1982) *Scientific Management: Job Design and Work Performance*, London: Academic Press.
Merkle, J. A. (1980) *Management and Ideology: The Legacy of the International Scientific Management Movement*, Berkeley, CA: University of California Press.
Prujit, H. D. (1997) *Job Design and Technology: Taylorism vs Anti-Taylorism*, London: Routledge.

Team-based pay

Team-based rewards are payments to members of a formally established team which are linked to the performance of that team. According to 1998 Chartered Institute of Personnel and Development research, around 8 per cent of organizations operate some form of team pay system, still very much a minority although many more were considering introducing some form of scheme. Under such schemes, the payments aim to clarify team goals, encourage group effort and co-operation, and recognize the team achievements. Schemes are often introduced to reinforce the organization's strategy of valuing teams and teamworking.

In a production environment, team targets have, in recent year, been extended beyond the traditional productivity measures to include other important measures such as quality, safety and savings on waste and energy.

The method of payment is most commonly to distribute a cash sum among team members either on an equal basis or according to their salary or grade. The cash sum is calculated either through the achievement of predetermined organizational and team objectives or by reference to defined criteria such as the Sun Life scheme where the sum is calculated from their customer service index.

Important aspects to consider in such schemes are the *size of the teams*, which should be small enough so each team member can feel that they make a genuine contribution; the *team definition*, so that membership is relevant and directly related to the task in hand; ensuring there are *no free-riders* through effective individual and collective feedback; and involving team members in the entire process from job design to systems of team bonuses. **JSk**

References and further reading

Armstrong, M. (2000) *Team-Based Pay*, London: CIPD.
Gross, S. (1995) *Paying Teams*, New York: Hay Publications/Amacom.
Brown, D. (1995) 'Team-based reward plans' *Team Performance Management* 1(1): 23–31.
Harrington, J. (2000) 'Team-based pay', in R. Thorpe and G. Homan (eds) *Strategic Reward Systems*, London: Financial Times Prentice Hall.

Team briefing

In common with issues such as empowerment, involvement and collective bargaining, the subject of team briefing is often subsumed within a larger discussion of participation. However, it may be sensible to extract the discussion of team briefing from the larger discussions of participation because team briefings tend to offer a very limited form of participation where managers attempt to make company information available to workers. A team briefing, therefore, might be regarded as a special kind of meeting where managers speak and workers are expected to listen. Normally these meetings involve a supervisor or line manager and a group of around a dozen employees. In the meeting the supervisor presents a brief to the workers. Typically the brief will contain some general company information (profit figures, market conditions etc), and some other more local matters, which are particularly relevant to the team, such as production targets. Team briefings may last for around 30 minutes, although meetings may be shorter than this.

Team briefings are associated with a range of relatively new management initiatives, such as **total quality management** (see separate entry) which require some degree of worker consent and commitment to be effective. Viewed in these terms team briefings may be regarded as a form of communication operated by line managers, which seeks to cascade information down through the lower levels of the organization. In cascading this information managers hope to increase worker loyalty and commitment to the goals of the organization as a whole.

Team briefings have aroused much controversy in the field of human resource management. For example, some unions have argued that managers use team briefings to reduce trade union voice in the workplace, since they assume a passive role for the workers receiving the briefing. Recognizing this characteristic, some unions in Britain, initially encouraged their members to boycott team briefings. More recently, however, unions in Britain have argued that it is possible to exploit weaknesses in the system of team briefing to foster a more active and two-way exchange between line managers and employees. Recognizing that line managers are often ill-trained and poorly equipped to deal with an assertive audience, unions have encouraged their shop stewards and their members to adopt a more active and critical approach to the briefings presented to them. **DSC**

References and further reading

Beale, D. (1994) *Driven by Nissan? A Critical Guide to New Management Techniques*, London: Lawrence and Wishart.

Cully, M., Woodland, S., O'Reilly, A. and Dix, G. (1999) *Britain at Work*: *As Depicted by the 1998 Workplace Employee Relations Survey*, London: Routledge.

Fucini, J. J. and Fucini, S. (1990) *Working for the Japanese*: *Inside Mazda's American Auto Plant*, Basingstoke: MacMillan.

Grenier, G. J. (1988) *Inhuman Relations*: *Quality Circles and Anti-Unionism in American Industry*, Philadelphia, PA: Temple University Press.

Marchington, M. and Wilkinson, A. (1997) *Core Personnel and Development*, London: Institute of Personnel and Development, Pt 5.

McCabe, D. and Black, J. (2000) ' "Something's gotta give give": trade unions and the road to teamworking', *Employee Relations* 19(2): 110–27.

Team development

The terms 'team development' and 'team-building' are sometimes used as synonyms and sometimes used by some writers to mean different things. Where the latter is the case, the distinguishing characteristic is taken to be the 'age' of the team, i.e. 'development' is what newly established teams experience and 'building' is what long-established teams need. This seems a distinction of limited use and value, though it can have some connections with relevant theory. The basic purpose of team development is to produce greater efficiency and effectiveness in the operation and outputs of groups of employees. The rationale rests on two related sets of assumptions. First, that working in groups, or teams, is somehow a more effective principle than individual working for organization and work design. Second, that it is possible to improve the functioning of such groups, as groups, in such a way that their improved group, or team, functioning will have a positive impact on their work functioning. Methods of team development have a major, though not exclusive, focus on interpersonal behaviour and relationships. The argument, or assumption, is that improving these will bring benefits to the work carried out by the team.

The evidence on the first set of assumptions is ambiguous. It is by no means certain that teams produce better results than individuals working separately and individually. The exception to this is perhaps where certain tasks or objectives can only be achieved by a group of individuals working collectively rather than separately. The analogy of a sports team is often used to illustrate where this is the case. However, while it might be clear that an individual hockey player for example cannot either play or win a match by him or herself, applying this principle in work organizations is more problematic. It is often the case though that individuals in work organizations, both separately and with their direct work colleagues, are subjected to team development activities without full consideration of whether they are, or need to be, a member of a team. The problem of defining the composition of teams in work organizations can be illustrated by a series of television adverts current at the time of writing. Members of staff of the Morrisons supermarket chain appear on screen and say 'My mission is to buy the best wines/produce the cleanest cabinets/ensure the bread is fresh' etc., with the store manager appearing last saying something like 'My mission is to deliver the best value to our customers'. Are these individuals members of the same team in the same way as the hockey player? All of that said, there is clear evidence in the UK that companies are attempting to apply the principle of teams in work design.

The evidence on the second set of assumptions is more clear, though not yet able to fully settle the question. Application of theories such as the well known 'forming, storming, norming, performing' stages of group formation, and more recent work on the role of personality-related preferences for roles adopted in teams, suggest that team functioning can be improved. Studies of these and similar approaches in practice also suggest that improved team functioning brings improvements to work performance. However, recent developments such as networked organizations and virtual teams, with associated decreases in or total lack of face-to-face interaction, present challenges to these established approaches to team development. **JS**

References and further reading

Belbin, M. (1996) *Team Roles at Work*, Oxford: Heinemann.
Belbin, M. (1996) *Management Teams: Why They Succeed or Fail*, Oxford: Heinemann.
Purcell, J. (1999) *People Management Implications of Leaner Ways of Working*, IPD Working Paper no. 15, London: Institute of Personnel and Development.
Stewart, J. (1996) *Managing Change through Training and Development*, 2nd edn, London: Kogan Page.
Walton, J. (1999) *Strategic Human Resource Development*, London: Financial Times Prentice Hall.

Teleworking

Teleworking is an alternative mode of work, enabled by the technological improvements and increase in use of information technology (IT) on one hand, and on the other hand, by an unconventional managerial approach, which takes it that work is what you do, not a place where you go. During the 1950s, the literature on technological new inventions in electronics and communication systems led to the idea that telecommunications, combined with computing technology, could enable work to be relocated away from the traditional office (Jones, 1957–58). Toffler (1980: 212) suggested that the information age 'could shift literally millions of jobs out of the factories and offices into which the Industrial Revolution swept them right back to where they came from originally: the home'. Widespread interest in teleworking started in the 1970s, when it was expected to be the 'next workplace revolution' in the 1980s. Interest continued to grow among employees, employers, transportation planners, communities, the telecommunications industry and many others. Among the reasons for the positive forecast are the qualities of teleworking – a results-based, trust-based mode of work. Technological developments makes it easier and enable more occupations to be performed from locations other than the employer base: apart from home there is the availability of telecommuting cottages and other work centres, as well as mobile work, when the office can be in the car or the suitcase.

By the turn of the twentieth century, the actual level of applying teleworking is low in the industrial states (below 10 per cent) and in many countries much lower. The reasons is perhaps due to Baruch and Nicholson's (1997) claim that there are four factors, all needs to be fulfilled simultaneously before teleworking can become feasible and effective:

1. *The job*: the nature of work and fit of technology for the specific work role.
2. *The organization*: how supportive the business culture is to homeworking arrangements, including the willingness and ability of workplace-based management to trust teleworkers.
3. *The home/work interface*: covering a diverse range of factors from the quality of family relations to the kind of physical space and facilities available.
4. *The individual*: fit of teleworking with personal attitude, values, norms, qualities and needs.

Most of the early writing on teleworking was focused on its innovative and positive influence (or expected impact). Recent views (e.g. Davenport and Pearlson, 1998) provide balanced reports, which open questions about the idea of 'best way' or suitability of teleworking to 'all'. The table below presents the possible benefits and shortcomings of teleworking. **YB**

Table: **Teleworking benefits and shortcomings**

Level	Possible benefits	Possible shortcomings and challenges
Individual	*Improved performance/higher productivity *Less time spent on commuting *Satisfying need for autonomy *Improved quality of working life (e.g. working environment) *Less work-related stress *More time with the family *Could be the only way to work at all (mothers of infants, disabled, etc.)	*Less opportunities for affiliation, detachment from social interactions *Less influence over people and events at workplace *Questionable job security and status *Fewer career development options *Lower 'visibility'/promotability *Work-related use of private space and resources *More home-related stress *Management of work–home interface without time/space buffers *More time with the family
Organizational	*Higher productivity *Wider labour market to draw upon *Space and overheads savings *Less absenteeism *Image of a flexible workplace *Legal requirements	*Control over teleworkers activities and monitoring performance * Control over health and safety *Need of alternative motivation mechanisms *Less committed employees *Loss of teamworking benefits
National	*Less commuting, less pollution, congestion, accidents *Support for local, in particular rural, communities *More people can work *Less discrimination	*The creation of an autistic society (i.e. individuals atomized and isolated from social institutions) *Need to adapt legal system

Source: Barruch (2001)

References and further reading
Baruch, Y. (2001) 'The status of research on teleworking and an agenda for future research', *International Journal of Management Review* 3(2) (in press).
Baruch, Y. and Nicholson, N. (1997) 'Home, sweet work', *Journal of General Management* 23(2): 15–30.
Jones, J. C. (1957–58) 'Automation and design' pts 1–5, *Design* 103, 104, 106, 108 and 110.
Toffler, A. (1980) *The Third Wave*, London: Collins.
Davenport, T. H. and Pearlson, K. (1998) 'Two cheers for the virtual office', *Sloan Management Review* 39(4): 51–65.

Tenure

Tenure is the length of time a person spends in a job. The overall length of tenure for an employer or the economy as a whole is jointly determined with the turnover or separation rate.

Tenure varies from job to job. For low-skilled occupations in which employment tends to be highly sensitive to cyclical changes in the economy, turnover is high and thus tenure low. Moreover, workers can be replaced at fairly low cost. In skilled occupations on the other hand, tenure tends to be higher as it may be difficult for workers with the appropriate skills to be replaced. In particular, where there are high turnover costs due to significant fixed costs of employment, it will be in firms' interests to take steps to retain its employees. These fixed employment costs include the costs of recruitment, selection, and training. In jobs where there is a high degree of firm-specific skills or human capital, tenure will also tend to be greater. These skills are often acquired as a result of experience and will have been gained at a cost to the firm, usually in the form of reduced productivity while they are being developed. Also, being firm specific, they will raise the employees' value only to the employing firm. It is therefore in the firm's interests to take steps to retain employees, reducing turnover and increasing tenure. This effect is closely related to the incentive to create an internal labour market (ILMs) within a firm or organization. Tenure is high in an ILM as employees tend to remain in the same job or with the same employer for many years.

Tenure also depends on workers' mobility. While tenure tends to be longer in highly skilled occupations, it is possible to conceive of situations in which skilled workers are highly mobile. Where they are in considerable demand for example, and the labour market is competitive, competition between employers may entice workers to move employer frequently, thus reducing tenure.

Recent studies suggest that tenure has fallen in the UK. Gregg and Wadsworth (1995) suggest a decline of about 20 per cent in median job tenure from 1975 to 1993. Part of the change is explained by the rise in female employment – women tend to have shorter job durations than men. It is also explained by the increasing number of men who are taking jobs of short-term duration. Thus the proportion of men with tenure of less than two years rose by 12 per cent in the period studied, and the proportion of men with job tenure of over 20 years fell from 19.6 per cent to 13.9 per cent of employees. The effects, however, have been concentrated at the low-skill end of the labour market, giving rise to the view that in the UK the labour market is increasingly becoming segmented into a primary sector of 'good' jobs, and secondary sector of insecure'bad' jobs. **SJ**

References and further reading
Booth, A. L., Francesconi, M. and Garcia-Serrano, C. (1999) 'Job tenure and job mobility in Britain', *Industrial and Labor Relations Review* 53(1): 43–60.
Burgess, S. and Rees, H. (1998) 'A disaggregate analysis of the evolution of job tenure in Britain 1975–1993', *British Journal of Industrial Relations* 36(4): 629–50.
Cockx, B., Van der Linden, B. and Karaa, A. (1998) 'Active labour market policies and job tenure', *Oxford Economic Papers* 50(4): 685–708.

Gregg, P. and Wadsworth, J. (1995) 'A short history of labour turnover, job tenure and job security, 1975–93', *Oxford Review of Economic Policy* 11(1): 73–90.

Neumark, D., Polsky, D. and Hansen, D. (1999) 'Has job stability declined yet? New evidence for the 1990s', *Journal of Labor Economics* 17(4): 29–40.

Theory X and Theory Y

Douglas McGregor extended Maslow's concept of the hierarchy of needs with his suggestion that needs can be facilitated by the leader or manager. This has the advantage of moving content theories of motivation away from their one-sided view that motivation is simply a reflection of the individual's genetic faculties or cultural awareness. McGregor's observations suggested that traditional managers often treated employees like children by failing to consider their ability to influence others. Consequently, they often failed to consider that subordinates had higher order social and self-actualization needs. His research, which was primarily focused on North America, suggested that leadership style was a significant catalyst to motivation. In particular he suggested that participative management can be achieved only if managers recognize their ability to influence. This led him to consider that managers broadly fall into two camps which he called Theory X and Theory Y.

Most managers in the early twentieth century appeared to McGregor to have adopted a Theory X mindset based on short-termist, control-driven management styles which determined their attitudes to subordinates. This mindset caried assumptions that people were, by nature, lazy, untrustworthy, resistant to change and needed to be led. This has been described as a carrot and stick approach which is limited to simplistic behaviours: be good and get rewarded, be bad and get punished.

Managers who practise Theory X tend to use certain limited tactics of control. These include the use of threat and punishment. By contrast, Theory Y managers operate with more optimistic assumptions of human nature. Thus, employees are viewed as having the potential for operating with autonomy, for being creative, for being committed. To quote McGregor (1960: 182): 'The essential task of management is to arrange organizational conditions so that people can achieve the goals best by directing their efforts to ward organizational rewards.'

MacGregor's Theory X and Theory Y is essentially about the way in which attitudes to work are formed through a process of influence that begins with leadership style and its positive impact on subordinates. This has also been referred to as the Pygmalion effect or as the self-fulfilling prophecy by which people can be influenced to achieve higher levels of personal ability (a fact well documented in the educational literature) and operate more effectively in an organizational context.

MacGregor's work echoes the seventeenth-century debates in political philosophy between Thomas Hobbs and John Locke. These debates imply that human nature either, in the Hobbesian view, needs to be controlled through explicit rules and sanctions or, in the Lockian view, was a product of its environment and thus open to change.

One dimension that was not considered effectively by MacGregor was national culture. Further research has revealed that cultural differences exist in management style. For example William Ouchi's investigation of Japanese management style indicates that collectivism characterises Japanese management. This is in contrast with the individualism expected by American organizations.

Ouchi calls this Japanese style theory Z. By contrast to the bureaucratic style of American organizations Japanese organizations carry assumptions and expectations related to:

- long-term employment
- a relatively slow process of a valuation and promotion
- the development of company specific skills

- implicit rather than explicit informal control mechanisms
- participative and consensual decision making
- individual responsibility.

Overall, Japanese environments tend to display a broad concern for the welfare of people rather than the hire and fire attitudes that appear to dominate Anglo-American organizations. **JG**

References and further reading

Khojasteh, M. (1993) 'Motivating the private vs public sector manager', *Public Personnel management* 22(3): 391–402.

McGregor, D. (1960) *The Human Side of Enterprise*, New York: McGraw-Hill.

Ouchi, W. G. (1981) *Theory Z: How American Business can Meet the Japanese Challenge*, Reading, MA: Addison–Wesley.

360° performance appraisal

360° appraisals have recently become an established part of the UK appraisal scene. The origins of 360° appraisal have been credited to the US army in the 1970s. Here military researchers found that peer opinions were more accurate indicators of a soldier's ability than were opinions of superiors. The term '360° appraisal' is used to describe the all-encompassing direction of feedback derived from a composite rating from peers, subordinates, supervisors and occasionally customers. It is normally conducted via an anonymous survey. There is a wide variation in what is appraised in 360° feedback. Many companies use fully structured questionnaires based upon models of managerial competency. Others employ a much less structured approach with appraisers responding to open questions, which ask for descriptions of the appraisee's 'major value-adding areas for the year', summaries of the manager's strengths, descriptions of key improvement needs and a call for other general comments. Unstructured systems of appraisal have advantages in tapping into key aspects of managerial performance. However, the danger of using an unstructured approach is that the popular but incompetent manager may well fare better than one who is highly effective but not particularly pleasant.

The appraisers mostly remain anonymous but some systems leave the option open to the appraiser whether or not to add their name to the appraisal form. It seems that 360° appraisal is now edging away from a management development tool and towards a broader organizational role. Increasingly, and controversially, organizations are also experimenting with linking 360° appraisal and managerial remuneration. Companies such as 3M and British Aerospace have been reported as introducing 360° appraisal and feeding the results into the formula for performance-related pay for managers.

Rather a lot is claimed for 360° appraisal and, as with many new initiatives, we have seen a rash of articles announcing how it can 'change your life' and deliver competitive advantage for the organization. The use of multiple raters with different perspectives, a sort of safety in numbers approach, often leads to the suggestion that it provides more accurate and meaningful feedback. However, here 360° appraisal may simply replace the subjectivity of a single appraiser with the subjectivity of multiple appraisers. 360° appraisal has proved especially useful for providing feedback for senior managers who are often neglected at the top in appraisal terms. However, it remains to be seen whether the benefits gained are outweighed by the considerable time, effort and costs involved. **TR**

References and further reading

Antonioni, D. (1996) 'Designing an effective 360–degree appraisal feedback process', *Organizational Dynamics* 25(2): 24–38.

London, M. and Beatty, R. W. (1993) '360–degree feedback as a competitive advantage', *Human Resource Management*, Summer–Autumn: 353–72.

Peiperl, M. (2001) 'Getting 360 degree feedback right', *Harvard Business Review* 79(1): 142–7.
Thatcher, M. (1996) 'Allowing everyone to have their say', *People Management* 2(6): 28–30.
Waldman, D. A. and Bowen, D. E. (1998) 'The acceptability of 360 degree appraisals: a customer-supplier relationship perspective', *Human Resource Management* 37(2): 117–29.

Total quality management (TQM)

Total quality management is a way of managing or philosophy of management drawing from the work of Crosby (1979), Deming (1986), Feigenbaum (1983), Ishikawa (1985), and Juran (1989). It is seen as an holistic and organization wide approach based on three fundamental principles:

1. *Customer orientation*: quality means meeting customer requirements, customers are both external and internal, and the orientation of quality management is to satisfy customers. This customer orientation provides a common goal for all organizational activities and members.
2. *Process orientation*: the activities performed within an organization can be broken down into basic tasks or processes (transformations of inputs into outputs). Basic processes are linked in series or 'quality chains' to form extended processes. The production process, for example, is modelled as an extended chain of interlinked basic processes. Organizations may be conceptualized as quality chains that cut across conventional internal boundaries such as functional specialisms (Oakland, 1993). In addition, each process in the quality chain has a customer, stretching back from the external customer through the various internal customers to the start of the series. Thus the customer focus identified above is a means of unifying processes as well as determining the objective of organizational activities (Grant, Shan and Krishnan, 1994).
3. *Continuous improvement*: satisfying customer requirements involves the continuous improvement of products and processes. The most effective means of improvement is to use the people who do the job to identify and implement appropriate changes.

These principles are implemented in a specific manner and the mode of implementation is itself one defining feature of TQM. Implementation is by means of appropriate improvement tools (statistical process control methods, process simplification and process re-engineering), measurement systems, (monitoring the cost of quality and customer satisfaction are novel metrics of TQM, in addition to the more traditional measurement of defects or variation) and management and organizational processes, (these include quality improvement or action teams, quality committees, cross-functional planning, self-inspection, exposure of employees to customers, more autonomous work units and collaborative quality improvement with suppliers). Quality planning is a component of strategic corporate management, while policy deployment ensures that quality policies at every level of the organization, right down to the appraisal of individual members of staff, derive from and are congruent with the corporate plan. The new organizational infrastructure is seen as a necessary condition for TQM: it both enables the operation of total quality management and ensures its continued survival (Hill and Wilkinson, 1995).

Total quality management practices have spread widely since the 1980s. The British evidence, is of widespread adoption of TQM practices in a partial fashion (Wilkinson *et al.*, 1998, Yong and Wilkinson, 1999). The difficulty is to know whether the partial state of many cases is due to the time it takes to change fully the way of managing onto TQM lines – estimates of up to seven years for TQM to become fully established in a company are not unusual – or the implementation of schemes that are simply piecemeal and will never develop into full TQM; or, indeed, whether TQM is essentially flawed as a management approach. The American evidence does appear to be more positive and this may explain why some writers have interpreted the reduced headline hype about TQM as a sign that it has been successfully 'normalized' – that is, total quality principles have become the new common sense about work (Greene, 1993). **AW**

References and further reading

Crosby, P.B. (1979) *Quality is Free*, New York: McGraw-Hill.
Deming, W. C. (1986) *Out of the Crisis*, Cambridge, MA: MIT Centre for Advanced Engineering Study.
Feigenbaum, A. (1983) *Total Quality Control*, 3rd edn, New York: McGraw-Hill.
Grant, R. M., Shan, R. and Krishnan, R. (1994) 'TQM's challenge to management theory and practice', *Sloan Management Review*, Winter: 25–35.
Greene, R. (1993) *Global Quality*, Milwaukee, WI: ASQC Quality Press/Homewood, IL: Business One Irwin.
Hill, S. and Wilkinson, A. (1995) 'In search of TQM', *Employee Relations* 17(3): 8–25.
Ishikawa, K. (1985) *What is Total Quality Control? The Japanese Way*, Englewood Cliffs, NJ: Prentice-Hall.
Juran, J. (1989) *Juran on Leadership for Quality*, New York: Free Press.
Oakland, J. (1993) *Total Quality Management*, 2nd edn, London: Heinemann.
Wilkinson, A., Redman, T., Snape, E. and Marchington, M. (1998) *Managing with TQM Theory and Practice*, London: Macmillan.
Yong, J. and Wilkinson, A. (1999) 'The state of total quality management: a review', *International Journal of Human Resource Management*, 10(1): 137–61.

Trade union de-recognition (see also Trade union recognition)

Union de-recognition is defined as a process of excluding trade unions a formal role in collective bargaining and consultation. This has witnessed a marginal increase since the late 1980s. Like union recognition, the scope and depth of de-recognition is variable. At one extreme is the withdrawal of bargaining and representational rights for all workers by management. Other forms of de-recognition exclude unions from negotiation but retain some consultative role, while in other cases de-recognition has been applied to certain sections of a workforce (Gall and McKay, 1994; Claydon, 1996). Marchington and Parker (1990: 217–24) comment on the managerial objectives as 'pushing negotiation down to consultation, and consultation down to communication'.

There are four broad reasons often cited by employers for union de-recognition (Gall and McKay, 1994; Claydon, 1996):

1. De-recognition occurs following company restructuring, merger or acquisition. Management use this process to realign industrial relations practices with new company structures (as in the different BT and water authority businesses following privatization).
2. Union membership and activity within an enterprise declines to such low levels that bargaining and negotiation becomes artificial.
3. Human resource management techniques promote a more individualistic rather than collectivist approach to labour relations. Thus management decide that unionization is no longer part of the organizational culture.
4. De-recognition is opportunistic. Management capitalise on declining union power and influence, and see de-recognition as a cost saving strategy.

The extent of union de-recognition is difficult to gauge. The Warwick University Company Level Industrial Relations Survey (CLIRS) found that 19 per cent of large companies in Britain had de-recognized unions between 1987 and 1990 (Marginson *et al.*, 1993). Most were in the engineering industry, although Claydon (1996) notes a pattern across chemical, publishing, water and financial service industries.

The latest Workplace Employee Relations Survey (WERS) shows that the decline in union membership cannot be explained by the marginal rise in de-recognition. Between 1990 and 1998, new recognition agreements were reported in 4 per cent of workplaces, while de-recognition accounted for 6 per cent of the companies sampled. Furthermore, it is important to note that a number of problems often occur after de-recognition. Line managers have reported increased workloads given the added responsibility for individual communication and consultation post de-recognition. Other issues include shop-floor tension and declining employee attitudes toward management.

Under the Employment Relations Act (1999), there are now legal procedures for de-recognition. An employer may seek to de-recognize a union after a three-year period following a recognition declaration (Lockton, 1999). The Central Arbitration Committee (CAC) of the Advisory, Conciliation and Arbitration Service can invoke a secret ballot to assess whether workers in a bargaining unit would like recognition to cease. The CAC also has the power to proceed with a ballot if it has evidence that at least 10 per cent of employees in a bargaining unit would like to end the bargaining arrangements. **TD**

References and further reading

Bacon, N. (1999) 'Union de-recognition and the new human relations: a steel industry case study', *Work, Employment and Society* 13(1): 1–7.

Cully, M., O'Reilly, A., Millward, N., Forth, J., Woodland, S., Dix, G. and Bryson, A. (1998), *Britain at Work: As Depicted by the 1998 Workplace Employee Relations Survey*, London: Routledge.

Claydon, T. (1996) 'Union de-recognition: a re-examination', in I. Beardwell (ed.) *Contemporary Industrial Relations*, Oxford: Oxford University Press.

Gall, G. and McKay, S. (1994) 'Trade union de-recognition in Britain: 1988–94', *British Journal of Industrial Relations* 32(3): 433–48.

Lockton, D. (1999) *Employment Law*, 3rd edn, London: Macmillan.

Marchington, M. and Parker, P. (1990) *Changing Patterns of Employee Relations*, Hemel Hempstead: Harvester Wheatsheaf.

Marginson, P., Armstrong, P., Edwards, P. and Purcell, J. (1993) 'Decentralisation, collectivism and individualism: evidence from the 1992 CLIRS', paper delivered at the British Universities Industrial Relations Association Annual Conference, University of York, July.

Trade union immunities

Contrary to popular belief, English law has never recognized a legal right to strike. However, recognized trade unions do have certain statutory immunity from prosecution when contemplating industrial action. Legally, the process of immunity is contained in the Trade Union and Labour Relations (Consolidation) Act of 1992, which states:

> An act done by a person in contemplation or furtherance of a trade dispute is not actionable in tort on the ground only:
>
> a) that it induces another person to break a contract or interferes or induces another person to interfere with its performance, or
>
> b) that it consists in his threatening that a contract (whether one to which he is a party or not) will be broken or its performance interfered with, or that he will induce another person to break a contract or interfere with its performance. (Trade Union and Labour Relations [Consolidation] Act, 1992, section 219)

Statutory protection does not grant trade unions or their members complete immunity for all or any criminal act. They can be prosecuted for criminal and civil acts that fall outside the legal definition, such breach of the peace or slander. The test is whether or not a union is acting in 'contemplation or furtherance of a trade dispute', and this has very specific meaning in the same 1992 Act:

A *trade dispute* is defined as:

a dispute between workers and their employer which relates wholly or mainly to one or more of the following:

a) terms and conditions of employment, or the physical conditions in which any workers are required to work

b) engagement or non-engagement, or termination or suspension of employment or the duties of employment, of one or more workers

c) allocation of work or the duties of employment between workers or groups of workers

d) matters of discipline

e) a worker's membership or non-membership of a trade union

f) facilities for officials of trade unions, and

g) machinery for negotiation or consultation, and other procedures, relating to any of the above matters, including the recognition by employers or employers' associations of the right of a trade union to represent workers in such negotiation or consultation in the carrying out of such procedures. (Trade Union and Labour Relations [Consolidation] Act, 1992, section 244[1])

This means that immunity is granted to the trade union (and its members) for action that conforms to the above definition. However, it should be recognized that the procedures and regulations covering industrial action are now extremely complex. Among other things, should a union fail to give an employer seven days' notice of intended action, following a ballot, then they lose the immunity given the requirements contained in the Trade Union Reform and Employment Rights Act 1993 (Lockton, 1999).

The legal position of trade union immunity is steeped in history. Traditionally, trade unions were viewed by the judiciary as criminal conspiracies, such that two or more people acting 'in contemplation' of a dispute would be 'in restraint of trade' and could face criminal (often harsh penal) penalties (Wedderburn, 1986; Whincup, 1991). The 1871 Union Act and the 1875 Conspiracy and Protection of Property Act repealed the criminal conspiracy of trade union action, although civil claims could be made against trade unions for 'inducing their members to break their contract of employment'. It was not until the passing of the Trade Disputes Act 1906 that this constraint was removed (now contained in the Trade Union and Labour Relations (Consolidation) Act 1992. **TD**

References and further reading
Lockton, D. (1999) *Employment Law*, 3rd edn, London: Macmillan.
Wedderburn, W. (1986) *The Worker and the Law*, London: Butterworth.
Whincup, M. (1991) *Modern Employment Law*, 7th edn, London: Butterworth.

Trade union recognition (see also Trade union de-recognition)

Trade union recognition is defined as 'recognition of a union by an employer or employers to any extent for the purpose of collective bargaining' (Employment Protection Act, 1975, c 71, section 11[2]). Prior to 1979 policy-makers believed that union recognition and voluntary collective bargaining was the best way to promote good industrial relations (Dickens and Bain, 1986). The 1971 Industrial Relations Act and the Employment Protection Act 1975 outlined procedures for the process of union recognition. Under these guidelines an independent trade union could refer recognition to the Advisory, Conciliation and Arbitration Service (ACAS), who could investigation and make recommendations to an employer. In practice, however, these procedures were rarely used and carried little legal enforceability (Wedderburn, 1986).

Recent research suggest that around 45 per cent of all workplaces in Britain recognize a union for bargaining over pay and terms and conditions, although there is substantial sector variation (Cully *et al.*, 1998: 92). Only 25 per cent of all private sector organizations recognize a trade union, whereas for the public sector this is 95 per cent. Moreover, union recognition appears to be a function of organizational size. In the latest Workplace Employee Relations Survey (Cully *et al.*, 1999), union recognition ranged from 33 per cent in the smallest workplaces to 76 per cent in the largest. It is also important to note that recognition is variable in both scope and depth (Brown *et al.*, 1998). This means that employers recognize unions for specific activities, such as discipline, grievance or health and safety representation but not necessarily full-blown collective bargaining.

The 1999 Employment Relations Act makes legal provision for statutory trade union recognition. The mechanisms for enforceable recognition are:

1. *Recognition by agreement*: in companies that employ 21 or more workers, an independent trade union can make a request to the employer for recognition. If there is no agreement after 28 days, ACAS can be called in to intervene.
2. *Recognition from an application to ACAS*: the Central Arbitration Committee (CAC) of ACAS assesses the extent to which a 'bargaining unit' exists for the purpose of recognition, should voluntary negotiations fail. The CAC has the responsibility to help both sides reach agreement about the bargaining unit within 28 days of the union's request, and consider whether the trade union has majority support of workers within the defined bargaining unit. If the CAC is satisfied, they can issue a declaration that the union is recognized for those workers. There is no agreed definition of a 'bargaining unit', although it should consistent with existing structures of management, and ideally avoid small fragmented groups of workers within an undertaking.
3. *Recognition ballots*: There are three broad factor which allow the CAC the discretion to conduct a ballot to assess the extent of support for trade union recognition:
   (a) if it thinks this is in the interests of good industrial relations;
   (b) a 'significant number' of employees within a bargaining unit inform the CAC they do not want trade union recognition; and
   (c) there is evidence that leads the CAC to conclude that a 'significant number' of union members do not want the trade union to bargain on their behalf.

The employer is obliged to co-operate with the ballot, and allow the union reasonable access to employees. If at least 40 per cent of those eligible to vote support union recognition, the CAC must issue a declaration that the union is recognized. Ballot costs are distributed evenly between the employer and trade union.

Trade union recognition is peppered with controversy. Earlier legal procedures carried little weight, and were often bypassed by both trade unions and employers as having 'no teeth'. The statutory recognition procedures contained in the Employment Relations Act (1999) have also come under criticism. On one hand, employers prefer the voluntary approach and view the law as impeding further regulation within the labour market. On the other hand, trade unions regard the 40 per cent voting threshold as unworkable. They suggest it will be extremely difficult to achieve recognition for workers in those organizations for which the law was intended, particularly in smaller undertakings where membership is low (or non-existent) and employers are extremely hostile.

Finally, it should be noted that the term 'recognition' is quite important. In law, it is an independent 'recognized' trade union that has rights, such as industrial action immunity, time off without the loss of pay for representatives to carry out union duties, and for shop stewards and health and safety representatives to receive training (Lockton, 1999). **TD**

References and further reading

Brown, W., Deakin, S., Hudson, M., Pratten, C. and Ryan, P. (1998) *The Individualisation of Employment Contracts in Britain*, DTI Research Series No 4, Department of Trade and Industry: London.

Cully, M., O'Reilly, A., Millward, N., Forth, J., Woodland, S., Dix, G. and Bryson, A. (1998) *Britain at Work*: *As Depicted by the 1998 Workplace Employee Relations Survey*, London: Routledge.

Dickens, L. and Bain, G. (1986) 'A duty to bargain? Union recognition and information disclosure', in R. Lewis (ed.), *Labour Law in Britain*, Oxford: Blackwell.

Industrial Relations Law Review (1978) *Grunwick Processing Laboratories* v. *ACAS* [ICR 231], *Industrial Relations Law Review* 38: 143–4.

Lockton, D. (1999) *Employment Law*, 3rd edn, London: Macmillan.

Wedderburn, W. (1986) *The Worker and the Law*, London: Butterworth.

Trade unions

Various definitions of trade unions have been suggested. Labour historians, the Webbs, saw them as *a continuous association of wage-earners for the purpose of maintaining or improving the conditions of their employment* (Webb and Webb, 1902: 1). Trade unions are defined for legal purposes in Section 1 of the 1992 Trade Union and Labour Relations (Consolidation) Act, and are referred to here as temporary or permanent organizations of workers principally concerned with the regulation of relations between their members and employers. Some unions have had wider class and political aims, whilst others have focused more narrowly upon the particular sectional interests of their members. There are many different types of unions in Britain, distinguished particularly by their recruitment strategies. However, collective bargaining has been a common feature of British trade union methods in the twentieth century. Trade union membership in Britain has declined dramatically in the 1980s and 1990s, from more than 13 million in 1979 to approximately 8 million 20 years later, though there is now evidence of a slight increase in membership.

Whilst union membership cannot be simply equated with union power, certainly a number of developments in the 1980s and 1990s have seriously weakened the unions. The collapse of manufacturing, prolonged high unemployment, extensive anti-union legislation and a less sympathetic relationship with the Labour Party have combined to pose very serious and considerable difficulties for the unions. Whether this loss of influence is permanent or temporary, and whether the way forward for unions is through a conciliatory or more militant approach to employers has been widely debated (e.g. Ackers, Smith and Smith, 1996). The predominant view is that the trade union movement in the Britain has been permanently weakened. However, the possibility of a gradual and partial return to full employment cannot be discounted, and with it trade union power and influence could improve significantly. (See also **Shop Steward** and **Trades Union Congress**.) **DB**

References and further reading

Ackers, P., Smith, C. and Smith, P. (eds) (1996) *The New Workplace and Trade Unionism*: *Critical Perspectives on Work and Organizations*, London: Routledge.

Certification Office for Trade Unions and Employers' Associations, *Annual Report of the Certification Officer*, London: Crown copyright.

Kelly, J. (2000) 'Unions in the new millenium', *Labour Research* 89(1): 11–13.

Labour Research Department (2000) 'The story of the unions in 20 minutes', *Labour Research* 89(1): 19–21.

McIlroy, J. (1995) *Trade Unions in Britain Today*, 2nd edn, Manchester: Manchester University Press.

Monks, J. (1998) 'Trade unions, enterprise and the future', in P. Sparrow and M. Marchington (eds) *Human Resource Management: The New Agenda*, London: Financial Times and Pitman.

Webb, S. and Webb, B. (1902) *The History of Trade Unionism*, London: Longmans.

Trades Union Congress (TUC)

The Trades Union Congress, founded in 1868, is essentially a confederation of trade unions, and most unions in Britain are affiliated to it. Its role has been described in terms of four aspects. These are as a regulator and supporter of its affiliated unions, as a provider of services to its affiliates (e.g. trade union education for union representatives), as a representative of union interests to government and other organizations (e.g. the Confederation of British Industry) and as a representative of union interests internationally (e.g. within the context of the European Union) (McIlroy, 1995: 46–7). The TUC holds an annual conference, elects a General Council to make decisions between conferences and establishes policy on a wide range of issues. A fundamental reorganization of the TUC took place at national level with a relaunch in 1994 (Heery, 1998). In attempts to regain some of its former influence, the TUC has focused upon new membership recruitment strategies and partnership concepts, and has recognized the potential of European Union to provide considerable advancement of rights and conditions in the workplace.

In Britain there is one central trade union confederation, in contrast to most countries which have several, based upon political, religious or manual/white-collar divisions. There are difficulties for unions that operate outside the TUC, and those which do so are mostly professional or staff associations and/or have no strike policies. In the 1970s the TUC's influence was considerable, and it contributed significantly to corporatist developments in British industrial relations, particularly through the Social Contract of that period. However, unlike previous post-war Conservative administrations, the Thatcher and Major governments of the 1980s and 1990s refused to recognize the TUC for consultative purposes. Combined with the loose relationship the TUC has with its affiliated unions, and the relatively arms length policy of New Labour towards the unions, these factors have done much to weaken the TUC's influence in recent years. (See also **Trade Unions.**) **DB**

References and further reading

Heery, E. (1998) 'The relaunch of the Trades Union Congress', *British Journal of Industrial Relations* 36(3): 339–60.

Labour Research Department (1999) 'Government backs TUC policy on partnership', *Labour Research* 88(7): 7.

Martin, R. (1980) *TUC: The Growth of a Pressure Group 1868–1976*, London: Clarendon Press.

McIlroy, J. (1995) *Trade Unions in Britain Today*, 2nd edn., Manchester: Manchester University Press.

McIlroy, J. (2000) 'The new politics of pressure: the Trades Union Congress and new Labour in government, *Industrial Relations Journal* 31(1): 2–16.

Trades Union Congress web site at http://www.tuc.org.uk

Training agreements

The question of who pays for the training of Britain's workforce is a regular topic of debate amongst academics, politicians and managers. Despite evidence suggesting that investment in training is associated with lower labour turnover, surveys of employers have indicated that the fear of poaching limits their expenditure on training. Consequently there are a wide variety of legal devices created by employers in their attempt to prevent poaching of key staff. Training agreements, however, focus specifically on the organization's investment in training, securing either the employee's continued service or a return of their training expenditure.

The training agreement is a legal instrument conceived by employers to establish the conditions under which they will be prepared to fund the training and development of an employee. Such agreements, normally only applied to training which leads to a recognized qualification, commit the employee to a defined period of employment in return for funding support. They impose a financial penalty on the employee's termination of employment within that defined period. Many also require the employee to successfully complete the training, imposing a penalty for voluntary withdrawal from the course or failure to gain the final qualification. Typically the amount of repayment is on a sliding scale, reducing from 100 per cent repayment on completion to 50 per cent after one year. This reducing scale is advisable as an overzealous penalty clause may be considered an unreasonable restraint of trade and consequently render the agreement unenforceable.

The rationale for the training agreement is somewhat complex. The expressed intention is to secure the investment in training, either by retaining the employee or by recovering the initial costs. However employers report that the most significant benefit is deterring the ill-conceived application for funding (Story and Redman, 1997). A requirement to sign an agreement provides a hurdle to test the employee's resolve and commitment both to the programme of study and to the organization. The agreement appears unlikely to impact on employee retention, although it does facilitate cost recovery. From the employee perspective, however, the key significance of signing an agreement is that it motivates them to complete their programme of study. Training agreements do little to improve, and may negatively affect an employee's commitment to the organization (Story and Redman, 1997). Organizations need to ensure that the terms of any training agreement represent an equitable exchange to reduce the possibility of creating employee resentment. **AS**

References and further reading
Redman, T. and Story, A. (2000) 'Training agreements and failure rates in university provided management development courses', *Human Resource Development International* 3(1): 101–7.
Story, A. and Redman, T. (1997) 'Training agreements: resolving under-investment in training?', *International Journal of Training and Development* 1(3): 1–17.

Training and development

Training and development may be seen as a form of management development which is primarily skills and current job related. The term 'management training development' (MTD) is often used to overcome semantic difficulties in differentiation. However, there is a fine line between 'training' (focused on learning activities to develop a skill) and 'development' (a broader interpretation of learning activity which explores the value of learning to the employee and the organization. It may not be a specific skill/education related activity but more about attitude). (See also **Management development**.) **ASm**

References and further reading
Hayes, J. and Allenson, C. W. (1996) 'The implications of learning styles for training and development: a discussion of the matching hypothesis', *British Journal of Management* 7(1): 63–74.
Patching, K. (1999) *Management and Organisation Development*, London: Macmillan.
Riding, R. and Mortimer, J. (2000) 'A study of the on-the-job training of production line operatives in manufacturing companies', *Internet Journal of Training and Development* 4(2): 111–23.

Training and Enterprise Councils (TECs)

The White Paper, 'Employment for the 1990s', proposed the establishment of TECs in England and Wales and Local Enterprise Councils (LECs) in Scotland. Training and Enterprise Councils were established to promote education, training and enterprise within the local context of economic and industrial development. Eighty-two TECs were created in England and Wales by the early 1990s to meet the needs of specific geographic areas. They were based on five principles:

- a locally based system
- an employer led partnership
- a focused approach
- an accent on performance
- an enterprise organization.

Funded by the government as independent companies, TECs are run by a board of directors comprising business and community leaders from the private sector, trade unions, education, the public sector, economic development and voluntary organizations. Training and Enterprise Councils aims are to provide the country with a skilled and enterprising workforce to develop growth and prosperity. Their priorities are concerned with meeting government targets for foundation and lifetime learning, reducing unemployment through skill development, stimulating education and training opportunities to meet the education targets and encouraging enterprise, particularly amongst small business and the self-employed. They promote a number of initiatives in support of the priorities above. Examples of initiatives are Investors in People, National Vocational Qualifications, Skills for Small Businesses.

Each TEC determines whether or not to bid for funds to take these initiatives forward, as priorities will vary from region to region. This can be confusing for the customer seeking, for example, funding support for a training programme as some TECs will support the programme while others will not. Amounts of funding awarded will also vary both from area to area and, within the same TEC, from year to year. It has also been a criticism that, being target led, the TECs may not always be as focused upon the needs of the local market as would be beneficial. Reform of the support systems to small and medium-sized enterprises (SMEs) is under way with the formation of the Small Business Service. Funding which currently goes through TECs is likely, in the future, to be managed by Learning Skills Councils which will have responsibility for meeting national targets. **AS**

References and further reading

Boocock, J. G., Loan-Clarke, J., Smith, A. J. and Whittaker, J. (1999) 'Management training and development in small and medium-sized enterprises: an assessment of the effectiveness of Training and Enterprise Councils in the East Midlands', *Small Business and Enterprise Development* 6(2): 178–90.

Jones, M. (1996) 'TEC policy failure: evidence from the baseline studies', *Regional Studies* 30(5): 509–32.

Jones, M. R. (1995) 'Training and Enterprise Councils: a continued search for local flexibility', *Regional Studies* 29: 577–80.

Rolfe, H., Bryson, A. and Metcalf, H. (1996) *The Effectiveness of TECs in Achieving Jobs and Qualifications for Disadvantaged Groups*, London: HMSO.

Vickerstaffe, S. and Parker, K. (1995) 'Helping small firms: the contribution of TECs and LECs', *International Small Business Journal* 13(4): 56–72.

Training audits

A training and development (T&D) audit provides a snapshot of T&D activity at a particular point in time. Evidence is gained from historical and current data, drawn typically from a lateral slice through an organization's functional areas and a vertical slice within each area. This enables identification of critical outcomes and trends throughout the organization. Comparisons with good practice indices provide the basis for future T&D planning and continuous improvement.

In the larger organization, a small audit team of internal and external personnel can offer an effective mix of expertise, knowledge and credibility. In the smaller enterprise, only one or two people should be needed. The immediate outcome of an audit should be a report concluding with recommendations to improve the present position. The report should also identify any gaps in existing information that require further research in order to determine appropriate action.

Every audit has its own focus and framework. The US-based Baldrige National Quality Award is concerned with quality in the business. It uses five criteria, or standards, in relation to human resource management and development, with performance indicators attached to each. The European Foundation for Quality Management's 'Business Excellence' model uses nine criteria. The Investors in People standard provides the most familiar audit framework in this country for assessing links between T&D and the business. It uses 12 criteria, each with performance indicators. Any audit should have a clear explanation of its focus and framework – if it has not, user beware!

Complete objectivity in auditing is impossible. All analysis depends on the exercise of human judgement, and all performance measures have subjective aspects. In their search for accuracy auditors must strike a sensible balance between gathering information on critical measures, achieving cost-efficiency, and maintaining an overall focus on continuous improvement of T&D. Saturation by information will tend to follow any attempt that involves too many measures, and/or a protracted search for too many data.

Another warning note: T&D activity is organized in different ways from one enterprise to another, its goals vary from one organization to the next and it operates in a wide range of cultural and business scenarios. Audit terminology and performance indicators must therefore fit their context and auditors must take key variables fully into account when choosing data sources, collecting and analysing data, and making recommendations. **RH**

References and further reading

Applegarth, M. (1991) *How to Take a Training Audit*, London: Kogan Page.

Fombrun, C. J., Devanna, M. A. and Tichy, N. M. (1984) 'The human resource management audit', in C. J. Fombrun., N. M. Tichy and M. A. Devanna (eds) *Strategic Human Resource Management*, New York: Wiley.

Harrison, R. (1999) *The Training and Development Audit: An Eight-Step Audit to Measure, Assess and Enhance the Performance of your Organisation's Training and Development*, Cambridge: Cambridge Strategy Publications.

Training credits

In member states of the European Union, the funding arrangements and systems are being scrutinized to find the most appropriate and cost effective ways to train and develop people for employment. Generally, financial funding for initial vocational training and opportunities for training and development for unemployed people, are guaranteed by the various governments within the member states. However, continuing training for those already in employment and the up-skilling of employees raises concerns of equity and accessibility of those who may wish to become more employment 'marketable' or who may have to acquire new skills or knowledge as a result of their jobs becoming redundant.

Within the UK, the introduction of training credits and vouchers was an approach to guarantee the training and development of young people entering the job market.

Training credits was also viewed as a way to encourage employers to employ, train and develop young people especially in areas of high unemployment. At the time a phenomenon occurred in some geographical areas of the UK: although there was high unemployment there were also considerable job vacancies because insufficient numbers of people had the necessary skills to be able to do the jobs available.

Training credits for young people were introduced in selected geographical areas of the UK in April 1991. The government's aims of the training credit scheme were to 'empower young people and increase their motivation, expand the number of young people in training and establish an efficient training market' (DfEE, 1991: 9). In 1993 the critical assessment and report of the first year pilot of training credits illustrated that only half of the young people who were eligible, actually took up training credits and that there was no evidence to suggest that the numbers and levels of qualifications have been raised.

It is important to remember that training credits are contributions towards the total cost of training; in most circumstances, the real cost of the training and development of the young person is substantially higher than the credit given. One of the criticisms of the scheme is that although young people should negotiate with their prospective employer about what training and development is to be provided, after employment commences, many young people are faced with no other option other than to accept the job that is offered. (This depends, of course, on the location/ region and economic conditions of the community in which the young person resides because of the fluctuation market/economic conditions).

There is no evidence to suggest that training credits have overcome the problems associated with young people getting a choice of jobs and training but reports from different areas of the UK do not give a universal picture of the benefits available to them. One aspect that has influenced the statistics is that more young people have opted to stay within the education system and are staying on either at school or college.

In some areas the advice given to young people has not been entirely appropriate. For example, there is evidence that young people have been advised to look for jobs in occupational areas where there is more chance of getting employment or training. This has led to young people been channelled into unsuitable types of work and training.

On the other hand, many organizations have used the training credits in positive ways to help young people gain employment. Tesco's is one such example where training is provided that leads to specific retail qualifications, mostly retail National Vocational Qualifications. The company has gone to great lengths to advertise their training and development opportunities for young people and, since the introduction of Individual Learning Accounts, have extended their training and development schemes to other adults. Tesco's training and development has been most successful especially in certain locations where shortage of suitable staff has exceeded Tesco's demand for labour. There are regional variations of course. **SR**

References and further reading
Atack, W. (1997) 'Tesco experiments with training credits', *IRS Employment Review: Employee Development Bulletin* 626, February: 7–9.
Department for Education and Employment (DfEE) (1991) *Directory March 1991, a Report on the First 12 Months: Upskilling of the Workforce*, Sheffield: DfEE.
Howard, M. (1993) 'Training Credits', *International Journal of Manpower* 12(4): 20–38.

Training needs analysis (TNA)

Training can be a wasteful and expensive activity if not carefully planned in line with organizational objectives and individual trainee needs. Therefore, organizations seeking to introduce training programmes need to consider their own requirements, the skills, knowledge and attitudes of the employee stock and appropriate means of closing any gaps identified. Training needs may be identifiable as corrections to a problem, i.e. a difference between what does happen and what should. Alternatively, needs may be more developmental and provide opportunity to explore new ideas in line with strategy.

The classic approach to TNA involves job analysis and definition, the establishment of performance standards, assessment of performance against the standards and identification of gaps. This systematic 'survey' approach is suitable particularly for the identification of skills training needs but may be insufficiently broad and too prescriptive for less tangible and obvious requirements involved, for example, in a culture change programme.

Ideally, training should result from a clear understanding of business objectives and a formal training needs analysis exercise might well start with a review of the business plan and discussions with senior management before moving on to discussions with potential trainees. It is this approach which the Investors in People (IIP) is seeking to develop as standard procedure within organizations. A proactive training department should work closely with senior management to ensure it tailors provision to changing requirements, rather than simply maintaining a suite of courses. 'Training', in the traditional sense, may not always be the solution to the issue.

In organizations without training departments, responsibility for training tends to lie with line management. Here, a proactive and developmental approach to performance management, including appraisal should help determine training needs. **ASm**

References and further reading

Bartram, S. and Gibson, B. (1994) *TNA: A Resource for Identifying Training Needs, Selecting Training Strategies and Developing Training Plans*, Aldershot: Gower.
Boydell, T. H. (1983) *A Guide to the Identification of Training Needs*, London: BACIE.
Kubr, M. and Prokopenko, J. (1989) *Diagnosing Management Training and Development Needs: Concepts and Techniques*, Geneva: International Labour Office.
Peterson, R. (1992) *Training Needs Analysis in the Workplace*, London: Kogan Page.
Robinson, D. G. and Robinson, J. C. (1989) *Training for Impact: How to Link Training to Business Needs and Measure the Results*, London: Jossey-Bass.
Truelove, S. (1997) *Training in Practice*, Oxford: Blackwell.

TUPE

This well-known acronym represents the Transfer of Undertakings (Protection of Employment) Regulations 1981 which were passed to implement the Acquired Rights Directive (77/187). The Directive was intended to ensure that the rights of employees were safeguarded when their employment was transferred from one employer to another. TUPE attempted to do this but not very successfully – as a result the Regulations have been amended because of complaints to the European Court that it did fully implement the Directive.

TUPE is the subject of numerous court cases, many of which are concerned with the application of the regulations to a particular set of circumstances. Before a transfer occurs good practice would dictate that legal advice is sought as to whether the transfer comes within TUPE. Unfortunately, because of the flexibility of interpretation of both TUPE and the Directive it is not always possible to give a certain answer. Specialist lawyers attempt to keep up to date with this very fast-moving area of law but new cases are heard every month which slighly shift the law in a different direction.

There must be consultation with employee representatives on the consequences of any proposed transfer and TUPE aims to put the transferee employer, as far as possible, in the same position as the transferor, so that all employment rights of the employees are transferred. This means that normally an employee cannot be dismissed because of a transfer, but there is the powerful defence of 'economic, technical or organisational reasons' (Regulation 8[1]).

The Acquired Rights Directive was amended in 2000 and TUPE will need to be amended again in 2001 to reflect these changes. One of the most significant changes is that liability for occupational pensions will also transfer to the transferee. **AB**

References and further reading
Hammond Suddards Edge (2000) *Transfer of Undertakings*, Legal Essentials Series, London: CIPD.
Web site at http://www2.dti.gov.uk/access/pl699/intro.htm

U

Unfair dismissal

The right not be unfairly dismissed is available to employees with one year's continuous employment at the 'effective date of termination'. The statutory provisions relating to unfair dismissal are set out in the Employment Rights Act and comprise three basic elements. First, there must be a *dismissal*, defined in section 95 of the Act as:

i)   termination by the employer, with or without notice;
ii) expiry of a fixed term contract without its being renewed;
iii) termination by the *employee* caused by conduct on the part of the employer (amounting to breach of a fundamental term of the contract of employment, either express or implied) which entitles the employee to resign – so-called 'constructive dismissal'.

If the employer does not admit that there has been a dismissal, it must be proved by the employee.

Section 98 of the Act then requires the employer to establish the reason for dismissal and lays down 'potentially fair' reasons relating to:

* capability (including ill health)
* conduct
* redundancy
* statutory prohibition, e.g. a driver loses his or her driving licence
* some other substantial reason of a kind to justify dismissal, e.g. refusal to go along with a business reorganization.

However, whilst it is not usually problematic for an employer to show a potentially fair reason, a dismissal will only be fair if in the circumstances the employer *acts reasonably* in treating this as a sufficient reason for dismissal. The question of reasonableness generally revolves around such issues as following a fair disciplinary procedure and investigating adequately in cases of misconduct; consultation, warning and fair selection in cases of redundancy; and determining accurately the medical situation as well as considering alternative jobs in the case of ill health dismissals.

No question of 'reasonableness' arises, and no qualifying period is required, if dismissal is for an automatically unfair reason such as:

- pregnancy and/or maternity
- trade union reasons
- 'whistleblowing' (Public Interest Disclosure Act 1998)
- asserting a statutory right
- raising health and safety issues
- refusal to work in contravention of the Working Time Regulations 1998.

Although the legislation provides for unfairly dismissed employees to be reinstated or re-engaged, in practice they are almost invariably awarded compensation. This normally comprises a basic award of up to £6300 and a compensatory award of up to £50000, although where dismissal is for whistleblowing or raising health and safety issues, the compensatory award has no ceiling. **JE**

References and further reading

Employment Rights Act 1996, London: HMSO.
Haddon v. *Van den Bergh Foods Ltd* [1999] IRLR 672.
Pitt, G. (1997) *Employment Law*, 3rd edn, London: Sweet and Maxwell, ch. 8.
Polkey v. *AE Dayton Services Ltd* [1987] IRLR 503.
Western Excavating v. *Sharp* [1978] ICR 221.

Unitarism

'Unitarism' was a termed coined by Alan Fox in 1966 to describe a particular management 'frame of reference' or perspective on the management of employees. This view sees the business organization as a team united by shared interests and values, with senior management as the sole source of authority and focus of loyalty. Such an approach has a problem comprehending structural conflict at work, for example, strikes or opposition to change. Expecting harmony between management and workers, it sees conflict as irrational and unnecessary. Unitarists tend to characterize 'trouble' of this sort in one of two ways. The first is to see it as the work of agitators or ringleaders who, to use a biological metaphor, have infected a healthy organism with an outside virus. Thus, Australians have often blamed strikes on the malign influence of British immigrants or 'winging poms', while in Britain during the 1970s, Communist shop stewards, like 'Red Robbo' at the Longbridge car factory, were seen as the cause of bad industrial relations. The logic of this position is a tough 'macho management' to weed out troublemakers. A second, more self-critical approach is to see conflict as a product of misunderstanding and bad management communications. This thinking has been the impetus behind many employee involvement initiatives during the 1980s and 1990s.

Fox argues that 'frames of reference' are of great practical import, since they influence management policy. In the case of unitarism, one consequence is a hostility to trade unions, as independent representative organizations for employees. Unions are regarded as opposition groups or factions, cutting across authority lines and as outside bodies interfering in the family relationship between management and their employees, and throwing up rival leaders to challenge management authority. For Fox and most other industrial relations writers, unitarism was a 'straw man', to stand for was an unrealistic, managerial view of the business organization, as compared to **pluralism** (see separate entry). In the 1980s, however, the scarecrow came to life, through the influence of US popular management thinking on excellence and human resource management. This more sophisticated neo-unitarism, cast managers as charismatic leaders who used employee involvement to win employee commitment. This tide has ebbed lately, and **social partnership** (see separate entry) seeks to blend pluralist and unitarist themes. **PA**

References and further reading

Ackers, P. (1994) 'Back to basics? Industrial relations and the enterprise culture', *Employee Relations* 16(8): 32–47.

Fox, A. (1966) 'Industrial sociology and industrial relations', *Royal Commission on Trade Unions and Employers Associations, Research Paper* 3, London: HMSO.

Guest, D. (1992) 'Right enough to be dangerously wrong: an analysis of the In search of Excellence phenomenon', in G. Salaman (eds), *Human Resource Strategies*, London: Sage.

Guest, D. (1995) 'Human resource management, trade unions and industrial relations', in J. Storey (ed.) *Human Resource Management: A Critical Text*, London: Routledge.

Marchington, M., Wilkinson, A., Goodman, J. and Ackers, P. (1992) *New Developments in Employee Involvement*, Employment Department Research Paper, Series no. 2.

Provis, C. (1996) 'Unitarism, pluralism, interests and values', *British Journal of Industrial Relations* 34(4), December: 473–95.

Upward appraisal

Upward appraisal is a relatively recent addition to performance appraisal practice in the UK. Although still far from common, the 1990s have witnessed the introduction of upward appraisal in range of UK companies. Upward appraisal is more common in the USA and appears to have spread from US parent companies to their UK operations. Upward appraisal involves the employee rating their manager's performance via, in most cases, an anonymous questionnaire. The process is anonymous to overcome employees' worries about providing honest but unfavourable feedback on managerial performance. Anonymity limits the potential for managerial retribution or what is termed the 'get even' factor of upward appraisal.

Advocates claim significant benefits for upward appraisal including improved managerial effectiveness and leadership through 'make your better feedback' and increased employee voice and empowerment. Equally, upward appraisal is seen as being more in tune with the delayered organization where managerial spans of control are greater and working arrangements much more diverse. In such situations employees are in much greater contact with their manager than the manager's manager and thus traditional top-down boss appraisal is seen as being less effective. Upward appraisal, because of the use of multiple raters, is also seen as being more robust to legal challenge of performance judgements. Given the increasingly litigious culture in the UK, it is surprising that performance appraisal methods and the systems in which they are embedded are not attacked in the courts more often.

Managers have been reported as not being especially fond of upward appraisal systems. In part this may stem form the career threatening use of upward appraisal schemes in some organizations. For example, one of BP Exploration's objectives in introducing upward appraisal was to return to individual contribution roles those managers 'clearly not cut out to manage people'. Often it appears to the manager on the receiving end of upward appraisal that, according to Grint (1993: 65) '"the honest opinions" of subordinates look more like the barbs on a whale harpoon than gentle and constructive nudges'. Such a lack of managerial acceptance of upward appraisal, especially at middle and junior levels of management, may go some way to explaining its relatively low uptake in the UK after a flurry of activity in the early 1990s. **TR**

References and further reading

Brajkovich, L. F. (1995) 'How truthful should you be when evaluating your boss?', *Academy of Management Executive* 9(4): 89–91.

Grint, K. (1993) 'What's wrong with performance appraisals? A critique and a suggestion', *Human Resource Management* 3(3): 61–77.

Redman, T. and Mathews, B. (1995) 'Do corporate turkeys vote for Christmas? Managers' attitudes towards upward appraisal', *Personnel Review* 24(7): 13–24.

Redman, T. and Snape, E. (1992) 'Upward and onward: can staff appraise their managers?', *Personnel Review* 21(7): 32–46.

Vision

Creating a vision is one of the most important aspect to of managing change. A vision should provide the purpose and reason for change by describing the desired future state the organization needs to take. The vision should energize commitment to change by providing a compelling rationale that seeks to direct effort. This effort should provide the organization's members with a felt need to change. However, if the vision is seen to be unrealistic it will itself become a barrier to change and will be counter-productive. A critical feature of creating a vision is its power to motivate. A much cited example in the political sphere is John F. Kennedy's vision to put a the man on the moon and return him safely to the earth by 1970. In the 1960s this vision provided both a major technical challenge to engineers and a valued change in direction to American aerospace policy.

It is generally argued that creating an effective vision is the first critical element of leadership. This is because the vision represents transformational leadership by mobilising direction through strategy.

In addition to strategic direction a vision often represents a ideals and values. Creating a vision is therefore a creative act and should involve intuitive thought processes that may even conflict and challenge existing ideas and practices. Consequently, a vision statement may include a mission or means to achive the vision, valued descriptions of the desired future which may include both performance criteria and social (cognitive, behavioural, values driven) outcomes.

In constructing such a process senior leaders may need to create special conditions for describing a desired future state by creating offside workshops or exercises that stimulate creative thinking. Although the vision statement may be detailed, it does not generally specify how the changes will occur. These details are part of the subsequent activity planning that occurs in managing the transition towards the desired future state.

Creating an efficient vision is sometimes referred to as strategic thinking. This is a process by which an organization's direction-givers cannot rise above the daily managerial processors and crises to gain different perspectives of the internal and external dynamics causing a change in their environment, and thereby cannot give more effective direction to the organization.

When management development seeks to develop strategic thinkers it is attempting to create innovative entrepreneurs. Strategic thinkers challenge conventional wisdom, and the processes often referred to as a lateral thinking.

The process of visualization is sometimes referred to as the conceptual map. This requires a holistic and methodical attitude involving key skills of:

- strategy formulation
- providing direction or orientation to others
- identifying best choices through decision techniques
- gathering information
- being creative with ideas
- identifying causal relationships
- planning the strategy
- selling the idea to others
- learning from the experience. **JG**

References and further reading

Argenti, J. (1993) *Your Organization: What Is It For?*, London: McGraw Hill.

Cummings, T. G. and Worley, C. G. (1997) *Organisational Development and Change*, Cincinnati, OH: South Western College Publishing.

Fowles, R. (1999) 'Creating a shared vision', *Total Quality Management*, July: 548–60.

Garratt, B. (1994) *Developing Strategic Thought*, London: McGraw-Hill.

Whistleblowing

This popular term is not found in any legislation but is used to describe giving information about an employer's workplace or activities to a third party, usually to prevent unlawful practices. An example that led to the law being amended was the abuse of children while in the care of social services.

There is a duty of confidentiality assumed in every employment relationship so that the general rule is that no information which could be regarded as confidential should be disclosed to an unauthorized person. There are certain exceptions, e.g. in relation to safety, but it is possible for an employer can obtain a court order to discover who has been leaking unauthorized information if it is published in the press.

Against the right of the employer to expect confidentiality to be maintained must be set the right of the public which requires to be informed of malpractice. This delicate balance was struck by the detailed wording of the Public Interest Disclosure Act 1998. This gives legal protection to workers in certain circumstances against dismissal or suffering a detriment if they make a disclosure in accordance with the Act. The Act lists the different types of protected disclosure e.g. a criminal offence has been, or is likely to be committed, and also prescribes a process which must be followed before the protection operates. The assumption is that the disclosure should be made in good faith to the employer or person whose conduct is of concern unless the worker believes that he or she will be subjected to a detriment as a result. The employer may prescribe some other person to whom the worker should make disclosure. Only if there is no such prescribed person is the worker entitled to disclose to some other body or person, e.g. a trade union or the media. **AB**

References and further reading

Industrial Relations Service (IRS) (2000) 'Whistleblowing: the early view from the tribunals', *IRS Industrial Relations Law Bulletin* 648, September.

Lewis, D. (1997) Whistleblowing at work: ingredients for an effective procedure, *Human Resource Management Journal* 7(4): 5–11.

Public Concern at Work (1996) *Whistleblowing, Fraud and the European Union*, London: Public Concern at Work.

Web site at *http://www2.dti.gov.uk/er/individual/pidguide-pl502.htm*

Work-based learning

There are different interpretations of what work-based learning actually means in practice. For example, there are suggestions and indeed much literature on experience at work, which does not separate this from learning at work as an ongoing process. Therefore it is important to illustrate that experience at work is generally associated with providing work experience for young people, either whilst they are still in full-time education or when they embark on a programme of learning at a college or university.

Work experience and work-based learning

The provisions that are made for young people to gain work experience is well documented and there are many organizations, of whatever employee numbers, who take on young people to gain this valuable experience from which they can identify some areas of interest for future employment prospects.

Work-based learning is also providing work experience but offers the opportunity to develop skills and knowledge that enables people to acquire a different set or level of skill and additional knowledge. In acquiring different skills and knowledge, people become more flexible regarding their employment prospects and, most importantly, develop as independent learners.

Important changes are taking place within organizations in the delivery of training and development, which substantiates the increasing emphasis on the workplace as a source of learning. This is manifest in a number of ways, one of which is the decline in the number of attendees at formal training and development courses. In many companies that have been researched, a formal off the job course is now being considered as the last option.

The concept of 'Sitting by Nellie', where the new employee sits and observes the trained and experienced worker, leaves the new employee to pick up the job skills as and when they can. This method is now being considered as a less expensive and more valuable way of training and developing new employees to the job role, irrespective of whether they are new to the company or transferred to a new job.

Job shadowing is a variation on how people can learn from work, although the greatest disadvantage here is that the learner is not 'allowed' to participate and merely observes the experienced person perform the job role. This can lead to boredom and disinterestedness and is therefore not as valuable as one where the learner can perform part(s) of the actual job role. In some professions, job shadowing is the only option because of the risks involved. For example, the medical profession or pilot training, though of course at certain stages of the learning process, these trainees also have the opportunity to perform the actual job role, under strict supervision.

Attachments to a particular department or job holder is becoming a popular method of developing managers, either as first-line managers or senior managers to director level. In a large number of the organizations surveyed, this method is used in preference to the more expensive off-the-job management development programmes. Suck skills and abilities being developed in this way include negotiation, persuasion, leadership and team-building. Depending on the size and type of organization, mentors are part of this work-based programme of learning.

The most pervasive manifestations for using work-based learning are the cost-reduction concerns of most organizations and the devolution of responsibility for training and development to line managers, though in some companies there is immense resistance. There is still the mindset that if one does not attend an expensive off-the-job course, then one has not been trained or developed. This is prevalent in some of the blue chip companies where there is still a bias towards the more formal management development and succession planning programmes. **SR**

References and further reading
Evans, K., Hodkinson, P. and Keep, E. (1997) *Working to Learn: A Work-Based Route to Learning for Young People*, London: Institute of Personnel and Development, pp. 55–6.
Felstead, A., Ashton, D. and Raper, P. (1997) 'Toward the learning organization? Explaining current trends in training practice in the UK', *International Journal of Training and Development* 1(1) March: 9–21.
Payne, J., Lissenbutgh, S. and Payne, C. (1999) 'Work-based training and job prospects for the unemployed: an evaluation of training for work', *Labour Market Trends* 107(7), July: 355–61.
Raelin, J. A. (2000) *Work-based Learning: The New Frontier of Management Development*, Reading, MA: Addison-Wesley.

Working time

Hours of work were not subject to any regulation in Britain until the Working Time Directive (93/104) was implemented by the Working Time Regulations 1998, as amended. The regulations govern not just working hours but also holidays and rest periods.

It is important to remember that employers may be flexible in the way the provisions apply to them as long as they have an agreement with their employees which was freely made.

There is a wealth of detail in the regulations but the basic provisions are as follows:

1. The *working week* should not exceed 48 hours including overtime, averaged out over a four-month period. There is potential for averaging over a longer period of time, e.g. up to 12 months if employees agree. This will be valuable if annual hours arrangements are used. Employers need to keep accurate records of actual hours worked and to make such records available to the competent authorities
2. *Rest breaks* should be provided in that each employee should be granted a rest break if working for six hours continuously and employees should have a rest break of 11 consecutive hours per 24 hours. Every week employees should have a rest period of 35 consecutive hours. This need not include a Sunday, although the Directive says this is 'preferable'. Calculation periods for rest breaks are negotiable, e.g. the 35-hour rest break might be calculated over a 14-day period rather than a seven-day period. The Department of Trade and Industry points out that workers are only 'entitled' to a break – they do not have to take it and this break can be unpaid. The timing of it can be left to employees.
3. *Holiday entitlement*: employees are entitled to four week's paid holiday a year from November 1999 (it was three weeks prior to this date). It is presumed bank holidays are included in this period. This annual leave may not be replaced by an allowance in lieu except where the employment relationship is terminated.

Provisions also cover night workers and monotonous work. Certain groups of workers, e.g. managers are exempt from all provisions and others, e.g. trainee doctors and air, rail and sea transport workers are being brought into the regulations over the next few years. **AB**

References and further reading
Hammond Suddards Edge (2000) *Working Time Regulations*, 2nd edn, London: Legal Essentials Series, London: CIPD.
Web site at http://www2.dti.gov.uk/er/work_time_regs/index.htm

World class manufacturing

The concept of 'World Class Manufacturing (WCM)' became popular in the 1990s and was publicised in fictional form by the work of Eli Goldratt. WCM also became the subject of extensive research by the academic community and a number of models of WCM were developed.

The underlying theory is that there are a series of practices and performance levels which, taken together, constitute BEST PRACTICE in WCM.

World Class companies are supposed to develop and utilise these practices and this is what makes them 'World Class'. Theorists believe that, if these practices can be uncovered and set out, then other companies can adopt these practices and so move towards becoming World Class companies themselves, thereby improving their competitive performance. The idea was particularly attractive to countries like the UK, which are dependent on export performance in an increasingly competitive global economy.

The problem lies in attempts to define WCM. It has proved an elusive concept. According to the Department of Trade and Industry (1995), WCM companies

> produce the right goods and services of the right quality, at the right price and right time, meeting their customer's needs more efficiently and effectively than other firms

This begs a number of questions of course. What do these terms mean in practice and how do you know when you get there?

Students of Human Resource management will be encouraged to learn that the same research emphasised the importance of 'leadership and good management of people in manufacturing success'.

The report identified 4 key characteristics of WCM companies:

1. They have visionary leaders who have fully communicated their business goals throughout the company and generated the necessary commitment at all levels.
2. They have a culture of INNOVATION that seeks continuous improvement in products and working methods.
3. Their business practices and processes are designed to achieve continually lower cost and product customisation, whilst retaining a clear competitive edge in price, quality, and service to the customer.
4. They have flexible and empowered employees, capable of performing multiple tasks at different levels of responsibilities.

Other models have been developed and are referred to below. The study by Voss and Hanson has been influential in helping companies to measure their performance against best practice in Europe and this model has been utilised by the Confederation of British Industry in developing a World Class manufacturing self-assessment benchmarking method called 'Manufacturing Probe', which has been widely used in the UK.

It remains unclear whether a full understanding of WCM has yet been developed and the extent to which any underlying model will, in any case, be transferable between companies and countries. **JB**

References and further reading

Department of Trade and Industry (June 1995) 'Manufacturing Winners: Creating a world-class manufacturing base in the UK'.

Voss, C. and Hanson, P. (1994) 'Made in Europe: A four nations best practice study', IBM Consulting Group/London Business School Publications.

Confederation of British Industry (1997) 'Fit for the future: How competitive is UK manufacturing?', CBI National Manufacturing Council Publications.

Keegan, R. and Lynch, J. J. (1995) 'World Class Manufacturing', Oak Tree Press Paperback.

Schonberger, R. J. (1996) 'World Class Manufacturing: the next decade, building power, strength and value', Free Press.

Goldratt, E. M. and Cox, J. (1993) 'The Goal', Gower Publishing Limited Paperback.

Goldratt, E. M. (1999) 'Theory of Constraints', North River Press, Incorporated Paperback.

Wrongful dismissal

A wrongful dismissal is a dismissal in breach of contract, and normally arises in one of two ways, the most common of which is where an employee is dismissed without notice or with less than the contractual period of notice provided for. However, dismissal without notice ('summary' dismissal) is not unlawful if either the contract provides for payment in lieu of notice or if the employee is guilty of gross misconduct. Whilst certain acts of gross misconduct tend to be company specific, others such as theft, serious acts of insubordination, misuse of company property and breaches of confidentiality are likely to apply to most jobs. If the contract of employment does not expressly provide for a notice period, a court or tribunal will imply a 'reasonable' period, which is normally dependent on length of service and status, and which may well exceed the statutory minimum notice periods set out in section 86 of the Employment Rights Act 1996. Dismissal during the currency of a fixed-term contract is also wrongful unless there is a provision for termination on notice.

Until employment tribunals were given jurisdiction in 1994 over breaches of contract where the employment relationship had terminated (now covered by the Industrial Tribunals Act 1996), claims of wrongful dismissal had to be brought in the civil courts. Damages normally relate to the loss of wages for the notice period or remainder of a fixed term less any monies earned during that time, and applicants are under a duty to take reasonable steps to mitigate their loss by seeking alternative employment. Employment tribunals cannot award damages of more than £25 000.

Where a dismissal is wrongful in the sense that it is in breach of a contractual disciplinary procedure, individuals have from time to time successfully sought an injunction in the civil courts to prevent the dismissal taking place other than in accordance with the contractual requirements. However, case law has ruled out the possibility that employees wrongfully dismissed in such circumstances could claim damages on the basis that had the correct procedure been followed they might not have been dismissed at all. **JE**

References and further reading
Deakin, S. and Morris, G. S. (1998) *Labour Law*, 2nd edn, London: Butterworths, pp. 396–438.

Jancuik v. Winerite Ltd [1998] IRLR.

Peace v. City of Edinburgh Council [1999] IRLR 417.

Pitt, G. (1997) *Employment Law*, 3rd edn, London: Sweet and Maxwell, pp. 176–80.

Wilson v. Racher [1974] ICR 428.

Further reading and useful web sites

General texts on human resource management

S. Bach and K. Sisson (eds) (2000) *Personnel Management*, 3rd edn, Oxford: Blackwell.

I. Beardwell and L. Holden (eds) (2001) *Human Resource Management*, 3rd edn, London: Pitman.

J. Bratton and J. Gold (2000) *Human Resource Management*, 2nd edn, London: Macmillan.

K. Legge (1995) *Human Resources Management: Rhetorics and Realities*, Basingstoke: Macmillan.

C. Mabey, G. Salaman and J. Storey (eds) (1998) *Strategic Human Resource Management: A Reader*, Buckingham: Open University Press.

M. Marchington and A. Wilkinson (2000) *Core Personnel and Development*, London: CIPD.

T. Redman and A. Wilkinson (eds) (2001) *Contemporary Human Resource Management*, London: Financial Times Prentice Hall.

R. Schuler and S. Jackson (eds) (1999) *Strategic Human Resource Management*, Oxford: Blackwell.

K. Sisson and J. Storey (2000) *The Realities of Human Resource Management*, 2nd edn, Buckingham: Open University Press.

P. Sparrow and M. Marchington (eds) (1998) *Human Resource Management: The New Agenda*, London: Financial Times Pitman Publishing.

J. Storey (ed.) (2000) *Human Resource Management*, 3rd edn, London: Routledge.

D. Torrington and L. Hall (1998) *Human Resource Management*, 4th edn, London: Prentice Hall.

International human resource management

G. Bamber and R. D. Lansbury (1998) *International and Comparative Employment Relations*, London: Sage.

C. Brewster and A. Hegewisch (eds) (1994) *Policy and Practice in European Human Resource Management*, London: Routledge.

T. Clark (1996) *European Human Resource Management*, Oxford: Blackwell.

P. Dowling, Welch, D. E. and Schuler, R. S. (1999) *International Human Resource Management*, Cincinnati, OH: South Western College Publishing.

P. Flood, M. Gannon, J. Paauwe (1996) *Managing without Traditional Methods*, London: Addison-Wesley.

C. Hampden-Turner and F. Tromperaars (1993) *The Seven Cultures of Capitalism*, London: Piatkus.

G. Hofstede (1994) *Cultures and Organisations*, London: HarperCollins.

G. Hollinshead and M. Leat (1995) *Human Resource Management: An International and Comparative Perspective*, London: Pitman.

R. Kandola and J. Fullerton (1998) *Diversity in Action: Managing the Mosaic*, 2nd edn, London: Institute of Personnel and Development.

P. S. Kirkbride (1994) *Human Resource Management in Europe*: *Perspectives for the* 1990s, London: Routledge.

M. Mendenhall and G. Oddou (2000) *Readings and Cases in International Human Resource Management*, 3rd edn, Cincinnati, OH: South Western College Publishing.

N. Phillips (1992) *Managing International Teams*, London: Financial Times Pitman Publishing.

P. Sparrow and J. M. Hiltrop (1994) *European Human Resource Management*, Hemel Hempstead: Prentice-Hall.

D. Torrington (1994) *International HRM*, London: Prentice Hall.

Employee reward

M. Armstrong (1999) *Employee Reward*, London: CIPD.

M. Armstrong and H. Murlis (1988) *Reward Management*: *A Handbook of Remuneration Strategy and Practice*, 4th edn, London: Kogan Page.

D. Brown (2001) *Reward Strategies*: *From Intent to Impact*, London: CIPD.

M. Cannell and S. Wood (1992) *Incentive Pay*, London: IPD.

D. Hume (1995) *Reward Management*, Oxford: Blackwell.

I. Kessler (1998) 'Payment systems', in M. Poole and M. Warner (eds) *The Handbook of Resource Management*, London: Thomson.

E. Lawler, (1990) *Strategic Pay*: *Aligning Organizational Strategies and Pay Systems*, San Francisco: Jossey-Bass.

T. Lupton and D. Gowler (1969) *Selecting a Wage Payment System*, London: Kogan Page.

J. Stredwick (1997) *Cases in Reward Management*, London: Kogan Page.

R. Thorpe and G. Homan (2000) *Strategic Reward Systems*, London: Financial Times Pitman.

R. Williams (1998) *Performance Management*, London: Thomson Learning.

Employee development

R. Bee and F. Bee (1994) *Training Needs Analysis and Evaluation*, London: IPD.

P. Bramley (1991) *Evaluating Training Effectiveness*: *Translating Theory into Practice*, Maidenhead: McGraw Hill.

C. Dean and Q. Whitlock (1992) A *Handbook of Computer-Based Training*, London: Kogan Page.

R. Harrison (1997) *Employee Development*, London: IPD.

D. Kolb, J. Osland and I. Rubin (1995) *Organisational Behaviour*: *An Experiential Approach*, 6th edn, Englewood Cliffs, NJ: Prentice-Hall.

E. Moorby (1992) *How to Succeed in Employee Development*: *Moving from Vision to Results*, Maidenhead: McGraw-Hill.

M. Pedler, J. Burgoyne and T. Boydell (1991) *The Learning Company*: *A Strategy for Sustainable Development*, London: McGraw Hill.

M. Reid and H. Barrington (1994) *Training Interventions*: *Managing Employee Development*, 4th edn, London: CIPD.

M. Tupson (1994) *Outdoor Training*: *For Employee Effectiveness*, London: CIPD.

S. Wood (ed.) (1988) *Continuous Development*, London: CIPD.

Employee resourcing

J. Bramham, J. (1994) *Human Resource Planning*, 2nd edn, London: CIPD.

D. Cooper and I. Robertson (1995) *The Psychology of Personnel Selection*, London: Routledge.

C. Fletcher (1997) *Appraisal*: *Routes to Improved Performance*, 2nd edn, London: CIPD.

A. Fowler (1996) *Employee Induction*: *A Good Start*, 3rd edn, London: CIPD.

P. Hom and R. Griffith (1995) *Employee Turnover*, Cincinnati, OH: South Western College Publishing.

A. Huczynski and M. Fitzpatrick (1989) *Managing Employee Absence for a Competitive Edge*, London: Pitman.

C. Jackson (1996) *Understanding Psychological Testing*, Leicester: British Psychological Society.

P. Lewis (1993) *The Successful Management of Redundancy*, Oxford: Blackwell.

M. Pearn and R. Kandola (1993) *Job Analysis*: *A Manager's Guide*, 2nd edn, London: IPM.

J. Skeats (1991) *Successful Induction*: *How to Get the Most from your New Employees*, London: Kogan Page.

M. Smith and I. Robertson, (1993) *The Theory and Practice of Systematic Personnel Selection*, London: Macmillan.

M. Smith, M. Gregg and D. Andrews (1989) *Selection and Assessment*: *A New Appraisal*, London: Pitman.

S. Taylor (1998) *Employee Resourcing*, London: CIPD.

C. Woodruffe (1993) *Assessment Centres*: *Identifying and Developing Competence*, 2nd edn, London: CIPD.

Employee relations

P. Blyton and P. Turnbull (1994) *The Dynamics of Employee Relations*, London: Macmillan.

M. Cully, S. Woodland, A. O'Reilly. and G. Dix. (1999) *Britain at Work*, London: Routledge.

D. Farnham (1993) *Employee Relations*, London: IPM.

A. Fox (1974) *Beyond Contract*: *Work, Power and Trust Relations*, London: Faber and Faber.

R. B. Freeman and J. L. Medoff (1984) *What Do Unions Do?* New York: Basic Books.

Institute of Personnel and Development (1997) *Employment Relations into the 21st Century*, London: Institute of Personnel and Development.

T. Kochan., H. Katz and B. McKersie (1986) *The Transformation of American Industrial Relations*, New York: Basic Books.

J. Purcell and B. Ahlstrand (1994) *Human Resource Management in the Multi-Divisional Company*, Oxford: Oxford University Press.

A. Scott (1994) *Willing Slaves?* Cambridge: Cambridge University Press.

B. Towers (1997) *The Representation Gap*, Oxford: Oxford University Press.

Useful web sites

General human resource management (HRM)

- http://www.ihrim.org/about/index.cfm Site for the International Association for Human Resource Information Management.
- http://www.cipd.co.uk The Chartered Institute of Personnel and Development web site for the professional body that represents personnel and development professionals in the UK.
- http://www.shrm.org/ The US Society for Human Resource Management's site.
- http://www.iop.unibe.ch/english/index.html Swiss-based site for the Institute for Organization and Human Resource Management.
- http://www.hrnetwork.co.uk A human resources (HR)-related new site.
- http://www.hrworld.com/ Online information source for HRM.
- http://www.HRnext.com/ A US site which has a free HR-specific search engine.

- http://www.the-hrnet.com/ A US web site for HR professionals.
- http://www.oneclickhr.com/ Example of a dot.com offering on-line HR solutions.
- http://www.ilo.org/ the International Labour Organization's web site.
- http://www.nbs.ntu.ac.uk.depts/hrm/hrm_link.htm A very useful site based at Nottingham Trent University with links to a wide range of HRM-related sites.
- http://www.hse.gov.uk/hsehome.htm The Health and Safety Executive's home page.
- http://www.dfee.gov.uk Department for Education and Employment home page

Sites based around HR journals and publications

- http://www.personneltoday.net/ links related to the magazine *Personnel Today*.
- http://www.incomesdata.co.uk Incomes Data Services Limited includes useful articles on HRM topics.
- http://www.hrhq.com/index.html/ A site from the US based *Personnel Journal* includes a searchable database of articles.
- http://www.peoplemanagement.co.uk/index.html The web-based version of the CIPD's publication.
- http://www.employment-studies.co.uk/ Provides extensive on-line summaries of the Institute for Employment Studies reports.
- http://www.journals.wiley.com/wilcat-bin/ops/ID1/0098-8898/prod *Employee Relations Law Journal* with titles of recent articles in this US journal.

Training and development related sites

- http://www.iipuk.co.uk/ Web site with materials and background on Investors in People.
- http://www.lifelonglearning.co.uk/ DfEE site promoting lifelong learning.
- http://nacett.org.uk/ Site for the National Advisory Council for Education and Training Targets.
- http://www.tsc.gov.uk/ The Training Standards Council web site.
- http://world.std.com/ Discussion and resources on the theory and practice of the learning organization.
- http://www.graffnet.co.uk/elsin2000/ A site supporting the European Learning Styles Information Network (ELSIN) with resources and materials related to learning and cognitive style.
- http://www.trainingzone.co.uk/ An online community offering news, jobs and discussion related to training issues.
- http://www.itol.co.uk/ Site for the relatively new Institute of Training and Occupational Learning.
- http://www.ahrd.org/ Site for the US Academy of Human Resource Development.
- http://www.astd.org/ Site for the US Society for Training and Development.
- http://www.cedefop.gr/ Site for the European Centre for the Development of Vocational Training.

Industrial relations and labour law related sites

- http://www.lawrights.co.uk/emp.html Law Rights – Employment Questions and Answers.
- http://www.eurofound.ie The European Foundation for the Improvement of Living and Working Conditions. Has a very useful online data base of European Works Councils.
- http://www.niesr.ac.uk/niesr/wers98/ Workplace Employment Relations Data Dissemination Service (currently the National Institute of Economic and Social Reseach).

- http://www.acas.org.uk/ The UK Advisory Conciliation and Arbitration Service site.
- http://www.igc.apc.org/strike/ The Strike Page provides news about ongoing strikes.
- http://www.labornet.org/workers/ Information on international industrial relations issues.
- ttp://dialspace.dial.pipex.com/town/estate/ac/742/ A resource for Trade Union activists, shop stewards and health and safety representatives.
- gopher://garnet.berkeley.edu:1250/00/.labor/.resource/.comp.ind Comparative Industrial Relations Source List.
- http://www.ilr.cornell.edu:80/ This provides information about industrial relations (IR) research in the school and a range of IR links.
- http://www.mailbase.ac.uk/lists-f-j/industrial-relations-research/ A UK-based forum for academic discussion on industrial relations.
- http://natlex.ilo.org/ NATLEX is a bibliographic database that contains information on national laws on labour, social security and related human rights. It covers a wide range of national labour law systems.

Diversity related sites

- http://www.cre.gov.uk/ Site for the Commission for Racial Equality.
- http://www.aimd.org/ The American Institute for Managing Diversity, a good site for exploring diversity issues in depth.
- http://www.eoc.org.uk/ Site for the Equal Opportunities Commission.
- http://www.careermosaic.com/cm/cm33.html Diversity Links for Women and Minorities from Career Mosaic.

Union sites

- http://www.tgwu.org.uk/ Site for the Trade and General Workers' Union.
- http://www.unison.org.uk/ Site for UNISON.
- http://www.msf.org.uk/ Site for the Manufacturing, Science and Finance Union
- http://www.tuc.org.uk/ The Trades Union Congress' site, organized around a 'virtual building'.
- http://www.aflcio.org/unionand.htm collection of union home pages and other relevant websites.

Employers sites

- http://www.cbi.org.uk Confederation of British Industry – the main British employer's body.
- http://www.eef.org.uk/ Site of the largest sector employer's organization in the UK.
- http://www.cia.org.uk/ site of the UK chemical industry's leading trade and employer organization.
- http://www.iod.co.uk/home.jphtml site of the organization representing UK senior managers.

General business sites

- http://wwwl.bnet.co.uk/ A general news source for business and management information.
- http://www.bized.ac.uk/ A source site for business and management information.
- http://www.hoovers.co.uk Free company information including financial statements and company profiles.
- http://www.inst-mgt.org.uk/ the Institute of Management's site has a useful gateway, 'Management Links' for relevant sites on the Internet.